STUDIES IN THE HISTORY OF CHRISTIAN MISSIONS

R. E. Frykenberg
Brian Stanley
General Editors

STUDIES IN THE HISTORY OF CHRISTIAN MISSIONS

Alvyn Austin
China's Millions: The China Inland Mission and Late Qing Society, 1832-1905

Michael Bergunder
The South Indian Pentecostal Movement in the Twentieth Century

Judith M. Brown and Robert Eric Frykenberg, *Editors*
Christians, Cultural Interactions, and India's Religious Traditions

Robert Eric Frykenberg
Christians and Missionaries in India: Cross-Cultural Communication Since 1500

Susan Billington Harper
In the Shadow of the Mahatma: Bishop V. S. Azariah and the Travails of Christianity in British India

D. Dennis Hudson
Protestant Origins in India: Tamil Evangelical Christians, 1706-1835

Ogbu U. Kalu, *Editor,* and Alaine M. Low, *Associate Editor*
Interpreting Contemporary Christianity: Global Processes and Local Identities

Donald M. Lewis, *Editor*
Christianity Reborn: The Global Expansion of Evangelicalism in the Twentieth Century

Jon Miller
Missionary Zeal and Institutional Control: Organizational Contradictions in the Basel Mission on the Gold Coast, 1828-1917

Andrew Porter, *Editor*
The Imperial Horizons of British Protestant Missions, 1880-1914

Dana L. Robert, *Editor*
Converting Colonialism: Visions and Realities in Mission History, 1709-1914

Wilbert R. Shenk, *Editor*
North American Foreign Missions, 1810-1914: Theology, Theory, and Policy

Brian Stanley
The World Missionary Conference: Edinburgh 1910

Brian Stanley, *Editor*
Christian Missions and the Enlightenment

Brian Stanley, *Editor*
Missions, Nationalism, and the End of Empire

Kevin Ward and Brian Stanley, *Editors*
The Church Mission Society and World Christianity, 1799-1999

Richard Fox Young, *Editor*
India and the Indianness of Christianity: Essays on Understanding—Historical, Theological, and Bibliographical—in Honor of Robert Eric Frykenberg

Robert Eric Frykenberg

India and the Indianness of Christianity

Essays on Understanding
— Historical, Theological, and Bibliographical —
in Honor of Robert Eric Frykenberg

Edited by

Richard Fox Young

William B. Eerdmans Publishing Company
Grand Rapids, Michigan / Cambridge, U.K.

Published 2009 by
Wm. B. Eerdmans Publishing Co.
2140 Oak Industrial Drive N.E., Grand Rapids, Michigan 49505 /
P.O. Box 163, Cambridge CB3 9PU U.K.

Printed in the United States of America

15 14 13 12 11 10 09 7 6 5 4 3 2 1

Library of Congress Cataloging-in-Publication Data

India and the Indianness of Christianity:
essays on understanding, historical, theological, and bibliographical,
in honor of Robert Eric Frykenberg / edited by Richard Fox Young.
p. cm. — (Studies in the history of Christian missions)
Includes bibliographical references and index.
ISBN 978-0-8028-6392-8 (pbk.: alk. paper)
1. Missions — India. 2. Christianity — India.
I. Frykenberg, Robert Eric. II. Young, Richard Fox.

BV3265.3.I525 2009
266.00954 — dc22

2009017340

www.eerdmans.com

Contents

Contributors

PETER B. ANDERSEN is Associate Professor in the Department of Cross-Cultural and Regional Studies, Faculty of Humanities, University of Copenhagen. He works on religion and has published on the Santals of West Bengal and Jharkhand and on the Christians of the former Danish settlement of Taragambadi (Tranquebar) in Tamil Nadu. He has also done survey-based research on religion and religious education in Denmark.

MICHAEL BERGUNDER is Professor and Chair, History of Religions and Mission Studies at the University of Heidelberg. His special fields of interest include the Pentecostal and charismatic movements, esotericism, and new religious movements in the global context, as well as the history of South Indian religions since the eighteenth century.

JUDITH M. BROWN is Beit Professor of Commonwealth History in the University of Oxford and a Professorial Fellow of Balliol College. Her research and writings have focused mainly on Indian politics in the twentieth century, particularly as seen through the life and thought of Mahatma Gandhi, and the career of Jawaharlal Nehru. She has also written on the modern South Asian diaspora.

JOHN B. CARMAN was a boyhood friend of Robert E. Frykenberg in South India and returned there for five years as an American Baptist missionary. From 1963 until his retirement in 2000, he taught comparative religion at Harvard Divinity School, serving from 1973 to 1989 as director of its Center for the Study of World Religions. He is the author of *The Theology of*

Ramanuja (1974) and *Majesty and Meekness: A Comparative Study of Contrast and Harmony in the Concept of God* (1994).

GUNNEL CEDERLÖF is Associate Professor of History at Uppsala University. Her work focuses on South Indian modern history, particularly legal and environmental history, labor relations, land rights and social mobilization among Dalits and indigenous people. Her work includes *Landscapes and the Law: Environmental Politics, Regional Histories, and Contests over Nature* (2008), *Bonds Lost: Subordination, Conflict, and Mobilisation in Rural South India, c. 1900-1970* (1997), and *Ecological Nationalisms: Nature, Livelihoods, and Identities in South Asia* (with K. Sivaramakrishnan, 2005).

DANIEL JEYARAJ is the Professor of World Christianity and Director of the Andrew F. Walls Centre at Liverpool Hope University. He is an ordained minister of the Diocese of Tirunelveli, Church of South India. He has pioneered research into the history and cross-cultural impact of the Royal Danish-Halle Mission (i.e., the Tranquebar Mission). His research interests include studies on bhakti religions of the Tamil people, inculturation, German literature, and non-Western expressions of Christianity in Asia and Africa.

CHANDRA MALLAMPALLI is Associate Professor of History at Westmont College (Santa Barbara). He is the author of *Christians and Public Life in Colonial South India, 1863-1937* (RoutledgeCurzon, 2004). His work explores the intersection of law, religion, and society in nineteenth-century South India.

GEOFFREY A. ODDIE is an Honorary Research Associate at the University of Sydney and the author of a range of books and articles on South Asian history. These include studies of Protestant missionaries, Hinduism, and religious conversion movements, mostly during the nineteenth century. Among his works are *Popular Religion, Elites, and Reform: Hook-Swinging and Its Prohibition in Colonial India, 1800-1894* and *Missionaries, Rebellion, and Proto-Nationalism: James Long of Bengal, 1814-87*. His most recent publication is *Imagined Hinduism: British Protestant Missionary Constructions of Hinduism, 1793-1900* (2006).

AVRIL A. POWELL is Reader in the History of Islam in South Asia in the Department of History at the School of Oriental and African Studies in the University of London, and Director of the Royal Asiatic Society. Her research focuses on socioreligious issues in nineteenth-century northwest India, with a particular interest in Muslims, missions, education, and the legacy of Mughal rule. Her Ph.D. thesis was published as *Muslims and Missionaries in Pre-Mutiny India* (London: Curzon, 1983). Papers presented to a workshop she co-organized in Dhaka, Bangladesh, she coedited as *Rhetoric and Reality:*

Gender and the Colonial Experience in South Asia (New Delhi: Oxford University Press, 2006).

WILBERT R. SHENK, author of *Changing Frontiers of Mission* (1999), is Senior Professor of Mission History and Contemporary Culture, Fuller Graduate School of Intercultural Studies, Pasadena, California.

BRIAN STANLEY is Professor of World Christianity in the University of Edinburgh and Director of the Centre for the Study of Christianity in the Non-Western World. He is the joint editor with Professor Frykenberg of the Studies in the History of Christian Missions series, and has written or edited a number of books on the history of Christian missions and world Christianity. Formerly he was Director of the Henry Martyn Centre in Cambridge.

ROSEMARY SETON was archivist-in-charge of archives and special collections at the School of Oriental and African Studies from 1979 to 2004. From 1999 to 2002 she directed the Mundus Project, a collaborative project that improved access to missionary collections at several important centers in the U.K., and created a Web-based guide to these materials at http://www.mundus.ac.uk. With Martha Smalley she compiled a manual for church and mission archives, is a partner of the Internet Mission Photography Archive Project (IMPA), and is a coconvenor of the recently founded seminar series *Christian Missions in Global History* at the Institute of Historical Research, University of London.

MARTHA LUND SMALLEY is Special Collections Librarian and Curator of the Day Missions Collection at Yale Divinity School Library. She is coauthor, with Rosemary Seton, of the *Rescuing the Memory of Our Peoples* archives manual and has conducted archives workshops worldwide. She also edits the Library's Occasional Publications, including *American Missionary Eyewitnesses to the Nanking Massacre,* and has contributed to digital projects related to mission photography and history.

RICHARD FOX YOUNG returned in 2000 from more than two decades of teaching in South and East Asia to join the faculty in History and Ecumenics at Princeton Theological Seminary where he holds the Timby Chair in the History of Religions. An Indologist by training, he works in mission studies, world Christianity, interreligious dialogue, and other contiguous areas. *Resistant Hinduism* (1981), *The Bible Trembled* (1995), and *Vain Debates* (1996) are three of his most widely cited research monographs on the encounter of Buddhists and Hindus with Christians in nineteenth-century South Asia.

INTRODUCTION

The Frykenberg Vamsavali: *A South Asia Historian's Genealogy, Personal and Academic, with a Bibliography of His Works*

RICHARD FOX YOUNG

Years ago, when the individual this volume honors was beginning to make his mark in South Asian studies, a senior colleague in the field, Hugh Tinker, reviewed a book called *Land Control and Social Structure in India* (1969), the first collaborative venture Robert Eric Frykenberg ever edited. Overall, Tinker was enthusiastic: "[the] book deserves to take its place in the mainstream of historical studies." There was, however, one thing — the "chapati English" of the editor and the other contributors (Bernard Cohn, Ainslee Embree, Thomas Metcalf, et al.): "almost every sentence is interlarded with Indian, Persian, and Arabic terms." The effect of unfamiliar words — *jamabandi, taccavi, waqf,* etc. — Tinker commented, was "withdrawal into the arcana of Orientalism."[1] The habit, however, was difficult to break, and anyway had nothing to do with academic obfuscation. Instead, it was Bob's way of expressing respect for the concrete particularities of the subjects he addressed, and his scholarship has long been marked by a reticence about India's translatability into supposedly cognate European categories and English terminology.

Those who hear Bob hold forth or read him in print know that his style, spoken and written, remains unapologetically hybrid. Still rich in terms evocative of India's ethos "under" British rule (Bob's first major publication dealt with that subject and ended with an eleven-page, fine-print glossary!), the Frykenberg lexicon is nowadays more Indo-English than ever. A word of pure

1. Hugh Tinker, *American Historical Review* 75, no. 2 (1969): 567.

Sanskrit pedigree that keeps popping up in works reflecting his increasing interest in the history of Indian Christianity is *vamsavali*, which I use in my title. Conventionally translated, *vamsavali* denotes something close to "lineage" or "genealogy." Bob employs it to convey the point that Indian Christianity as a social phenomenon becomes embodied — empirically and generationally — in actual Indian family lives. The word also occurs when Bob discusses an individual's intellectual or spiritual line of descent, whether a figure from history or another historian.[2] As a historian, Bob himself has a *vamsavali* worth recalling in each of these respects.

I

Born in 1930 in "Ooty" (Ootacamund, in the Nilgiri Hills of Tamil Nadu), Bob enjoyed the privilege of a multicultural upbringing in South India where his parents — Carl, a Swedish immigrant to America, and Doris, a first-generation Swedish American from Minnesota — served as Baptist missionaries among the Telegu-speaking peoples of Andhra Pradesh. Although Bob received his early education in the Palni Hills near Madurai at an English-medium school for missionary children (now called Kodaikanal International School), Andhra got into Bob's blood, as it were. The ethos of home, where he lived when school was out of session, was evangelical in profession and practice (Carl and Doris went out as American Baptists but later became Conservative Baptists). This, however, was no deterrent to Bob's immersion in the Telegu language, which he spoke quite fluently as a youth, or to his fascination with the pluralistic cultures he experienced firsthand in the South. Just in shuttling back and forth between Andhra and Tamil Nadu, Bob made

2. *Vamsavali* is used in all three ways in one of Bob's most recent essays, "The Lineage of an Evangelical Leader," which appeared in a Festschrift entitled *World Evangelization and Christian Leadership* (New Delhi, 2005), edited by J. T. K. Daniel to honor South Indian Methodist pastor and theologian Sam Kamelson. When exactly Bob adopted *vamsavali* into his vocabulary I am unsure. It may have been around the time he worked on the family records of a South Indian catechist with a graduate student of his, John J. Paul, which they reported on in a joint article, "A Research Note on the Discovery of Writings by Savariraya Pillai, a Tamil Diarist of Mid-Nineteenth-Century Tinnevelly," *Journal of Asian Studies* 44, no. 3 (1985): 521-28. Also noteworthy in this respect is Bob's encouragement and support (with funds from a grant provided by the Pew Charitable Trust of Philadelphia) for Indian-initiated research on Indian Christian *vamsavalis* under the auspices of the Bishop Stephen Neill Research Centre in Palayamkottai. From this project came David and Sarojini Packiamuttu's *Tirunelveli's Evangelical Christians: Two Centuries of Family* [Vamsavali] *History* (Bangalore, 2003), for which Bob wrote the introduction.

multiple passages through several "Indias" (as I heard him say on one occasion). In 1942, when the Japanese invasion of Burma threatened India's security, the family evacuated to the United States where Bob continued his schooling in Massachusetts and at Wheaton Academy in Illinois. When the war ended, Bob's parents returned to India for another round of service.

Instead of Wheaton College, the expected trajectory for a Wheaton Academy graduate, Bob enrolled at Bethel, a Baptist college in St. Paul, Minnesota. Afterward, considering the possibility of a "call" to parish ministry, Bob studied at Bethel Seminary and received ordination at a Minneapolis church, Grace Baptist. Concurrently, he completed a master's degree in political science at the University of Minnesota (and married Carol, whom he met at Bethel). Though active in lay ministries down to the present (as, for example, chair of the board of directors of "Pres House," a campus ministry at the University of Wisconsin in Madison), Bob felt the "pull" of academics and commenced a program of doctoral studies in political science at the University of California, Berkeley, where he worked with Richard L. Park, an India specialist. Unhappy with the "theory wars" that divided Berkeley's faculty, Bob was ripe for change; he had already passed his qualifying exams, but four years at Berkeley had left him disenchanted. Around this time, Bob became acquainted with Percival Spear, a historian of India on sabbatical from Cambridge; on Spear's recommendation, Bob was awarded a Rockefeller fellowship to study in London at the School of Oriental and African Studies. Under Kenneth Ballhatchet, Bob completed a dissertation on Andhra "under" British rule (Richard Park had had a role in suggesting the project, but London was the better place to pursue it). I shall return to Bob's dissertation momentarily; what should be noted is that Bob (like others from around the world in his generation of India scholars) flourished under "the unrestrained freedom of thought" Ballhatchet encouraged, unlike Berkeley.[3] That freedom included the possibility of pioneering the kind of historiography that would characterize his studies of modern India in the years ahead. After a brief stint at the University of Chicago, Bob moved in 1962 to the Madison campus of the University of Wisconsin where the Department of Indian Studies (renamed South Asian Studies in 1973) had been founded a few years earlier. Of that university, Bob is now an emeritus professor, having done much to make it one of America's top-ranked regional-studies institutions.

3. Robert Eric Frykenberg, *Guntur District, 1788-1848: A History of Local Influence and Central Authority in South India* (Oxford, 1965), p. vii.

II

In Chicago, Bob was able to burnish his London dissertation, which the Clarendon Press published in 1965 as *Guntur District, 1788-1848: A History of Local Influence and Central Authority in South India.* On the reading lists of many universities where courses on modern India are offered, the book has become a classic. One reason is that Bob's research demonstrated that a district study might produce more promising results in certain respects than an all-India macro-study or a village-based micro-study. Although Guntur, the district he selected, falls into today's Andhra Pradesh, Bob's first home, in colonial India Guntur was a somewhat distant administrative appendage attached to Madras Presidency. As a young scholar working on colonial India's political, social, and cultural history, Bob focused on Guntur "under" British rule, where modern innovations in the collection of revenue appeared to have hardly any impact at all on traditional systems. Besides having a firsthand feel for Telegu culture and society made vivid by Bob's distinctive prose (the book with the eleven-page, fine-print glossary I referred to earlier is *Guntur District*), the book retains the status it achieved because of the cutting-edge historiographical model Bob employed. Eric Stokes, an early reviewer who taught modern India at Cambridge, described it as "grass roots history."[4] In a recent overview of the history of South Asian historiography for the new *Oxford History of the British Empire,* Bob himself speaks of *Guntur District* as a study that worked "Indocentrically" from the "bottom up" instead of "Eurocentrically" from the "top down."[5]

However denominated, a change of perspective like Bob's involves serious questions about agency and causality, indigenous and exogenous. The overall effect was to call into doubt the certainty exuded by earlier "imperial" historians that India had been "under" British rule in any unqualified sense: no longer, Bob argued, could Indian history be written as if events had been planned in advance by sovereigns and orchestrated on the ground by civil servants. As Bob's *Oxford History* essay further clarifies, his argument in *Guntur District* had been that "the Raj was an *Indian* institution" (emphasis added) in terms of day-to-day reality.[6] Audacious at the time (and the reason ever since for quotation marks around the word "under"), the claim had solid evidential

4. Eric Stokes, "A New Approach to Indian History," *Historical Journal* 10, no. 3 (1967): 460. Most academic reviews appear without titles; significantly, this one did, with a rather bold one at that, for Bob himself would be the first to acknowledge that he had been inspired by the work of Percival Spear in the 1930s.

5. Robert Eric Frykenberg, "India to 1858," in *Oxford History of the British Empire,* vol. 5, *Historiography,* ed. Robin Winks et al. (Oxford and New York, 2001), p. 200.

6. Frykenberg, "India to 1858," p. 204.

backing. Bob had rummaged through mountains of archival material in London, New Delhi, and Madras, not, as Stokes aptly observed, to find out "what one clerk said to another," but rather to ascertain whether Indian agency had been overlooked or undervalued. Bob's "symbolic label" for the broader relevance of his local study to India "under" British rule beyond Guntur came to be called the "White-Ant Principle." Although the version I use comes from a slightly later work, one can understand why, in Stokes's view, Bob's "bias" in favor of indigenous agency and local initiative could be considered "revolutionary." He had, for instance, focused considerable attention on the role of Maratha Brahmins known as *Deshasthas,* who became indispensable to the British as *dubashes* (lit., "bilingual people," i.e, "interpreters" or "cultural intermediaries"). To Stokes, writing in 1969, earlier historiographical approaches had begun to seem disappointingly "antediluvian":[7] "The white ant is a tiny creature of tremendous energy and silence. It joins with its tiny termite brothers. These in silent combination devour the interior of the stoutest wooden structure, leaving it a hollow shell without necessarily destroying its outer form. The white ant typifies what happened in South India when energetic and silent forces, in combination, made hollow mockery of the stout administrative structures of successive systems of regal and imperial power."[8]

As a good dissertation should, Bob's opened up a whole range of related interests, vectoring out from the seminal work he had done on Guntur. Until he gave himself free rein to pursue research on the history of Indian Christianity, essays appeared in clusters around several correlative topics. One was the Protestant missionary movement as a stimulus for radical social change in eighteenth- and nineteenth-century South India;[9] a second had to do with the ways in which Christian initiatives (exogenous and indigenous) in the same period and region contributed to the rise of modern Indian educa-

7. Stokes, "A New Approach," p. 460.

8. Robert Eric Frykenberg, "Village Strength in South India," in *Land Control and Social Structure in India,* ed. Robert Eric Frykenberg (Madison, Milwaukee, and London, 1969), p. 246. For the original version of the "White-Ant Principle," see Frykenberg, *Guntur District,* pp. 231-44.

9. Samples of this variety include the following: (1) "The Impact of Conversion and Social Reform upon Society in South India during the Late Company Period: Questions concerning Hindu-Christian Encounters," in *Indian Society and the Beginnings of Modernisation, c. 1830-50,* ed. C. H. Philips and M. D. Wainwright (London, 1976), pp. 187-243; (2) "Conversion and Crises of Conscience under Company Raj in South India," in *Asie du Sud, Traditions et changements: VIth European Conference on South Asian Studies, Serves 8-13 Juillet 1978,* ed. Marc Gaboreieau and Alice Thorner (Paris, 1979), pp. 311-21; (3) "On the Study of Conversion Movements: A Review Article and a Theoretical Note," *Indian Economic and Social History Review* 17, no. 1 (1980): 121-38.

tion;[10] and a third evolved in the aftermath of Ayodhya (1992) when Bob was associated with the Chicago Fundamentalism Project (directed by Martin Marty and Scott Appleby) and worked on the emergence of modern militant Hinduism, compelled by a parallel concern for the future of Christian and other religious minority communities.[11]

Naturally enough, behind, beneath, and beyond these projects, contemporary historiographic trends remain one of Bob's most persistent interests. In this connection, *History and Belief* (Grand Rapids and Cambridge, 1999) merits attention; in it, Bob invested a lifetime of reflection on — as the subtitle goes — *The Foundations of Historical Understanding.* Of this work, Mark Noll, a historian of American Christianity, has written: "[the author] combines a stalwart belief in the possibility of knowledge about the past with careful diffidence about the limits of such knowledge."[12] To another reviewer, however, China specialist Paul Cohen, Bob's "diffidence" bordered on "the very cognitive relativism [the author] elsewhere forcefully rejects."[13] A passage like the following may have been the kind Cohen had in mind: "Historical understandings are never absolute and never complete. They are always tentative — sometimes highly so and sometimes hardly at all. Historical knowledge, in technical terms, is never entirely certain. It is never entirely free from question. This always being so, in some measure, the task of the historian is to maximize plausibility."[14] Cohen may have a point, but his exegesis is

10. In this cluster, see (1) "Modern Education in South India, 1784-1854: Its Roots and Its Role as a Vehicle of Integration under Company Raj," *American Historical Review* 91, no. 1 (1986): 37-65; (2) "The Myth of English as a 'Colonialist' Imposition upon India: A Reappraisal with Special Reference to South India," *Journal of the Royal Asiatic Society,* no. 2 (1988): 305-15; (3) "The Halle Legacy in Modern India: Information and the Spread of Education, Enlightenment, and Evangelization," in *Missionsberichte aus Indien im 18. Jahrhundert: Ihre Bedeutung für die europäische Geistesgeschichte und ihr wissenschaftlicher Quellenwert für die Indienkunde,* ed. Michael Bergunder (Halle, 1999), pp. 6-29.

11. See, for example, (1) "Hindu Fundamentalism and the Structural Stability of India," in *Fundamentalisms and the State: Remaking Polities, Economies, and Militance,* The Fundamentalism Project, vol. 2, ed. Martin E. Marty and R. Scott Appleby (Chicago, 1993), pp. 233-55; (2) "Accounting for Fundamentalisms in South Asia: Ideologies and Institutions in Historical Perspective," in *Accounting for Fundamentalisms: The Dynamic Character of Movements,* The Fundamentalism Project, vol. 4, ed. Martin E. Marty and R. Scott Appleby (Chicago, 1994), pp. 591-616; (3) "Gospel, Globalization, and Hindutva: The Politics of 'Conversion' in India," in *Christianity Reborn: The Global Expansion of Evangelicalism in the Twentieth Century,* ed. Donald M. Lewis (Grand Rapids, 2004), pp. 108-32.

12. Mark A. Noll, *International Bulletin of Missionary Research* 21, no. 3 (2001): 134.

13. Paul A. Cohen, *American Historical Review* 103, no. 2 (1998): 482.

14. Robert Eric Frykenberg, *History and Belief: The Foundations of Historical Understanding* (Grand Rapids and Cambridge, 1996), p. 8.

off the mark. I would rather he had said the opposite: instead of cognitive relativity, Bob's bête noire would be cognitive absolutism. This he thinks of as being especially prevalent in postcolonial and subaltern historiographies. "Diffident" about the limits of historical understanding (his own included), Bob bristles at theory-driven historiographies that overstep — in his judgment — the boundaries of evidential plausibility.[15]

While oscillations between historiographic binaries — Eurocentric and top-down versus Indocentric and bottom-up — are bound to occur, today's theory wars have brought out in Bob a tendency to react as if he were the Lone Ranger. That he stands in good company has been pointed out even by his critics.[16] Still, consider Bob's review of *The British Conquest and Dominion of India* (London, 1989) by Penderel Moon, which addresses one of Bob's long-standing interests. In it, Bob ruminates on the rise of "theoretical scholasticism," and Moon reminds him of how different historiography used to be: "What Moon wanted to write was an 'old fashioned, conventional history, concentrating on the deeds, motives, and thoughts of the principal . . . [British] actors in the drama of events rather than on the almost unmoving background of the mass of the [Indian] population against which they played their parts'" (p. 9). Bob's tolerance for this kind of "antediluvian" approach (as Stokes might say), which is hardly Indocentric or bottom-up (as Bob

15. This was evidently Bob's quarrel with Gauri Viswanathan's *Masks of Conquest: Literary Study and British Rule in India* (New York, 1988), in *American Historical Review* 97, no. 1 (1992): 272-73, wherein he remonstrates as follows (note that Bob had devoted considerable attention to the rise of modern education in South India; n. 10, *supra*): "With astounding certainty, bereft of critical scrutiny, the author's eyes seem closed to anything but a monolithic motivation (with an implied collective guilt). Viswanathan's position is that knowledge is power — without meaning apart from relations of power by which it is determined. Awkward facts or contexts are not allowed to stand in her way. . . . The possibility that Viswanathan's own discourse may itself be a monocultural or Eurocentric imposition, precisely the same kind of 'Orientalism' against which Edward Said inveighed, seems to elude her." Similar comments made by Bob in his *Oxford History* essay elicited a retort in Viswanathan's defense from Douglas M. Peers in "Is Humpty Dumpty Back Together Again? The Revival of Imperial History and the Oxford History of the British Empire," *Journal of World History* 13, no. 2 (2002): 451.

16. Vinay Lal, "Subaltern Studies and Its Critics: Debates over Indian History," *History and Theory* 40 (February 2001): 141-42. Though Bob is an outspoken critic, Lal includes him among a number of prominent modern India historians "who characterize Said's intellectual framework as totalizing, supposedly without the awareness . . . that [colonial] control and domination were never absolute, and that everywhere communities offered resistance to regimes of power by strategic and imaginative interpretations of local traditions and customs." I acknowledge Lal for inspiring my reference to the Lone Ranger syndrome.

would say), speaks volumes about his disenchantment with Saïdian-inspired historiographies. On these, Bob pronounced a blistering indictment in "History as Rhetoric: A Disputed Discourse" (chapter 10 of *History and Belief*). The historiographies indicted there, Moon at least eschews (and still arrives at conclusions congenial to Bob's):

> Not for him those "tropes of discourse," with their theoretical sails so high and their empirical keel (or ballast) so shallow and light that they could capsize in the face of any contrary puff of wind. Not for him those sweeping and conveniently vague scholastic wranglings over "colonialism" and "capitalism" and "orientalism" and "world systems," with their flagellistic devilings about how much collective evil, guilt, and shame should be atoned for. Rather, with fascinatingly informed, if opinionated, insight and with warm-blooded enthusiasm, he was convinced that the Indian empire, was itself an accident "unplanned and unpremeditated [which] came about by the operation of natural instincts."[17]

III

On today's theory wars, contributors to this volume may feel (and probably do) that the jury is still out, and that Bob's perspectives and participation may not accurately reflect our own opinions or styles. We readily identify with Indocentric, bottom-up historiographies and share many of Bob's reservations about Eurocentric, top-down approaches, but most of us (maybe all of us) feel that being situated somewhere in between is better than manning the barricades at either extreme, and that selective adaptation from postcolonial and subaltern historiographies enriches our research without making us one-eyed, elitist, or Euro-exclusive. Having said this, I hasten to add that Bob may be *the* historian (certainly, one of the foremost) most responsible for promoting studies of intercultural and interreligious interactions (Indo-Euro-American, Hindu-Muslim-Christian) in the South Asian context. He may also be the one who has done the most to bring questions having to do with the *Indianness* of Indian Christianity to the table for historiographic discussion (Bob's *Oxford History* essay makes this kind of case).[18] That, I believe, is why each contributor would agree that being "adopted" into the Frykenberg *vamsavali* is an association we appreciate. Going back at least to the 1980s,

17. Robert Eric Frykenberg, *Victorian Studies* 33, no. 4 (1990): 652.
18. Frykenberg, "India to 1858," pp. 206-11.

Bob has encouraged our work and galvanized our energies at conferences[19] and in collaborative publication projects.[20]

Bob himself has been galvanized and encouraged by contact with Andrew Walls of Edinburgh, Lamin Sanneh of Yale, and other scholars involved in African religions, mission studies, and world Christianity. Acknowledging in his *Oxford History* essay that "Christian missions and missionary history have never generated as much attention for India as for Africa,"[21] Bob seeks to rectify the imbalance not only by organizing conferences and editing books but also by asking comparative questions and absorbing insights from scholars whose historiographies are grounded more explicitly in theology than his are. Speaking for myself as one who came to the "religious" academy from the "secular" (distinctions that may seem irrelevant outside American higher education), Bob's experiences mirror my own in certain respects. Of these, the realization that Afrocentric, bottom-up historiographies concur with the ones he developed for South Asian Christianities is perhaps the most illuminating and liberating, although such historiographies derive from a specific biblical hermeneutic.[22] Walls's conceptualization of Christianity's "translat-

19. Kodaikanal in 1984, Oxford in 1999, panels of the European Association of Modern South Asian Studies in Copenhagen, Prague, and Edinburgh in the 1990s, brought some contributors to this volume together for the first time. Bob's involvement in two large-scale projects, NAMP (North Atlantic Mission Project) and CWC (Currents in World Christianity), administered by Brian Stanley of the Henry Martyn Centre, Cambridge, as well as Bob's coediting with Brian of Studies in the History of Christian Mission (the series in which this volume appears), deserve special mention.

20. *Christians, Cultural Interactions, and India's Religious Traditions,* coedited with Judith Brown (Grand Rapids, Cambridge, London, 2002), and *Christians and Missionaries in India: Cross-Cultural Communications since 1500* (Grand Rapids, Cambridge, London, 2003).

21. Frykenberg, "India to 1858," p. 207.

22. As I have written elsewhere, "One of the most noteworthy changes in the historiography of world Christianity is the shift in emphasis from Western transmission of the gospel to non-Western appropriation, from missionaries to converts, and from mission to church." Richard Fox Young, "Christian Spirituality in Africa, Asia, Latin America, and Oceania," in *The Blackwell Companion to Christian Spirituality,* ed. Arthur Holder (Oxford, 2005), p. 158. Older historiographies of non-Western Christianity, which placed a high value on Western transmission, correlate with the Eurocentric, top-down varieties Bob renounced. Analogously, the newer historiographies, which put a high value on indigenous appropriation, match the Indocentric, bottom-up varieties Bob embraced. My discussion of *Guntur District* in section II mentioned that Bob believed that India's modern history could not be written "as if events had been planned in advance by sovereigns and orchestrated on the ground by civil servants." Insofar as India's modern Christian history is concerned, Bob would likewise agree that it cannot be written as if events had been planned in advance by prelates (ABCFM, BMS, CMS, administrators, etc.) and orches-

ability," based on John's Gospel (1:14, "The Word became flesh and dwelt among us"), has freed Bob to speak of the incarnation as the transempirical basis for the empirical *Indianness* of Indian Christianity in ways that would have been out of place when Bob was writing *Guntur District* and beginning to make his mark in South Asian studies as a young scholar. Note how his idiom has changed: "[T]here could never be such a thing as a 'Christian' in the abstract or in general. Christians, either as individuals or as members of a community, could only be known and understood in concrete, local, and specific terms. They could experience, and be experienced or described, only in nonabstract terms. Each Christian was (and is) a person with a reality and specificity of face and name and place, with a specificity of birth and blood (*vamsha:* lineage)."[23] The passage is redolent of Bob's personal, intellectual, and spiritual *vamsavali,* ever open, always expansive. His early conditioning in South India where he was exposed to the concrete particularities of culture, religion, and society is readily apparent, his Indocentric, bottom-up historiographic predisposition, and his recovery of a more pronounced theological "voice."

At this writing, just months after Bob's hefty contribution to the Oxford History of the Christian Church, a series edited by Henry and Owen Chadwick, the jury is still out on how *Christianity in India: From the Beginnings to the Present* is going to be received. All will surely agree, however, that a work of such prodigious scope has not been attempted since Stephen Neill's two-volume work came out from Cambridge University Press in the mid-1980s.[24] For a history that has the present as its horizon, a hiatus of that duration needs a good deal of filling in, for in the last few decades Indian Christianity has hardly been standing idle. With characteristic modesty, Bob acknowledges that "there are many in India whose authority to write about some particular facet of Christianity in India is much greater than that of the author of this work [viz., Bob himself]. Yet, when all is said and done, there is no single person today, nor has there ever been a person, whose expertise and grasp and insights were sufficiently vast as to embrace the entire subject of

---

trated on the ground by missionaries. Bob is thus a prime example of the happy confluence of historiographies that can occur when scholars of the two academies, secular and religious, engage each other in constructive conversation.

23. Robert Eric Frykenberg, "Introduction," in *Christians and Missionaries in India,* p. 12. In context, Bob was here referring to the Tamil evangelicals of late-eighteenth- and early-nineteenth-century South India on whom he has lavished so much attention.

24. Stephen C. Neill, *A History of Christianity in India,* vol. 1, *The Beginnings to 1707* (Cambridge, 1984), vol. 2, *1707-1858* (Cambridge, 1985). Bob's review of Neill is found in *Journal of Asian Studies* 46, no. 1 (1987): 195-97.

this study."[25] Still, this 564-page volume will remain Bob's most rigorous and vigorous exemplification of his hallmark historigraphical principles: "It is *Indian* Christians, or Christian communities *within* the continent, together with *their* institutions, with which this work is primarily concerned. Alien, non-Indian, non-indigenous names have become important to the narrative only insofar as their actions or words are seen as having been consequential for Indian Christians or Indian Christian institutions."[26]

And while the jury will be out for a good while longer, *Christianity in India* has made the pages of the *Times Literary Supplement* in a substantial review by a friend and colleague, Brian Stanley, Professor of World Christianity in the University of Edinburgh, a coeditor along with Bob Frykenberg of Studies in the History of Christian Missions, the series in which this Festschrift happens to be appearing. In the following extract, Stanley captures much of what is most distinctively Frykenbergian about Bob's magnum opus:

> Foreign missionaries emerge from Frykenberg's pages as too few in number, fallible in capacity, and potentially disruptive in their political impact to play the role cast for them by much Western historiography and contemporary Hindu vituperation. They were at best leaky conduits of information, imperfectly transmitting knowledge in both directions between India and Europe. Or, to adopt another of the author's metaphors, they were mere catalysts of hidden and slow-burning processes of religious change which usually burst into flame decades after the initiating missionary had passed from the scene. When Christianity did take deep root in a particular location through movements of group conversion, it did so because of local agency. Sometimes the agents of the gospel were high-born men or women of learning, such as the great Tamil poet, Nellaiyan Vedanayakam Sastriar, or, later in the nineteenth century, Ramabai Sastri Dongre, a brilliant woman who before her conversion was awarded the honorific title of "Pandita" on account of her unrivalled mastery of classical Sanskrit learning. Perhaps more frequently, they were people of humble, even polluting, birth, unlettered and often unremembered apostles who spread the word of the gospel using a down-to-earth vocabulary of salvation, which spoke of freedom in Christ from fear of demons, from the terrors of sickness and the grave, and from oppression by caste Hindus. But in almost every case

25. Robert Eric Frykenberg, *Christianity in India: From the Beginnings to the Present,* Oxford History of the Christian Church (Oxford, 2008), p. 455.

26. Frykenberg, *Christianity in India,* p. 461.

> where the Church saw growth, it did so, not because of external imposition but through local appropriation and indigenization of the Christian message.[27]

Later, as he rounds off his review, Stanley restates the question that Bob was so invested in figuring out: "Is Christianity an Indian religion?" Then, aware that there are skeptics who will need to be convinced, he dispenses some apt advice: "Read this book and you may change your mind."[28] And so, read ours as well; it will, we trust, have the same good effect.

27. Brian Stanley, "Thomas's Tribes," *Times Literary Supplement,* no. 5524 (February 13, 2009): 24.

28. Stanley, "Thomas's Tribes," p. 24.

Bibliography

Books and Monographs

1965 *Guntur District, 1788-1848: A History of Local Influence and Central Authority in South India* (Oxford: Clarendon).

1968 *Today's World in Focus: India* (Boston: Ginn and Co.).

1996 *History and Belief: The Foundations of Historical Understanding* (Grand Rapids and Cambridge: Eerdmans).

2008 *Christianity in India: From Beginnings to the Present,* Oxford History of the Christian Church (Oxford: Oxford University Press).

Edited Works

1969 *Land Control and Social Structure in Indian History* (Madison, Milwaukee, and London: University of Wisconsin Press; revised and enlarged edition, New Delhi: Manohar, 1978), with introduction, xiii-xxi.

1975 *India's Imperial Tradition* (Madras: Indo-British Society).

1977 *Land Tenure and Peasant in South Asia: An Anthology of Recent Research* (Madison: University of Wisconsin Press; reprint, New Delhi: Orient Longman, 1981), with introduction, "Analytical and Historical Perspectives," pp. 1-16.

1985 *Studies of South India: An Anthology of Recent Research and Scholarship,* coedited with Pauline Kolenda (Madras: New Era Publications).

1986 *Delhi through the Ages: Essays in Urban History, Culture, and Society* (New Delhi and Oxford: Oxford University Press). Editor's introduction, "The Study of Delhi: An Analytical Introduction and a Historiographic Overview," pp. xx-xxxix, and "The Coronation Durbar of 1911: Some Implications," pp. 369-90. (Reprinted as part 4 of *The Delhi Omnibus* [New Delhi and Oxford: Oxford University Press, 2002].)

2002 *Christians, Cultural Interactions, and India's Religious Traditions,* coedited with Judith Brown, Studies in the History of Christian Missions (Grand Rapids: Eerdmans; London: RoutledgeCurzon).

2003 *Christians and Missionaries in India: Cross-Cultural Communication since 1500, with Special Reference to Caste, Conversion, and Colonialism,* Studies in the History of Christian Mission (Grand Rapids: Eerdmans; London: Routledge-Curzon), with introduction, "Dealing with Contested Definitions and Controversial Perspectives," pp. 1-32.

Pandita Ramabai's America: "Conditions of Life in the United States," translator, Kshitija Gomes; translation editor, Philip C. Engblom (Grand Rapids and Cambridge: Eerdmans), with a "Biographical Introduction" by R. E. Frykenberg, pp. 1-54.

Contributions to Other Works

1969 "The Ryotwari System and Social Organization in the Madras Presidency," with Nilmani Mukherjee, in *Land Control and Social Structure in Indian History,* edited by Robert E. Frykenberg (Madison and London: University of Wisconsin Press), pp. 217-26. (Reprinted in the *Indo-British Review* 10, no. 2 [1983]: 45-49.)

"Village Strength in South India," in *Land Control and Social Structure in Indian History,* edited by Robert E. Frykenberg (Madison and London: University of Wisconsin Press), pp. 227-47.

1975 "Integration of South Asia: The Indian Empire," "Subjugation of Southeast Asia: Under European Rule," "The Awakening of East Asia," "Breakup of Empire in South Asia: The Emergence of India and Pakistan," "Loss of Empires in Southeast Asia: Conflicts and New States," "China and Japan in the Twentieth Century," all in *European History in a World Perspective,* edited by Shepard Bancroft Clough, 3rd ed. (Lexington, Mass.: Heath), pp. 1350-1417, 1614-1700.

1976 "The Impact of Conversion and Social Reform upon Society in South India during the Late Company Period: Questions concerning Hindu-Christian Encounters," in *Indian Society and the Beginnings of Modernisation, c. 1830-50,* edited by C. H. Philips and M. D. Wainwright (London: School of Oriental and African Studies), pp. 187-243.

"The Last Emergency of the Raj," in *Indira Gandhi's India,* edited by Henry C. Hart (Boulder, Colo.: Westview Press), pp. 36-66.

1977 "'Company Circari' in the Carnatic, c. 1799-1859: The Inner Logic of Political Systems in India," in *Realm and Region in Traditional India,* edited by Richard G. Fox (Durham, N.C.: Duke University, Program in Comparative Studies on Southern Asia), pp. 117-64.

"The Silent Settlement in South India, 1793-1853: An Analysis of the Role of Inams in the Rise of the Indian Imperial System," in *Land Tenure and Peasant in South Asia,* edited by Robert E. Frykenberg (New Delhi: Orient Longman), pp. 37-53.

1979 "Conversion and Crises of Conscience under Company Raj in South India," in *Asie du Sud, Traditions et changements: VIth European Conference on South Asian Studies, Serves 8-13 Juillet 1978,* edited by Marc Gaboreieau and Alice Thorner (Paris: Colloques Internationaux du Centre National de la Recherche Scientifique), pp. 311-21. (Reprinted in *The Indo-British Review* 18, no. 1 [1990]: 67-81.)

"The Morphology of Madras as a City-State," in *The Rise and Growth of the Colonial Port Cities of Asia,* edited by Dilip Basu (Santa Cruz: University of California, Center for South Pacific Studies), pp. 94-96, 109-122.

1984 "The Socio-political Morphology of Madras: An Historical Interpretation," in *Changing South Asia: City and Culture,* edited by K. A. Ballhatchet and J. B. Harrison (London: SOAS, University of London; Hong Kong: Asian Research Service), pp. 21-41. (Reprinted in the *Indo-British Review* 11, no. 2 [1985]: 5-37.)

1985 "Education as an Instrument of Imperial Integration during the Company's Raj in South India," *Indo-British Review* 12, no. 2: 58-85.

"State, Empire and Nation in South India: Demythologizing as a Scholar's Enterprise," in *Region and Nation in India,* edited by Paul Wallace (New Delhi: Oxford University Press and IBH Publishing Company), pp. 60-84.

"US Bibliographical and Microfilming Programs in South Asia: A Retrospective Examination of SAMP [South Asia Microfilming Project]," in *South Asian Studies, Papers Presented at a Colloquium, 24-26 April 1985,* British Library Occasional Papers 7 (London: British Library), pp. 159-64.

1986 "New Light on the Vellore Mutiny," in *East India Company Studies: Papers Presented to Professor Sir Cyril Philips,* edited by Kenneth Ballhatchet and John Harrison (Hong Kong, 1986), pp. 207-31.

"What Rajaji Represents within the Context of South India's History: An Introductory Essay," in *Rajagopalachari: Gandhi's Southern Commander,* edited by Antony Copley (Madras: IBHS), pp. 3-22.

1987 "Conflicting Norms and Political Integration in South India: The Case of the Vellore Mutiny," *Indo-British Review* 13, no. 1: 51-63.

1988 "Revivalism and Fundamentalism: Some Critical Observations with Special Reference to Politics in South Asia," in *Fundamentalism, Revivalists, and Violence in South Asia,* edited by James Warner Bjorkman (Riverdale, Md.: Riverdale Press; New Delhi: Manohar), pp. 20-39.

1989 "The Emergence of Modern 'Hinduism' as a Concept and as an Institution: An Appraisal with Special Reference to South India," in *Hinduism Reconsidered,* edited by Gunther Sontheimer and Hermann Kulke (Heidelberg: South Asia Institute; reprint, New Delhi: Manohar Books, 1997), pp. 1-29.

"India's Past Seen 'from Below,'" *Journal of Imperial and Commonwealth History* 17, no. 3: 433-37.

1993 "Hindu Fundamentalism and the Structural Stability of India," in *Fundamentalisms and the State: Remaking Polities, Economies, and Militance,* Fundamentalism Project, vol. 2, edited by Martin E. Marty and R. Scott Appleby (Chicago: University of Chicago Press), pp. 233-55.

1994 "Accounting for Fundamentalisms in South Asia: Ideologies and Institutions in Historical Perspective," in *Accounting for Fundamentalisms: The Dynamic Character of Movements,* Fundamentalism Project, vol. 4, edited by Martin E. Marty and R. Scott Appleby (Chicago: University of Chicago Press), pp. 591-616.

1995 Specialist editor for approximately 400 entries for British India in *The Blackwell Dictionary of Evangelical Biography,* edited by Donald M. Lewis, 2 vols. (Oxford: Blackwell Reference).

1999 "The Halle Legacy in Modern India: Information and the Spread of Education, Enlightenment, and Evangelization," in *Missionsberichte aus Indien im 18. Jahrhundert: Ihre Bedeutung für die europäische Geistesgeschichte und ihr wissenschaftlicher Quellenwert für die Indienkunde,* edited by Michael Bergunder (Halle: Verlag der Franckeschen Stiftungen zu Halle), pp. 6-29.

"India," in *World History of Christianity,* edited by Adrian Hastings (London: Cassell; Grand Rapids: Eerdmans), pp. 147-91, 546-48.

"India in the Aftermath of Ayodhya: Historical Implications and Constitutional Stability," in *History and Politics: Millennial Perspective; Essays in Honour of Kingsley de Silva,* edited by Gerald Peiris and S. W. R. de A. Samarasinghe (Kandy, Sri Lanka: International Centre for Ethnic Studies).

2000 "The Construction of Hinduism as a 'Public' Religion: Looking Again at the Religious Roots of Company Raj in South India," in *Religion and Public Culture: Encounters and Identities in Modern South Asia,* edited by Keith E. Yandell and John J. Paul (Richmond, Surrey: Routledge), pp. 3-26.

2001 "The Anecdote as the Essence of Historical Understanding," in *Faith and Narrative,* edited by Keith E. Yandell (Oxford: Oxford University Press), pp. 116-37. (Previously published in Robert E. Frykenberg, *History and Belief* [Grand Rapids and Cambridge: Eerdmans, 1996], pp. 96-122.)

"Benoy Kumar Sarkar, 1887-1949: Political Rishi of Twentieth Century Bengal," in *Explorations in the History of South Asia: Essays in Honour of Dietmar Rothermund,* edited by Georg Berkemer et al. (New Delhi: Manohar), pp. 197-217.

"Christians in India: An Historical Overview of Their Complex Origins," in *Christians and Missionaries in India: Cross-Cultural Communication since 1500, with Special Reference to Caste, Conversion, and Colonialism,* Studies in the History of Christian Mission (Grand Rapids: Eerdmans; London: Routledge-Curzon), pp. 33-61.

"India to 1858," in *Oxford History of the British Empire,* vol. 5, *Historiography,* edited by Robin W. Winks et al. (Oxford and New York: Oxford University Press), pp. 194-213.

2003 "Historical Introduction," in *Tirunelveli's Evangelical Christians: Two Centuries of Family* (Vamshavazhi) *Traditions,* edited and translated by David and Sarojini Packiamuthu (Bangalore: SAIACS Press), pp. xiv-xxxviii.

2004 "Gospel, Globalization, and Hindutva: The Politics of 'Conversion' in India," in *Christianity Reborn: The Global Expansion of Evangelicalism in the Twentieth Century,* edited by Donald M. Lewis (Grand Rapids: Eerdmans), pp. 108-32.

2005 "Christian Missions and the Raj," in *Missions and Empire,* Oxford History of the British Empire, Companion Series, edited by Norman Etherington (Oxford, 2005), pp. 107-31.

"Christians and Religious Traditions in the Indian Empire," in *World Christianities, c. 1815-1914,* edited by Sheridan Gilley and Brian Stanley, Cambridge History of Christianity, vol. 8 (Cambridge, 2005), pp. 473-92.

"Hindutva and the Aftermath of Ayodhya: Dangers of Political Religion and Religious Nationalism," in *Nationalism and Hindutva: A Christian Response; Papers from the 10th CMS Consultation,* edited by Mark T. B. Laing, Indian Contextual Theological Education Series 28 (Delhi: ISPCK; Pune: Centre for Mission Studies, Union Biblical Seminary), pp. 3-34.

"Sam Kamaleson: The Lineage of an Evangelical Leader," in *World Evangelization and Christian Leadership: A Festschrift in Honour of the Rev. Dr. Samuel T. Kamaleson,* edited by J. T. K. Daniel (Delhi: ISPCK), pp. xvii-xxxvi.

2006 "Naga Baptists: A Brief Narrative of Their Genesis," in *Baptist Identities: Inter-*

national Studies from the Seventeenth to the Twentieth Century, edited by Ian M. Randall et al. (Carlisle: Paternoster), pp. 213-40.

Articles

1962 "British Society in Guntur during the Early Nineteenth Century," *Comparative Studies in Society and History* 4, no. 2: 200-208.

1963 "Traditional Processes of Power in South India: An Historical Analysis of Local Influence," *Indian Economic and Social History Review* 1, no. 2: 122-42. (Reprinted in *State and Society: A Reader in Comparative Political Sociology,* edited by Reinhold Bendix [Boston: Little, Brown]; second reprinting in *Aspects of Deccan History,* edited by V. K. Bawa [Hyderabad: Institute of Asian Studies, 1975].)

1965 "Elite Groups in a South Indian District: 1788-1858," *Journal of Asian Studies* 24, no. 2: 261-81. (Reprinted in *Indo-British Review* 10, no. 1: 42-57.)

1968 "Elite Formation in Nineteenth Century South India," in *Proceedings of the First International Conference on Tamil Culture and History,* edited by S. Arasaratnam (Kuala Lumpur: University of Malaysia Press).

1976 "The Logic of Imperium in India," *Indo-British Review* 6, no. 2: 39-58.

1979 "Bell-Weather of Change: The Role of Telegus in Times of Turbulence and Transition," *Itihas* [Hyderabad] 7: 93-103.

1980 "On the Study of Conversion Movements: A Review Article and a Theoretical Note," *Indian Economic and Social History Review* 17, no. 1: 121-38.

1981 "World Hunger: Food Is Not the Answer," *Christianity Today* 25, no. 11: 36-39.

1982 "On Roads and Riots in Tinnevelly: Radical Change and Ideology in Madras Presidency during the 19th Century," *South Asia* 4, no. 2: 34-52.

"Sovereignty and the 'Sikka' under the Raj: Minting Prerogative and Imperial Legitimacy in India," coauthored with J. S. Deyell, *Indian Economic and Social History Review* 19, no. 1: 1-25.

1985 "Religion and Company Raj in South India," *Fides et Historia* 17: 6-37.

"A Research Note on the Discovery of Writings by Savariraya Pillai, a Tamil Diarist of Mid-Nineteenth-Century Tinnevelly," with John J. Paul, *Journal of Asian Studies* 44, no. 3: 521-28.

1986 "Modern Education in South India, 1784-1854: Its Roots and Its Role as a Vehicle of Integration under Company Raj," *American Historical Review* 91, no. 1: 37-65.

"Rising Expectations among the World's Poor," *Christianity Today* 30, no. 1: 61-71.

1987 "The Concept of 'Majority' as a Devilish Force in the Politics of Modern India," *Journal of Commonwealth and Comparative Politics* 25, no. 3: 267-74.

1988 "The Myth of English as a 'Colonialist' Imposition upon India: A Reappraisal with Special Reference to South India," *Journal of the Royal Asiatic Society*, no. 2: 305-15.

1993 "Constructions of Hinduism at the Nexus of History and Religion," *Journal of Interdisciplinary History* 23, no. 3: 523-50.

"Hindu Fundamentalism: Is It a Religious or National Movement?" *Ethnic Studies Report* 11: 1-20. (Separately reprinted as *Religion, Nationalism, and Hindu Fundamentalism: The Challenge to Indian Unity* [Kandy, Sri Lanka: International Centre for Ethnic Studies].)

1996 "The Genesis of the 'Andra Movement' and the Formation of Andhra: A Case Study of the South," *Calcutta Historical Journal* 18, no. 1: 35-63.

1997 "Contesting the Limits of Tolerance, Intolerance and Toleration: Some Observations on Fundamentalism," *South Asian Survey* 4, no. 1: 13-24.

1999 "The Legacy of Christian Friedrich Schwartz," *International Bulletin of Missionary Research* 23, no. 3: 130-36.

2005 "India under the Raj," "The Faith 'Goes Native': How Indigenous Christian Movements Radically Transformed Entire Communities," "The Social Context: Caste and 'Color,'" and "A Timeline of Christianity in India," all in *Christian History and Biography*, issue 87: 15, 21-24, 26-27, 28-29.

2007 "Hiebert, Paul G., 1932-2007," *International Bulletin of Missionary Research* 31, no. 3: 128-29.

"Setting the Captives Free: Oppressed Women around the Globe Await Those Willing to Carry on the Legacy of Pandita Ramabai," *Christian History and Biography*, issue 94: 17-18.

2008 "Avarna and Adivasi Christians and Missions: A Paradigm for Understanding Christian Movements in India," *International Bulletin of Missionary Research* 32, no. 1: 14-18, 20.

Reviews and Review Essays

1962 Bearce, George D., *British Attitudes towards India, 1784-1858* (London, 1961). *Journal of Asian Studies* 21, no. 4: 571-72.

1965 Ikram, S. M., *Muslim Civilization in India,* edited by Ainslie T. Embree (New York, 1964). *Journal of Modern History* 37, no. 3: 360-61.

"India at the Turn of the Century" (review essay: Singh, Hira Lal, *Problems and Politics of the British in India, 1885-1898* [New York, 1963]; Edwardes, Michael, *High Noon of Empire: India under Curzon* [London, 1965]; Das, M. N., *India under Morley and Minto: Politics behind Revolution, Repression, and Reforms* [London, 1964]; Wasti, Syed Razi, *Lord Minto and the Indian Nationalist Movement, 1905-1910* [Oxford and New York, 1964]; Aziz, K. K., *Britain and Muslim India: A Study of British Public Opinion vis-à-vis the Development of Muslim Nationalism in India, 1857-1947* [London, 1963]). *Victorian Studies* 9, no. 4: 393-403.

1966 Mukherjee, Nilmani, *The Ryotwari System in Madras, 1792-1827* (Calcutta, 1962). *Journal of Economic History* 26, no. 3: 393-95.

Singhal, Satish C., *Muslim Communities in Gujarat: Preliminary Studies in Their History and Social Organization* (New York, 1964). *American Historical Review* 71, no. 2: 649-50.

1967 Braibanti, Ralph, et al., *Asian Bureaucratic Systems Emergent from the British Imperial Tradition* (Durham, N.C., 1966). *American Historical Review* 73, no. 2: 570-71.

"Studies of Land Control in Indian History" (review essay: Habib, Irfan, *The Agrarian System of Mughal India: 1556-1717* [Bombay, 1963]; Chandra Gupta, Sulekh, *Agrarian Relations and Early British Rule in India: A Case Study of Ceded and Conquered Provinces (Uttar Pradesh), 1801-1833* [Bombay, 1963]; Mukherjee, Nilmani, *The Ryotwari System in India, 1792-1827* [Calcutta, 1962]; Kumar, Dharma, *Land and Caste in South India: A Study of Agricultural Labour in the Madras Presidency during the Nineteenth Century* [Cambridge, 1965]). *Economic Development and Cultural Change* 15, no. 3: 347-53.

1968 Tinker, Hugh, *Experiment with Freedom: India and Pakistan, 1947* (London, 1967). *Pacific Affairs* 41, no. 2: 298-300.

1969 Grover, B. L., *A Documentary Study of British Policy towards Indian Nationalism, 1885-1909* (Delhi, 1967). *Journal of Asian Studies* 28, no. 4: 881-82.

Seal, Anil, *The Emergence of Indian Nationalism: Competition and Collaboration in the Later Nineteenth Century* (New York, 1968). *American Historical Review* 74, no. 3: 1065-66.

Sundaram, K., *Studies in Economic and Social Conditions of Medieval Andhra (A.D. 1000-1600)* (Madras, 1968). *Journal of Asian Studies* 28, no. 3: 637.

1970 Hardgrave, Robert L., Jr., *The Nadars of Tamilnad: The Political Culture of a Community in Change* (Berkeley and Los Angeles, 1969). *American Historical Review* 75, no. 4: 1169-71.

1971 Singhal, D. P., *India and World Civilization* (East Lansing, Mich., 1969). *American Historical Review* 76, no. 3: 741-42.

1972 "The Partition of India: A Quarter Century After" (review essay: *The Transfer of Power, 1942-7*, vol. 1, *The Cripps Mission, January-April 1942*, edited by Nicholas Mansergh and E. W. R. Lumby [London, 1970]; Hodson, H. V., *The Great Divide: Britain — India — Pakistan* [New York, 1971]; *The Partition of India: Policies and Perspectives, 1935-1947*, edited by C. H. Philips and Mary Doreen Wainwright [Cambridge, Mass., 1970]). *American Historical Review* 77, no. 2: 463-72.

1974 Gallagher, John, et al., eds., *Locality, Province, and Nation: Essays on Indian Politics, 1870-1940* (Cambridge, 1973). *Journal of Asian and African Studies* 9: 244-46.

1975 Laird, Michael A., ed., *Bishop Heber in Northern India: Selections from Heber's Journal* (Cambridge, 1971). *American Historical Review* 80, no. 1: 170-71.

Jannuzi, F. T., *Agrarian Crisis in India: The Case of Bihar* (Austin, Tex., 1974). *Agricultural History* 49: 674-75.

1976 "Before and after the Transfer of Power" (review essay: Mansergh, Nicholas, et al., eds., *Constitutional Relations between Britain and India: The Transfer of Power, 1942-7*, vols. 1-6 [London, 1970-76]). *South Asia*, n.s., 1, no. 1: 110-13.

Bhatia, K., *Indira: A Biography of Prime Minister Gandhi* (New York, 1974). *Historian* 38, no. 1: 196-97.

Mansergh, Nicholas, and E. W. R. Lumby, eds., *The Transfer of Power, 1942-7*, vol. 4, *The Bengal Famine and the New Viceroyalty, 15 June 1943–31 August 1944* (London, 1973). *American Historical Review* 81, no. 1: 196-97.

Mansergh, Nicholas, and Penderel Moon, eds., *The Transfer of Power, 1942-7*, vol. 5, *The Simla Conference: Background and Proceedings, 1 September 1944–28 July 1945* (London, 1974). *American Historical Review* 81, no. 3: 648-49.

Nanda, B. R., *Nehrus: Motilal and Jawaharlal* (London, 1962). *Historian* 38, no. 1: 350-51.

"Reconstructing the History of South India" (review essay: Washbrook, D. A., *The Emergence of Provincial Politics: The Madras Presidency, 1870-1920* [Cambridge, 1976]; Baker, Christopher John, *The Politics of South India, 1920-1937* [Cambridge, 1976]; Washbrook, D. A., and C. J. Baker, *South India: Political Institutions and Political Change, 1880-1940* [Delhi, 1975]). *Modern Asian Studies* 12, no. 4: 687-701.

1978 Baker, Christopher John, *The Politics of South India, 1920-1937* (New York, 1976); Washbrook, David A., *The Emergence of Provincial Politics: The Madras Presidency, 1870-1920* (New York, 1976). *American Historical Review* 83, no. 1: 257-58.

Pridmore, F., *The Coins of the British Commonwealth of Nations to the End of the*

Reign of George VI, 1952, part 4: *India,* vol. 1: *East India Company, Presidency Series, c. 1642-1835* (London, 1975), coauthored with J. S. Deyell. *Journal of Asian Studies* 37, no. 3: 555-56.

Worswick, Clark, and Ainslie Embree, *The Last Empire: Photography in British India, 1855-1911* (Millerton, 1976), coauthored with D. Herwaldt. *Journal of Asian Studies* 37, no. 2: 390-91.

1980 Gray, J. C. F., *Tranquebar: A Guide to the Coins of Danish India, circa 1620 to 1845* (Lawrence, Mass., 1974), coauthored with J. S. Deyell. *Journal of Asian Studies* 39, no. 1: 391.

1982 Hockings, Paul, *Ancient Hindu Refugees: Badaga Social History, 1550-1975* (New York, 1980). *American Historical Review* 87, no. 2: 521.

Oddie, G. A., ed., *Social Protest in India: British Protestant Missionaries and Social Reforms, 1850-1900* (Columbia, Mo., 1978). *Journal of Asian Studies* 41, no. 2: 395-96.

1985 "Caste, Morality and Western Religion under the Raj" (review essay: Forrester, D. B., *Caste and Christianity: Attitudes and Policies of Anglo-Saxon Protestant Missionaries in India* [London and Dublin, 1979]; Boudens, R., *Catholic Missionaries in a British Colony: Successes and Failures in Ceylon, 1796-1893* [Immensee, 1979]; Ballhatchet, K., *Race, Sex, and Class under the Raj: Imperial Attitudes and Policies and Their Critics, 1793-1905* [New York, 1980]). *Modern Asian Studies* 19, no. 2: 321-52.

1987 "Christianity in India before the Eighteenth Century" (review essay: Brown, L., *The Indian Christians of St. Thomas: An Account of the Ancient Syrian Church of Malabar* [Cambridge, 1982]; Neill, Stephen, *A History of Christianity in India: The Beginnings to AD 1707* [Cambridge: 1984]; Thekkedath, J., *History of Christianity in India,* vol. 2 [Bangalore, 1982]). *Fides et Historia* 19: 42-48.

Neill, Stephen C., *A History of Christianity in India: 1707-1858* (Cambridge, 1985). *Journal of Church and State* 29: 141-43.

Neill, Stephen C., *A History of Christianity in India: The Beginnings to A.D. 1707* (Cambridge, 1984); Neill, *A History of Christianity in India: 1707-1858* (Cambridge, 1985). *Journal of Asian Studies* 46, no. 1: 195-97.

Baker, Christopher John, *An Indian Rural Economy, 1880-1955: The Tamilnad Countryside* (Oxford, 1984). *Agricultural History* 61, no. 4: 108-9.

1988 Arasaratnam, Sinnappah, *Merchants, Companies, and Commerce on the Coromandel Coast, 1650-1740* (Delhi, 1986). *Pacific Affairs* 61, no. 4: 699-700.

Crawford, S. Cromwell, *Ram Mohan Roy: Social, Political, and Religious Reform in 19th Century India* (New York, 1987). *Journal of Church and State* 30: 591-92.

Kozlowski, Gregory C., *Muslim Endowments and Society in British India* (Cambridge, 1985). *Economic Development and Cultural Change* 36, no. 3: 613-14.

1989 Akbar, M. J., *Nehru: The Making of Modern India* (London and New York, 1988). *Chicago Tribune,* Sunday, April 23, Books, p. 6.

Penner, Peter, *Robert Needham Cust, 1821-1909: A Personal Biography* (Lewiston, N.Y., and Queenston, Ont., 1987). *Victorian Studies* 32, no. 2: 258-59.

Wink, Andre, *Land and Sovereignty in India: Agrarian Society and Politics under the Eighteenth-Century Maratha Svarajya* (Cambridge, 1986); Stokes, Eric, *The Peasant Armed: The Indian Rebellion of 1857* (Oxford, 1986). *Journal of Imperial and Comparative History* 17, no. 3: 432-36.

1990 Dirks, Nicholas B., *The Hollow Crown: Ethnohistory of an Indian Kingdom* (Cambridge, 1987). *Journal of Asian Studies* 49, no. 1: 181-82.

Moon, Penderel, *The British Conquest and Dominion of India* (London, 1989); Metcalf, Thomas R., *An Imperial Vision: Indian Architecture and Britain's Raj* (Berkeley, 1989). *Victorian Studies* 33, no. 4: 652-54.

Pearson, M. N., *The New Cambridge History of India: The Portuguese in India* (Cambridge, 1987); Bayly, C. A., *The New Cambridge History of India: Indian Society and the Making of the British Empire* (Cambridge, 1988); Marshall, P. J., *The New Cambridge History of India: Bengal, the British Bridgehead* (Cambridge, 1987). *American Historical Review* 95, no. 4: 1270-71.

1991 Naipaul, V. S., *India: A Million Mutinies Now* (New York, 1991). *Chicago Tribune,* Sunday, January 6, Books, p. 5.

Moon, Penderel, *The British Conquest and Dominion of India* (London, 1989). *Journal of Asian Studies* 50, no. 1: 190-91.

1992 Viswanathan, Gauri, *Masks of Conquest: Literary Study and British Rule in India* (New York, 1988). *American Historical Review* 97, no. 1: 272-73.

1993 Ward, Richard E., *India's Pro-Arab Policy: A Study in Continuity* (New York, 1992). *Middle East Studies Association Bulletin* 27, no. 1: 70-71.

1994 Reeves, Peter, *Landlords and Governments in Uttar Pradesh: A Study of Their Relations until Zamindari Abolition* (New York, 1992). *American Historical Review* 99, no. 3: 955-56.

Webster, John C. B., *A History of Dalit Christians in India* (San Francisco, 1992). *International Bulletin of Missionary Research* 18, no. 2: 85-86.

1996 McLane, John R., *Land and Local Kingship in Eighteenth-Century Bengal* (Cambridge, 1993). *Journal of the Economic and Social History of the Orient* 39, no. 2: 200-201.

1997 Metcalf, Thomas R., *Ideologies of the Raj* (Cambridge, 1994). *Journal of Asian Studies* 56, no. 1: 237-38.

Young, Richard F., and Subramaniam Jebanesan, *The Bible Trembled: The Hindu-Christian Controversies of Nineteenth-Century Ceylon* (Vienna, 1995); Young, Richard F., and G. P. V. Somaratna, *Vain Debates: The Buddhist-Christian Controversies of Nineteenth-Century Ceylon* (Vienna, 1996); Amaladass, Anand, and Richard F. Young, *The Indian Christiad: A Concise Anthology of Didactic and Devotional Literature in Early Church Sanskrit* (Anand, Gujurat, India, 1995). *International Bulletin of Missionary Research* 21, no. 3: 138-39.

2000 Mani, Lata, *Contentious Traditions: The Debate on Sati in Colonial India* (Berkeley and Los Angeles, 1998). *International History Review* 22, no. 3: 647-48.

Panda, Chitta, *The Decline of the Bengal Zamindars: Midnapore, 1870-1920* (Oxford, 1996). *American Historical Review* 105, no. 5: 1719-20.

Perry, Cyndy L., *Nepali around the World: Emphasizing Nepali Christians of the Himalayas* (Kathmandu, 1997). *International Bulletin of Missionary Research* 24, no. 3: 142-43.

Viswanathan, Gauri. *Outside the Fold: Conversion, Modernity, and Belief* (Princeton, 1998). *Journal of Asian Studies* 59: 790-91.

2001 Irvin, Dale T., *Christian Histories, Christian Traditioning: Rendering Accounts* (Maryknoll, N.Y., 1998). *International Bulletin of Missionary Research* 25, no. 3: 136-37.

2002 Heideman, Eugene P., *From Mission to Church: The Reformed Church of America Mission in India* (Grand Rapids, 2001). *International Bulletin of Missionary Research* 26, no. 3: 136.

Kort, Wesley A., *Faith and Narrative* (Oxford, 2001). *Religion and Literature* 34, no. 2: 111-15.

2003 Cox, Jeffrey, *Imperial Fault Lines: Christianity and Colonial Power in India, 1818-1940* (Stanford, Calif., 2002). *International Bulletin of Missionary Research* 27, no. 3: 141.

2006 Cooper, Randolf G. S., *The Anglo-Maratha Campaigns and the Contest for India: The Struggle for Control of the South Asian Military Economy* (New York, 2003). *American Historical Review* 111, no. 4: 1155-56.

Zupanov, Ines G., *Missionary Tropics: The Catholic Frontier in India (16th-17th Centuries)* (Ann Arbor, 2005). *International Bulletin of Missionary Research* 30, no. 4: 213-14.

2007 Gross, Andreas, et al., eds., *Halle and the Beginning of Protestant Christianity in India*, vol. 1, *The Danish-Halle and the English-Halle Mission;* vol. 2, *Christian*

Mission in the Indian Context; vol. 3, *Communication between India and Europe* (Halle, 2006). *International Bulletin of Missionary Research* 31, no. 3: 163.

Moffett, Samuel Hugh, *History of Christianity in Asia,* vol. 2, *1500-1900* (Maryknoll, N.Y., 2005). *International Bulletin of Missionary Research* 31, no. 1: 52.

Wendt, Reinhard, ed., *An Indian to the Indians? On the Failure and the Posthumous Success of the Missionary Ferdinand Kittel (1832-1903)* (Wiesbaden, 2006). *International Bulletin of Missionary Research* 31, no. 2: 108-09.

2008 Collins, Paul M., *Christian Inculturation in India* (Aldershot, U.K., 2007). *Church History* 77, no. 4: 1118-20.

Kumaradoss, Y. Vincent, *Robert Caldwell: A Scholar-Missionary in Colonial South India* (Delhi, 2007). *International Bulletin of Missionary Research* 32, no. 4: 218-19.

2009 Sanneh, Lamin, *Translating the Message: The Missionary Impact on Culture,* 2nd ed., revised and expanded (Maryknoll, N.Y., 2008). *International Bulletin of Missionary Research* 33, no. 1: 42.

CHAPTER 1

Indian Participation in Enabling, Sustaining, and Promoting Christian Mission in India

DANIEL JEYARAJ

A Tamil proverb asks: *oru kai taTTināl ōcai eLumpumā, irukai taTTināl ōcai eLumpumā?* ("Can applause be effected with one hand, or with both hands?"). Obviously, ovation can be produced only with both hands, and at least two things are necessary to create an effect. This proverb refers to the basic fact of interdependence. Nothing can happen in isolation, but only in relation with other realities. This truth of interdependence is also applicable to the Christian missionary enterprise. Both missionaries and their converts collaborate to establish and continue a Christian presence in a new place. The principle of interdependence is a suitable hermeneutical tool to interpret available Christian missionary reports. The following essay evaluates the work of the Lutheran missionaries in the Danish colony of Tranquebar in South India (1620-1845) and relates it to the contribution of two Tamil Christian leaders. This essay is based on the information found in the *Hallesche Berichte* (i.e., *Halle Reports,* the first German Lutheran mission journal, 1708-1767), archival records kept in various European archives, and other published essays.

Christian Missionary Historiography and Local Agency

Christian missionary historiography is an art of storytelling in which the narrator and the readers play decisive roles. The perspectives of the narrator and the expectations of the readers shape the selective perspectives, starting point, emphasis, and goal of storytelling. Generally, the narrator, who knows the mind-set of the hearers, interprets the stories in such a way that the readers would have little trouble understanding the specifics of the story within the worldviews. If the subject matter of the story is far removed from the worldviews of the readers, it is likely that they would perceive the details of people, culture, and religion that are mentioned in the story in black and white categories such as "we" and "they," "ours" and "theirs," and "here" and "there." It is not always easy to bridge the ethnocentric gap between the subjects of the story in a faraway place and the readers of the story in another place. Further, reports on spiritual matters were also written fully knowing that they would also have socioeconomic and political implications. Christian missionaries have always tried to interconnect people of different cultures and countries with one another, and the intensity and level of their success vary greatly.

Similarly, Christian missionary historiography, written from the perspective of a sending agency, tends to highlight the "heroic achievements" of its self-sacrificing representatives engaged in cross-cultural missionary work. By attempting to describe the nature of other peoples, missionaries generally illustrate their own attitudes, and religious, cultural, and intellectual condition. Christian missionary historiography portrays the missionaries as those who easily master the language of another people, study their literature, and document their customs and thus excel in every aspect of their cross-cultural work. On the other hand, the contributions of the native converts are minimized. They are presented as illiterate, naive, spiritually blind, wavering, stubborn, and uncivilized. But a fresh analysis from the perspective of those who "received" the gospel of Jesus Christ and intelligently chose to become the followers of Jesus Christ often represents another story: the major actors in authentic missionary enterprises were not only the missionaries from outside, but above all the local converts. These converts permitted the missionaries from outside to share their sociocultural space, taught them the local language, explained to them the complexity of their socioreligious thought patterns and lifestyle, and thus tried to bridge the gap between the missionaries and themselves. The converts were the hosts and the missionaries were the guests. Hence, the missionaries could enjoy and benefit from the generosity and hospitality of their hosts. These hosts ensured the very survival and "success" of their "guests," and they were no mere objects and passive beneficiaries of the Christian mission, but were the creators of their own destiny and — under the guidance of the Holy Spirit — the destiny of their newfound Christian faith. The following two representative leaders contributed to the growth, expansion, and consolidation of Tamil Lutheran Christianity.

Savarimuthu, Founder of a Mission School (Cuddalore)

The name Savarimuthu ("Xavier, the Pearl") indicates that this individual was a Roman Catholic Christian who perhaps belonged to the Madurai Mission that was founded by Roberto de Nobili (1577-1656). Niekamp, who has summarized the *Halle Reports,* narrates that Savarimuthu was a fisherman from the harbor city of Nagapattinam. There he heard of the news that the Lutheran Pietists were preaching the message of Jesus Christ in Tranquebar. Consequently, he went to Tranquebar in 1709, decided to leave the Roman Catholic Church, and joined the Lutheran congregation in Tranquebar. In the following year he was appointed a teacher in the mission school in Tranquebar.[1] This experience equipped him to found a Christian school in the English colony of Cuddalore, not far from Tranquebar.

Cuddalore was an important administrative and commercial center for the English East India Company (EIC), which was housed in Fort St. David. The officers there looked for ways to execute an express order of their company dated September 5, 1698. This order required the local officers to establish schools and appoint teachers in all colonies in India so that the children of the company officers and their native servants could be educated.[2] In addition, the members of the Society for Promoting Christian Knowledge (SPCK, founded in 1698 in London) requested the governors of the British colonies to establish appropriate schools for children. The SPCK, which had published the *Propagation of the Gospel in the East* (1709-18), containing several letters and reports of the Tranquebar missionaries,[3] knew of the mission schools in Tranquebar. The educational goals of the Anglican SPCK in London and the Lutheran missionaries in Tranquebar were similar in content and scope. Both groups viewed the schools as the major place "to lay the Foundations of true Christianity," to prepare the "Disciples for the future Service of Christ's Church," and also to bring "in the Use of Books among Christians in the East

1. Johann Lucas Niekamp, *Kurzgefaßte oder Historischer Auszug der Evangelischen Mißions-Berichte aus Ost-Indien von dem Jahr 1705 bis zu Ende des Jahres 1736 mit zwey dazu nöthigen Land-Charten und einer Vorrede Herrn Gotthilf August Franckens* (Halle, 1740), p. 329.

2. Lambeth Palace Library, SPG Papers, vol. ix., fols. 204r-204v: "Extract of the Company's Charter Dated 5th September 1698."

3. B. Ziegenbalg and J. E. Gründler, *Propagation of the Gospel in the East — Being an account of Two Danish Missionaries Lately sent to the East-Indies for the conversion of the Heathens in Malabar in several letters to their correspondents in Europe, containing a narrative of their voyage — Rendered into English from the High Dutch & dedicated to Corporation for Propagating the Gospel in Foreign Parts,* 2 pts. (London, 1709-10; 3rd ed., 1718).

Indies."[4] The SPCK conveyed its desire to start schools in British colonies in India to George Lewis and William Stevenson, two chaplains of the EIC in Madras, and these chaplains decided to contact the Tranquebar missionaries with a request for able teachers to start new schools.

After Bartolomäus Ziegenbalg (1683-1719), one of the founders of the Tranquebar mission, had traveled back to Europe (1714-15), Edward Harrison, the Governor of the EIC in Madras (1711-17), invited Johann Ernest Gründler of the same mission to establish a charity school in Madras and educate Tamil orphans and children of the Tamil slaves who worked for the Europeans. However, Gründler could not accept this invitation, as he thought he could not decide this matter on his own for two reasons: In the absence of his senior colleague Ziegenbalg, who was in Europe at that time, he did not want to make independent decisions. Secondly, he thought he might not be able to find an able schoolteacher, who would be willing to establish and oversee the operation of a mission school in Madras. However, after Ziegenbalg returned to Tranquebar in 1716, the EIC in Cuddalore once again requested the Tranquebar missionaries to send an able teacher. They deputed Savarimuthu to establish a mission school in Cuddalore and lead it. After a few years of successful existence, the school had to be closed down because some of the EIC officers understood that the school, as a Danish institution, could not be tolerated in a British colony.[5]

Even though Savarimuthu did not have an easy time in Cuddalore, he accomplished his task, which at that time no European wanted to face. One of his lasting contributions to the Tamil church was identifying and training Arumugam ("six-faced man," 1698/99–1745). Arumugam was a Shaivite who belonged to the socially respected Pillai caste. It seems that Savarimuthu's low-caste status as a fisherman did not deter Arumugam from learning from him. Arumugam received Tamil Christian books from Savarimuthu. When

4. B. Ziegenbalg and J. E. Gründler, *A Letter to the Reverend Mr. George Lewis, Chaplain to the Honourable East India Company at Fort St. George giving an Account of the Method of Instruction Used in the Charity-Schools of the Church Called Jerusalem in Tranquebar By the Protestant Missionaries there. Translated from the Portuguese — Copy printed at Tranquebar* (London, 1715), p. 2.

5. SPCK Archival Records, Tranquebar Mission, ME Cr. 3, p. 64. T. Wendoy and W. Leeke, two EIC officials in Cuddalore, wrote on December 27, 1725, to SPCK, saying that "The protestant [i.e., English, Anglican] inhabitants of Fort St. David do not like the school work carried on by the Danish Hand. Though Rev. Stevenson planned it well in his time, now it is under present circumstances the schools for heathens [i.e., the Tamils] are impractical." Later another school was established, but when the French captured Cuddalore in 1758, there was no prospect of its recovery. Missionary John Z. Kiernander therefore left Cuddalore, and went to Calcutta.

Arumugam's father, a merchant by profession, lost his trade in Cuddalore, Arumugam went to Tranquebar. There he met Ziegenbalg, who baptized him in 1718 and gave him the symbolic name Aaron. When the missionaries and Tamil Christians discussed the matter of choosing and ordaining a Tamil Christian leader as their pastor, they suggested the name of Savarimuthu along with Aaron. However, Savarimuthu, being conscious of his age (at that time forty-seven) and above all his caste, withdrew his nomination and agreed that his student Aaron be ordained.[6] Consequently, Aaron was ordained on December 28, 1733, and became the first Tamil Lutheran pastor. Though Savarimuthu's school in Cuddalore existed but for a short time, it paved the way for the establishment of schools in other EIC colonies. For example, Benjamin Schultze (1689-1760) left Tranquebar and established a charity school in Madras (1726), which existed for a long time. Thus, Savarimuthu's ministry in Cuddalore was significant for the future of the Tamil church.

Rayanayakkan, Founder of the First Lutheran Church in Tanjore

Another person who facilitated Aaron's ordination was Rayanayakkan ("Imperial Prince," 1700-1771). Rayanayakkan,[7] whose name is generally written as Rajanaikkan ("Royal Prince"),[8] was the grandson of a Roman Catholic. A wandering *pandaram*, who was most probably a Jesuit missionary of de Nobili's Madurai Mission and catered to the spiritual needs of the low-caste people in the Tamil country, was the first person who had apprised Rayanayakkan about the Lutheran missionaries in Tranquebar. This *pandaram* had also lent him the New Testament in Tamil, which had been translated by Ziegenbalg and printed in Tranquebar (1714). Rayanayakkan also read Ziegenbalg's public letter (1709) entitled *Parāparavastuvākiya saruvēcuran cōlamadalalattilē vācamāyirukkira tamilarellārukkum eluti*

6. Niekamp, *Kurzgefaßte*, p. 415.

7. The author of this essay transliterates the name Rayanayakkan as it is found in Tamil palm-leaf manuscripts that are kept in the Royal Library, Copenhagen, Denmark.

8. The life and work of Rayanayakkan have already been narrated, and the present essay does not repeat all the details but adds significant information not available elsewhere. Cf. Reinhold Vormbaum, *Eingeborene Lehrer des Evangeliums in Ostindien* (Düsseldorf, 1851), pp. 5-40; Heike Liebau, "Tamilische Christen im 18. Jahrhundert als Mitgestalter sozialer Veränderungen, Motivationen, Möglichkeiten und Resultate ihres Wirkens," in *Akteure des Wandels: Lebensläufe und Gruppenbilder an Schnittstellen von Kulturen*, ed. Petra Heidrich and Heike Liebau (Berlin, 2001), pp. 19-44.

anuppina nirupam ("The letter written by Sarveshvara, the Supreme Being and sent to all the Tamils living on [the Coast of] Coromandel").[9] Ziegenbalg had written this letter from the perspective of the prophets of the Old Testament, who spoke in the name of YHWH-God. His letter emphasizes the omnipresence, omniscience, and omnipotence of God, who does not tolerate any form of image worship. It considers the Tamil poets the primary agents of image worship, because their poetry perpetuates it. This letter also presents the poets as standing under the influence of the Evil One, who opposes the worship of the invisible God but insists on image worship. Finally, this letter encourages the readers to change their mind (in Tamil: *manacai-t tiruppu,* "repent") from worshiping the images to worshiping the true God as portrayed in the Bible.

> How can I save you, if [you] do not accept my grace? I cannot save you. My righteousness will not compel any one of you. I have come to your land during this time to preach the true Veda so that neither you nor your children can blame me saying that I did not try to save you. Hence, discern the signs of this time, and let me, the Sarveshvara, save you. Is it not enough that you walked for many years on wrong paths? Is it not enough that you still walk in darkness, whereas the light has come near you? Is it right that you continue to hear the false Vedas even though the true Veda has been brought to you?[10]

It seems that Rayanayakkan understood the teachings of the Tranquebar missionaries, and corresponded with them. Whenever he had doubts, he requested clarification, and they sent him written answers. Thus, their relationship grew strong.

Rayanayakkan was a professional soldier, and was employed in the army of Serfoji I, alias Sarabōji (1711-29), the king of Tanjore. He was a *cervaikkaran* ("captain, commander of a division of an army"). Serfoji I waged several wars against the Tamil princes of the small kingdoms Pudukottai, Ramanathapuram, and Madurai, and assisted the Maravar prince Bhavani Shankar in re-

9. A palm-leaf manuscript copy of this letter is kept in the Mission Archives of the Francke Foundations in Halle: AFSt/P TAM 37, Leaves 207v-220. For a German translation see Alwin Gehring, *Bartholomäus Ziegenbalg: Der Vater der Evangelischen Tamulenmission, Jubiläumsausgabe,* 2nd rev. ed. (Leipzig, 1907), pp. 99-104. Gehring entitles his translation "Ziegenbalgs Traktat: Brief Gottes, des Allherrn, an alle in Tscholamandala wohnenden Tamulen."

10. Palm-leaf manuscript, Royal Library, Copenhagen, Cod. Tamul 5829, fols. 22vff. Gehring, *Bartholomäus Ziegenbalg,* p. 103.

gaining his sovereignty. Hence, his armies were constantly on the move. Around 1726 Rayanayakkan's army division was stationed near Poraiyar, a village three kilometers from Tranquebar, and he wanted to make use of the opportunity to personally get to know the Lutheran missionaries, and often went to them for religious discussions. It seems that he and the missionaries spoke about the distinctive elements of Roman Catholicism and Lutheran Pietism.

The second half of 1727 was an important time for Rayanayakkan. He decided to leave the Roman Catholic Church and join the Lutheran church in Tranquebar. When other Roman Catholics came to know of Rayanayakkan's change of faith, they physically attacked him and his family, accusing them of ulterior motives. In one of those attacks his father was killed. In spite of these and other hardships, he gave up his appointment as a *cervaikkaran* and became a catechist — even without any formal theological training in the seminary in Tranquebar (established in 1716).

It seems that some of his colleagues in the army — most of them Roman Catholics — decided to follow his example. Three of them — Nanamuthu ("Spiritual Pearl"), Nanayutam ("Spiritual Weapon"), and Rajappan ("Royal Father," i.e., Peter) — came to Tranquebar to meet the Tranquebar missionaries. On July 20, 1727, they were sent back to Tanjore in "the name of God." After they had returned to Tanjore, they also became the ambassadors of Lutheranism. Rayanayakkan himself worked as a catechist in the area of Madevipattinam, and by the end of 1727 the Lutheran congregation in Madevipattinam consisted of fifteen persons.

This was the beginning of the first Lutheran church in the kingdom of Tanjore, which was the citadel of Shaivism. Serfoji I and his predecessors were ill-disposed toward the Roman Catholics in their kingdom and had earlier prohibited their subjects from being converted.[11] In that context, Rayanayak-

11. Leon Besse, *Father Beschi of the Society of Jesus, His Times and His Writings with a Portrait* (Trichinopoly, 1918), p. 22. Besse states that King Shahaji of Tanjore (1682-1711) persecuted the Roman Catholic Christians so much that he was known as the "Nero of Tanjore." See also James Hough, *The History of Christianity in India from the Commencement of the Christian Era*, vol. 2 (London, 1839), pp. 430-36. Hough explains the immediate reason for this persecution. In 1701, the Roman Catholic Christians in Pondicherry staged their annual drama. They gathered together in front of a Hindu temple where they enacted the legend of Saint George and how he trampled on the divine images in the Greek city of Delphi. The Hindus there were so afraid that they approached King Shahaji for support. Immediately, King Shahaji passed an edict prohibiting his subjects from converting to Roman Catholicism. This edict was in force for a long time. Twelve years later, Ziegenbalg wrote about the fear that non-Christians in the kingdom of Tanjore still felt; they did not dare to come to any Christian church. Cf. Ziegenbalg's diary, entry dated April 30, 1713, in B. Ziegenbalg, *Diarium und Konferenzbuch von 1706 bis 1719 von Ziegenbalg und Gründler*

kan and his colleagues broke down the barriers of prejudice and intolerance. It is evident that Rayanayakkan's reputation contributed to the growth of a small congregation in Tanjore. This is noteworthy because previously no Lutheran missionary was allowed to cross the borders of the kingdom of Tanjore and travel to the capital city. For example, in September 1709, Ziegenbalg tried to cross over from Tranquebar and enter the kingdom of Tanjore. The customs officials stopped him and turned him back. Had they not heard him speak with them in Tamil, they would have arrested and put him in a prison.[12] Tamil converts like Rayanayakkan could accomplish what the foreign missionaries could not.

The Royal House in Tanjore took note of the growing number of Lutherans not only in Tranquebar, but also in certain parts of the kingdom of Tanjore. They wanted to know more about this new group of Christians. In November 1721, Telunguraja, a maternal uncle of King Serfoji I, sent a messenger to Benjamin Schultze in Tranquebar to inquire about Lutheranism. Schultze sent gifts to Telunguraja,[13] but did not go to Tanjore. However, soon after the first Lutheran congregation was established in Tanjore, Telunguraja sent another invitation to the Tranquebar missionaries, and in March 1728 missionary Christian Friedrich Preßier (1697-1745) visited the Royal House in Tanjore, dined with the members of the Royal House, attended a marriage function, and gave the bridegroom a copy of the four Gospels and the Acts of the Apostles (printed in Tranquebar in 1714).[14] It seems that by that time at least some members of the Royal House had changed their attitude toward Christians in general and the Lutherans in particular. Preßier then called upon the Lutherans in Tanjore and returned to Tranquebar. His visit must have boosted the work of Rayanayakkan and his colleagues. By October 1731 there were 414 Lutherans in the kingdom of Tanjore who were under the care of Rayanayakkan and his eight colleagues.[15] The growing number of the Lutherans in Tanjore posed another challenge: the administration of the sacraments of baptism and Eucharist. Hence, the Tranquebar missionaries and the Tamil Lutherans felt the need for an ordained Tamil pastor.

(Copenhagen, National Archives, call number: Reg. 107.Laeg.6). King Serfoji I continued the religious policy of his immediate predecessor.

12. *Halle Reports,* vol. 1, 4th Continuation, p. 171, and 6th Continuation, p. 268.

13. Mission Archives of the Francke Foundations, Halle, Germany, I B 2:13: Schultze's manuscript says the gifts he had sent to Telunguraja were a dog and a pistol.

14. Arno Lehmann, *Es begann in Tranquebar,* 2nd ed. (Berlin, 1956), p. 239.

15. *Halle Reports,* vol. 3, 32nd Continuation, preface. By 1731 the Lutherans in Tanjore were divided into five administrative blocks. Rayanayakkan was directly in charge of 116 Lutherans.

When the question of ordination was discussed, the names of Savarimuthu, Rayanayakkan, and Aaron were suggested. Savarimuthu and Rayanayakkan were Pariahs by birth and the stigma of their status as outside the caste system influenced the decision-makers, including the German missionaries, to choose Aaron, who was a Pillai, belonging to the Vellalar-Shudra community, which was perceived to be of higher status. The decision-makers thought that while a Pariah would be willing to receive the Eucharist from the hands of a Vellalar pastor, the Vellalar people would not take it from the hands of a Pariah pastor. Gotthilf August Francke (1696-1769), the director of the Francke Foundations in Halle, wondered why Rayanayakkan, whose work was thus far successful, could not be ordained. He was told that they had indeed discussed this matter, but the caste differences between the high-caste and low-caste Tamils were so great that the differences between the farmers and normal citizens in Europe were hardly comparable. The missionaries assured Francke that they had tried to remove all ill feelings of the high-caste Shudra Christians toward the low-caste Pariah Christians.[16] However, caste differences still lurked behind the Christian facade. In spite of this fact, when Aaron was ordained on December 28, 1733, Rayanayakkan, three other catechists, and their helpers (Tamil: *utavikkarar*) stood around Aaron and supported him. They pledged that they would continue to carry out his instructions and cooperate with him in extending the reign of God among the Tamil people.[17]

It seems that Rayanayakkan suffered from the fact that his birth-based *jati* (caste subgroup) as a Pariah prevented him from being fully recognized in administering the affairs of the church in Tanjore, which he founded. He had to depend on Aaron and request him to celebrate the Eucharist in his church. He was disappointed.[18] At times he tried to join the Moravian missionaries, who on their way to the Nicobar Islands landed near Tranquebar and began their long residency there.[19] The Lutheran Pietists from Halle and their leader, G. A. Francke, could not accept the Moravians, who wished to reform the Pietists in Tranquebar. Further, G. A. Francke and Count Nikolaus Ludwig Zinzendorf (1700-1760) grew up together in Halle. However, when they took up two different institutions and sent out missionaries, their opinions

16. *Halle Reports,* vol. 4, 48th Continuation, pp. 1503-4.

17. Archives of the Tranquebar Mission kept in the Library of the Evangelical Lutheran Mission, Leipzig, Germany, Box 23, and the document entitled "Um die Ordination Aarons 22 Seiten."

18. Liebau, "Tamilische Christen," p. 27: Liebau explains that most of Rayanayakkan's problems had to do with alcohol and indebtedness.

19. Liebau, "Tamilische Christen," pp. 27-28.

were divided. The differences between Francke and Zinzendorf also affected the Tranquebar missionaries. In this context they did not approve of Rayanayakkan's associations with the Moravians. After forty-four years of missionary work, Rayanayakkan died on September 29, 1771.

Besides establishing and supervising the local congregations in the kingdom of Tanjore, Rayanayakkan had also been engaged in intellectual questions. His intense sense of "conversion" from Roman Catholicism to Lutheranism and his repeated encounters with other Roman Catholics led him to ask practical questions regarding the history of Christianity. His contact person was Christoph Theodosius Walther (1699-1741), who came as a missionary to Tranquebar in 1725. Rayanayakkan asked Walther (1728) to write a history of Christianity beginning with a chronological description of the events in the Old and New Testaments, and narrating the origin of ecclesiastical ceremonies, customs, and festivals, the origins of the Protestant Reformation, and the "transplantation" of the church to India. Walther was pleased that Rayanayakkan undertook this study.[20] After seven years of work, Walther published the first book in Tamil on the history of Christianity (1735).[21] Without Rayanayakkan's persistent questioning and patience, this book might not have been printed. It consists of two parts: the first is short and interprets the history of the Old Testament in terms of preparation of Jesus Christ; the second is long (pp. 65-438) and begins with the history of the New Testament, and then explains the history of the early church, the church fathers, the emergence of the Roman Catholic Church, and the significance of the Protestant Reformation. The book continues with a detailed description of the European missionary enterprise in three continents. It tells of work in Asia through the Portuguese in India and China, the French in Thailand, the Dutch in Sri Lanka and Taiwan, and the Danes in Tranquebar. It mentions the major Portuguese missionary work in the Congo and Ethiopia in Africa. And it details the French and British missions working in different parts of America. The book also includes a section that deals with the life of the apostles of Jesus Christ who are not mentioned in the New Testament. It explains the marks of a true and a false church. Rayanayakkan's questions prompted Walther to engage in an unprecedented missiological research project and see the place of the Lutheran missionary work in Tranquebar within the larger context of the European transcontinental missionary enterprise.

20. *Halle Reports,* vol. 3, 26th Continuation, p. 13.

21. C. T. Walther, *Rerum in Ecclesia Inde Ab Orbe Condito Ad Nostram Usque Aetatem Gestarum Notitiam Exhibens Historia Sacra quae per Septem Periodus & Veteris & Novi Testamenti, [. . .] In gratiam exercitatiorum in Ecclesia Tamulicae* (Tranquebar, 1735).

In 1732, Walther mentioned another of Rayanayakkan's contributions: it seems that Rayanayakkan was familiar with the art of composing metrical poems in Tamil. He followed the common genre of *ammanai*[22] and composed songs on the passion of Christ, and entitled his manuscript *Yēsu nātarudaiya pādupadutalin ammānai* ("Ammānai about the sufferings of the Lord Jesus").[23] Roman Catholic poets, especially the Italian Jesuit Constantin Josef Beschi (1680-1747, since 1709/10 in the Tamil country), had previously composed several Tamil *ammanai* poems in honor of the Virgin Mary. It is possible that Rayanayakkan imitated the style of these or other Roman Catholic poems and composed his *ammanai* on the passion of Jesus Christ. It is also reported that when the Lutherans in Tanjore celebrated the festival of Pentecost in 1748, they sang several edifying songs on the Holy Spirit, which were composed by Rayanayakkan.[24] It is regrettable that none of Rayanayakkan's poems are now preserved. However, three years after Rayanayakkan died, Vedanayagam Sastriyar (1774-1867), who later composed numerous lyrics in Tamil that are still sung in Tamil churches, was born. Vedanayagam Sastriyar may have known at least some of the poems that Rayanayakkan had composed.

Even though Rayanayakkan's Tamil poems are not available, five of his monthly work reports have survived. These reports are written on palm leaves. Rayanayakkan narrates his work during the Tamil months of Adi, Avani, Purattaci, Aipaci, and Margali of the year 1743.[25] A brief examination of these Tamil reports reveals the fact that Rayanayakkan used local bhakti religious concepts to explain the distinctive aspects of Christian faith. For example, he paraphrased Acts 4:12[26] as follows: "There is no *motcam* without Jesus." The Sanskrit loanword *moksha* ("emancipation, final release from worldly existence") was known and is still known to all Tamils. However, the new content that Rayanayakkan assigned to this word means that it was not a

22. *Ammanai* is a kind of girls' game, in which they keep a number of balls in the air. While some balls rise, others fall down. The girls catch the falling balls and throw them up.

23. Manuscript Department, Royal Library, Copenhagen: Ny.Kgl.S. 589C.40 [104 opt]. The information on this palm-leaf manuscript bears the number 28, and is found in the fourth part entitled "Recession der von den Missionaries verfertigen Ole-Bücher [i.e., palm-leaf manuscript books] — theils größere, theils kleinere."

24. Michael Meier, *Johann Lucas Niekamps Kurzgefaßte oder Historischer Auszug der Evangelischen Missions-Berichte aus Ostindien, von dem Jahr 1737 bis zu Ende des Jahrs 1767 fortgesetzt* (Halle, 1772), p. 274.

25. Manuscript Department, Royal Library, Copenhagen: Cod Tamul 5836, Cod Tamul 5837, Cod Tamul 5838, Cod Tamul 5839, and Cod Tamul 5840.

26. Acts 4:12 reads as follows: "There is salvation in no one else, for there is no other name under heaven given among mortals by which we must be saved" (NRSV).

mere release from worldly existence, but salvation in the sense of eternal preservation and safety. Further, Rayanayakkan insisted that *parakati* ("the highest goal," "heavenly refuge") was available only in Jesus. Every person, including the mahatmas ("great-souled," "eminent people"), could attain this *parakati* only in and through Jesus Christ.[27] Thus, Rayanayakkan could indigenize biblical concepts and help his hearers understand the distinctive aspects of Christian beliefs.

A report for the year 1747 summarizes various activities of Rayanayakkan. Regularly, he met Hindus, Muslims, and Roman Catholics and invited them to become the followers of Jesus Christ. As a convert, he did not view the Roman Catholics as Christians. This problematic approach raised opposition. Once he was attacked and his books were taken away. He requested an influential Muslim (German: *Rittermeister*), whom he had known as a colleague serving in the army of the king of Tanjore, to solve the problem. In response, this Muslim leader arrested the Roman Catholic priest who had planned the attack on Rayanayakkan. Soon several Roman Catholics protested against this arrest and threatened to kill themselves if their priest was not released immediately. They also pledged themselves to take revenge on Rayanayakkan. Amidst these and other challenges Rayanayakkan continued his work. Whenever he went to the Royal House in Tanjore, he met with influential Muslim officials (e.g., "Mirusa-Saibhu," "Cusada-Saibhu," and the like), gave them an Arabic version of the New Testament, and discussed various aspects of faith with them. Once he came across a group of "Waruger," who were probably the Wadugar (Telugu-speaking immigrants from the kingdom of Vijayanagar). These people believed neither in God nor in hell, neither in soul nor in heaven. They did not smear on their forehead either *tiruniru* or *tirunamam,* the characteristic marks respectively of Shaivites and Vaishnavites. He spoke with them about the history of creation, human sin, and the consequences of this sin, and invited them to consider accepting Jesus Christ as their Savior.[28]

Whenever Rayanayakkan spoke with the people of the bhakti religions, he did not argue using the philosophical concepts of Shaivism and Vaishnavism (e.g., Shaivasiddanta), but dealt with puranic stories, which portray the rivalry between Shiva and Vishnu.[29] Rayanayakkan knew the socioreligious

27. Manuscript Department, Royal Library, Copenhagen: Cod Tamul 5836, palm leaf 3v.

28. Meier, *Johann Lucas Niekamps Kurzgefaßte,* pp. 293-96.

29. Manuscript Department, Royal Library Copenhagen: Cod Tamul 5836, palm leaf 15v. In one conversation with the Tamils, Rayanayakkan asked: "If Rama is an incarnation of Vishnu, why did he not know where Sita was? How could Vishnu be transformed into a woman and mislead Shiva?"

and cultural mind-set of the people and could address them on various levels. People in general and the Pariahs in particular respected him. In 1750, the soldiers of the king of Tanjore camped near his home; in an ensuing conflict his home was destroyed, and Rayanayakkan had to move to a different place. He wrote to the Tranquebar missionaries that in the time of trouble he desired to be with Christians. Hence, he stayed near a cremation ground. All the Pariahs of the place gathered together and elected him to be their arbitrator.[30] The Lutherans in the city of Tanjore were happy to have Rayanayakkan as their leader. In 1748, Diago, the second Tamil Lutheran pastor (ordained in 1741), visited the Lutherans in and around Tanjore and celebrated Easter and Pentecost with them.[31] These kinds of religious celebrations had been unthinkable in 1709. Within forty years a big change in the attitude of the people occurred, largely due to the work of Tamil Lutherans.

Rayanayakkan was a lay Christian leader who had not undergone any formal theological training, yet he accomplished much more than any of his Christian contemporaries in Tanjore. He took special care to train younger colleagues. One of his assistants was his own brother Anandan ("the Joyful"). Another assistant was Savariappan ("Father Xavier"), a local convert from the Roman Catholic church in Tanjore. Rayanayakkan supervised the work of the catechist Sinnappan ("Minor/Lesser Father" = Paul in comparison to Peter) first in the capital city of Tanjore and after 1746 in the temple city of Kumbagonam near Tanjore.[32] It seems that Rayanayakkan's colleagues respected him and were willing to learn from him.

In 1742, Rayanayakkan and his colleague Alagappan ("handsome Father") founded a school in Tanjore. This school was situated on a street that was frequented by high-caste Shudras and low-caste Pariahs. Alagappan was the main teacher of this school,[33] and it was open to any child irrespective of religious affinity. As a result, not only Christians but also Hindus and Muslims sent their children to study in this school. In 1746, Devanesan, another Tamil Christian, joined Alagappan to look after the welfare of the school. It is reported that "Sultaniappan," a Muslim general in the army of the king of Tanjore, characterized the school as a "work of love" that was established by people who had come there from faraway places. Others criticized the school

30. Meier, *Johann Lucas Niekamps Kurzgefaßte*, pp. 321-22.

31. Meier, *Johann Lucas Niekamps Kurzgefaßte*, p. 274.

32. Niekamp, *Kurzgefaßte*, p. 330. Moreover, Sinnappan's three monthly reports, written on palm leaves, are now kept in the Manuscript Department, Royal Library, Copenhagen: Cod Tamul 5844, Cod Tamul 5845, and Cod Tamul 5849.

33. *Halle Reports*, vol. 5, additional material to 58th Continuation, p. 1524. This report is dated January 4, 1744.

as being a means of converting people. In the midst of public recognition and blame, the school flourished. During this time, other mission schools also existed in different places in the kingdom of Tanjore. For example, twenty-six children were in the school at Tiruppāladuthurai, who were taught by Muthu and Diago. Rayanayakkan supervised all these and other schools in the kingdom of Tanjore.[34] These mission schools signified a radical move in the direction of intercaste, and interreligious, mixing, and fostered the spirit of mutual understanding and tolerance.

Building on Indian Foundations

Another unexpected event seems to have deepened the change of public attitude toward the Lutherans. In 1755, the king of Tanjore appointed Johann Wilhelm Berg as a major in the army with European soldiers under his authority. Berg was a Lutheran from Hamburg. Earlier he had married a Portuguese widow in Tranquebar, and used to participate in the Lutheran services and receive the sacrament of Eucharist. He persuaded the king of Tanjore to issue a written permission for the Tranquebar missionaries to come to Tanjore and administer the sacraments because many of the European soldiers under his command were Protestants. Due to this permission, Diago and missionary Jacob Klein could publicly celebrate a Good Friday service and the Eucharist (on March 31, 1755) in a temporary shed erected on the grounds where Major Berg stayed. Gradually, the Lutheran Christians in Tanjore were recognized as forming a distinct religious group, and could coexist with Hindus, Muslims, and others. Rayanayakkan and his colleagues contributed to the change of attitude.

One year after the death of Rayanayakkan the famous missionary Christian Frederich Schwartz (1726-98, from 1750 in Tranquebar) settled down permanently in Tanjore.[35] There he built his mission on the foundations of Rayanayakkan and other Tamil colleagues. In 1769, Schwartz personally met King Tulajaji (1763-87) in his palace and discussed God's two modes of revelation: through nature and the Word of God. Later, he solemnized the marriage of Major Berg's daughter in the presence of the king. In 1771, the Muslim army of the Nawab of the Carnatic besieged Tanjore and captured Tulajaji. Tulajaji had already asked Schwartz to take care of his adopted son Serfoji II. In 1772,

34. Meier, *Johann Lucas Niekamps Kurzgefaßte,* pp. 243-44.

35. Wilhelm Germann, *Missionar Christian Friedrich Schwartz — Sein Leben und Wirken aus Briefen des Halleschen Missionsarchivs* (Erlangen, 1870).

Schwartz moved to Tanjore, looked after the welfare and education of Serfoji II, and ensured his rule (1798-1832), for which act of kindness the Royal House of Tanjore remains grateful to him even to this present day.

In conclusion, the following can be said about the interaction between Tamil Christians and German missionaries in eighteenth-century South India. The *Halle Reports* and other reports and diaries of the missionaries portray Tamil Lutherans as those who were in need of the missionaries. In reality, the non-Indian missionaries were dependent on the goodwill and hospitality of the Tamil people. The missionaries believed that they could radically change the Tamil society. Soon they realized that the millennia-old system of caste resisted every attempt to change. The missionaries were outsiders to the caste system. But the Tamil converts were exposed to the sociocultural consequences of conversion. Most of the Tamil Lutherans came from the low-caste Pariah castes. Although they did not hesitate to live with the stigma of their *jati*, they dared to take up a new identity as Christians. In spite of these and other limitations, Tamil Lutherans were courageous in sharing the message of Jesus Christ with their non-Christian neighbors. Their interaction with the common people, their attempts to indigenize the Christian message, and above all their attempts to live the ideals that they had been preaching resulted in the origin of new congregations, especially in places where the European missionaries could not go. The missionaries needed the Tamil Christians, and the Tamil Christians, in turn, needed the missionaries. Both of them needed the help of other (Indian and non-Indian) Christians, who understood them and dared to assist them. Together they accomplished many useful things. Hence, a balanced Christian missionary historiography gives equal importance to the missionaries and to the "missionized." As mentioned earlier, at least two hands are necessary to make applause.

CHAPTER 2

"Ancient Churches" and Modern Missions in the Nineteenth Century

WILBERT R. SHENK

Throughout the nineteenth century one of the widely canvassed topics was methods of missionary work. The prevailing assumption was that proper methods would ensure success in missionary work.[1] This discussion was set within the horizon of the "heathen" or "uncivilized" world. Sometimes a distinction was drawn between the peoples of the great historical cultural traditions — including India and China — and those of traditional ethnic societies. But this did not alter the essential task. The obligation laid on the Christian church was to take the gospel from the Christian West to the non-Christian continents and lands.

The encounter of Christian missions with India furnishes the longest continuous engagement by Western missions with one of the oldest of the large-scale religio-cultural traditions. Viewing India as a major laboratory for testing missionary methods, it has been suggested that the three greatest exemplars of missionary methods were Francis Xavier (1506-52), Christian Friedrich Schwartz (1726-98), and William Carey (1761-1834). Xavier and Schwartz employed the method of widespread preaching and baptizing while Carey's goal was to establish a "red-hot centre from which the light and influence of Christianity might radiate throughout a gradually widening circle."[2]

1. Cf. C. H. Robinson, *History of Christian Missions* (Edinburgh, 1915), chap. 1. Missionary conferences typically included sessions on mission methods. Cf. *Report of the Centenary Conference on Protestant Missions, London, 1888*, vol. 2, ed. James Johnston (London, 1889). Many of the sessions were devoted to reports and discussions of the main methods and means of missionary work in vogue at that time.

2. This formulation is from Louis G. Mylne, *Missions to Hindus: A Contribution to the*

Broadly speaking, evangelization was conceptualized either as a process of spreading the Christian message rapidly and widely, followed by mass baptisms, or as a patient building up of committed local congregations. During the first two decades of the nineteenth century, methods of missionary work revolved around preaching, teaching, and publishing — the latter being regarded as essential to the success of the other two.

William Carey had crystallized his missionary approach quite early into five points: (1) preach the gospel widely, using all appropriate methods; (2) support preaching by translating and distributing the Scriptures in the vernacular languages; (3) establish a local church as soon as possible; (4) the missionary must study thoroughly the culture and language of the peoples being evangelized; and (5) make the training of indigenous leaders a priority.[3] In fact, Carey's formulation was widely shared in the early nineteenth century, and this became the dominant model of modern missions. The specific methods would be debated and new ones added, but the superstructure was set in place early in the nineteenth century.

It comes as something of a surprise, then, to read in Eugene Stock's *History of the Church Missionary Society* that "As far back as 1802, a Bristol friend had written to the young Society, — 'Would it not be an object well worthy the attention of your Missionary Society, to attempt the revival of Spiritual and Evangelical Religion in the Greek Church?'"[4] Unfortunately, Stock does not indicate who the letter writer was and gives no background that would place this inquiry in historical context. What is noteworthy about this intervention is that the writer dares to suggest that this newly established missionary society pursue a course of action that appears not to fit at all into the expectations of the day concerning missionary work. In the event, various influences combined so that within two decades the Church Missionary Society (CMS) made the revival of the "ancient churches" an important dimension of its work. Stock devotes an entire chapter to CMS efforts to revive the Eastern churches.[5] The roots of this alternative method go back at least a hundred years.

In this essay, I will argue that this strategy derived mainly from two sources. First, it was a birthright child of Pietist-Puritan impulses at the beginning of the eighteenth century that held together mission and an ecumenical

---

Study of Missionary Methods (London, 1908), and is cited by Robinson, *History of Christian Missions*, p. 14. Apparently the phrase quoted by Robinson is from Mylne.

3. Stephen Neill, *A History of Christian Missions* (Harmondsworth, 1964), p. 224.

4. London, 1899, vol. 1, p. 222.

5. This included "ancient churches" in India, Greece, Turkey, and later Egypt and Ethiopia.

vision of the church. Second, it took on new life as a result of the "Christian Researches" movement that was initiated by Claudius Buchanan (1766-1815) in India and became the primary model of mission for the CMS in Kerala, South India, the Middle East, and Ethiopia, and was emulated by the American Board of Commissioners for Foreign Missions and the American Presbyterian Mission in the Middle East in the early decades of the nineteenth century. The archbishop of Canterbury established a mission that related to the Assyrian Church of the East after 1868. This largely forgotten experiment in forging an alliance between these "ancient churches" and Western mission agencies is a reminder that the ecumenical and missional impulses arise from a common source and should never be treated as antagonists.

The Halle-London-Boston Connection: Missionary and Ecumenical

The turn of the eighteenth century was a time of pulsating religious ferment. In Europe, Great Britain, and North America concerned churchmen were engaged in an earnest transatlantic discussion of the urgency of reviving the Christian faith.

Heinrich W. Ludolf (1655-1712), former personal assistant to the Danish Prince George, husband of Princess (later Queen) Anne, is credited with taking the first steps in forging the London-Halle connection in the early 1690s.[6] His passion was to see a "Universal Church" arise, and he believed the work of August Hermann Francke (1663-1727) at Halle was a model for this "pan-confessional" Christianity that promoted inward personal piety and practical application of the faith. During the 1690s Ludolf traveled widely throughout Europe as well as Russia and the Middle East.[7] As a result of his observations, he became especially interested in promoting renewal of the Russian and Greek Orthodox churches.

The interests of Ludolf and Francke were complementary and intertwined. Francke was a man of extraordinary energy, vision, and ability to organize. His goal was to establish a "Universal Seminary" in which a cadre of young preachers would be trained to carry the message of new life in God

6. Daniel L. Brunner, *Halle Pietists in England: Anthony William Boehm and the Society for Promoting Christian Knowledge* (Göttingen, 1993), p. 42. This is the fullest account of the establishment of the Anglican-Pietist relationship.

7. The range of Ludolf's contacts is quite astonishing. For example, Brunner (*Halle Pietists in England,* pp. 43-44) lists the connections Ludolf made in Great Britain in the 1690s. He used his relationship with Prince George to full advantage in contacting Anglican bishops, university principals and professors, and SPCK leaders.

throughout the world. Such a seminary at Halle would draw together Pietists and awakened Orthodox churches and prepare a new generation for missionary work. As a renewal movement, Pietism was less interested in proper ecclesiastical protocol and correct theology than in promoting vital Christian faith expressed in practical piety wherever possible. Francke and Ludolf nurtured this ecumenical vision of awakening the somnolent churches of historical Christendom by transforming individuals and thereby renewing Christian faith and energizing the church for its missionary task.[8]

In 1696, Josiah Woodward published *An Account of the Rise and Progress of the Religious Societies in the City of London,* in which he advocated the revival of religion and the "reformation of manners."[9] When Woodward brought out the revised third edition of this influential work in 1701, he reported on Francke's multifaceted ministries at Halle as examples of vital Christianity — clear evidence of Ludolf's success in publicizing Pietist renewal and building up a network of relationships.

Thomas Bray (1658-1730) was appointed commissary of the Church of England to the colony of Maryland in 1696 and visited the colony briefly in 1700. Bray took the lead in founding the Society for the Promotion of Christian Knowledge (SPCK) in 1699 and the Society for the Propagation of the Gospel in Foreign Parts (SPG) in 1701. Within two months of the launch of the SPCK, Ludolf arranged contact between Halle Pietists and the SPCK, and Francke and Ludolf became corresponding members of the SPCK.[10] This relationship would grow and remain an important bridge between the Anglican missionary societies and the German Pietists well into the nineteenth century.

In 1701 a young German Pietist, Anton Wilhelm Boehm (1673-1722), was installed as chaplain of the German Lutheran Royal Chapel at St. James, London.[11] He had received his theological training at Halle under A. H. Francke, who had a direct hand in arranging Boehm's appointment to London. Following in the footsteps of Ludolf, in London Boehm quickly became associated with the SPCK and the SPG. At his death in 1722, an SPCK secretary wrote: "[Boehm] was the first promoter of those two excellent Designs the

8. Martin Schmidt, "Ecumenical Activity on the Continent of Europe in the Seventeenth and Eighteenth Centuries," in *A History of the Ecumenical Movement, 1517-1948,* ed. Ruth Rouse and Stephen Neill (London, 1967), pp. 100-101.

9. Josiah Woodward, *An Account of the Rise and Progress of the Religious Societies in the City of London. And of the Endeavours for Reformation of Manners Which have been made therein,* 2nd ed. (London, 1696; enlarged ed., 1698).

10. Brunner, *Halle Pietists in England,* pp. 44-45.

11. Brunner, *Halle Pietists in England,* pp. 49-56.

Protestant Mission to the E. Indies and the Impression of the N. Testament in Arabick having by his good offices with the Society prevailed with them to espouse the furthering of them. He was the life and soul of our Correspondence in religious affairs with Germany and Denmark."[12] Boehm's genius as a publicist and network builder soon made London the hub for exchanges between the Continent, Great Britain, North America, and India. His abilities as a translator enabled a multilateral exchange of letters and other writings.[13]

Cotton Mather (1663-1728), leading Puritan pastor in New England, was also kept abreast of these new missionary societies. His friend in London, Edward Bromfield, was involved in the founding of SPCK as well as a fellow commissioner with Mather of the Corporation for Propagating the Gospel in New England and Adjacent Parts. When Mather published his *Magnalia Christi Americana,* a history of the church in New England, in 1702, he arranged to send copies immediately to A. H. Francke, an indication that Mather was aware of this Pietist leader and wanted to engage with him. Mather's history included a biography of John Eliot (1604-90), pioneer Puritan missionary to the Native Americans of Massachusetts.

It is not clear exactly when the two men began exchanging personal correspondence. At first the Germans had reservations about the character of American Christianity, and Mather was evidently concerned to reassure them that Christian faith in the New World was authentic Pietism.[14] When in February 1709 Mather again sent his latest publications to "Dr. Franckius, in Saxony," the tone suggested that this was a well-established pattern of relationship.[15]

In 1705 Boehm had published an English translation of Francke's book *Pietas Hallensis,* an account of the development of a hospital, charity schools, and orphanage at Halle.[16] Francke emphasized that "the *main scope* [*sic*] of

12. W. O. B. Allen and Edmund McClure, *History of the Society for Promoting Christian Knowledge, 1698-1898* (New York, 1970; original, 1898), p. 232. The rest of the sentence reads: "and the distressed Protestants from the Palatinate found a common father in him to commiserate them under all their Hardships but especially for keeping up a sense of Religion among them by an Evangelick ministry when they should be transplanted into the wild parts of America."

13. Ernst Benz, "Ecumenical Relations between Boston Puritanism and German Pietism: Cotton Mather and August Hermann Francke," *Harvard Theological Review* 54 (1961): 160-62, pays special tribute to Boehm's crucial role.

14. Richard F. Lovelace, *The American Pietism of Cotton Mather* (Grand Rapids, 1979), pp. 33-34.

15. *Diary of Cotton Mather,* vol. 2 (New York, 1957), p. 23.

16. Brunner, *Halle Pietists in England,* pp. 82-87. This publication was to have a considerable career. Instead of reprinting the entire work, it was subsequently abridged and released in three parts. Boehm updated the work to take into account the most recent developments.

the whole Undertaking . . . is nothing else but the Salvation of Souls and their Conversion to life everlasting."[17] His goal, summed up in the title of his treatise on educating children, was "to guide children 'to true piety and Christian wisdom.'"[18] To achieve this goal Francke depended on teachers who modeled and taught the Pietist ideals. One immediate result of the publication of the book was that it generated financial support among the English-speaking world for Francke's institutions. Later, young British men were sent to Halle to be educated by Francke; and charity schools were set up in Great Britain, Ireland, and North America based on the Halle model.

At this time, King Frederick IV of Denmark had decided to establish a mission to India, and he turned to the Halle Pietists for help. Francke handpicked Heinrich Plütschau and Bartholomäus Ziegenbalg for this new venture. They arrived in India in July 1706 and set to work using the methods Francke had taught them at Halle: education and translation and distribution of the Scriptures. These were regarded as the primary means of conversion.

At first the English-speaking world was largely unaware of this initiative. But the missionaries regularly sent letters to Denmark and Germany, and these were published and distributed. In London Boehm translated the missionaries' letters into English in order to promote the Tranquebar Mission in Great Britain. In 1709, he collected these letters and published a small volume titled *Propagation of the Gospel in the East* and dedicated it to the Society for the Propagation of the Gospel and its president, Archbishop Thomas Tenison, evidently in the hope that the SPG would ally itself with the Tranquebar Mission.[19] In the event, the SPG declined on the legal ground that its charter authorized it to work only in North America. Thereupon, Boehm turned to the SPCK. On September 7, 1710, the SPCK accepted Ziegenbalg and Plütschau as corresponding members.

Propagation of the Gospel in the East consisted of ten missionary letters and an essay by Boehm, "A Preliminary Discourse concerning the Character of a Missionary." Echoing the concern of H. W. Ludolf, Boehm addressed "'the sad Fate of the Eastern Churches' in the Levant, of whom St. John had written in Revelation ii-iii, and warned the European Churches that it was of little avail 'to have the Name and Form of an Orthodox Communion, without

17. Brunner, *Halle Pietists in England*, p. 84.

18. Brunner, *Halle Pietists in England*, p. 93.

19. See John Foster, "The Ecumenical Significance of A. W. Boehm, 'The Propagation of the Gospel in the East,'" *Oecumenica: Jahrbuch für ökumenische Forschung 1968* (Gütersloh, 1968), pp. 117-32, for an analysis of the multiple revisions and expansion of Boehm's book over more than a decade and a discussion of Boehm's essay.

the Life and Power which should attend it.'"[20] Within nine years, two more parts had been added and the work had been reprinted several times.

German church historian Ernst Benz has argued that in the correspondence exchanged between Cotton Mather and A. H. Francke "we find the first attempts to develop a theology of missions and to understand missions as a global task involving all Protestant churches."[21] Benz's main point is that previously the missions had developed in isolation from one another. Now theologians and mission leaders were grappling with the issues being raised by these developments from a global perspective.

Writing to Mather in 1714, Francke reports that he has in his possession a letter written by Increase (father of Cotton) Mather, July 12, 1687, which gives an account of John Eliot's work among the Native Americans "which I have read with singular Satisfaction." Francke goes on to describe the progress of the Tranquebar mission and encourages Mather to correspond directly with the missionaries at Tranquebar, giving them "a full Account of all such *Methods* [*sic*] as hitherto have been made use of for converting your *West India* [*sic*] Heathens to the Christian Faith."[22] Francke also requests that Mather share his views with the Halle-London folk as well.

In 1721 Mather published his book *India Christiana,* a compilation of a report on the current status of Christian work among the Native Americans and a lengthy letter to Bartholomäus Ziegenbalg dated December 31, 1717. Unfortunately, Ziegenbalg died before the letter arrived. It fell to his colleague, Johann Gründler, to write a substantial reply to Mather, dated December 10, 1719. Mather reproduced this letter in *India Christiana.* In his letter to Ziegenbalg, Mather identified the core of his theology of mission as the "Everlasting Gospel": (a) the triune God is the basis and goal of life; (b) Jesus Christ is the only redeemer of humankind; and (c) the essence of Christian faith is love for all people.[23]

This emphasis on the "Everlasting Gospel" causes Mather to conclude that in non-Christian lands the missionary's task is to preach only the gospel and

20. Brunner, *Halle Pietists in England,* p. 103.

21. Benz, "Ecumenical Relations," p. 178. This judgment will be challenged by those who claim that the pioneer in this regard is Gisbertus Voetius (1589-1675), who developed a comprehensive theology of mission in his five-volume work: *Selectae Disputationes Theologicae* (1843). See Jan A. B. Jongeneel, "The Missiology of Gisbertus Voetius, the First Comprehensive Protestant Theology of Missions," *Calvin Theological Journal* 26 (1991): 47-79.

22. Benz, "Ecumenical Relations," p. 179.

23. This formulation appears in several of Mather's writings. Benz helpfully displays two parallel versions in "Ecumenical Relations," pp. 188-92.

not the doctrinal formulations that separate denominations from one another. His ecumenical vision is set forth in this passage:

> . . . this is the very First born of my Wishes; nor is there any thing that I more wish, or have more Earnest desires for, than this: That all the Servants of GOD, who *Do and Endure* many Things for the *Evangelizing* of the World, may Exhibit unto the whole *World* the *Pure Maxims* of the *Everlasting Gospel,* and would Preach unto the Nations, the *Weightier Matters of the Gospel,* and the *Wheat* well cleansed from the *Chaff,* and from those *Lesser Matters,* whereabout Good Men, may and often do carry on their Disputations.
>
> 'Tis most certain, That the *Christian Religion* is no other than the Doctrine of Living to GOD by CHRIST, and is a *Practical Thing* rather than a meer *Theory,* the intention whereof is, to animate a Real Solid, Vital PIETY, and Call forth such as ly *dead* in their Sins, unto a *Godly, & a Sober, & a Righteous Life.*[24]

Independently of Mather, the Moravian leader, Nikolaus Zinzendorf (1700-1760), arrived at the same conclusion. Indeed, Zinzendorf would develop a more comprehensive and articulated theology, strategy, and methodology of mission that was thoroughly ecumenical in spirit.[25] Moravian missions were widely publicized through missionary accounts. These missions were far-flung and helped create an awareness of the "uttermost parts" that hitherto had been lacking. The Moravian model of mission was to exert considerable influence on the pioneers of the modern mission movement from the late 1700s onward. William Carey drew directly on Moravian concepts and principles. When the London Missionary Society was founded in 1795, its "fundamental principle" was to introduce no particular ecclesiastical system but rather to leave to converts the decision as to the form of church government.

In the autumn of 1744 Christian ministers in Scotland issued a call to their churches to join in united prayer for the coming of the kingdom of God. They concluded

> that the providence of God, at such a day, did loudly call upon such as were concerned for the welfare of Zion, to united extraordinary applications to the God of all grace, suitably acknowledging him as the foun-

24. Cotton Mather, *India Christiana* (Boston, 1721), p. 66.

25. A J. Lewis, *Zinzendorf the Ecumenical Pioneer: A Study in the Moravian Contribution to Christian Mission and Unity* (Philadelphia, 1962), especially chaps. 5 and 6.

> tain of all the spiritual benefits and blessings of his church, and earnestly praying to him, that he would appear in his glory, and favor Zion, and manifest his compassion to the world of mankind, by an abundant effusion of his Holy Spirit on all the churches, and the whole habitable earth, to revive the true religion in all parts of Christendom, and to deliver all nations from their great and manifold spiritual calamities and miseries, and bless them with the unspeakable benefits of the kingdom of our glorious Redeemer, and fill the whole earth with his glory.[26]

This group decided to put out a circular containing the proposal that for the next two years ministers and their congregations would agree to dedicate time each week for intercession and, each quarter, Tuesday would also be given to this purpose. The proposal met ready response. Young people became involved by establishing special prayer groups. After two years a group of ministers printed a memorial: *A Concert for Prayer, to Be Continued for Seven Years.* This pamphlet was circulated widely in Scotland and England as well as in America.[27]

Fortunately, this proposal caught the imagination of Jonathan Edwards, widely respected pastor-theologian, who responded by writing a book, *An Humble Attempt to Promote Explicit Agreement and Visible Union among God's People, In Extraordinary Prayer For the Revival of Religion, And the Advancement of Christ's Kingdom on Earth, Pursuant to Scriptural Promises, And Prophecies Concerning the Last Time.*[28] When it was published five Boston pastors signed the preface. It exerted profound and sustained influence throughout the Western world. Edwards based his appeal on Zechariah 8:20-22 and then built his case by assembling a wide array of prophetic texts from the Old Testament. Appealing to millennial impulses, he argued that God had not yet revealed the "latter-day glory." This would happen only when God's people united in prayer.

Edwards's initiative played an important role in preparing the way for the emergence of the modern mission movement in various ways. At the time Edwards was writing *An Humble Attempt,* the young David Brainerd, known for his missionary work among the Native Americans, was on his deathbed in

26. Jonathan Edwards, *An Humble Attempt to Promote Explicit Agreement and Visible Union of God's People in Extraordinary Prayer,* in *The Works of Jonathan Edwards,* vol. 5, ed. Stephen J. Stein (New Haven, 1977), p. 321.

27. This section draws on the fine article by R. Pierce Beaver, "The Concert for Prayer for Missions: An Early Venture in Ecumenical Action," *Ecumenical Review* 10 (1958): 420-27.

28. First published in Boston in 1747.

the Edwards home. Brainerd implored his congregation to accept Edwards's proposal, which they did. Subsequently, Edwards, in editing *The Life of David Brainerd,* included the latter's deathbed appeal to his congregation. Generations of readers were inspired by this example.

While many churches on both sides of the Atlantic followed the proposed pattern of weekly and quarterly prayer meetings, there was variety. The Association of Baptist Churches in Northampton, England, for example, initiated a prayer movement in 1784 "for the general revival and spread of religion."[29] John Sutcliffe, pastor of the young William Carey (1761-1834), was active in this movement. The founders of the London Missionary Society in 1795 urged that the first Monday night of each month be set aside for prayer for missions. This "concert of prayer," which drew together Christians of many traditions, remained an important force in the missionary movement through the 1820s.

William Carey's "pleasing dream" in 1806 has been called "the most startling missionary proposal of all time."[30] Writing from Serampore, India, to Andrew Fuller, secretary of the Baptist Missionary Society, Carey urged Fuller to take the lead in convening "a meeting of all denominations of Christians at The Cape of Good Hope somewhere about 1810."[31] Visionary that he was, Carey projected a series of decennial international and interdenominational missionary conferences. Fuller dismissed this proposal out of hand "as one of bro'r Carey's pleasing dreams."[32] Even the rather limited missionary work of the eighteenth century had already produced examples of the practical issues and conflicts that arise when more than one mission agency attempts to work in the same area. In spite of the theological visions of Cotton Mather and Count Zinzendorf, ecclesiastical loyalties proved to be highly resilient and the vast majority of missionaries dutifully sought to replicate exactly what had been drilled into them by the sending church. Living in a missionary situation in India, Carey was in daily contact with colleagues from various ecclesiastical traditions. He surely was aware of both the problems and the possibilities of collaboration. It would take nearly a century, and only after missionary conferences had been instituted in the 1850s, before issues of cooperation began to be addressed and a system of comity worked out. These two impulses

29. Beaver, "The Concert for Prayer," p. 425.

30. Ruth Rouse, "William Carey's 'Pleasing Dream,'" *International Review of Missions* 38 (1949): 181. P. G. J. Meiring, "William Carey's Pleasing Dream," *Missionalia* 21 (1993): 219-28, written to commemorate the bicentennial year of Carey's journey by way of the Cape of Good Hope and arrival in India, offers a suggestive reflection on the multiple dimensions of what Carey's proposal entailed.

31. Rouse, "William Carey's 'Pleasing Dream,'" p. 181.

32. Cited from S. Peace Carey, *William Carey* (London, 1934), pp. 268-69.

— the *missionary* and the *ecumenical* — though arising from a single source, were uneasy allies. Nonetheless, the Puritan-Pietist heritage remained a salient force.

"Christian Researches" and "Ancient Churches"

While living in London in 1790, Claudius Buchanan had experienced a religious awakening and came under the influence of John Newton.[33] Newton's friend Henry Thornton also took an interest in Buchanan and offered to support him while he studied for the ministry at Cambridge. Inevitably, he came under the influence of Charles Simeon, vicar of Holy Trinity Church and evangelical activist. The East India Company (EIC) barred missionaries from India, but Simeon and his friends found a way around this restriction by recruiting for the EIC chaplaincy — a service the Company was required by law to maintain — young evangelicals who shared their passion for missions. Buchanan completed his studies at Cambridge in 1795 and a curacy in 1796. He arrived at Calcutta in March 1797.

From the beginning, Buchanan did not find his duties as chaplain fulfilling. He studied the Bengali language and began to acquaint himself with others in Bengal who shared his missionary interests. Senior chaplain David Brown and William Carey were among his confidants and collaborators. Brown and Buchanan were involved in the founding of Fort William College, and Carey joined them in establishing an extensive Bible translation program under college auspices. Buchanan was also concerned about the lack of a satisfactory ecclesiastical arrangement in India. While the East India Company opposed any change, Buchanan and others were determined to change the company charter. In 1805, Buchanan submitted to the bishop of London a proposal for the establishment of the Anglican Church in India "as a means of perpetuating the Christian religion among our own countrymen; and as a foundation for the ultimate civilizing of the natives."[34] This proposal was warmly welcomed in London but strongly resisted by the EIC and its supporters.

33. This section is based on Wilbert R. Shenk, "Claudius Buchanan, 1766-1815: Laying the Foundation for an Indian Church," *Mission Legacies: Biographical Studies of Leaders of the Modern Missionary Movement,* ed. Gerald H. Anderson (Maryknoll, N.Y., 1994), pp. 255-63.

34. This phrase is taken from the title of the 176-page brief Buchanan submitted to Bishop Porteus: *Memoir of the Expediency of an Ecclesiastical Establishment for India: both as the means of perpetuating the Christian religion among our own countrymen; and as a foundation for the ultimate civilizing of the natives* (London, 1805).

As an outgrowth of the Bible translation projects proposed for Fort William College, in 1806 Buchanan requested, and was granted, a leave of absence by the governor-general to engage in research. The indefatigable Buchanan had already corresponded with various people across the Indian Subcontinent as well as other parts of Asia, gathering information about the religious and cultural conditions. Buchanan was especially concerned to establish the status of Christianity and other religions in the region. He noticed that the reports coming in frequently contained contradictory information and, therefore, personal follow-up was required. Buchanan was especially interested in knowing the situation with regard to scriptures in the vernacular languages. He proposed to make an inventory of all the scriptures available for the various religions. Buchanan carried out two arduous journeys between 1806 and 1808, covering much of southern India and Sri Lanka. He gathered information on Hinduism, Judaism in India, Roman Catholicism, Protestantism, and Syrian churches.

Having lost his wife and several children, and in poor health himself, Buchanan returned to Great Britain in 1808. The timing was critical. His return home allowed him to get the report of his field research ready for press. Buchanan's findings were published as *Christian Researches in Asia* in 1811 and proved to be an immediate publishing success. Within two years it had gone through twelve editions.[35] Buchanan's great contribution was to bring the existence of India's ancient churches to the attention of the English-speaking world. What is more, his book became a model for a stream of such "research" reports.

The East India Company charter was coming up for renewal in 1812, and all of Buchanan's expert knowledge of India and skill as a publicist would be called on to lead the struggle by the pro-missionary forces determined to amend the EIC charter to allow Christian missions to conduct missionary work in India.[36] In the end, the pro-missionary side won. One of the first results was the establishment of the bishopric of Calcutta in 1813.

On his first journey to southern India in October 1806, Buchanan visited the Syrian Christians in Travancore and Malabar, who had "been settled there from the early ages of Christianity."[37] Buchanan was aware that three centuries earlier Vasco da Gama had had contact with these people in 1503. Subsequently, the Dominicans had succeeded in bringing most of the Syrian Chris-

35. Last republished in 1858.

36. Allan K. Davidson, *Evangelicals and Attitudes to India, 1786-1813: Missionary Publicity and Claudius Buchanan* (Oxford, 1990), gives a full account of this campaign to get the EIC charter amended and the role of Buchanan in it.

37. Claudius Buchanan, *Christian Researches in Asia,* 3rd ed. (Edinburgh, 1812), p. 99.

tians into the Roman Catholic Church. After 1550, the Jesuits became the dominant Roman Catholic influence and a Jesuit became archbishop of the church in the early 1600s. The rigorous efforts of the Jesuits to bring the Syrians into complete conformity with Rome resulted in a backlash. In 1653 the Indians expelled the Jesuits and took steps to have their bishops consecrated through the church of the Middle East. The Catholics did succeed in recouping a part of the Syrians who had broken away. The existence of the traditional Mar Thoma Church, claiming to have been founded by the apostle Thomas, had largely faded from view.

Buchanan had two declared purposes for his visit: (1) to determine what historical materials and biblical manuscripts the Mar Thoma Christians had, and (2) to assess whether this church might be enlisted in the task of translating their scriptures into the vernacular languages.[38]

In his conversations with church leaders, Buchanan observed their poverty and "the air of fallen greatness." The senior priest acknowledged their plight: "The glory of our Church has passed away; but we hope your nation will revive it again." Buchanan replied, "the glory of a Church could never die, if it preserved the Bible."[39] Buchanan offered to supply them with copies of the Syriac Bible, but what interested him most was their interest in producing a new translation. Good Protestant that he was, he was convinced that placing the Scriptures in vernacular translation in the hands of the people would lead to an ingathering.

Later it was recognized that Buchanan had been naive in certain respects by accepting at face value much of what the Syrians had told him.[40] But what he did accomplish was to introduce this ancient church sympathetically to a world that was unacquainted with it and to advocate continuing helpful collaboration. H. W. Ludolf and A. W. Boehm would have been firm supporters of this move. Buchanan's *Christian Researches* laid the foundation for a policy and missionary methods that called for European missionary societies to work for the revival of the "ancient churches" in order that they would carry out the evangelization of their societies since they would be able to do so far more effectively than the foreign missionary.

In the first fifteen years of its existence the (Anglican) Church Missionary Society (CMS) received several proposals for engaging in the renewal of ancient churches. Finally, it was decided that they should concentrate these "re-

38. Buchanan, *Christian Researches,* p. 103.

39. Buchanan, *Christian Researches,* p. 109.

40. E.g., Stephen Neill, *History of the Church in India, 1707-1858* (Cambridge, 1985), p. 239, says Buchanan drew several wrong impressions and passed these along to his readers.

vival" efforts on the churches of the East. The rationale that underlay CMS's conclusion was "that the revival of the Eastern Churches would undoubtedly have an effect on the Mohammedan and Heathen World."[41]

During his travels Buchanan was assisted by Colonel Macaulay, British resident at Travancore. In 1813, Macaulay's successor, Colonel John Munro, put forward a plan to establish a college to train Syrian Christians as ministers as well as teachers. Munro secured land and financial support for constructing the buildings. In 1816, the first two missionaries were sent to establish this program. The CMS instructed its missionaries "not to pull down the ancient Church and build another but to remove the rubbish and repair the decaying places."[42]

At the time of his death in 1815, Buchanan was contemplating traveling throughout the Middle East for the purpose of writing a report on religious conditions in Greece, Turkey, and Egypt. In response to this developing vision, CMS assigned William Jowett to Malta in 1815 "to inquire into the state of religion in the Levant, and to suggest methods for translating and circulating the Scriptures, and other ways of influencing the Oriental Churches."[43] His instructions were to (1) gather information about the religious situation in the Mediterranean world, and (2) investigate the most effective means of evangelization. Sensitive that they were sending the young missionary into an area where the Roman Catholic Church was dominant, the CMS counseled him to exercise great discretion. He was to study all the ancient churches: "Greek, Jacobite or Syrian, Coptic, Abyssinian, Armenian, Nestorian. Then the Mohammedans." And he was to establish relationships with leaders of the churches and seek to open correspondence between Anglican prelates and these heads of Middle Eastern churches. In summary, says Stock, "It was, indeed, to the Eastern Churches that the Society chiefly looked for the future evangelization of the non-Christian populations in the neighbouring Asiatic and African countries."[44] Jowett remained in Malta for fifteen years, and among his many literary efforts was *Christian Researches in the Mediterranean, Syria, and the Holy Land* (1820).[45]

Eugene Stock records that "Abyssinia had long been in the thoughts of the

41. Eugene Stock, *History of the Church Missionary Society* (London, 1899), 1:222.

42. Stock, *History*, 1:233, citing CMS instructions to missionaries.

43. Stock, *History*, 1:224.

44. Stock, *History*, 1:225.

45. This genre of writing would continue to be produced. William Ellis published a four-volume *Polynesian Researches* (London, 1829). The most famous of all and marking the end of an era was David Livingstone's *Missionary Researches and Travels in South Africa* (New York, 1858).

Church Missionary Society."[46] In 1817, CMS acquired a manuscript in Ethiopic[47] of a portion of the Old Testament. A linguistic expert, Samuel Lee, later professor of Arabic at Cambridge, prepared a brief history of the Ethiopian Coptic Church as a briefing for the CMS.[48] In 1820, William Jowett was able to purchase a manuscript copy of the Amharic Bible. Finally, in 1830, CMS missionary Samuel Gobat was able to reach Ethiopia and begin a ministry based largely on distribution of the Scriptures in Amharic.[49] Illness forced Gobat to return to Europe. Despite great difficulties in reaching the country and constant health problems, other missionaries worked in Ethiopia during the following decade. J. L. Krapf was the last of this heroic company. He moved to Mombasa in 1841.

Even though the policy did not yield the results originally envisaged, it would shape CMS response throughout this region for many years. Furthermore, it was adopted by other missionary societies as well. When the American Board of Commissioners for Foreign Missions (ABCFM) sent its first missionaries — Pliny Fisk and Levi Parsons — to the Middle East in 1819, it gave careful instructions on how the missionaries were to go about their work.[50] Following the lead of the CMS, the ABCFM accepted the premise that evangelization of the wider population could most effectively be accomplished by first reviving the ancient churches.[51] After a promising start, the American missions ran into difficulty. The ancient churches rather quickly cooled to these efforts by outsiders to reform them. The missionaries found allies among the local Christians. These "dissidents" longed to see their church revived and were attracted by this new spirituality; they sided with the missionaries. Having broken rank with the traditional church, they were marginalized and, naturally, turned to the mission for aid and comfort. Eventually, the ABCFM decided it had no recourse but to form a new church. The First Evangelical Armenian Church in Constantinople was organized July 1, 1846, with thirty-six Armenians as charter members. This pragmatic step did not mean the ABCFM repudiated its original commitment. The Board's long-serving secretary, Rufus Anderson (1796-1880), insisted on the priority of *preaching* as the most efficient method of

46. Stock, *History,* 1:351.

47. A Semitic language used in the Ethiopian Coptic Church.

48. Published as an appendix to the CMS Annual Report for 1818.

49. *Samuel Gobat, Bishop of Jerusalem: His Life and Work. A Biographical Sketch* (New York, 1885), chap. 4.

50. [Rufus Anderson], *Memorial Volume of the First Fifty Years of the American Board of Commissioners for Foreign Missions* (Boston, 1861), pp. 229-33.

51. William E. Strong, *The Story of the American Board* (Boston, 1910), chap. 5.

evangelization but recognized that this was not possible in certain situations.[52] In his history of ABCFM missions to the Middle East, Anderson concluded that "the main work of winning races to Christianity must be performed by men of the same race. . . . [T]he original plan of the mission to Turkey has been more promising of good, than any other; namely, that of operating upon the Mohammedans through regenerated churches planted in the communities where they dwell."[53] In reality, experience did not render a clear verdict. The ABCFM had also run up against interethnic conflicts and rivalries that made it inadvisable, for example, to send an Armenian to evangelize the Turks.

When the American Presbyterian Mission entered Egypt in 1854, the question of what the mission was to do in relation to the ancient Coptic church had a clear answer. The mission set its sights on evangelizing the Coptic Christians and founding the Coptic Evangelical Church.[54]

Undoubtedly, the most sustained experiment in forging a "helping" relationship by a European church with one of the ancient churches was the archbishop of Canterbury's Assyrian Mission.[55] This initiative was the fruit of a series of contacts that began in the 1820s and 1830s, including an agent of the British and Foreign Bible Society (BFBS) and the intrepid Joseph Wolff, missionary to the Jews, who visited the region for the first time in 1825.[56] The BFBS agent in Constantinople, Henry Leeves, met a Chaldean bishop in 1822 who was returning from a visit to Rome. The BFBS made various attempts to work with these churches to produce and distribute vernacular translations of the Scriptures. Other explorations were carried out during this time, including that of ABCFM missionaries H. G. O. Dwight and Eli Smith.[57] Finally, in 1868 the Church of England took under consideration an appeal to

52. Paul W. Harris makes this point in *Nothing but Christ* (New York, 1999), pp. 50-53, 72-76.

53. Rufus Anderson, *History of the Missions of the American Board of Commissioners for Foreign Missions to the Oriental Churches*, vol. 2 (Boston, 1873), p. 484.

54. Stanley H. Skreslet II, "The American Presbyterian Mission in Egypt: Significant Factors in Its Establishment," *Journal of Presbyterian History* 64 (1986): 84.

55. J. F. Coakley, *The Church of the East and the Church of England* (Oxford, 1992). Coakley indicates that "the earliest stirrings of interest in an acquaintance with the Church of the East in the nineteenth century can be traced to the Church Missionary Society" and cites Stock, *History*, 1:221-35.

56. Cf. Joseph Wolff, *Missionary Journal of the Rev. Joseph Wolff, Missionary to the Jews*, 3 vols. (London, 1829).

57. Eli Smith, *Researches of Eli Smith and H. G. O. Dwight in Armenia: including a Journey through Asia Minor and into Georgia and Persia, with a visit to the Nestorian and Chaldean Christians of Oormiah and Salmas*, 2 vols. (Boston, 1833).

give aid to the Assyrian Church of the East.[58] Eighteen years later, a mission was established when two missionaries were sent out in June 1886 to assist this church. The archbishop of Canterbury took something of a risk since the Assyrian Church of the East was linked historically with Nestorius, fifth-century bishop of Constantinople. A part of the logic for establishing this relationship was that the American Board, representing American Congregationalists, and the Protestant-leaning CMS did not appreciate the historical episcopacy that was important to both the ancient churches and High Church Anglicans.[59] This relationship lasted until 1938. The Assyrian Church of the East became a member of the World Council of Churches in 1950.

Conclusion

A century before the launch of the modern mission movement, a group of visionaries dreamed of a movement that would unify Christian churches as they joined together for world evangelization. This grand vision, introduced in the 1690s, of linking world evangelization to the revitalization of the ancient churches had an impressive durability. They insisted that the *ecumenical* and *missionary* dimensions of the *missio Dei* belonged together.

In the first place, the fact that it has proved difficult in experience to hold these two dimensions together in no way invalidates the theological and missiological integrity of the vision. Rather, it stands as a permanent challenge to rise above the conventional habits of thought and ecclesiastical parochialism in order to strive for "the more excellent way."

A second observation is that the reasons given for pursuing either task — be it the ecumenical or the missionary — separate from the other, have been predominantly pragmatic rather than theological. Both sides have regarded church and mission as separable realities. A defective ecclesiology underlies both.

In the third place, this study underscores the power of ignorance and prejudice. The "ancient churches" typically had long lived in isolation from other Christians and as cultural enclaves. The Western missionary societies responded out of sincere motives but with only the most superficial under-

58. Cf. Hervé Legrand, "Assyrian Church of the East," in *Dictionary of the Ecumenical Movement,* ed. Nicholas Lossky et al., 2nd ed. (Geneva, 2002), pp. 69-70, for a sketch of this church and its relationship to other ancient churches.

59. Coakley, *Church of the East,* pp. 18-53, traces the interplay between traditional ecclesiastical and theological rivalries leading up to the founding of the archbishop of Canterbury's Assyrian Mission.

standing of the "ancient churches." Furthermore, they naively assumed that the "ancient churches" would quickly and gladly receive the resources they had to offer. The Western missionary societies and their missionaries did not recognize sufficiently the need for patience and a profound knowledge of the tradition and history of these churches as prerequisites to any action on their part.

Finally, although the world context has changed in significant ways, each of these criticisms applies with equal force to ecumenical and missionary action in the twenty-first century. These nineteenth-century experiments will repay careful study.

CHAPTER 3

Empire and Misinformation: Christianity and Colonial Knowledge from a South Indian Hindu Perspective (ca. 1804)

RICHARD FOX YOUNG

To anyone who keeps abreast of the literature on Indian history, it will be obvious that the title of my essay can make no claim to originality. It occurred to me from reading C. A. Bayly's *Empire and Information*,[1] a work of rich, archival texture, which I believe to be an exemplary model, historiographically, for the proper alignment of theory with data. Overall, *Empire and Information* is a book that concerns itself with indigenous information systems and how they were utilized (manipulated, exploited, etc.) by the British in order to sustain the Leviathan that the Raj became. From intelligence gathering to postal systems, Bayly leaves almost nothing out. My first acquaintance with the book came when I was working on India's interactions with Europe and Christianity (via missionary agency) in the area of science;[2] as it turned out, Bayly and I had coincidentally worked on some of the same individuals (mainly Company servants) and learned communities (Brahmins in Benares and Malwa). As I expected, however, Bayly was way ahead of me, archivally (and otherwise). In his chapter "Physicians and Astronomers," I read of one "P. Raghaviah," the South Indian author of an early-nineteenth-century treatise that attempted a

1. C. A. Bayly, *Empire and Information: Intelligence Gathering and Social Communication in India, 1780-1870* (Cambridge, 1996).

2. Richard Fox Young, "Receding from Antiquity: Hindu Responses to Science and Christianity on the Margins of Empire, 1800-1850," in *Christians and Missionaries in India: Cross-Cultural Communication since 1500*, ed. Robert E. Frykenberg (Grand Rapids and London, 2003), pp. 183-222.

reconciliation of Indian and European astronomy, whose manuscript Bayly had found in the Oriental and India Office Collections (London).

The more I learned about Ragaviah, the clearer it became that science was less of an interest to him than public administration; moreover, this undeservedly obscure individual was clearly prime material for a micro-study of what might happen when British information systems failed: what, for instance, might an indigenous informant do to rectify misinformation about India, especially when the appropriation of it made colonial administrators incompetent and arrogant? Ragaviah's concerns had an institutional focus, and the crux was: young recruits educated at the College of Fort William (Calcutta) were being graduated to govern India without a proper understanding of Hindu jurisprudence *(dharmashastra);* symptomatically, the misunderstanding had to do with suttee/*sati,* which in the evangelical ethos of the College had become emblematic of India's civilizational inferiority and the urgency of its Christianization. Archival materials, fortunately, are abundant enough to work the subject from both directions, the College's and Ragaviah's. Under the first heading, "Orientalism and Orientalization at the College of Fort William," I differentiate "orientalism," the late-eighteenth-, early-nineteenth-century study of Indian antiquity through its languages and literatures, from "orientalization," the construction of India as Europe's radical "other" for hegemonic, colonial purposes, to show that while both were evident at the College, Ragaviah embraced the one but rejected the other. Under the second heading, "The Honour of Being a 'Hindoo,'" I inquire into the identity Ragaviah began to evince in responding to India's orientalization. Finally, under the third heading, "The Hollowing of History," I discuss what it means to me to work archivally with a figure like Ragaviah in relation to contemporary debates about colonial historiography.

Orientalism and Orientalization at the College of Fort William

Early in 1802, at what became a fixture of Calcutta's public life throughout the later years of Richard Wellesley's tenure as governor-general (1798-1807), city notables gathered in the stately Town Hall to witness an event without precedent. The occasion marked the first anniversary of the College of Fort William, a Wellesley-initiated project so ambitious that contemporaries referred to it as the "University of the East."[3] Such praise was premature; informed of

3. On the origins and vagaries of the College of Fort William, see David Kopf, *British Orientalism and the Bengal Renaissance: The Dynamics of Indian Modernization, 1773-1835* (Berkeley, 1969).

the College as a fait accompli, the East India Company's Court of Directors was incensed. By the time Wellesley sailed home, the wonder he had wrought was considerably scaled down. The reasons were various. To Charles Grant (1746-1823), the Clapham evangelical whose image of "Hinduism" could hardly be described as cordial,[4] the seemingly uncritical, humanistic orientalism that Wellesley patronized had been decoupled, disastrously, from British Christianity's civilizing mission. As much as the Company's fledgling administrators needed a knowledge of "oriental" languages (the raison d'être of the College), they needed even more to keep themselves anchored in British values and the Christian faith. Grant associated orientalism with Indianization,[5] and thus to think of India as being on a civilizational par with Europe, or, worse yet, to think of "Hinduism" as being competent to revitalize itself without first being baptized into Christianity, seemed subversive. In the absence of institutional safeguards, Grant argued, the College might undermine the identity and integrity of the impressionable recruits who were sent out to govern India.[6]

Grant's reaction to the occasion of 1802 remains unknown. What transpired, however, would have confirmed his worst fears — but only some. What the occasion marked was actually more than simply an anniversary; it was the first of the annual "oriental disputations" that students of the College conducted publicly and solely in oriental languages (Persian, Hindustani, Sanskrit, and Bengali, among others); as we shall see, the disputations were "public" in more senses than one, but on this day they took place in the presence of the governor-general, the distinguished linguists of the faculty, and

4. Grant's (mis)perceptions of "Hinduism" were inscribed in a frequently reprinted memo of 1792: "Observations on the State of Society among the Asiatic Subjects of Great Britain, particularly with respect to Morals, and on the means of Improving It." See Ainslee Thomas Embree, *Charles Grant and British Rule in India* (New York, 1962), pp. 141-57.

5. When I speak of orientalists, I mean those of the late eighteenth century: William Jones (1746-94; founder of the Asiatic Society), Charles Wilkins (1749-1836; translator of the *Bhagavad Gita*), the early Nathaniel Brassey Halhed (1751-1830; translator of *A Code of Gentoo Laws*), and Henry Theodore Colebrooke (1765-1837; founder of Vedic and Vedantic studies). All were Grant's contemporaries. Wilhelm Halbfass, *India and Europe: An Essay in Understanding* (Albany, N.Y., 1988), p. 62, says their lines of inquiry were "typical of deism and the Age of Enlightenment."

6. For Grant's concerns about the College, which aggravated a long-standing quarrel with the governor-general, see Embree, *Charles Grant*, pp. 205-30. The clash turned into a victory for Grant. As a counterbalance to the College, the directors opened Haileybury, the Company's training school in Hertford. Haileybury cadets were to be grounded in the routine collegiate subjects of the day under the watchful eye of a faculty dominated by the Anglican clergy. Only when thus inoculated were they sent out to master the languages in situ.

the pandits whose patience was rewarded by the fluency of the few and tried by the stammering of the many.[7] Grant might have agreed with William Carey (1767-1837), the polylingual Baptist of Serampore who taught Bengali and Sanskrit at the College, when he characterized these disputations as more interesting than anything happening in the universities of Europe;[8] nevertheless, some of these youthful perorations would have struck him as alarmingly orientalist. W. B. Martin, for instance, speaking in Bengali, "On Whether the Asiaticks Are as Capable of as High a Degree of Civilization as the Europeans," affirmed that they were, echoing a theme from William Jones:

> [W]e see that literature, taste, and science originated in Asia, and by a gradual diffusion, in the course of time, spread themselves over Greece and Italy. Such then having been once the state of the sciences and arts among the Asiaticks, it cannot be unreasonable to suppose, that their ability still remains unhurt and vigorous; and that those sparks of genius, hitherto smothered or enfeebled by the noxious climate of oppression, might under the congenial influence of a milder government and more favourable laws, again be fanned into a flame.[9]

One could do a lot of unpacking with a dense "imperial" text like this; the trope of "oriental despotism" is there, a perennial favorite among all students; as Rosane Rocher has observed: "For all its emphasis on oriental languages, Fort William College was a training-school for imperial-minded administrators, and its imperial founder [Wellesley] acknowledged it when he stated 'the College must stand or the Empire must fall.'"[10] Still, for a context like this, the text evinces a remarkable openness to the past of Indian antiquity, so much so that its eloquence belies amateurishness; it is, in fact, a juvenile bastardization of Jonesian orientalism, which did not actually attribute to India the

7. The scene in all its pomp is described by the College vice-provost, Claudius Buchanan, in Hugh Pearson, *Memoir of the Life and Writings of the Rev. Claudius Buchanan, D.D.* (London, 1819), 1:175-76.

8. *Primitiæ Orientalis: Being the Essays and Disputations of the Students of the College of Fort William* (Calcutta, 1803-4), p. 115.

9. *Essays by the Students of the College of Fort William in Bengal, to which are added the Theses Pronounced at the Public Disputations in the Oriental Languages on the 6th February, 1802* (Calcutta, 1802), p. 166. Martin, a stellar student, attained high office as assistant to Wellesley.

10. Rosane Rocher, "British Orientalism in the Eighteenth Century: The Dialectics of Knowledge and Government," in *Orientalism and the Post-Colonial Predicament: Perspectives on South Asia*, ed. Carol A. Breckenridge and Peter van der Veer (Philadelphia, 1993), p. 218.

civilizational priority that Martin did.[11] Had it not been for this, however, Martin's disquisition would have been an unmitigated indictment, as arrogantly sweeping in its essentialization of "Hinduism" as its cross-cultural caricatures were crudely condescending. To the trope of Islamic "tyranny," those of "braminical priestcraft" and "oriental indolence" must be added; infanticide and especially suttee/*sati* — "Thousands of human victims have been known, annually to smoke on the polluted altars of their horrid deities"[12] — elicit from him a smug self-righteousness. As we shall see, the shades of difference between orientalists and evangelicals were rather indistinct, having mainly to do with the way Indian antiquity was envisioned. Thus, even though Martin also spoke of Christianity as the hammer and anvil that would "knock off the fetters of Braminical hypocrisy and pride,"[13] his overall orientation was symptomatically orientalist, if also tinged with evangelicalism and dyed in the colors of imperialism.

As P. J. Marshall rightly observes, evangelicals in the early 1800s grew increasingly disenchanted with orientalism.[14] Wellesley's adversary, Charles Grant himself, was a prime example. Anticipating trouble, Wellesley handed Grant a sop — the institutional safeguards he would ask for anyway. Before the Court had even been apprised of the College, two Church of England Clapham evangelicals, David Brown (1763-1812) and Claudius Buchanan (1766-1815), who had been appointed Company chaplains under Grant's patronage, were already installed as provost and vice-provost. Brown, who was in overall charge of the students' spiritual welfare, was learned in the older orientalism of biblical languages; though he had received mentoring from William Jones in the study of Sanskrit, his views on "Hinduism," for which he felt "utter disgust," had hardened.[15] Buchanan, who taught classics and European history, was a brilliant publicist for missions and the evangelical campaign against suttee/*sati;* even to Grant, however, his anti-Hindu tirades seemed imprudent.[16] In the aftermath of the Vellore Mutiny (1806) when

11. "Jones' views were dominated by the idea that India itself was not the original home of the religious and philosophical tradition of the West, but rather represented an old offshoot of an original source common to both East and West." Halbfass, *India and Europe,* p. 63.

12. *Essays by the Students* (1802), p. 113.

13. *Essays by the Students* (1802), p. 118.

14. P. J. Marshall, *The British Discovery of Hinduism in the Eighteenth Century* (Cambridge, 1970), pp. 41-42.

15. On Brown, coincidentally the father of Charles Philip Brown (1798-1884), a renowned "Christian Orientalist," see Peter L. Schmitthenner, *Telugu Resurgence: C. P. Brown and Cultural Consolidation in Nineteenth-Century South India* (New Delhi, 2001), pp. 36-41.

16. So incendiary were Buchanan's sermons that they had to pass the Company's cen-

Grant's Parliamentary opponents sought to lay the blame on missionary defiance of the Company's policy of religious "neutrality," the offices Brown and Buchanan held were abolished. Nevertheless, in these early years evangelical influence in the College was far from inconsiderable; from chapel to classroom, the only individuals to whom all the students would have regularly related was this pair of uncompromising, evangelical clergymen.

Institutional influence is hard to assess; so are student predispositions. To complicate matters further, there was another formidable evangelical in the College who makes the standard binary opposition between evangelicals and orientalists less tenable. This was William Carey, Martin's Bengali professor whose contempt for "Hinduism" was matched by his disciplined exploration of its languages and literatures. Some of both may have rubbed off on Martin, though it did not dampen his enthusiasm for Jones. On the whole, however, it seems probable that Brown, Buchanan, and Carey collectively imbued the College with a more distinctively evangelical ethos than is ordinarily recognized; it seeps out of the disputations most conspicuously when one reads them through the hermeneutic of the evangelicals' obsession with India's "dreadful Practices," suttee/*sati* in particular. It cannot be entirely coincidental that in 1799, just before Wellesley brought him to the College, Carey witnessed a widow immolation for the first time;[17] that around the same time as the disputations of 1802 he was collecting statistics on "victims";[18] or that Claudius Buchanan would circulate those statistics in a barrage of pamphlets to shame Parliament into action (ineffectually, it turned

sors before they could be published. Grant's loss of confidence in him is related in Embree, *Charles Grant,* pp. 240-48 passim.

17. Like those of most observers, Carey's reports on suttee/*sati* accentuated the lurid details (but not voyeuristically). In this first experience of being an eyewitness, the details describe an event that cannot be called "involuntary" in any simplistic sense: "[S]he in the calmest manner mounted the pile and danced on it, with her hands extended, as if in the utmost tranquility of spirit." *Periodical Accounts Relative to the Baptist Missionary Society* 2 (1801): 26-27.

18. On January 5, 1802, one month before the oriental disputations, the Serampore Mission announced the following: "Government have instituted an enquiry into the murders of the Hindoos, and brother Carey has been requested to present all his information on the subject. Some suppose that 30,000 widows are burnt annually with the bodies of their husbands: others say, about 25,000. Brother C. is endeavoring to ascertain it as near as can be." *Periodical Accounts Relative to the Baptist Missionary Society* 2 (1801): 241. Though these estimates were wildly off the mark, more sensible calculations were soon forthcoming (n. 19, *infra*). Serampore's campaign against this and other "dreadful Practices" is discussed in E. Daniel Potts, *British Baptist Missionaries in India, 1793-1837: The History of Serampore and Its Missions* (Cambridge, 1967), pp. 139-68.

out).[19] For evidence, I adduce an essay from 1802 by Thomas Newnham (b. 1778), who addressed the same theme as Martin's, only this time in English. More than the others, this would be the essay that reflects the views of Brown, Buchanan, and Carey.

Newnham, who was later posted to the presidency of Fort St. George (Madras), excelled at "Tamoul" and placed first in the examinations. The following year, he declaimed in that language "On the Custom of Hindu Women Burning Themselves on the Decease of Their Husbands," taking second prize.[20] Although his English essay does not qualify as an oriental disputation, it hardly matters; in most cases, only the English versions found their way into print. Those for which the originals survive, indicate that the students were mostly unable to think in anything but English. Like Martin, Newnham trots out the usual colonial tropes, scatters offensive generalizations like birdseed — "To vegetate in sloth is the delight of the Hindoo"[21] — and sees Christianity as India's salvation: "The only effectual expedient for the improvement of this idolatrous and deluded people appears to be the civilizing influence of the Christian religion."[22] Were it not for the un-Jonesian way he envisions Indian antiquity, Newnham would be heir to the same vulgarized orientalism as Martin's: "If the arts had been carried to a high degree of perfection, some traces of that perfection would have remained. . . . I mean not to assert, that many of the arts known and esteemed in Europe, have not had their origin in this country: it is probable that Hindoostan was one of the first countries which emerged from barbarism. But there is no appearance of its having at any former time greatly excelled that degree of civilization, such

19. The system was rudimentary but methodical. "Native" assistants stationed at strategic locations within a thirty-mile radius of Calcutta tallied a total of 438 widow immolations for 1803. These and other Serampore statistics were announced to the world in Baptist publications; none caught the attention of the British public more than Buchanan's *Christian Researches in Asia* (London, 1811). The ensuing outcry prompted Parliament to require the Company to undertake a similar survey, preliminary to a final decision on whether suttee/*sati* should be abolished — a dilemma long postponed. Statistics for the next decade are analyzed in Anand Yang, "Whose Sati? Widow Burning in Early 19th Century India," *Journal of Women's History* 1 (1989): 8-33.

20. The *Primitiæ Orientalis* of 1803 does not include Newnham's "Tamoul" disputation; one in Sanskrit by William Chaplin, another of Carey's students, is found on pp. 51-66. Chaplin was too much a gradualist to be in full sympathy with Carey: "If any thing ever could succeed amongst a people so much the slaves to bigotry and superstition, it must be the divine influence of the Christian religion. But time alone can effect this great object, and *it would be equally unjust and impolitic to make use of power to deprive men of the enjoyment of religious freedom*" (p. 65, emphasis added).

21. *Essays by the Students* (1802), p. 132.

22. *Essays by the Students* (1802), p. 141.

as it is, which exists at this day."[23] While this kind of slam on Jonesian orientalism — thou-shalt-know-India-by-its-fruits — imbues the text with an evangelical orientation, its construction of India as Europe's "other" is itself undeniably and pejoratively orientalizing, by which I mean, following C. A. Bayly, "the creation of 'essentialized' stereotypes and modes of classification which abstract social characteristics from complex local identities for the sake of ruling":[24]

> When writing on the progress of national refinement, how is a standard for civility to be fixed? It has been generally accounted that those countries alone are civilized, where laws have been framed for the protection of life and for the safety of property. That country therefore can never be called civilized, where the priest stands before the altar of his idol, with his hands reeking with the blood of the newly slaughtered victim; whose laws permit the son to expose to the flood the being who gave him birth, when oppressed by years, and unable to labour for the support of life; where the youthful widow is compelled to finish a short life upon the pile of her deceased husband, or else must survive his loss in ignominy or servitude; where human sacrifices are offered up to appease the demon of destruction; and where the woman who has been long barren, offers her first born to her God, by exposing it to the birds and beasts of prey, or suffering it to be carried away by the flood of the Ganges.[25]

For a text like this, which catalogues most of the "dreadful Practices" that colonial discourse routinely deplored, one needs a theory but also a context. Fortunately, at the end of the segment quoted, an asterisked comment provides a clue for understanding how orientalization could occur: "Many of these unnatural cruelties were perpetrated publicly in the presence of Europeans at the last Hindoo festival, in the Island of Saugor, in December 1801." An incident of the kind alluded to, which must have set the College abuzz with rumor, did in fact occur; according to a police report filed twelve days after the disputations, "The number of victims destroyed amounted to no less than 39" — enough to send a shudder through the spine of a green recruit. Although Government was first apprised of the Saugor "sacrifices" in 1793, no action was taken until Wellesley's Council took the matter in hand; six

23. *Essays by the Students* (1802), pp. 126-27.
24. Bayly, *Empire and Information*, p. 369.
25. *Essays by the Students* (1802), pp. 130-31.

months later, Regulation 6 of 1802 declared the "dreadful Practice" a criminal offense on grounds of not being "sanctioned by the Hindoo law."[26] The way I read Newnham, anxiety wears the mask of indignation; this would come from not seeing how justice could be administered to a people whose jurisprudence violated "cultural sense." Newnham would eventually have to apply this law, just as every Company judge and magistrate had had to since 1792. Although it was, more precisely, not Hindu law but Anglo-shastric law, the consequences for him of actually having to apply this hybrid, using College "Tamoul" in the court of Cuddapah in the South, I put aside for later.

Unless I am mistaken, my analysis has something in common with C. A. Bayly's interpretation of India's orientalization as (in part) a "panic response" to "the information gap" (deficit, vacuum, etc.) during times of perceived crisis.[27] To Fort William students, "sanctioned by the Hindoo law" must have made justice sound disarmingly simple to administer. Being accustomed to English common law, the gap between the texts of Indian antiquity *(dharmashastras)* would have seemed more like a gulf. For years, judges and magistrates had nothing better to turn to than *A Code of Gentoo Laws*, Nathaniel Brassey Halhed's 1776 translation of a panditic legal encyclopedia in Sanskrit. Had Newnham consulted the *Code* for guidance on how to adjudicate a case of suttee/*sati*, he would not have found law *(naya)* as such but dharma: "It is proper for a Woman, after her Husband's Death, to burn herself in the Fire with his Corpse; every Woman, who thus burns, shall remain in Paradise with her Husband Three *Crore* and Fifty *Lacks* of Years, by Destiny; if she cannot burn, she must, in that Case, preserve an inviolable Chastity; if she remains always chaste, she goes to Paradise; and if she does not preserve her Chastity, she goes to Hell."[28] Halhed's commentary, moreover, would hardly have helped: "The Terms of the Injunction as there set forth are plain, moderate and conditional: 'It is proper for a Woman to burn with her Husband's Corps [*sic*];' and a proportionate Reward is offered in Compensation for her Sufferings. Notwithstanding the Ordinance is not in the absolute Style of a Command; it is surely sufficiently direct to stand for a Religious Duty; the only Proof that it is not positive is the proposal of inviolable Chastity as an Alternative, though it is not to be taken for an Equivalent." Com-

26. "Papers relative to Infanticide, by Drowning, Practised by the Hindoos at *Saugor*, and other Places: 1794-1820," *House of Commons Papers on East India Affairs, Hindoo Infanticide* (London, 1824), p. 137. Carey had long agitated for the same legislation. See Potts, *British Baptist Missionaries*, pp. 140-42.

27. Bayly, *Empire and Information*, pp. 365ff.

28. Nathaniel Brassey Halhed, *A Code of Gentoo Laws, Or Ordinations of the Pundits* (London, 1776), p. 286.

pounding the problem, Halhed shrouded the commentary with a veil of inscrutability and implied that suttee/*sati* was still fairly prevalent:

> The Bramins seem to look upon the Sacrifice as one of the first Principles of the Religion, the Cause of which it would hardly be orthodox to investigate. There are however several Restrictions with respect to it, as that a Woman must not burn herself if she is with Child, nor if her Husband died at a Distance from her, unless she can procure his Turban and Girdle to put it on at the Pile, with other Exceptions of the same Nature, which they closely conceal from the Eyes of the World, among the other Mysteries of their Faith. But we are convinced equally by Information and Experience, that the Custom has not for the most Part fallen into Desuetude in India.[29]

Naturally, "Information and Experience" differed; H. T. Colebrooke's essay of 1795, "On the Duties of the Faithful Hindu Widow," contradicted Halhed, claiming "happily the martyrs of this superstition have never been numerous."[30] In a surprise reversal, Colebrooke omitted this one line from his *Digest of Hindu Law* of 1801, which otherwise reproduced the earlier essay unabridged.[31] The *Digest* surpassed the *Code* by extracting a broader swath of shastric precepts; some were even accompanied by panditic commentaries. They were, however, mutually discrepant; judges and magistrates who lived by the common-law principle of *stare decisis* ("to stand by decided matters") would not only have found the laws they were duty-bound to uphold disconcertingly un-English, they would also have felt morally compromised when called upon to enforce them.[32]

Newnham's essay was a "traveling" text that went back to Europe where it was published in 1804 by the *Monthly Review.* A London literary periodical with orientalist pretensions, its editor gushed at being able "To behold the victor bowing to the institutions, laws, and manners of the conquered peo-

29. Halhed, *Code of Gentoo Laws,* pp. lxx-lxxi.

30. H. T. Colebrooke, "On the Duties of a Faithful Hindu Widow," *Asiatic Researches* 4 (1795): 219.

31. H. T. Colebrooke, *A Digest of Hindu Law, on Contracts and Successions: with a Commentary by Jagannatha Tercapanchanana* (Calcutta and London, 1801), 2:451-97.

32. My understanding of Anglo-shastric law and the dilemmas of colonial jurisprudence comes from J. Duncan M. Derrett, *Religion, Law, and the State in India* (New York, 1968), pp. 274-320; Jörg Fisch, "Humanitarian Achievement or Administrative Necessity? Lord William Bentinck and the Abolition of Sati in 1829," *Journal of Asian History* 34 (2000): 109-34, has been likewise informative.

ple." Because of its much-needed "information with respect to the Natives," Newnham's essay received the *Monthly Review*'s seal of approval.[33] From London, the essay returned to India, ostensibly "authenticated." Cross-culturally, however, it traveled less successfully, which brings my essay to "Partheputt Ragaviah Charry" (Parthepat Raghaviah Acharya), who stepped into the public arena to contest India's orientalization by offering, civilly and collegially, to fill in the information Newnham lacked.

The Honor of Being a "Hindoo"

To even think of resurrecting Ragaviah from the archival tomb necessarily presupposes a certain historiographical disposition; disinclined to hamstring myself before the tomb is opened, I leave such considerations aside until the data reaches "critical mass." That being said, the mass *is* meager and miscellaneous; besides the review of the *Monthly Review*, the only remains of Ragaviah are a few items of correspondence scattered across the European Manuscripts and the Mackenzie Collection of the Oriental and India Office Collections (OIOC) of the British Library. Because the materials range only from 1803 to 1807, a diachronic account is ruled out; had Ragaviah lived into the 1820s, I suspect he might have been active in founding one of the several literary societies that came into existence in Madras in that decade (Ragaviah's last letter puts forward a proposal to do exactly that; see n. 59). He identifies himself as a "native of Madras," but the correspondence is mainly from "Seringapatam" (Srirangapatnam) in Mysore; references to "Hurry-har" (Harihar) in northern Mysore and Fort St. George indicate that Ragaviah was on the move. The correspondence is from him but not to him; there is, significantly, correspondence about him. Ragaviah cultivated a network of high-level British contacts: (1) William Kirkpatrick (1754-1812), Persian interpreter to the commander of the Bengal army, British resident at Hyderabad, assistant to Wellesley, professor of Persian at the College of Fort William, and presumably the person through whom Ragaviah heard about the *Monthly Review;* (2) Thomas Strange (1756-1841), chief justice of the Madras Supreme Court, scholar of Anglo-shastric law, Sanskritist; and (3) Colin Mackenzie (1753-1821), Madras engineer, surveyor of Mysore and Madras, pack rat and collector extraordinaire who vacuumed up vast amounts of historical material from South India (textual, epigraphical, numismatic, etc.), including Ragaviah's Newnham review, which tells us that Ragaviah was not only a *sub-*

33. *Monthly Review* 43 (February 1804): 190-97.

ject of interest but also an *object* of research.[34] Additionally, Ragaviah talks about corresponding with Arthur Wellesley (1769-1852), the future duke of Wellington, younger brother of the governor-general; at the time, Wellesley was with the Madras army. With the exception of Strange, the others had all been present at the battle of Seringapatam in 1799, which ended the Fourth Anglo-Mysore War. To Strange, Ragaviah writes on subjects of orientalist interest; Kirkpatrick is a patron, the "Pagoda Tree"; about Mackenzie, more can be added later.

Thanks to Robert E. Frykenberg, I am able to identify Ragaviah as a Teluguized Maratha, a *Deshastha* ("of the land," i.e., of Maratha lineage but acculturated outside the Maratha heartland); *Deshasthas* were a Brahmin community that long enjoyed a monopoly over the upper echelons of the British administrative apparatus throughout the South, just under the British themselves.[35] Evidently, however, Ragaviah had not yet reached the top and was shaking his "Pagoda Tree" in the hope of finding a more remunerative position. Being a "secular" Brahmin involved in worldly *(laukika)* affairs, Ragaviah's letters to Kirkpatrick are engagingly chatty; he alludes to turmoil in Mysore and laments the death of the British resident, Josiah Webbe (1767-1804). Most of all, he strategizes: Arthur had written to Richard; Richard said through Arthur that something might open up in the Maratha country; Arthur had left Madras for Calcutta; Arthur was leaving Calcutta for England; he would be going to Calcutta to see Richard himself, because it looked like Arthur had not done what he promised. That is how it goes (surnames and honorifics omitted), always in a vivid, delightfully idiosyncratic prose. *Deshasthas* were noted for their English skills, and Ragaviah complained to Kirkpatrick that the Company was squandering its resources on "the study of

34. Of Kirkpatrick, Strange, and Mackenzie, Mackenzie is the figure of greatest interest to contemporary scholarship. See Matthew Edney, *Mapping an Empire: The Geographical Construction of British India, 1765-1843* (Chicago and London, 1997), pp. 152-55. The Mackenzie Collection has been described as "the largest set of sources for the study of early modern historical anthropology of southern India." Nicholas B. Dirks, "Colonial Histories and Native Informants: Biography of an Archive," in *Orientalism and the Post-Colonial Predicament*, p. 281. To some scholars, Mackenzie represents colonialism masquerading as science; for the view that "collecting" India was a collaborative, Indo-European project, see Robert E. Frykenberg, "The Halle Legacy in Modern India: Information and the Spread of Education, Enlightenment, and Evangelization," in *Missionsberichte aus Indien im 18. Jahrhundert: Ihre Bedeutung für die europäische Geistesgeschichte und ihr wissenschaftlicher Quellenwert für die Indienkunde*, ed. Michael Bergunder (Halle, 1999), pp. 22-24.

35. Personal communication, 03/08/98. Frykenberg has written extensively on *Deshasthas* in *Guntur District, 1788-1848: A History of Local Influence and Central Authority in South India* (Oxford, 1965), passim.

vernacular languages among the Gentlemen" (viz., students of Fort William); instead, it ought to "encourage the natives to acquire a proficiency in the English language and literature." The British, he claimed, "never have much to say"; it would be better for both sides if more of the talking were done by "Natives": "esteem and friendship will be added to obedience and civility."[36]

Unfortunately, there is no clue as to how and where Ragaviah acquired English. Frykenberg's studies on South India suggest that it might have been a mission school or government *kachcheri.* Adducing evidence that "The origins of modern education in South India lay in Northern Europe,"[37] he demonstrates that while the Company dithered, Protestant missionaries had been opening schools up and down the Coromandel Coast since the early eighteenth century, beginning at Tranquebar. Under Christian Friedrich Schwartz (1726-98), a German missionary, the Society for the Promotion of Christian Knowledge operated schools in several princely states in the vicinity of Madras (Tanjore, Sivaganga, Ramnad); Ragaviah could have been one of the many *Deshasthas* who flocked to those schools and then joined the Company.[38] One wonders, however, because even though Ragaviah had more than a nodding acquaintance with Western astronomy (a subject much-taught in mission schools as a way of undermining "Hinduism"), he evinces no interest in Christianity at all. A *kachcheri* education, the second possibility, therefore looks just as likely. For this, Frykenberg provides the example of Vennelacunty Soob Row (b. 1784), a *Deshastha* who rose from the lowly position of *gomashta* (accountant) in the *kachcheri* of Masulipatam to become chief pandit of the Madras High Court, renowned for his love of Shakespeare, though he had no formal English education.[39] That Ragaviah rose as high as Row seems doubtful; the "Pagoda Tree" shook out very little that I can see. Though he hoped for better, Ragaviah appears mainly to have shuttled back and forth between Seringapatam and Madras, apparently in the role of *dubashi* ("person of two languages"), calling on the auditor and paymaster at Fort St. George on his client's behalf, which appears to have been the military. In and of itself, that role goes a long way to explain why Ragaviah stepped forward to supply the information Newnham lacked. Frykenberg explains: "*Dubashis* were double agents. The very nature of their duties as confidential servants and commercial inter-

36. Kirkpatrick papers, Ragaviah to Kirkpatrick, undated (ca. 1806), Mss. Eur. F228/20, OIOC.

37. Robert E. Frykenberg, "Modern Education in South India, 1784-1854: Its Roots and Its Role as a Vehicle of Integration under Company Raj," *American Historical Review* 91 (1986): 40.

38. Frykenberg, "Modern Education," pp. 41-42.

39. Frykenberg, "Modern Education," pp. 46-47.

preters to British Company officers made them so. As go-betweens, their very success depended upon their ability to resolve differences, compromise opposing interests, avoid stalemates, and conclude agreements. As mediators, they drew foreign minds and alien cultures together."[40] One wonders, however, whether being the "glue" between cultures caused Ragaviah to become "unstuck" from his own. "I have been so much brought up among you," he writes to Kirkpatrick, "that I unawares forget myself an Hindoo."[41] It may be, as Frykenberg claims of *Deshasthas* generally, that they were, by virtue of their status in the Company, as socially distanced from other Hindus as the British themselves.[42] Ironically, however, despite wanting more, proximity to British power and prestige appears to have made Ragaviah increasingly self-conscious that he was, and ever would be, a "Hindoo."

"Hindoo" is a word that Ragaviah uses frequently and ecumenically. I have the impression, however, that it makes him uncomfortable; he admits that his people are considered "superstitious," even though he thinks them "religious." In one instance, he speaks of India as being inhabited by "Hindoos" but adds a word from Sanskrit in parentheses, *Curmataus,* which appears to be the Anglicized plural of *karmatha,* meaning "diligent in ritual action" — a superb way of clarifying what it is for "Hindoos" to be "religious."[43] Ragaviah's sectarian affinities do not admit of specification, except that he was vaguely Vedantic and partial to the *Puranas,* which is hardly out of the ordinary. Of all his papers, the most curious is "Essay on Hindoo Geography," addressed to Justice Strange. Eccentric and eclectic, it could hardly be clearer that Ragaviah was no pandit. Evidently ignorant of the astronomy of antiquity *(jyotihshastra),* he makes no reference to its systematic treatises *(siddhantas);* instead, he appears to have derived some of his knowledge about "Hindoo Geography" (*bhugola,* into which he subsumes *khagola,* celestial geography) from Jones's *Asiatick Researches,* although he claims not to think very highly of it. Due to having had a mission-school education or from having been among "Gentlemen" of the Company, Ragaviah is already a convinced — and yet reluctant — Copernican. The geocentricity of the *Puranas*

40. Frykenberg, *Guntur District,* pp. 34-35.

41. Kirkpatrick papers, Ragaviah to Kirkpatrick, undated (ca. 1806), Mss. Eur. F228/20, OIOC.

42. Frykenberg, *Guntur District,* p. 8.

43. I take it that *Karmatha,* a rare word, corresponds to the more common *karmabhumi,* which designates "India" as the geographical locus of soteriologically efficacious action. Kirkpatrick Papers, P. Ragaviah to William Strange, 12/27/1803, Seringapatam, Mss. Eur. F228/20, OIOC. Until otherwise indicated, subsequent citations come from the same document.

is obsolete for him; still, he feels compelled to "reconcile" the differences and not merely report them.

Overawed by Europe, he speaks of the "Enlightened western nations" doing their science with the "tedious labour of an enterprising Navigator or the deliberate Travells of an Engineer," while that of his people is "founded upon the fertility of imagination, [the] power of traversing the universe in Ideal Balloons [*sic;* an allusion to hot-air balloons, introduced around this time from Europe?]." Europe's science and India's are like "Heaven to Earth," but Ragaviah's way to save the *Puranas* from obsolescence is not to relegate them to the transempirical domain of religion, out of science's way; instead, he suggests that the world of the *Puranas* — a flat, circular plane with the massive Mount Meru at the center, surrounded by seven concentric continents, each one separated by an ocean — might actually be compatible with the heliocentric universe. Meru would be the sun, the concentric continents the "orbits of planets," and the oceans "the vacuum" of space. It is ingenious and perhaps unprecedented, although within the Indian tradition to make the *Puranas* and *Siddhantas* agree, the flat earth of the one had often been folded around the globe of the other; this was fairly commonplace. By "eccentric" and "eclectic," I do not mean Ragaviah was closed to correction or supplementation; clearly, he was active in the intercultural exchange of knowledge, which is consistent with his role as a *dubashi.* Contemporaneous documents from the Mackenzie Collection confirm how rare it was in Mysore to be so unbiased toward the science of non-Hindus; even learned *jyotishis* claimed that Islamic and — a fortiori — European astronomy "have their Origin from Ours."[44] Receptivity like Ragaviah's could be easily misconstrued in tradi-

44. C. V. (Cavelli Venkata) Boria, Mackenzie's principal assistant, recorded the following in 1801 from two Telugu Brahmins of "Ballaghaat": "In former times, a Bramin named Moosal Maha Moonee was profoundly skilled in all sciences, by the Destiny of God he cohabited with a concubine of inferior caste and begot her several sons and daughters; from natural love for his family and children, he wished to receive them into the tribe of Bramins that they might at all times be in good society, but the other Bramins refused to admit them. . . . The Moonee dissatisfied with the Brahmins taught his Children Astronomy, Geography, Medicine, Philology and several other arts and Sciences . . . and directed them to follow his Doctrine for ever and established Customs, Laws, [and] Regulations for them in all things in opposition and directly contrary to the Laws of the Bramins. Hence the Mussulmuns acting in all things in opposition to the Bramins are called their enemies. If the Bramins dedicate their attention to the Sun, they direct theirs to the moon and if the Bramins worship the Cow, they kill it. In this manner they are still in opposition to the Bramins as the descendents of Moosal Maha Moonee. Hence they are called Mussulman to this day." Mackenzie Mss., vol. 15, fols. 275-58, "Brief Account of the Astronomy of the Hindoos of the Deckan," OIOC.

tional communities; transgressors were sometimes threatened with sanctions.[45] It appears, however, that Ragaviah's encounter with the science of Europe did nothing to jeopardize his sense of being "Hindoo": "It would . . . appear blasphemous in me as [a] Religious Descendent of Divine Bruhma if I do not place as much or in a comparative degree, more belief in the one than in the other."

Newnham's essay elicits from Ragaviah a more complex and vigorous response to being "Hindoo"; the stakes are now higher than they were with Justice Strange, whose orientalist curiosity he could indulge on a somewhat equal basis. Newnham's catalogue of "dreadful Practices" is where his critique begins: "As these are very severe charges against the Hindoos, *of whom I have the honour to be one,* I should imagine that any information I could offer to refute them in any degree may be acceptable to the public, and Mr. Newnham would himself be pleased to find that the British Government in India have a better description of the People than what superficial information represents them to be."[46] Beneath the restraint — "honour" is the language of the "Gentlemen" with whom he associated — there is, I submit, a trace of disappointment but none of despair. The frustration he evinces has less to do with marginality than with redundancy, as if the College of Fort William had become sufficient unto itself and no longer needed the *Deshasthas* who served the Company with the same impartiality that characterized their service to the Marathas and Mughals. What hurts, it seems, is that Ragaviah seeks the patronage that faithful service deserves, but receives none. The fact that Mysore has fallen, the most recent kingdom to succumb to British power, does not trouble him; what does, is that Newnham, representing an "enlightened Western nation," has been misinformed, has only had access to "limited knowledge," and is now regarded as an authority. Seeing himself as the man of the moment, Ragaviah offers to fill in the gaps. More is involved, however, because foreign rule is evidently to him not only a matter of power but also of karmic or yugic predestination, which suggests familiarity with the *Bhavishyapurana*'s interpolated passages referring to the British in Calcutta.[47] While Ragaviah responds to the tropes of "oriental indolence" and "brahminical priestcraft" in the Newnham essay, his more symptomatic concerns are administrative and jurisprudential:

45. For examples, see Young, "Receding from Antiquity," pp. 200-06.

46. Kirkpatrick papers, item no. 2, undated, "In *The Monthly Review* for 1804," Mss. Eur. F228/20, OIOC. Unless otherwise specified, all subsequent references come from the same document.

47. Ludo Rocher, *The Puranas* (Wiesbaden, 1986), p. 153.

> I beg leave to observe that the Hindoo laws are copious and blended in some measure in all our books upon various subjects, which we call sacred, altho' we have volumes of them distinctly: on examining the whole, an impartial lawyer would find that it provides for every case with an impartial Eye. . . .
>
> As I have already premised the Sastras are copious and from their equivocal style, our devine Legislators gave us an opening to reform any part of them as change of circumstances and vicissitude of time may suggest, our devine authors of Sastras foresaw that the climate, the Religion, and the immemorial customs of the country must render the natives unfit for our native life and therefore must subject them to be governed by foreigners: with such an idea, they composed laws and regulations, rather flexible.
>
> Hence where the sastras sanction a virtuous and chaste woman to sacrifice herself on the burning pile of her husband in virtue of the solemn oath committed by her on the day of marriage to the effect that his (the husband's) will will be hers and that she will follow his fate, then they shift by expressing that every act or attempt to bring unnatural death would be considered suicide and the soul of the person so dying will be transmigrated into vermin and evil spirits for ages, and wiser regulations are made for a widow now to conduct herself after the demise of her husband; on the above Principles, our Vadantics and enlightened part of the Hindoos gave up the custom of *sahagamanum* [concremation], as they consider it was formed exclusively for Chatrias, who were very jealous of their women.

Here, Ragaviah turns to the miscellaneous "dreadful Practices" in Newnham's catalogue:

> 1st. To refute this charge is in the power of every reader that has the least knowledge in our Pooranums and customs. The Hindoo law forbids the killing any thing that has life in it. Our Vedams and 18 Pooranums besides Oopaporanums all cry out against it. The custom of placing Mareyama, an infernal demon . . . at the end of every village and cities originated from an idea among the vulgar Sudras and Parriars that she is tutelary god of village, house, children and diseases, and to her they sacrifice that which they eat: such an act is not sanctioned by the Sastras nor tolerated by the Bramuns, Bhagwat Ramayanam and other sacred Pooranums contain not the least ground or vestige of any such ceremonies.

> With regard to the charge 2nd, it is true that some obscure motive induced the authors of our Sastras to give sanction for an old man borne down with years to discharge his tottered carcase in the confluence of the Ganges where the rapid current will effect the intended purpose with a degree of easiness. But as I have already said, no Vadantics, or man of virtue, would think of this. It is only those who cannot review their past life without horror who expect forgiveness by this supposed holy death.
>
> We abhor nothing so much as killing an animal, nor do our Sastras tolerate the sacrifice of an humane being nor does custom sanctify it. Every European that has been in the country will bear an evidence to this, and therefore the imputation of humane sacrifices is unfounded in the extreme: but villains and blasphemers may commit crimes of this kind in every part of the world.
>
> With regard to the 5th accusation, nothing of the kind is to be traced in our Pooranums, for if any woman was to be so barbarous as to commit her first fruit of connubial love to the waves of the Ganges, it proceeds from a local custom established among a certain class of people in a particular district for the Sastras abhor it as much as the generality of Hindoos, and in this part of the Peninsula such a thing is unheard of.

Ragaviah's Brahminical snootiness and Sanskritizing bias are too self-evident to require comment; there is, however, enough in these passages to warrant some conclusions about the information he wanted Newnham to have. An important clue comes from the repeated insistence that the *shastras* are "copious." I do not think Ragaviah means by this the *manyness* of the dharmashastric texts; it is, rather, their *complementarity.* That the texts promulgate a plethora of precepts is obvious; less obvious is that some pertain to the karmically oriented *(karma-* or *pravrittimargis),* others to "salvation"-seekers *(moksha-* or *nivrittimargis).* My analysis and my contention — that Ragaviah wanted to convey both the "theological anthropology" behind the bifurcation and its relevance to jurisprudence — is indebted to a discussion of suttee/*sati* by J. Duncan M. Derrett, who proposes that "the *shastra* through recognizing and sanctioning both outlooks [viz., *karma/moksha, pravritti/nivritti*], also provided a theoretical reconciliation between them."[48] With this in mind, one can see that Halhed's *Code* and Colebrooke's *Digest* never crossed the hurdle of the manyness of the texts; the missing postulate that Ragaviah provides is that to be "copious" is not a vice but a virtue. Had this gap been filled in,

48. Derrett, *Religion,* p. 69.

Newnham might have been able to see the "cultural sense" behind Hindu law, and this in turn would have enhanced his credentials as an administrator: "The ability to distinguish between injunctions directed to a better rebirth and injunctions directed to avoiding rebirth is an ability which the *shastra* would regard as supreme."[49]

While Derrett is right, and Ragaviah speaks positively of "flexibility" and "equivocation," he is equally clear that the virtue of being "copious" can also be a vice; in this sense, the "theoretical reconciliation" Derrett speaks of turns out to look more like a temporary standoff between irreducibly different religious ends that cannot coexist: one must give way to the other. At the most obvious level, the issue is one of "custom" versus "law." As a Brahmin, Ragaviah shows himself an inveterate textualizer: custom cannot sanctify, cannot make a wrong a right. The argument, a very nuanced one, is not from law *(naya)* to dharma, but from dharma to law. Above all, it is the "Vadantics," whom he glosses as "men of virtue," who know best that "salvation"-seekers are superior to the karmically oriented (widows who burn, widow-burners, etc.) with respect to the goals they value; "Vadantics," therefore, have the dharmic responsibility of curbing the excesses of their inferiors. This is why Ragaviah believes that Hindu law, which seems to transcend time, is not immutable, and that India is amenable to "reform" — a most unusual word for a *dubashi* from Seringapatam speaking before the rise to prominence of Ram Mohun Roy (1772-1833) in Calcutta. It is, moreover, why he thinks it worth his while to engage Newnham publicly, to fill in the missing information, because in his view there is a convergence of mutual interest between the British and right-minded "Hindoos" in seeing India rid of "dreadful Practices." It would be left to Ram Mohun to recognize and assess the relevance of Christianity to the project of "reforming" India; to Ragaviah, evidently, Christianity under the British was as immaterial to matters of governance as Islam under the Mughals.[50]

The Hollowing of History

By saying that Ragaviah envisioned a convergence of interest between India's underlords and its British overlords, I do not mean that he spoke for India; nor do I mean that non-Brahmins would not have contested the inferiorizing

49. Derrett, *Religion,* p. 69.

50. Under the Mughals, "there was no question of administering Islamic law as such to non-Muslims." Derrett, *Religion,* p. 279.

rhetoric of Ragaviah's "theological anthropology." Specifically with respect to suttee/*sati*, the post-1829 protests of the Calcutta *Dharma Sabha* (Society for the Promotion of Dharma; dominated by non-Brahmins) demonstrates the vitality of the karmically oriented cohort in the public most directly affected by abolition;[51] this was the cohort that most tenaciously contested Ram Mohun's Vedantic prioritization of "salvation" seeking, which shares an affinity with Ragaviah's and made Ram Mohun a target for the "pro"-suttee/*sati* forces who overestimated his influence with the British.[52] By the same token, I am not suggesting that Ragaviah's perception of British interests was necessarily the same as theirs; on the other side of the colonial divide, there may have been near unanimity that reform was overdue, but none on how it should be effected, immediately or gradually, or otherwise.

Some twenty years later, as is well attested, the dilemma was still there, debated interminably. In 1825, for example, Justice Strange, who had sent Ragaviah's review of the *Monthly Review* to Colin Mackenzie, authored one of the century's classic textbooks on Anglo-shastric law, which declared at the conclusion to the chapter "On Widowhood" that suttee/*sati* was "a subject fitter for abolition, than for regulation."[53] Still, the onus of regulation continued to fall on judges and magistrates like Thomas Newnham, now of the criminal court at Cuddapah in a territory recently ceded to the Company by the nizam of Hyderabad. In 1820, he can be found reporting to Fort St. George the number of suttees/*satis* in his *zilla* (district) since 1816; there had been "only" two — "Nursumma," aged forty, and "Dasoo," eighty, Brahmins of "Mudannapullee" — and this statistically "negligible" figure elicits from him what is, in effect, a de-orientalizing retraction of the claim he had made as a green recruit at the College of Fort William: "There are . . . many cruel superstitions common to Bengal that are nearly unknown among the inhabitants of this part of India." It can only be coincidental that this brings him closer to Ragaviah's position of two decades earlier, but experience had per-

51. On the *Dharma Sabha* and its protest against the abolition of suttee/*sati*, which has its roots in the non-Vedantic traditions of karmically oriented action, see Kopf, *British Orientalism*, pp. 266-72. Even though it was "pro"–suttee/*sati*, Kopf is right in refusing to characterize the *Sabha* as "anti-modern" or "reactionary"; the issues had rather to do with "theological anthropology": karmically oriented action versus "salvation"-oriented selfless action.

52. For the full complement of Ram Mohun's anti–suttee/*sati* tracts, see *The Essential Writings of Raja Rammohun Ray*, ed. Bruce Carlisle Robertson (Delhi, 1999), pp. 113-72. On the question of Ram Mohun's role in Bentinck's decision to abolish suttee/*sati*, Fisch, "Humanitarian Achievement," p. 130, argues that his influence was negligible.

53. William Strange, *Elements of Hindu Law* (London, 1825), 1:241.

haps taught him the importance of "complex local identities" (hearkening back to Bayly) — but only perhaps. Elsewhere, his report again represents the essentialization of suttee/*sati* as a defining feature of "Hinduism," despite being "nearly obsolete" in the *zillah* (as in the south generally); as such, it can only be regulated but not abolished because for "Hindoos" the act of "self sacrifice" *is and ever would be* "true religion." As a judicial officer duty-bound to uphold to the law, Newnham adheres not to the spirit of the *shastras*, as Ragaviah would have liked, but to the word; still, claiming to be "relieved" to report that Nursumma's and Dasoo's immolations were "perfectly voluntary," Newnham cannot mask his abhorrence for the "barbarous funeral."[54] As Jörg Fisch observes, in the long run regulation was administratively impracticable because "British officials would have to administer a legal distinction [between voluntary and involuntary suttee/*sati*] which would be absolutely contrary to their moral views."[55]

When it comes to policy, it would be groundless to argue that Ragaviah's was a voice that the Company heeded. His case, however, is instructive in at least two ways. To begin with, even though C. A. Bayly's contention that British India was an "Empire of Opinion"[56] can stand on its own evidence, the attention I have given Ragaviah serves as a caution to historiographies that characterize the production of colonial knowledge as if it were made in Britain, imposed from above, and passively accepted. To say that colonial knowledge was open to correction and supplementation may of course be an altogether different matter, for while we have seen that Ragaviah and his interlocutor Justice Strange interacted on nearly equal terms with respect to orientalist curiosities, going up against the *Monthly Review* was a more asymmetrical contest. In and of itself, however, the "mere fact" that Ragaviah was contesting the Newnham essay in Seringapatam almost as soon as the ink was dry in London is enough to suggest that Europe's ideological orientalizers were not an irresistible juggernaut who crushed a hapless and unresisting India beneath their wheels. Proximity to British power and prestige did not inoculate Ragaviah against the Company's incompetence or arrogance: where information was missing, it was provided; when ethnocentric complacency became insufferable, he had, in his words, the "penetration to see into insults offered, and spirit to resist it."[57] Before the fi-

54. *Parliamentary Papers Relating to East India Affairs, Relative to the Burning of Females on the Funeral Piles of Their Husbands* (London, 1823), pp. 96-98 passim.

55. Fisch, "Humanitarian Achievement," p. 114.

56. Bayly, *Empire and Information*, p. 313.

57. Kirkpatrick papers, item no. 2, undated, "In *The Monthly Review* for 1804," Mss. Eur. F228/20, OIOC.

nal drift into archival obscurity,[58] Ragaviah can again be glimpsed advocating the establishment of a "literary society" to promote "native involvement" in a collegial exchange with "Gentlemen" of the Company, only this time with more approval for the Fort William model: "The terms of association between the Europeans and Natives were established at first on a liberal and inviting footing, the Pundits flocked round the Gentlemen who wished for information and communicated it without reserve, a circumstance which must have contributed to the success with which the Gentlemen persevered in their studies."[59]

At the threshold between empire and imperium, voluntary associations of the kind Ragaviah proposed would soon be perceived by the British with alarm; the Hindu Literary Society of the 1830s, one of the first of its kind to actually get off the ground and become a formidable force, mobilized thousands of Madrasis to petition Government for institutions of English education where study of the Bible would not be made compulsory.[60] Although my

58. Since writing this essay in 2004, I have found that Ragaviah did not "drift into archival obscurity" quite so precipitously. A year after the OIOC correspondence comes to an end, Sir James Mackintosh (1765-1832), registrar of the Bombay court (earlier a renowned political commentator and later a long-serving Whig parliamentarian), passed through Seringapatam where he met Ragaviah ("Ragoboyah") and recorded the gist of their conversations in a letter dated February 28, 1808 (see *Memoirs of the Life of Sir James Mackintosh,* 2 vols. [Boston, 1853], 1:393-94). One thing the two had a common interest in was the *Monthly Review,* to which Mackintosh had been a frequent contributor. Their conversations ranged widely, from the religious (pilgrimage) to the philosophical (utilitarianism). Described as "a clerk (and a rich one too) in the military pay-office," Mackintosh's Ragaviah is clearly a cosmopolitan figure, at home in two worlds: "He speaks English as well as if he had been born in Middlesex, with the additional advantage of being free from cockneyism. He has a library of English writers; but he complained to me that no philosophical works were brought out to India, except those of the most common and popular sort, such as Locke, which he had read. . . . He seems accurately informed of their metaphysical doctrines, though not naturally of that subtlety of understanding, which makes a metaphysician. We had discussions on the *Dwita* [*sic*] and *Adwita* [*sic*], or the sect among them who allow two substances, — *Spirit* and *Matter;* and that which allows only one, — *Spirit,* or rather the mere fact of thought. The latter he allowed to be the most numerous and refined, though he is a *Dwita,* or Dualist. He promised, under my inspection, to translate the best abridgment of Hindu Logic, which if he does, I will publish." Nothing in the letter contradicts my characterization of Ragaviah as "vaguely Vedantic"; it is of interest, however, that Ragaviah described himself to Mackintosh as a "Dualist" (and therefore a follower of Madhva). But, since all varieties of Vedanta share the same "theological anthropology," this too would not materially affect my interpretation of Ragaviah on suttee/*sati.*

59. Ragaviah to Strange, "Proposal for a Literary Society at Madras by a Native of Madras," Seringapatam, 06/04/1807, Mackenzie Mss., vol. 176, OIOC.

60. R. F. Young and S. Jebanesan, *The Bible Trembled: The Hindu-Christian Contro-*

hunch as to Ragaviah's involvement in such societies cannot be verified, the Hindu Literary Society may in some way reflect the kind of vision he had. Likewise, I cannot verify why Justice Strange, who received the proposal, did not lend it his support. Instead, it was forwarded to Colin Mackenzie, who added it to his collection of South Indian curiosities, to be catalogued, accumulate dust, and — if we are to believe Nicholas Dirks, who has written a "biography" of the Mackenzie Collection — undergo "sedimentation." Since by this he means the loss of "native voices" and the erasure of India's history, the point I would like to end with is suggested to me by a comment of Robert E. Frykenberg's about "orientalism in reverse."[61] I see this in Dirks's dogmatic preoccupation with colonialism as a contaminant, which forces him to disassociate the biography *of* the archives from the biography *in* the archives and to make unsustainable claims to the effect that "Natives could only be informants; native knowledge only the stuff of anthropological curiosity."[62] My essay on an essay on an essay is therefore predicated on the belief that historiography cannot have it both ways, that·is, cannot reject the archives and still claim to work with them. To do so would be worse than sedimenting voices like Ragaviah's — it would be, and is, the hollowing of history.

versies of Nineteenth-Century Ceylon (Vienna, 1995), pp. 81-100. On the Hindu Literary Society, see Frykenberg, "Modern Education," pp. 52-53.

61. Robert Eric Frykenberg, *History and Belief: The Foundations of Historical Understanding* (Grand Rapids and Cambridge, 1996), pp. 287-302.

62. Nicholas B. Dirks, "Colonial Histories," p. 310.

CHAPTER 4

Creating Christian Community in Early-Nineteenth-Century Agra

AVRIL A. POWELL

In 1813, the year the East India Company's new charter facilitated the opening up of north India to Protestant missionary activity, a new Christian community came into being in the heart of the old Mughal city of Agra. The increase of evangelical influence in the vicinity, much of it from military men, was of some help, but this community owed its sudden growth to the combined efforts of two men, one Indian and one Scottish. ʿAbd al-Masih (ca. 1769-1827), born in nearby Delhi, was a newly baptized convert from a scholarly Muslim family. His colleague, Daniel Corrie (1777-1837), was one of the half-dozen "pious chaplains" serving the East India Company who since the late 1790s had been introducing Calcutta, the Company's headquarters in north India, to some new evangelistic agendas. The fledgling community created in the northwest in 1813, soon after the arrival of these two, remained influential in Agra city until the late 1820s, although it suffered fluctuating fortunes during even that short period. It is the argument of this paper that, however short-lived, this community was in some significant respects unique in the early history of Protestant missionary activity in north India. The following discussion aims to evaluate in particular the indigenous input into the founding and shaping of this particular community. It draws on previous work but seeks to probe the character of the new convert community primarily as a social organism rather than as the object of missionary attention.[1] ʿAbdul Masih's extensive journals and correspondence, originally

1. Avril A. Powell, *Muslims and Missionaries in Pre-Mutiny India* (London, 1993), chaps. 3–4; "Processes of Conversion to Christianity in Nineteenth Century North-Western In-

written in Hindustani (Urdu) and forwarded to the Church Missionary Society (CMS) in London, which employed him in Agra from 1813 to 1825, constitute the main source for the study.[2]

Agra's Christian Past

Unlike many other cities and villages of northern India where Protestants commenced preaching in the early nineteenth century, Agra had already experienced considerable Christian and missionary influence. The graveyards and chapels of Armenian and Portuguese merchants witness to the city's economic and political attractions under Mughal hegemony, yet by the early nineteenth century Agra's "once flourishing Armenian colony" had practically disappeared.[3] That some Armenians remained in the city until the middle of the nineteenth century is evident, however, both from tomb transcriptions and from ʿAbdul Masih's journals, though there is no evidence of institutionalized religious practice. The Jesuit settlement established in Agra in the late six-

dia," in *Religious Conversion Movements in South Asia: Continuities and Change, 1800-1900*, ed. Geoffrey A. Oddie (London, 1997), pp. 15-55.

2. ʿAbdul Masih's journals and letters have been consulted in the translated manuscript versions deposited in the CMS collection (North India) at the University of Birmingham (CI/E; E1-2; CI1/0194), and in the abridged versions that appeared in the *Missionary Register* (hereafter *MR*), from 1814 until 1826. Most of his journals and letters were translated and abridged in Calcutta by Daniel Corrie and other evangelicals, including Robert Mertyns Bird. The Urdu originals are no longer extant. The early journals were dictated to Corrie and bear the latter's strong mark, Corrie recording, "I keep a journal of his public labours," December 17, 1812. The later letters seem to be close literal translations, retaining some Persianisms and colloquialisms that were then pruned editorially from the abridged journal entries before publication. The precise extent of editorial intervention is impossible to determine. Even so, ʿAbdul Masih's record, particularly after 1815, remains unmatched for its longevity, detail, and frankness among early Protestant convert accounts of their own missionary roles in India. Eugene Stock dubbed his journals "the *pièce de résistance,* sometimes for months together, in the new *Missionary Register.*" Stock, *The History of the Church Missionary Society,* 3 vols. (London, 1899), 1:183.

3. Following Akbar's patronage to Armenian merchants, a chapel and college had been established in Agra, but during the eighteenth century there was an exodus of the merchant community to seek greater profits in up-and-coming commercial centers such as Calcutta and Madras. Mesrovb Jacob Seth, *Armenians in India from the Earliest Time to the Present Day* (Calcutta, 1937); E. R. Hambye, *History of Christianity in India,* vol. 3, *Eighteenth Century* (Bangalore, 1997). Bhaswati Bhattacharya, working on "Armenian-European Relationships in India, 1500-1800," considers that migration occurred even earlier when the court moved from Agra to Delhi. Personal communication, March 15, 2005.

Contemporary watercolor of ʿAbdul Masih [ʿAbd al-Masih] (ca. 1769-1827), Muslim convert, Anglican clergyman. Artist unknown. Henry Martyn Center, Cambridge (on permanent loan from Ridley Hall, Cambridge).

teenth century, as the result of Emperor Akbar's interest in Christianity, had a more long-standing influence on making Christian beliefs and religious practices known to its citizens. The earlier Jesuit presence, in spite of their withdrawal from north India on papal instruction in the late eighteenth century, was to affect the new Protestant community in various ways.

Much is now known about the religious and cultural interface between the early Jesuits and the Mughal court through studies of the religious and the artistic dimensions of their encounter.[4] Little has come to light, in con-

4. Edward Maclagan, *The Jesuits and the Great Mogul* (London, 1932), remains the classic account of the Mughal-Jesuit encounters, supplemented by Arnulf Camps, *Jerome Xa-*

trast, concerning Jesuit contacts with nonelite Indians, particularly on the peripheries of their "court" missions in Agra and Lahore. Yet gradual realization of the failure of their mission's primary goal of drawing the Mughal elites to Christianity had soon turned Jesuit attention to those the Jesuit historian Paul Jackson describes as "lesser" folk.[5] Further substantiation of the composition of these Jesuit congregations is difficult, but several studies have emphasized the significance of liturgical and ceremonial observances in first drawing the interest that led to the slow creation of Catholic communities, coming from varied social backgrounds, around the Jesuit churches. "Most of the converts," noted Edward Maclagan, were drawn "by the ceremonial activities of the Mission," notably the public and elaborate celebration of the main Christian feast days.[6] The introduction of these practices, according to Arnulf Camps, was "a well-considered plan of Xavier's," who consciously promoted "the full and public display of liturgical and extra-liturgical ceremonies in the Mogul Mission."[7] Paul Jackson has commented on Camps's findings more recently: "It may come as quite a surprise to many to read that the actual converts of the period were not won over by rational argument, nor by Jerome Xavier's Persian writings, nor by any other 'out-reach' program, but by the sight of the Christian community celebrating the Christian Mysteries together."[8] Such insights into "the conversion of the common people," in the face of the more usual view of the Jesuits solely as court missionaries, are very useful to the concerns of this paper in drawing attention to the creation of a Christian public space in Mughal Agra that did not entirely disappear and would later influence the contours of Protestant activity in the same city.[9]

---

vier, SJ, and the Muslims of the Mogul Empire: Controversial Works and Missionary Activity (Schöneck-Beckenried, 1957), and J. Correia-Afonso's translations of correspondence from Latin, Portuguese, and Italian, for example, *Letters from the Mughal Court: The First Jesuit Mission to Akbar (1580-1583)* (Bombay, 1980). Recent study includes Gauvin Alexander Bailey, *The Jesuits and the Grand Mogul: Renaissance Art and the Imperial Court of India, 1580-1630* (Washington, D.C., 1998).

5. Paul Jackson, S.J., "Jesuits at the Mughal Court," in *Vidyajyoti: Journal of Theological Reflection* 44 (1980): 108-13.

6. Maclagan, *Jesuits*, pp. 275-76.

7. Camps, *Jerome Xavier*, pp. 235-36. Among other displays and ceremonies discussed by Camps were visits to the paintings of the *Madonna del Popolo* and the *Adoration of the Magi* in the Jesuit church at Agra; the public display of the manger at Agra in 1604; the washing of feet during Lent; processions of flagellants; music and fireworks; funeral rites (pp. 206, 209, 228-32, 237ff.).

8. Jackson, "Jesuits," p. 113.

9. Camps, *Jerome Xavier*, p. 246.

Members, first of the Carmelite Order and later of the Capuchin Order, replaced the Jesuits in this region. Yet from the mid seventeenth through most of the eighteenth century, the daily life of the various Catholic congregations, apart from those supported through the patronage of the well-known Catholic convert the Begam Samru at Sardhana, near Meerut, now seems lost to history.[10]

By the time ʿAbdul Masih and Daniel Corrie reached Agra in 1813, most Catholics, variously numbered around the city at about a thousand, were nominally under Capuchin authority. Though the Capuchins would strengthen their presence again in the mid–nineteenth century with the building of a cathedral in Agra, their own historians testify both to their earlier ineffectiveness and to internal dissensions, which go far to explain any subsequent exodus to the new Protestant community in their midst. One Capuchin had explained his wish to abandon his post in 1794 because "his converts had never exceeded twenty, and were now only twelve, consisting of his own servants, and a few Hindus who had lost their caste."[11] By the mid-1820s there were only five missionaries to serve the whole vicariate of Tibet-Hindustan. The three and a half thousand souls they nominally shepherded were described as "scattered all over the vast territory of the Vicariate like lost sheep."[12] Unsurprisingly, some "native Christians" who would later be drawn to the Protestant services had already received baptism according to Catholic rites but were only loosely integrated into any "Christian community" and were ripe for new influences, if not apostasy.[13]

Apart from the transfer of some communicants between such congregations, it should be questioned whether there is evidence of textual transmission from the spate of scriptural translation in the early phases of Catholic activity to the new phase of biblical translation and dissemination in the early nineteenth century. Studies of the later Protestant initiatives in religious printing give the impression both that the Catholic missions were little interested in circulating the Scriptures and commentaries for individual consumption, and that those that did materialize prior to the spread of vernacular presses had disappeared, either through deliberate destruction or simply through the ravages of climate and time, leaving a tabula rasa for a new gen-

10. John Lall, *Begam Samru* (New Delhi, 1997).

11. Fr. Juvenal to Thomas Twining, November 1794, in *Travels in India a Hundred Years Ago,* ed. William H. G. Twining (London, 1893), p. 204. On the Capuchins in Agra, see Fr. Fulgentius Vannini, *Hindustan-Tibet Mission* (New Delhi, 1981), pp. 171-227.

12. Father Antonine's report, October 20, 1825, in Vannini, *Hindustan-Tibet Mission,* pp. 199-200.

13. Vannini, *Hindustan-Tibet Mission,* p. 202.

eration of evangelists who centered their mission on the dissemination of the biblical "word." Some identifiable portions of Scripture and catechisms, the work of the early Jesuits, which were still circulated in the early eighteenth century, could no longer be found in north India by the end of that century.[14] Yet, that some Indian Muslims were already well informed of the Christian Scriptures has been shown by Gulfishan Khan's study of Muslim travelers in Europe in the eighteenth century.[15] Certainly, some of the "new Christians" baptized by ʿAbdul Masih after 1813 would comment that they first heard of Christianity when handed portions of the Scriptures by Catholic priests.

ʿAbdul Masih's New Christian Community

The history of ʿAbdul Masih, whose conversion was the only one directly attributable to the influence of Henry Martyn, the "first modern missionary to Mohammedans," is well known in outline. During his residence in north India from 1806 to 1810, Martyn, inhibited both by Company regulations as a chaplain and by temperamental hesitancies, failed in his original objective of drawing Muslims to Christianity.[16] Instead, his energies were concentrated on the translations of the Bible and liturgy into Arabic, Persian, and Urdu, for which he is most remembered today, the printed versions of which were to play a significant part in the creation, after his own death, of the Christian communities examined here. ʿAbdul Masih, known then by his Muslim birth name as Shaikh Salih, asked Martyn for baptism after reading the Scriptures while binding Bibles in Martyn's workshop, but was refused on the ground that he displayed insufficient evidence as yet of true conversion. Colleagues in Calcutta knew better: after Martyn's departure from India, Salih received baptism as an Anglican and was taken on by the CMS as a catechist.[17] The Calcutta evangelicals very soon decided that their new colleague would be better suited to a ministry in his own northwestern homeland, where his knowledge of the classical and vernacular languages would be valued by those

14. Camps, *Jerome Xavier,* pp. 194-95.

15. Gulfishan Khan, *Indian Muslim Perceptions of the West during the Eighteenth Century* (Karachi, 1998), chap. 4.

16. S. Wilberforce, ed., *Journals and Letters of the Rev. Henry Martyn,* 2 vols. (London, 1837); J. Sargant, *A Memoir of the Rev. Henry Martyn, B.D.,* 2nd ed. (London, 1819); C. Bennett, "The Legacy of Henry Martyn," *International Bulletin of Missionary Research* 116 (1992): 10-15.

17. On ʿAbdul Masih's conversion, baptism, and training in Calcutta, see Powell, "Processes of Conversion," pp. 31-36.

to whom he would preach. Agra was chosen less for its Christian past than for its importance after the Company conquest, as a British military headquarters, where the presence of the army was guaranteed to stimulate a renewal of Indian commercial activity.[18] Their arrival in 1813 coincided with a year of local "scarcity," though not on the scale of the famine of 1837. The indigenous interest in Christianity that followed came as a surprise to evangelicals in Calcutta and Britain.

For requests for baptism from members of a variety of Indian communities and castes followed almost instantaneously on the arrival of ʿAbdul and Corrie in Agra in 1813. Before long, a distinct Christian community was recognizable, which nevertheless overlapped in certain respects the "native Christian" communities that had come into existence under Catholic auspices. Thomas Thomason, a Company chaplain and CMS activist, like Corrie, rejoiced from Calcutta after his colleagues' arrival in Agra, that "a bright day seems to be rising in those parts." He attributed a success that seemed to contrast with Martyn's failure to the complementary skills and sense of brotherhood of the Corrie–ʿAbdul Masih partnership.[19] What kind of community sprang into being so rapidly, and did it have any counterparts in this period and location?

The British had taken possession of Agra following victories over the Marathas in 1803. Many accounts emphasized the city's "ruined" state. No permanent chaplain had been appointed and a formal missionary station was as yet prohibited. A Serampore Baptist missionary, John Chamberlain, had recently caused Company displeasure, resulting in his return to Calcutta under guard, for some injudicious preaching within the Agra fort.[20] Corrie and ʿAbdul immediately fared better because of the former's status as station chaplain. Marriages, funerals, and the occasional service were conducted from an improvised chapel within the Mughal fort, Corrie's task being to develop such rudimentary facilities into a permanent place of worship. Any "native Christians" in the vicinity were welcome to worship, together with the Europeans, in the Agra fort, where a school for Indian boys was soon established. Two weeks after arrival Corrie reported that "a great many servants of the gentlemen who live in the fort" came to hear "Hindoostani worship" conducted by ʿAbdul, who later preached outside the fort to "multitudes of Natives."[21]

18. On Agra's change of character, and attractions to migrants during early British rule, see Mark Juergensmeyer, *Radhasoami: The Logic of a Modern Faith* (Princeton, 1991), p. 15.

19. Rev. T. T. Thomason, Calcutta, October 9, 1813, *MR* (1814): 187-88.

20. For Chamberlain's account of his misfortunes, see William Yates, *Memoirs of Mr. John Chamberlain, late Missionary in India* (Calcutta, 1824).

21. Corrie and Abdul, journal, April 4, 1813, *MR* (1814): 192.

Almost immediately the pair began to look for a building in the heart of the bazaar where a more accessible place of worship, a school, and, importantly, a *serai* for passing travelers might be established. The old house they eventually found, soon widely known as "ʿAbdul Masih's *katra*" in recognition of the stamp that the new catechist quickly put upon the locality, was to prove excellent for their purposes. This *katra,* variously referred to as a "court" or "marketplace," was said to have functioned during Mughal times as the residence of the head eunuch of the royal court.[22] Though semiruined, its open hall and cell-like subsidiary rooms were easily adaptable. Apart from its central location in the busy bazaar, "situated in the middle of the principal street in Agra," it had some distinct advantages:

> The north side of the Kuttra or Court, next the street, consists of a gateway with folding doors, and two shops. Over the gateway and shops, Abdool Meseeh resides: the entrance to his dwelling is by stairs from within the Court: it comprises an open hall, with a room on each side, and servants' apartments connected with them. . . . on the east side, which consists of five narrow cells . . . some of the converts reside. . . . on the south side, a building was erected for divine worship, about fifty feet long, by twenty-two wide, and sixteen high within. The side towards the court is built with five arches, which render it open to all who assemble in the Court: *people passing in the street can also see the congregation assembled, and thus many have been attracted to enter and hear.*[23]

Although services would continue to be held in the fort, and later in the newly built cantonment church, this *katra* became the hub of Protestant activity in Agra. Remarkable, in comparison to the segregation of many mission churches from British congregations, and to the earlier Catholic practices, was the extent to which fort and *katra* were to prove interchangeable, with Indian Christians continuing to attend the fort services as before and British officials coming to take the sacraments from ʿAbdul Masih at the Hindustani services in the *katra,* especially in the frequent absence of a chaplain. Although some of Corrie's successors took little interest, other chaplains revived his partnership with ʿAbdul. John Irving, the last chaplain to serve in Agra during ʿAbdul's lifetime, testified in 1824 to "the comfort of having such

22. A *katra* is "a piece of land that is enclosed and peopled." John T. Platts, *Dictionary of Urdu, Classical Hindi, and English* (Oxford, 1930). Corrie called the site "Boottats Kuttra," a derivation from "bhootistan," or graveyard. In 1970, its site could no longer be identified. See M. E. Gibbs, *The Anglican Church in India* (New Delhi, 1972), pp. 40-41.

23. Rev. Daniel Corrie, "Remarks on India," *MR* (1816): 22, emphasis added.

a man as Abdool always at hand," stressing the reciprocity involved in administering the sacrament to Indian Christians in his own cantonment church followed by his riding regularly to the *katra* to learn Persian and Hindi with ʿAbdul, where he and various laymen also assisted with the management of the school.[24]

An important factor in maintaining continuity when chaplains were unavailable or uninterested was the role played in the mission by the British community, notably by young evangelical officers, among them Lieutenant Alexander Macdonald, who described himself as an "acting parson."[25] By no means unique, such lay "patrons and protectors" (Corrie's terms) were particularly influential in Agra, an important city to which no European missionary was appointed by the CMS until 1838. Particularly energetic support came from Nathaniel Wright, an indigo planter, resident in the vicinity from 1794 until the 1820s, who lent his engineering skills to the problems presented by decaying *katra* buildings subject to annual monsoon damage.[26] Such lay patrons would play crucial roles when things went wrong: ʿAbdul recorded gratefully, after a period of tense relations with a Eurasian catechist, that the lieutenants now seconded to assist him, "treat us as Mr Corrie did."[27]

If the British component in the *katra* community was important, what was the social composition of a nascent Indian congregation that, numbering about fifty only a year after ʿAbdul's arrival, maintained, in spite of some significant defections, similar numbers until his final departure in the mid-1820s? In examining conversion patterns in Agra at this time, the wider north Indian context should be noted. The Serampore Baptists, established in Lower Bengal since the 1790s, had struggled to gain converts during their first few years, but numbers peaked from 1813 to 1817, simultaneously with the apparent "takeoff" in Agra. The Baptists then registered a sharp dip for the next few years.[28] A spate of high-caste conversions, triggered among Calcutta Hindus by Alexander Duff of the Scottish Free Church, would raise

24. John Irving to Daniel Corrie, Agra, April 19, 1824: CI1/076/149.

25. Lt. Alexander Macdonald was active in evangelical causes wherever he was posted. Thomason described him as "a pious zealous agent, one of the best we could employ." Thomason to J. Pratt, n.d., circa November 1815: CI1/E14.

26. The Wrights appear to have undergone a collective religious transformation, giving up cards and backgammon for family prayers, as a result of earlier Baptist influences. They remained staunch supporters of evangelical enterprises in the city but were particularly helpful to ʿAbdul. Yates, *Memoirs,* pp. 321, 336.

27. ʿAbdul, journal, January 1, 1816: CI1/E/17a.

28. Total Baptist baptisms in the whole of India were calculated at 1,407 between 1800 and 1821, only half of which were Indians. See E. D. Potts, *British Baptist Missionaries in India, 1793-1837* (Cambridge, 1967), p. 36.

evangelical optimism once more, but not until the early 1830s. Evangelicals, always struggling to make any headway in Lower Bengal, understandably welcomed rather wistfully the news from Agra of an almost immediate breakthrough.

Closer to Agra, triggered also by the preaching of chaplains and native catechists, was a conversion phenomenon among the Satnamis or Sadhs, a Hindu sect living near Meerut. Its rapid but ephemeral character, though set in a rural context, allows some comparisons with the processes almost simultaneously at work in Agra. Evangelical agency was provided in this case too by a recent convert, Anand Masih, a Brahmin, and by the British officer, Lieutenant Macdonald, who proved so supportive in Agra.[29] Yet unlike Meerut, where the converts were drawn from a single community, seemingly following a respected "leader" into baptism, the Agra converts spanned a considerable social range, including groups considered to be particularly inaccessible to Christian influence. ʿAbdul's records allow the charting of changes in composition even over the short existence of this Agra congregation.

Most surprising to those excited by the new prospects in Agra was the baptism of half a dozen Muslim males of the *ashraf*, or "well-born" and, usually, highly learned stratum of Muslim society.[30] Of *shaikh* lineage himself, ʿAbdul belonged to this stratum, as did the recruits from the Lucknow branch of his family who chose to join him in baptism, including two nephews, Inayat and Shamsher Rahim.[31] ʿAbdul's own *ashraf* credentials, particularly his education in the traditional Islamic sciences and languages, undoubtedly helped him gain an initial hearing among Muslims who usually ignored or spurned missionary advances. Other factors were influential too. A *yunani* physician, a *haji* as well as a *hakim*, in service with the nearby Jat Raja of Baratpur, was baptized as Talib Masih Khan in July 1813.[32] He had "once led a party to fight for Islam," he said, suggesting a particularly strong commitment to the faith of his birth, and hinting at some undefined *jihadi* activity during his pilgrimage to Mecca, possibly during the military campaigns in Arabia

29. The role of the native catechist, the Reverend Anand Masih (formerly Permanand), bears useful comparison with ʿAbdul Masih's role in Agra. Abha Singh, "Accommodation and Resistance: Satnamis, Christian Missionaries and Religious Plurality" (unpublished paper).

30. Comprising, in India, *sayyids* (descendants of the Prophet); *shaikhs* (descendants of his Companions); Mughals; and Pathans.

31. Most of his family appears to have remained Muslim, but joined him in Christian prayers when he visited Lucknow.

32. Corrie and ʿAbdul, journal, July 24-25, 1813, *MR* (1814): 294-96; August 22, 1813, *MR* (1814): 328-30.

that accompanied the spread of the Wahhabis in the mid–eighteenth century. He disclosed that long before his meeting with ʿAbdul he had been given an Arabic Old Testament by a Catholic priest belonging to a French military household in the area, an instructive case in point of the continuities between earlier Catholic and new Protestant missionary activity. Conversion had followed when he read the Persian gospels, given to him by a Baptist missionary in the version prepared by Henry Martyn. Clearly, earlier encounters, seemingly fruitless at the time, had prepared the way: he "came out" when two new evangelists, one of them a learned *ashraf* convert from Islam himself, seemed to make this socially possible. Even so, as Corrie reported, his baptism was to cause a "sensation" in the city.

A second Muslim, equally learned, had no such Christian contacts before he met ʿAbdul. Significantly, Maulawi Muhammad Fazil took the initiative by visiting ʿAbdul in April 1813 to challenge him to produce evidence from the Gospels for the Sonship of Christ. When ʿAbdul had read some New Testament passages, Fazil asked for a copy of the liturgy "that he might see our manner of worship."[33] Such an interest in Christian praxis was to prove common among ʿAbdul's subsequent inquirers, whatever their social backgrounds, in contrast to later phases of encounter in northwest India, by which time Christian "custom" held no further surprises and intellectual, doctrinal, and textual disputes had become all-important. The earlier emphasis may arguably be attributed to the daily manifestations of "practice" in the *katra* compound noted above as visible to "people passing in the street." Certainly Muhammad Fazil, for one, attended the *katra* daily until late September, inquiring "minutely into every subject of objection" until he requested baptism as "Fazil Masih," or "Learned of Christ," the ceremony presumably taking place before a mixed British and Indian congregation. Shortly before, Fazil's wife had sent for ʿAbdul, complaining that her husband "does nothing now but talk of religion." Rather than berate ʿAbdul, she asked him instead for a Gospel in order to try to understand Fazil's distress. She did not, it seems, subsequently seek baptism for herself.[34]

Other *maulwi* converts included Mansoor, from Rampur, a "man of great learning and of consideration among his nation," who was baptized by Corrie in early 1814. Another, Barkat Allah, was considered by Thomason "by far the most engaging next to Abdool" of all the converts.[35] There were several others of similar status within their own communities, "Mahomedans of the first re-

33. April 5, 1813, *MR* (1814): 192.

34. ʿAbdul and Corrie, journal, September 19-26, 1813, *MR* (1814): 446-47.

35. Thomason to Corrie, August 31, 1815: CI1/E/6.

spectability," as Corrie called them.[36] Sufficient circumstantial detail survives to categorize them as a distinct and unexpected conversion phenomenon, the roots of which should be sought as much in contemporary Muslim movements of inquiry and reform as in ʿAbdul's social and intellectual rapport with them. For Agra was at the heart of a region shortly to be roused by the preaching of a movement urging "return" to the textual roots of Islam in the Qur'an and the *hadith* ("traditions" of the Prophet). Curiosity about Christianity might well be felt by learned Muslims simultaneously with the spiritual concerns that subsequently fed into Syed Ahmad Barelvi's newly formed Tariqa-i Muhammadiyya movement.[37] What was unprecedented was that any such concerns should result in taking the step, particularly difficult for an *ashraf* Muslim, of accepting Christian baptism.

Apart from this remarkable *maulwi* component, the most socially distinct group of new converts came from lowly origins on the fringes of Hindu society. Such converts were, characteristically, members of the textile-working communities of the Agra hinterland who can be identified occupationally as contributing twelve men who were mainly poor weavers, and eighteen women who were spinners, to a total *katra* congregation numbering about forty-five in 1815. The weavers were probably Koris, a community of "very low" status, living in the environs of Agra, where they wove coarse cloth, with some diversification into agricultural labor or landholding as tenants.[38] Others, belonging to what Corrie called "the Labouring Orders of the people," included local cultivators from neighboring villages.[39] Efforts by ʿAbdul Masih to ensure occupational continuity, and hence adequate subsistence after baptism, included the provision of spinning wheels for the women, the employment of the men on weaving projects, and the hiring of land on which to employ the cultivators. Corrie reported after only six months that the wives of the new converts "spin thread . . . which our friends here buy of them," a further indication of lay commitment.[40] ʿAbdul recorded shortly afterward that

36. E.g., Hydar ʿAli, from Lucknow, where he had known ʿAbdul, baptized by Corrie in August 1814. *MR* (1815): 409.

37. Kenneth W. Jones, *Socio-Religious Reform Movements in British India* (Cambridge, 1989); Qeyamuddin Ahmad, *The Wahhabi Movement in India*, 2nd ed. (Delhi, 1994).

38. They almost certainly belonged to the Kori community, later described by the ethnologist William Crooke as "the Hindu weaver caste" he found settled in great numbers in Agra, Mathura, and their vicinity. The 1891 census listed 52,000 Koris in Agra and Mathura districts combined. W. Crooke, *The Tribes and Castes of the North-Western Provinces and Oudh*, 4 vols. (Calcutta, 1896), 3:316-21.

39. Corrie, "Remarks on India," *MR* (1816): 23.

40. Corrie to Udny, Thomason, Agra, July 1, 1813: CI/E/14.

"the newly baptised have been employed in the cultivation of land which we hired . . . all who have joined themselves to us are set to one kind of labour or another."[41] Such measures of social engineering fell short, however, of the integrated "Christian village" ideal, experiments with which would first occur in Agra district only in the aftermath of the 1837 famine.

ʿAbdul and Corrie did attract some interest among individuals of higher-caste identity, but in spite of many ensuing discussions, few of these then sought baptism. Corrie attributed this to fear of repercussions, surmising in 1825 that many Hindus were by then closet Christians. Communities less prone to such fears often did show interest, notably the many fakirs with whom ʿAbdul conversed, and the disciples of the various spiritual guides both Hindu and Muslim who resided with their devotees on the fringes of Agra oblivious to the constraints that affected caste Hindus. These too, though disposed to listen, seldom saw any reason to take matters further, some probably being the more ready as a result to seek spiritual solace in other revival movements.

There was also some recruitment from the struggling congregations of "native Christians" already baptized by Catholic priests, consisting mainly of descendants of Portuguese and French families. In the first months of the mission Catholic women were engaged to catechize some of the new converts, but seemingly without changing their sectarian identity themselves.[42] In Agra, as in the rest of India, Catholic-Protestant relations were frequently hostile: ʿAbdul Masih's journals are no different. He certainly rejoiced over "sinners" won from the Catholic fold, although he did not actually enumerate them as "converts." Capuchin records reveal the other side, exemplified in Antonine Pezzoni's lament that as the vicar apostolic of Agra he "was forced to see members of his flock gradually drifting away from the practice of their religion or becoming Protestants, because he had no one to cater to their spiritual needs."[43] In such circumstances a drift to the new Protestant mission is hardly surprising. Consequently when, in 1825, ʿAbdul administered the Easter Eucharist at the *katra* church, it was to a congregation that included Roman Catholics and Armenians. On another occasion he preached in Urdu to a mixed audience of Europeans, local Christians, Roman Catholics, and Armenians, and recorded visits to various Catholic communities along the Ganges.[44] That the traffic was probably two-way, and that the intra-Christian

41. ʿAbdul, journal, August 29, 1813: CI/E/17.

42. ʿAbdul, journal, September 23, 1813, *MR* (1814): 447.

43. Vannini, *Hindustan-Tibet Mission,* p. 202.

44. In 1820 some Roman Catholics reminded him that "you have led astray many of

boundaries remained very fuzzy, is implicit in a missionary visitor's surmise in 1818 that the Protestant congregation in the *katra* included some insincere "females of the Rom. Cath. persuasion, who secretly attend also at Padre Angelo's."[45]

A section of the community that crossed sectarian boundaries was the school population that surfaced spasmodically in the *katra* and cantonment compounds. Schooling was offered to the sons of adult converts, and as elsewhere, drew from other communities eager to obtain a free education. In 1818, among about forty pupils in one of the schools, a dozen were Roman Catholic and several Armenian.[46] The Eurasian children of drummers in the Company's regiments, married to Indian women, contributed to the enrollment. All categories were deemed by the evangelicals in need of Christian as well as secular teaching. Initially Corrie and ʿAbdul envisaged a higher level of teaching for the brightest boys, including Persian and English, as a ladder to social betterment as translators and teachers, and in the case of the converts, to responsibility within a growing Christian community whose most pressing need was leadership.

Community Dynamics

In spite of considerable evangelical excitement in 1813, ʿAbdul and Corrie's new Christian community had a checkered history after the first flush of baptisms, weakening almost to the point of collapse several times before final decline in the late 1820s. Critics of the mission would have had it buried even by 1817. A more nuanced understanding, bringing into the frame various causal factors, will be suggested here. Five stages may be distinguished: its phenomenal first eighteen months, 1813-14, under the joint leadership of ʿAbdul and Corrie; a decade of fluctuating fortunes from 1814 to 1824, when ʿAbdul was often bereft of support, and during which assistance both from the British community and from his Indian congregation proved crucial but fitful; a resurgence of optimism in 1824-25 in anticipation of the visit to Agra of Bishop Heber and ʿAbdul's Anglican ordination in Calcutta; followed by a final loss of vitality when ʿAbdul failed to return to Agra after his ordination, ending in his death in Lucknow in 1827.

---

the Agra Christians . . . you once disputed with Padre Antonio about ten years ago." Journal, December 1820: CI1/0194/5.

45. John Adlington to Corrie, Agra, February 13, 1818: CI1/E1/104.

46. Adlington to Corrie, Agra, February 13, 1818: CI1/E1/104.

Much of the confidential correspondence between evangelicals, and even some of the published journal reports, conveyed the view that having originated and proved so immediately successful in a partnership, the mission could only fail after Corrie left Agra in late 1814. Such a view not only undervalues ʿAbdul, but reflects a racist perception of the necessity of European agency and an exaggerated sense of Corrie's indispensability.[47] That a working partnership could in fact be reconstituted in others' hands would be shown when a similarly inclined "pious chaplain," John Irving, was able to rediscover synergies with ʿAbdul as late as 1824. Irving, ʿAbdul Masih confided to Corrie, "shows such a kindness and love to me as you used to do."[48]

Successes

The most convincing refutation of those, such as Thomas Thomason, who considered that ʿAbdul on his own would not manage to hold the nascent community together lies in consideration of his special qualities of leadership as well as his alleged weaknesses. Many contemporary accounts remarked on the combination of personal attributes that explains this remarkable Christian's influence. British accounts, with the exception of those of Thomason, were unanimous in attributing to ʿAbdul Masih almost saintlike qualities as a Christian exemplar, stressing his transparent piety and honesty, and his daily living out in public of a "Christian life."[49] In practical terms the various efforts he made to provide employment for his converts, and his readiness to dip into his own pocket for people in demonstrable need, whether Christian or not, certainly won him hearts. Such vaunting of his Christian virtues tended to tip over into sentimentality, especially in the eulogies in the *Missionary Register*, yet they are reflected in most letters written by those who

47. Thomason wrote that "in losing their beloved Corrie, the converts at Agra lost their head, their guide, their support, and their father." A military "friend of missions" posted in Agra expressed a common British racial assumption in suggesting in relation to Abdul's now lone role, that a native convert should not be expected to be as effective as a European. Capt. Robertson to CMS, December 7, 1815, *MR* (1816): 333-34. *Memoirs of the Right Rev. Daniel Corrie, LLD . . . by His Brothers* (London, 1847); Angus Macnaghten, *Daniel Corrie, His Family and Friends* (London, 1969).

48. ʿAbdul to Corrie, Agra, May 6, 1824: CI1/0194/3.

49. If accounts of ʿAbdul Masih based on missionary records seem eulogistic, some qualifications can be found. Even Corrie, generally a devotedly strong supporter of his former colleague, made a confidential suggestion to a colleague who would have to deal with him, that Abdul shared the deference and diffidence he felt was a characteristic of all natives in relation to Europeans, and as a consequence sometimes appeared to lack drive.

were closest to him, whose effusions concerning "our dear ʿAbdool" acknowledged a rare presence in their midst. A much-quoted description by the Meerut chaplain, Henry Fisher, reported the enigma of a man, "remarkably handsome with an air of Asiatic piety tempered by a sweetness of demeanour perfectly fascinating."[50] Bishop Heber helped to create a lasting orientalist stereotype in his representation of ʿAbdul Masih in 1825, whose "long eastern dress, his long grey beard, and his calm resigned countenance, give him already almost the air of an apostle."[51] Those closest to him went behind the physical facade to recognize the spiritual strengths that explained his influence. John Irving, the chaplain, recorded "the comfort of having such a man as Abdool always at hand. . . . the more I see of him the more I have reason to respect him so unassuming and yet so steady."[52]

If the same qualities were unlikely to endear him equally to his former coreligionists, other traits seemed to retain their respect. His ancestry assured him considerable interest within his old community. Former acquaintances as well as some of his Muslim relatives continued to seek him out. If their motives were curiosity or horror at his apostasy, reacquaintance reaffirmed some respect for him even while some decried his change of identity and whipped up hostility for him.[53] Related to his ancestral status was his command of Arabic and Persian. He used the latter to converse with those he described as "Moghul travellers" and to teach his school classes, thus successfully reaccrediting himself according to scholarly norms. When conversing with *ashraf* Muslims, he found that his own history often made a favorable impression by providing an entrée for discussing religion. His formal reports show, even in translation, a preference for Persianized forms of polite and effusive address. His tombstone in Lucknow, bearing a Persian inscription, symbolizes the value he attached to his cultural past.

While maintaining a scholarly image, he clearly commanded a common touch. Henry Martyn's Hindustani New Testament was valued by him principally because "this translation is intelligible to all."[54] But he preferred to com-

50. Cited by Andrew Cheap to Sec., CMS, Knaseborough, December 3, 1817: CMS. G/Ac3 (Oct-Dec. 1817).

51. Reginald Heber, journal, January 12, 1825, in *Bishop Heber in Northern India: Selections from Heber's Journal,* ed. M. A. Laird (Cambridge, 1971), p. 247.

52. John Irving to Corrie, Agra, April 19, 1824: CI1/076/149.

53. He recorded many intermittent instances of Muslim hostility, mentioning especially the local *qazi,* yet recent work on this region has not identified ʿAbdul Masih as an object of deep concern to local Muslims. Personal communications from Margrit Pernau and Abida Awan, August-December 2004.

54. ʿAbdul to Corrie, September 5, 1822: CI1/0194/1. After his death a European mis-

pose hymns and devotional poems in Hindustani according to "native measures" rather than English translations. ʿAbdul's letters, even in translation, convey the homeliness of his idiom, replete with proverbs and Hindustani sayings. A favorite phrase to describe the meditation on Scripture and "secret prayer" that he practiced was "I'm employed in mending my net."[55] His mixing of biblical parable and local folklore is shown in a rather despondent letter in which he finds "the parable of the fig-tree without fruit exactly suitable to my own condition," and the pressure of further spiritual instruction on his heart to be "like a well known saying in Hindoostan, 'The wetter the blanket the greater the weight.'"[56] His critic, Thomason, reported "a sermon in rhyme" he heard ʿAbdul give at the *katra* as "above the comprehension of the greater part," but judging by other reports it was Thomason who was more likely to have been out of his depth in Hindustani verse, rather than the congregation.[57]

It cannot be claimed, however, whatever the popularity and accessibility of his poems and hymns, that ʿAbdul was able to make the original contributions to Christian scholarship that some later converts from Islam would do.[58] His only scholarly contributions were, jointly with Corrie, some commentaries in Hindustani on Saint Matthew's Gospel and some epistles, notably Romans and Hebrews, none of which appear to be extant. Saint Matthew was the text most frequently discussed in his religious encounters and the one to which he had paid the closest attention. These translations were circulated in manuscript copies, an example being a Hindustani abridgment of Martyn's *Book of Common Prayer* that ʿAbdul "used in manuscript" before Corrie gave it for correction in Calcutta prior to publication.[59] His overshadowing by other translators probably reflected his lack of both Hebrew and Greek. Yet, it was his constant usage and distribution of Martyn's printed Hindustani translations that ensured that the Christian Scriptures became known in circles where the Bible was still not widely known. The chaplain, David Brown,

---

sionary used "part of Abdool Messeeh's Versified Translation of the conversation with Nicodemus" during discussion with Muslims at a *mela*. Charles Friend, journal, April 16, 1829, *MR* (1830): 154.

55. E.g., journal, January 15, 1825, *MR* (1826): 392.

56. ʿAbdul to J. Pratt and Committee, Agra, January 1, 1816: CI1/E/17a.

57. Thomason to Corrie, Calcutta, August 31, 1815: CI1/E/6.

58. E.g., Rev. Maulvi ʿImad ud-din's contribution to Urdu tract literature on Christian themes, as well as his translations of Scripture and commentaries in the Punjab from the late 1860s to 1900.

59. *A Compendium of the Book of Common Prayer* (in Persian) (Calcutta, 1814). See T. H. Darlow and H. F. Moule, *The Historical Catalogue of the Printed Editions of Holy Scripture in the Library of the British and Foreign Bible Society*, 2 vols. (London, 1903-11), vol. 2, pt. 3.

in earlier preparing him for baptism, had identified in "the unassisted study of the Scriptures" both the source of ʿAbdul's attraction to Christianity and the core of his subsequent evangelistic method.[60] Although later commentators stressed a strand of Islamic rationalism that would prove persuasive with other Muslims, it seems that "scripturalism" was his evangelistic bedrock.[61] There are numerous references in ʿAbdul's journals to the scriptural texts he was either asked to produce or thought appropriate for inquirers. Corrie recorded that he preferred to take "a whole chapter to explain, rather than a single verse, and reads the chapters as lessons between prayers."[62]

Although he was almost daily engaged in what he called "discourse" or "conversation" with individuals, he refused from the start of his mission any invitation to consciously engage in "dispute."[63] Reluctant to itinerate except when journeying to and from Lucknow and Calcutta, he usually waited for inquirers to come to him, thus avoiding any suggestion of provocation. Corrie emphasized ʿAbdul's reluctance to dwell on negative features of other religions, for "he never enters into the histories of their supposed prophets or gods," recognizing the hostility such forms of bazaar preaching would arouse.[64]

His reputation spread, carried by those he had engaged in conversation, his journals showing examples of the "networking" that resulted. One morning in 1815, for example, he recounted, when he was about his daily routine of leading the service and setting the boys to their schoolwork, "a handsome well-dressed young man, with several attendants, entered the Kuttra, and enquired, 'Where is Abdool Messeeh?'" He identified himself as "Ramdyal Brahmin," saying he had

60. David Brown [ed. Mrs. Brown], *Memorial Sketches: with a Selection of His Sermons, Preached at Calcutta* (London, 1816), p. 77.

61. Lyle L. Vander Werff, *Christian Mission to Muslims — the Record: Anglican and Reformed Approaches in India and the Near East, 1800-1938* (Pasadena, 1977), p. 39.

62. Corrie, "Account of Abdool Messee's method of promoting Christianity," *MR* (1815): 372.

63. E.g., he replied to a *maulwi* who came to "dispute," that he would not dispute, first, because he might not be able to understand "every difficulty" in the Gospels; second, "because, should they engage in dispute, he might say something that would offend, and so be guilty of a breach of hospitality." This *maulwi* then brought his son a second time "to hear this New Way." Corrie and Abdul, journal, April 2, 1813, *MR* (1813): 191.

64. In Christian company, however, he shared the contemporary evangelical tendency to criticize the "errors" of other religions, criticizing for example, in his ordination sermon in 1820, various Muslim, Hindu, and "Portuguese" practices as incapable in their "externality" of achieving salvation. Sermon on 2 Cor. 5:16-20, appendix 6, *Proceedings of the Church Missionary Society for Africa and the East, 1821-1822* (London, 1822), pp. 248-57.

"come a long way to see you: I heard of you in Jaypore." It transpired that he wanted to find out more about Christianity but feared his family's reaction. He left with a copy of one of the Epistles, never, apparently to return.[65] 'Abdul recorded in detail many such distant inquiries. A *maulawi* in Kashmir asked two "Mogul travellers" to procure for him in Agra copies of the Gospels and Psalms in Persian and Urdu.[66] By the time 'Abdul left Agra in 1825, he felt he had won over even those most disposed to object to Christian evangelism, his entrée into local society symbolized by an invitation to a Muslim wedding, which after his first refusal, was repeated with the promise of a separate room so that he might avoid the dancing and other customary wedding practices that would compromise his Christian values. Those gathered in the room, "learned in Religion and wealthy, all received me with respect."[67] Editorial interventions, intended to reassure readers of missionary journals in Britain that the gospel was indeed making progress in India, probably exaggerated some responses.

An innovative aspect of 'Abdul's evangelism, as Graham Kings has suggested, was his transparent use of his medical skills as an evangelistic tool at a time when few other missionaries had adopted the strategy.[68] A watercolor portrait of him was possibly painted in his improvised clinic. 'Abdul himself frequently alluded to his practice of "cures." He had probably taken up the role of *hakim* quite unself-consciously, some training in *yunani* medical traditions being part of the traditional education of the Muslim *ashraf* class. By his early days in Agra he had amassed a collection of more than fifty books on medicine, quickly becoming known in the region as a dispenser of remedies, frequently without a fee if he surmised the patient was unable to pay. Neither he nor his observers commented on whether his "cures" drew from *yunani* rather than from allopathy, but his reference to reading "the Physical book called Dafool Imraz" (Dispeller of Diseases) with one Dr. Child, the local physician, is suggestive of a *yunani* ingredient.[69] Alexander Macdonald, his sympathetic military "minder," reported to Corrie in 1816 that, "Having acquired some knowledge of medicine . . . he commenced Doctor and having made two or three successful cures he soon got a number of patients. He takes that opportunity of conversing with them and having a talent for dialogue they listen willingly but many of them when well never think of returning."[70]

65. Corrie and 'Abdul, journal, January 3, 1815, *MR* (1816): 26.

66. 'Abdul, journal, April 8, 1825, *MR* (1826): 398.

67. Abdul, journal, April 1, 1825, *MR* (1826): 397.

68. Graham Kings, "Abdul Masih: Icon of Indian Indigeneity," *International Bulletin of Missionary Research* 23 (1999): 66-69.

69. 'Abdul to Corrie, Agra, May 6, 1824: CI1/0194/3.

70. A. Macdonald to Corrie, Agra, February 10, 1816: CI1/E1/20.

Clearly this was a strategy ʿAbdul had adopted on his own initiative in the vacuum left by Corrie's departure, otherwise the lieutenant would have had no reason to explain it so intricately to Corrie. ʿAbdul, in describing his daily routine about this time, mentioned that having taken care of divine service and the teaching of children in the *katra,* "afterwards I unworthy creature am employed in administering medicine to the sick." The link he perceived between evangelism and medicine he spelled out as follows:

> There is a well known proverb in India. "Where there is no tree a shrub will even count for one." It is for this reason as there is no English physician of the Christian faith who can turn his attention to the state of the poor in this town that I having exerted myself for their spiritual welfare continue to carry on my endeavours for their bodily health, for the sake of Jesus' name, who is able to free from sickness spiritual and bodily. 300 persons have by God's goodness obtained relief since I have attempted this wherefore the people of the town begin to be very friendly to me and are coming to the Christian hospital. . . . and may the Holy spirit grant that as the people are collected for their bodily welfare so they may come forward for the advantage of their souls.[71]

Corrie advised the CMS to raise ʿAbdul's salary, as his modest pay was disappearing on medicine dispensed to poor patients and on other means of assistance. Rivalry was apparently caused by his thus setting up as a Christian *hakim,* notably the "resentment of the principal Native Physician of the city, who is . . . of considerable repute among the Natives."[72] A second physician, one Hakim Hyder al-din who had earlier shown some interest in ʿAbdul's teachings, later attacked his reputation. Whatever the professional opposition, he nevertheless managed to play a significant part in establishing an association between medicine and evangelism, and the *katra* became known as a clinic as well as a place of worship, a school and a *serai.*

Unfortunately, ʿAbdul was unable to treat successfully his own growing catalogue of physical ills. His journals suggest that his activities were constrained as early as 1818, even though he managed, with the help of lay assistants, to continue a skeleton program in the *katra.* Though Bishop Heber seemed impressed with the station on a brief visit in 1825, it was hardly the center of Christian takeoff anticipated by evangelicals. When ʿAbdul remained in his family home in Lucknow following his Anglican ordination in

71. ʿAbdul Masih to J. Pratt and committee, Agra, January 1, 1816: CI1/E/17a.
72. *MR* (1817): 424-25.

1825, the Agra community began to experience serious difficulties in projecting its Christian identity.

Failures

Some reasons for such failure were implicit in the community characteristics already discussed even when seemingly at its most successful. Staking much on the phenomenon of a rapid clutch of high-status conversions, the inexperienced CMS visionaries had failed to ensure their integration within the *katra* community. On his precipitate departure Corrie had dispersed most of the *ashraf* converts, apostle-like he hoped, to Calcutta and elsewhere, ostensibly for training as translators and catechists. Such a premature exodus had an undermining effect in Agra itself, so that, as the Calcutta evangelicals realized too late, "the Native Christian Society at Agra may be said to have been, in a manner, broken up."[73] More seriously, most who were transferred and several who remained, then abandoned their Christian identities shortly afterward. Such was the case with Hakim Talib Masih Khan, who, after being sent to Meerut, renounced Christianity by 1816 and returned to his former medical service with the nearby raja of Bharatpur. Similarly Fazil Masih, in spite of his tortured period of inquiry prior to baptism, left within a year to become a disciple of a local Sufi *pir*, possibly influenced by his fretting wife and relatives.[74] Maulawi Mansoor, who maintained his Christian identity, was sent to Calcutta to learn Hebrew, and then successively to Bareilly, Lucknow, and Ghazipur, much against his own wishes, to fulfill CMS plans. Even he never came up to expectations, causing problems wherever he was posted. Munshi Barkat Allah, regarded as the most steady and promising of all, very soon died. Some converts maintained their *katra* linkages but did not contribute to the running of the community.

Agra and ʿAbdul were thus deprived of the kind of scholarly reinforcement that a new and potentially controversial center of religious activity urgently required. Meanwhile no further baptisms of their caliber and status occurred. Such returns to Islam seem to have been related to pressures from local Muslim critics, such as the *hakims* already mentioned, as well as to dissatisfaction with their new roles and status within the Christian community.

73. First circular letter of the Corresponding Committee, Calcutta, February 2, 1817, *MR* (1817): 340-43.

74. ʿAbdul described some of the defections in a letter to London, Agra, January 1, 1816: CI1/E/17a.

By the mid-1820s the movement of internal Islamic reform, externalized in nervous British minds as a movement of jihad, was certainly gathering recruits in this region under Syed Ahmad Barelvi, with whom ʿAbdul had once conversed on the question of jihad.[75] If a convert such as Hakim Talib Masih Khan had earlier abandoned "a party to fight for Islam" in order to join ʿAbdul Masih's *katra* community, there were certainly local influences at work to encourage him back into newly reformed Islamic modes of religious expression.[76] Yet the precise effects of Islamic revival are hard to gauge as Christianity was seldom specifically mentioned in the movement's literature. Nor has recent scholarship on Muslim movements uncovered any specific hostility to ʿAbdul Masih's evangelistic activities that might have fueled efforts to draw the converts back to Islam.

However, there are some signs in ʿAbdul's own journals that tolerance of him was lessening in the city even during the apparent recovery in the mid-1820s. Early objections to the mission's extension of its property around the *katra* now resurfaced more vigorously. In 1824, one of the bungalows was set alight, and objectors used their influence with the city's *qazi* and the *kotwal* to prevent ʿAbdul from purchasing more land behind the *katra*. This was resolved in the mission's favor and the extensions proceeded. The mission survived but on a permanent knife-edge, protected to a considerable extent by the British presence; otherwise one commentator said, "they would have risen upon him." Such hostility should be balanced, however, against the continuing interest of individual Muslim inquirers and such evidence as the wedding invitation, discussed earlier, that was pressed on ʿAbdul at just this time.

ʿAbdul probably received a balanced sense of the spectrum of Muslim opinion about him when he overhead, while apparently asleep, both praise and invective from a group of Muslim guests who had stayed with him. "The Father and son took my part; while the others called me an Infidel and a Hyp-

75. ʿAbdul, journal, January 28, 1825, *MR* (1826): 393. Although ʿAbdul referred to this "spiritual guide" as "Saeud Mahomed Hage," the circumstantial details he gives about his recent return from Mecca wanting "war on the Christians" suggest he was indeed Syed Ahmad Barelvi.

76. See Ahmad, *Wahhabi Movement in India,* chap. 1, for the origin and spread of Barėlvi's movement. Ahmad noted Muslim disaffection in a line from Bareilly down to Tonk circa 1815, and a general tendency toward "seeking solace in religiosity" at the time when the converts were reverting to Islam. Barelvi started to take *baiʿat* from disciples in Delhi in 1818. No specific links have been found between former converts and this *tariqa,* but there are suggestions in ʿAbdul's journals that some of the increased hostility he encountered came from this source.

ocrite, deserving of death." All, however, proceeded on their journey, carrying copies of Saint Matthew's Gospel and a prayer book, suggesting that whatever the Muslim feeling against him, it never reached boiling point.[77]

Meanwhile, a gradual change in social composition from a "top-down" emphasis on elite converts to a congregation consisting predominantly of illiterate and poor textile workers may have adversely affected Muslim interest, while reinforcing disdain from higher-caste Hindu observers. Scarcely any of the higher-caste inquirers maintained their interest, let alone requested baptism. If the size of the community remained stable at between forty and fifty, the proportion of members from the low-caste textile and cultivating occupations increased. The few new members noted in 1818 were mainly weavers and spinners.[78] If his scholarly skills in Persianate culture were now rather wasted, ʿAbdul himself certainly showed no disdain, rather the opposite, mentioning by name in his letters each member, female and male, of his *katra* community, and paying special attention to those who were physically incapacitated. At his most despondent in 1816, he took care to provide details about the death of one Munoo, a leper, "the latchet of whose shoes I was not worthy to unloose," and for whom he built a brick tomb in the *katra* garden.[79] Journal editors, however, did not always share such solicitude, choosing not only to abbreviate his references to converts from lower social strata but also giving less attention than before to Agra, its mission, and its once eulogized "native" missionary as new concerns worldwide pushed this now faltering project into the background.

A related factor was the failure of the educational program to achieve the material and spiritual uplift of the low-caste converts. It was hoped that, learning Persian and English, some boys would be thus qualified as translators. Six Christian boys were subsequently sent to a school for training teachers in Calcutta. However, there is no further mention of these boys or of any future occupational outcome. Basic schooling in Hindustani, and sometimes in English, nevertheless continued, ʿAbdul taking some of the lessons and examining the pupils with the help of his British patrons, but handing over day-to-day management increasingly to superintendents, British or Eurasian, assisted by convert schoolmasters.

Although the *katra* school never actually closed, and new schools mushroomed momentarily in other parts of the city, the educational program experienced the difficulties common to many experiments in missionary- and

77. ʿAbdul Masih, journal, April 1-5, 1825, *MR* (1826): 397-98.

78. J. Adlington to Corrie, February 13, 1818: CI1/E1/104.

79. ʿAbdul to J. Pratt and Committee, Agra, January 1, 1816: CI1/E/17a.

government-sponsored schooling. In spite of references to innovative methods of teaching, adequately qualified teachers proved impossible to recruit and retain. There is little evidence of hostility to Christianity, but pupil numbers, consisting of Christian converts, Catholics, and Armenians as well as Hindus and Muslims, fluctuated around thirty to sixty in each school without growing further. Paradoxically, after ʿAbdul's death, when the community was otherwise at its weakest, the schools appear to have experienced a new growth, with encouragement from a new generation of British patrons. An Indian catechist and poet, Faiz Masih, a convert first from Hinduism to Islam and then to Christianity, managed to open three girls' schools. Nevertheless, these were short-lived initiatives.

Deficiencies in the CMS itself, and its agents in India, also prevented the consolidation and expansion of the community. It seems obvious, in retrospect, that the mission, whatever its recruitment problems, should have reinforced its Agra outpost with a missionary replacement for Corrie. This never happened despite promises, and despite ʿAbdul's strong wish for a permanent European partner. Internal rivalries also played an undermining part, following the arrival of a Eurasian catechist whose bad relations with ʿAbdul seem to have influenced some of the Calcutta CMS supporters against the latter. From this incident emerged Thomas Thomason's otherwise inexplicable denigration of ʿAbdul as "in danger of giving way to indolence. . . . There was a plump and sleek appearance about him which he had not in Calcutta which rather denoted a habit of self-indulgence."[80] It was on a visit to Agra at this time that Thomason criticized ʿAbdul's *katra* sermon, as discussed above, and opined that "[Abdul] has nothing of an interesting nature to communicate."[81] ʿAbdul was certainly at a low point, debilitated and depressed by Corrie's loss. But other sources qualify Thomason's criticism, particularly the letters of the young military officers who gave practical help in the schools, and who reported positively on the state of the Agra community. There seems no doubt, however, that the CMS's neglect of this fragile community contributed significantly to the reduced state of the mission.

Conclusions

The *katra* remained the center of low-key Christian activity in Agra for about ten years after ʿAbdul's departure and death, but references to his "scattered

80. Thomason to Corrie, Calcutta, August 31, 1815: CI1/E/6.
81. Thomason to Corrie, Calcutta, August 31, 1815: CI1/E/6.

flock" were now reminiscent of similar Catholic laments.[82] Of the approximately one hundred Indians converted under ʿAbdul and Corrie's influence, thirty to forty, despite defections, remained in the vicinity of the *katra*, attending spasmodically its services and schools, and providing continuity through their children and grandchildren's adherence to Christianity. Faiz Masih proved no ʿAbdul Masih: he remained in the Agra vicinity until at least 1840, sometimes preaching to Hindus in nearby Mathura, but only one letter was received by the CMS.[83] As no reports followed between 1832 and 1841, scarcely anything is known of the community. British residents and military officers kept some schools open and occasional services were held, but the indigenous community was on the verge of extinction. Other locations now seemed better suited to the CMS's evangelistic programs, notably Krishnagar in Bengal where a mass "awakening" was just beginning, and nearby Karnal, where Anand Masih, noted earlier as an evangelist of the Satnamis, still provided leadership.

Entirely new factors explain the sudden renewal of attention to Agra in the late 1830s. Agra's elevation to capital of the newly established North-Western Provinces, in preference to Delhi, certainly helped, but it was the famine of 1837-38, unprecedented in its destructive effects, that intensified missionary efforts in the vicinity. At this moment of crisis the bishop of Calcutta felt able to anticipate "every prospect of the Kattra regaining the character which it used to bear in the days of Corrie and Abdul Messeeh," despite "so long a decline."[84]

As a result, the CMS mission to Agra did revive: the *katra* became again in the 1840s and 1850s a center of encounter with local Muslims, but of a combative and controversial kind in which ʿAbdul would never have joined. Meanwhile, two new institutions perceived as offering longer-term evangelistic outcomes soon eclipsed the *katra*'s significance. The first, an orphanage for famine victims, established with workshops, a printing press, and schools in the nearby Christian village of Sikandra, became the focus of missionary

82. Report on Agra, *MR* (1830): 105.

83. "Papers of Indian Christians": CI1/019/21. Faiz's "confession of faith," October 12, 1817, sent to the CMS by Corrie, remains one of few records of north Indian converts still extant in the original Urdu: CI1/E/82a.

84. The bishop wrote dramatically of a degree of "decline" in Agra during which, "no sooner were the pillars [Corrie and ʿAbdul] removed, as I am informed, than the whole fabric fell to ruin; successive years defaced what faint traces were left, till, within a very short period of the present time, hardly a single vestige remained to show that a Mission had ever existed." "Visit of the Bishop of Calcutta to the Mission," *Church Missionary Record* (1841): 89-94.

attention until 1857, when it was destroyed in the Rebellion. The second, St. John's College, opened in 1853 in the new civil lines, remains today a center of Anglican higher educational activity. The *katra* community in the heart of the Agra bazaar was reactivated to some extent after attacks on it in 1857, but its latter-day importance was mainly symbolic. Many children had been removed to the orphanage schools at Sikandra, and after the Rebellion, together with a new generation of parents, to a Christian village near Allahabad that replaced Agra as the provincial capital. As Agra city declined again into an administrative backwater, so too did its significance to missionary societies.

ʿAbdul Masih, however, remains an icon of Anglican identity even though no full memoir making use of his manuscript journals and letters was ever published, and the site of his *katra* community cannot even be identified in today's bazaar. Yet he is memorialized in mission histories as the first Indian pastor to receive Anglican ordination, even "the first C.M.S. missionary in India."[85] Such ascriptions reflect the uniqueness of the community he created with Daniel Corrie in Agra, yet which has never received the attention it deserves, as one of the earliest communities of Protestant converts in the northwest of India. This paper is a contribution to recovering that significance.

85. Stock, *History,* 1:312.

CHAPTER 5

An "Ardour" of Devotion: The Spiritual Legacy of Henry Martyn

BRIAN STANLEY

> Amidst all the discords which agitate the Church of England, her sons are unanimous in extolling the name of Henry Martyn. And with reason; for it is in fact the one heroic name which adorns her annals from the days of Elizabeth to our own. Her apostolic men, the Wesleys and Elliotts [*sic*] and Brainerds of other times, either quitted, or were cast out of her communion. Her *Acta Sanctorum* may be read from end to end with a dry eye and an unquickened pulse. Henry Martyn, the learned and the holy, translating the Scriptures in his solitary bungalow at Dinapore, or preaching to a congregation of five hundred beggars, or refuting the Mahommedan doctors at Shiraz, is the bright exception.[1]

That sweeping verdict was delivered in 1844, at the height of the ecclesiastical tumult created by the Oxford Movement, by James Stephen, undersecretary of state at the Colonial Office, later Regius Professor of Modern History in the University of Cambridge, and one of the most notable sons of the Clapham Sect. In Stephen's reckoning, heroism had been in decidedly short supply in the Church of England, but Henry Martyn had single-handedly made up much of the deficit through an exemplary spiritual ardor that was admired by Tractarian and evangelical alike. In three places in this famous essay on the Clapham Sect, Stephen applies the word "ardour" to Martyn: at Shiraz in Persia he is said to

1. James Stephen, *Essays in Ecclesiastical Biography,* 2 vols. (London, 1853), 2:338-39. Stephen's essay "The Clapham Sect" was first published anonymously as a review article in the *Edinburgh Review* 161 (1844): 251-307.

have labored for twelve months "with the ardour of a man, who, distinctly perceiving the near approach of death, feared lest it should intercept the great work for which alone he desired to live"; Martyn's character is described, inter alia, as that of "a man born to love with ardour and to hate with vehemence"; and, most colorful of all, Martyn's spirituality is portrayed in the following hyperbolic terms: "Insatiable in the thirst for freedom, holiness, and peace, he maintained an ardour of devotion which might have passed for an erotic delirium, when contrasted with the Sadducean frigidity of other worshippers."[2]

One does not have to read very far in nineteenth-century Anglican ecclesiastical history before coming across evidence of what can only be described as the "cult" of Henry Martyn. The central motif of that cult is one of Martyn as the ideal embodiment of self-sacrificing missionary ardor. It is a cult that has left its mark on Victorian literature: the forbiddingly pious figure of Saint John Rivers in Charlotte Brontë's *Jane Eyre* (1847) is almost certainly modeled on Martyn.[3] Much less well known, and deservedly so, is the second-rate novel by the romantic novelist Harriet Parr (1828-1900), writing under the pseudonym Holme Lee. *Her Title of Honour* (1871) tells the heartrending story of the doomed romance between the Reverend Francis Gwynne (alias Henry Martyn) and Miss Eleanour Trevelyan (alias Lydia Grenfell). The novel adheres slavishly to historical accuracy and ends with the hero's solitary death in "Tocat."[4] The cult continued to flourish into the late Victorian period, as is evidenced by the seemingly automatic decision in 1887 to name the hall erected next to Holy Trinity Church in Cambridge (where Martyn had served as curate), in order to provide a meeting place for university associations in support of foreign missions, the Henry Martyn Memorial Hall. Two sermons were preached in Cambridge to mark the opening of the hall in October 1887. Neither was by a recognized member of the evangelical party, though both preachers were known for their decided Protestant sympathies. The first, preached as a University sermon in Great Saint Mary's Church on Sunday the 16th, was by Dr. Charles John Vaughan, dean of Llandaff and master of the Temple. Vaughan referred to Martyn's story as "the hero-life of my boyhood" (Vaughan's father, Edward Thomas Vaughan, was a leading evangelical clergyman and near-contemporary of Martyn at Cambridge).[5]

2. Stephen, *Essays in Ecclesiastical Biography,* 2:337, 339, 342.

3. See Valentine Cunningham, "'God and Nature Intended You for a Missionary's Wife': Mary Hill, Jane Eyre and Other Missionary Women in the Nineteenth Century," in *Women and Missions: Past and Present; Anthropological and Historical Perceptions,* ed. Fiona Bowie et al. (Oxford, 1993), pp. 96-97.

4. Holme Lee, *Her Title of Honour* (London, 1871).

5. *The Mission Field* 33 (1888): 35. On E. T. Vaughan, see *The Blackwell Dictionary of*

The second sermon, preached in Holy Trinity Church on the following evening, was by Henry Montagu Butler, the master of Trinity College, and Vaughan's successor as headmaster of Harrow School from 1859 to 1885.[6] Butler cited the same passage from James Stephen with which this essay began, and went on to consider why Martyn's life was so worthy of remembrance. His answer, in timeworn homiletical fashion, had three points. First, asserted Butler, Martyn was "not the greatest Clerical Missionary of the Church of England, but he was the first." Although John Wesley and George Whitefield "made attempts at missionary work in America," Martyn was, Butler assured his congregation, "the first clergyman of the Church of England — at least since the Reformation" to devote his life to "gathering together in one the children of God that were scattered abroad."[7]

In point of fact, Martyn was *not* the first Anglican clerical missionary; he was, approximately, the 411th. In the course of the eighteenth century, 410 ordained missionaries served the Society for the Propagation of the Gospel, mostly in North America and the Caribbean, all of them missionaries of the Church of England, though not all were English.[8] It is true that most of them had the primary responsibility of ministering to British persons in the colonies; their evangelistic duties toward the indigenous inhabitants were secondary to their role as colonial chaplains. But much the same, of course, was true of Henry Martyn, whose official duties as a chaplain of the Honorable East India Company were strictly confined to ministry to the Company's officials, British soldiers, and their families. By the 1880s, when British missionary horizons were firmly fixed on Africa and the Orient, earlier generations of Anglican missionaries who had crossed the Atlantic to the then heathen Americas seemed not to count. What stuck in the memory was the extraordinary difficulty faced by the Church Missionary Society (CMS) in its early years in finding any Anglican clergyman willing to sacrifice prospects and possibly life on the foreign field: the first ordained Anglican to be sent out by the CMS was William Greenwood, who was appointed to North India in 1815, nearly three years after Martyn's

---

Evangelical Biography, ed. Donald M. Lewis, 2 vols. (Oxford, 1995), 2:1135-36. For C. J. Vaughan's churchmanship, see F. D. How, *Six Great Schoolmasters* (London, 1904), p. 162.

6. On Butler, see *Henry Montagu Butler: Master of Trinity College Cambridge, 1886-1918; A Memoir* (London, 1925). The author describes his father as "a strong Protestant" (p. 86).

7. H. M. Butler, *Henry Martyn: A Sermon Preached in Trinity Church, Cambridge, October 17th, 1887* (Cambridge, 1887), p. 4.

8. D. O'Connor et al., *Three Centuries of Mission: The United Society for the Propagation of the Gospel, 1701-2000* (London and New York, 2000), pp. 27-28.

death.[9] Martyn, though never formally a missionary, appeared in retrospect to be the pioneer, the one whose self-immolation on the altar had ignited the flame of the evangelical Anglican missionary devotion that the Henry Martyn Hall had been erected to nourish at its original Cambridge source. The prime mover behind the erection of the hall was John Barton, vicar of Holy Trinity Church from 1877 to 1893, and for fifteen years before that a CMS missionary in north India; Barton was a key figure in encouraging the explosion of interest in foreign missions in late Victorian Cambridge.[10]

Butler's second and third points are less susceptible to challenge. Martyn was, in the second place, a man of "rare holiness," one who, in Thomas Thomason's famous words penned from Calcutta to Charles Simeon, "shines in all the dignity of love, and seems to carry about him such a heavenly majesty, as impresses the mind beyond [all] description."[11] Third, there was the legacy of Martyn's work during the seven years of his Company chaplaincy. This was to be measured not so much in numbers of Indian converts won through preaching, where (not surprisingly, in view of the role chaplains were supposed to fulfill) the harvest was meager. Indeed, commented Butler with some discernment, "perhaps, though it would have grieved him to think so, he was less fitted for this special function of winning, of attracting souls to Christ." Rather, Martyn's achievement must be assessed in terms of his translation work. The sedentary labor involved in his translations of the New Testament into Hindustani (Urdu) and Persian — Butler makes no reference to that into Arabic that Martyn supervised — was "not what he had thought of when he left Cambridge," but this reorientation of his missionary commission was accepted, "even with ardour," as part of the divine will.[12]

Butler's sermon suggests appropriate lines of inquiry in this investigation of Martyn's spiritual legacy. First, when and how did the cult of Henry Martyn develop? Second, what was it about his piety as recorded in his biographies that proved so magnetically attractive to nineteenth-century Christians, and not simply to those of evangelical convictions? Third, how far is it possible to peel away the layers of hagiography and recover something of the

9. Church Missionary Society, *Register of Missionaries . . . and Native Clergy, from 1804 to 1904* (n.p.: Church Missionary Society, privately printed, [1896]), p. 5.

10. On Barton, see Andrew Porter, "Changing People, Changing Places," *International Review of Mission* 88 (1999): 392-95.

11. Butler, *Henry Martyn*, pp. 6-7. For the original words of Thomason's eulogy, written on reunion with his Cambridge friend in Calcutta in November 1810, see John Sargent, *The Life of the Rev. T. T. Thomason, M.A.* (London, 1833), p. 183.

12. Butler, *Henry Martyn*, p. 7.

"real" Henry Martyn? How was he regarded by those who met him in north India and Persia, where his missionary years were spent?

In answer to the first question, it might plausibly be suggested that Martyn's virtual canonization was largely posthumous. Many of those who secured a lasting place in the pantheon of nineteenth-century missionary heroes did so because they died in harness, most often violently at the hands of the "natives," or sometimes (as in Martyn's case) pathetically isolated from all European company, finally succumbing to the rigors of a harsh climate. John Williams at Vanuatu in 1839, Allen Gardiner in Tierra del Fuego in 1851, John Coleridge Patteson in the Santa Cruz Islands in 1871, David Livingstone at Chitambo's village in 1873, James Hannington in Busoga in 1885, and James Chalmers in Papua New Guinea in 1901 form an apostolic succession of British missionary heroes whose violent or pathetic deaths came to be interpreted, with more or less explicitness, as martyrdoms, and whose lives gained added luster as a result. It is tempting to see Henry Martyn as the first link in that chain of Protestant missionary martyrs. However, none of the classic biographies from John Sargent's famous *Memoir* onward characterize Martyn *primarily* as a missionary martyr, although occasionally the title of martyr is given to him:[13] perhaps the obvious homophone of "Martyn the martyr" was simply too trite to be contemplated.

If we may partially anticipate here the answer to our third question, there is, moreover, evidence that even in his lifetime Martyn was regarded as an individual of prodigious sanctity as well as intellect. This was clearly the case within the Cambridge circle of the disciples of Charles Simeon that nurtured his piety, and remained so when some of those disciples were transplanted to India. David Brown, the first of the evangelical chaplains in Bengal, said of him at the end of the five months Martyn spent under his roof in Calcutta in 1806: "a more heavenly-minded young man I never saw."[14] "This bright and lovely jewel," as Thomason called him,[15] sparkled even more brightly in Calcutta than in Cambridge. Of greater significance, however, is the fact that those from outside the evangelical fold who met Martyn passed specific comment on his sanctity, even if some of them found it a little hard to stomach. Listen, for example, to these extracts from the journal of the utilitarian philosopher and lawyer Sir James Mackintosh, the recorder of Bombay, to whom Martyn was introduced on arrival in Bombay from Calcutta in February 1811

13. E.g., Clement Carlyon, *Early Years and Late Reflections,* 4 vols. (London, 1836-58), 3:20-21.

14. James Hough, *The History of Christianity in India from the Commencement of the Christian Era,* 5 vols. (London, 1845-60), 4:90.

15. Sargent, *Life,* p. 183.

by his shipboard companion, Mountstuart Elphinstone. Mackintosh's Christian sympathies were of a distinctly liberal hue,[16] but it seems from the journal entries as if Martyn slowly grew on him:

> [February] 24th, Sunday. — Elphinstone introduced me to a young clergyman, called Martyn, come round from Bengal on his way to Bussora, partly for health, and partly to improve his Arabic, as he is translating the Scriptures into that language. He seems to be a mild and benevolent enthusiast — a sort of character with which I am always half in love. We had the novelty of grace before and after dinner, all the company standing.
>
> March 1st. — Mr Martyn, the saint from Calcutta, called here. He is a man of acuteness and learning; his meekness is excessive, and gives a disagreeable impression of effort to conceal the passions of human nature.
>
> [March] 18th, Sunday — "Padre" Martyn, the saint, dined here in the evening; it was a very considerably more pleasant evening than usual; he is a mild and ingenious man. We had two or three hours' good discussion on grammar and metaphysics.[17]

It is possible that by denominating Martyn a "saint" Mackintosh was merely recognizing his theological affiliation to the "Saints" of the Clapham Sect, and highly likely that he was writing with his tongue in his cheek. But he does not spell "saint" with the capital *S* that was customarily applied to Wilberforce's followers in Parliament: Mackintosh does not appear simply to be identifying Martyn as a member of the evangelical club. The way he refers to him suggests rather that by 1811 Martyn was already known in the higher echelons of East India Company society for his conspicuous sanctity, even if that sanctity evoked a wide range of reactions. His sainthood was not merely posthumous.

Nevertheless, there is no doubt that, to put it crudely, Martyn died at, or very nearly at, the right moment. James Stephen, sensitive as he was to the political dimensions of missionary affairs, noted that news of his death reached England in 1813 during the parliamentary debates on the renewal of the East India Company's charter.[18] The same issue of the *Missionary Register* in April 1813 that contained Martyn's obituary also printed the text of petitions from

16. Carlyon, *Early Years*, 3:125.

17. *Memoirs of the Life of the Right Honourable Sir James Mackintosh*, ed. Robert James Mackintosh, 2 vols. (London, 1835), 2:89, 95.

18. Stephen, *Essays in Ecclesiastical Biography*, 2:344.

all the British missionary societies urging that the charter be revised to make provision for the protection or support of Christian missionaries in the Company's territories, and also reports of public meetings in major cities convened for the same purpose.[19] However, the reports of Martyn's death came too late to impact the petitions themselves. They were not too late to influence the debates in the House of Commons over the "pious clause" that made provision for persons seeking to introduce "useful knowledge" and "religious and moral improvement" in British India, but the absence of reference to Martyn by William Wilberforce and other speakers in those debates suggests that his death made little direct contribution to the outcome, even though there is retrospective evidence that Charles Grant and his supporters used Martyn's career as an argument in favor of amending the charter to ensure that Britain did her religious duty to India.[20] It is at least clear that the solemn news from Armenia combined with the fervor induced by the charter campaign to raise British Christian enthusiasm for the evangelization of India to a new peak in the years following 1813. That fervor helps to explain the extraordinary success of John Sargent's *Memoir of the Rev. Henry Martyn, B.D.*, which first appeared in 1819 and went through twelve British editions by 1835. Sargent's adulatory biography, which contains substantial but carefully selected extracts from Martyn's journals, did a great deal to establish the cult of Henry Martyn. A copy of Sargent's work in Keighley public library was probably the source of Charlotte Brontë's portrait of St. John Rivers.[21] More copious and significantly more revealing extracts from the journals appeared in Samuel Wilberforce's two-volume edition of Martyn's *Journals and Letters*, published in 1837, but Wilberforce's work, though well received, appears not to have had the same popular impact, perhaps because it was not sufficiently distinct in content from the existing biography; certainly Wilberforce's book is far rarer today than Sargent's *Memoir* in one of its many editions.[22]

We turn, second, to the question of what were the ingredients of Martyn's piety that proved so compelling to the readers of his life story in the nineteenth century. The simplest answer is that Martyn is portrayed as having pursued the ideal of holiness with a single-minded intensity that all evangelicals admired but few could match. In the age of seriousness, he appeared to be the serious Christian par excellence. The pursuit of holiness brooked no half-measures. As

19. *Missionary Register* 1 (1813): 107-44.

20. George Smith, *Henry Martyn Saint and Scholar: First Modern Missionary to the Mohammedans, 1781-1812* (London, 1892), p. 516 n.

21. Cunningham, "God and Nature," p. 96.

22. *Journals and Letters of the Rev. Henry Martyn, B.D.*, ed. Samuel Wilberforce, 2 vols. (London, 1837); hereafter *Journals and Letters.*

his schoolmate at Truro Grammar School and Cambridge contemporary, Clement Carlyon, put it, "Martyn was never an idle man, and his misfortune, if it be right to use such a term in his case, seems to have consisted in his not knowing how to realize a middle course — that happy mean which it is, indeed, so difficult to attain."[23] Martyn had no time for the happy mean, and most Anglicans loved him for it. Nineteenth-century evangelicals have acquired a certain notoriety in some circles for their suspicion that anything pleasurable is likely to be sinful: Leslie Stephen, for example, said of his father, James, that "he once smoked a cigar and found it so delicious that he never smoked again."[24] Martyn's life shows something of the same attitude, but on a plane that transcends triviality and bears most obvious comparison with the Catholic saints and mystics. Consider, for example, this extract from Martyn's journal for February 17, 1804, when he was serving as curate at Lolworth:

> A despicable indulgence in lying in bed this morning gave me such a view of the dangerous softness of my own character, that I resolved on my knees, to live a life of far more self-denial than I had ever yet done, and to begin with little things. Accordingly, I ate my breakfast standing at a distance from the fire, and stood reading at the window during the morning, though the thermometer stood at the freezing point. I was so cold that I did not get on much in my work of sermon; but the effect on the flow of my thoughts was very surprising, the tone and vigour of my mind rose rapidly.[25]

For Martyn, however, self-denial was desirable not as an end in itself but as a function of his consuming passion for obedience to the will of God. Once the missionary direction of that divine will for his life had become plain to Martyn, as it had by the end of 1802, his life story combines the central evangelical dynamic of a concern to proclaim the gospel to those who have never heard it with the Catholic ascetical motif of rigorous denial of the flesh and all worldly comforts. That combination is the key to the unique attraction he exerted on the generation of evangelical Anglicans whose theology evolved and mutated in the years between his death and the Oxford Movement of the 1830s and 1840s. As the evangelical party in the Church of England grew steadily more numerous and politically influential, it also became more pre-

23. Carlyon, *Early Years,* 1:12.

24. *Dictionary of Evangelical Biography,* 2:1049.

25. *Journals and Letters,* 1:94. This passage is cited in part in John Sargent, *A Memoir of the Rev. Henry Martyn, B.D.,* 12th ed. (London, 1835), p. 59.

pared to compromise with the ways of the world, more closely absorbed with the instrumentality of a myriad of different societies set up to evangelize the nations and transform the moral fabric of industrial Britain, and gradually less concerned with the essentials of Christian holiness. Martyn's life stood as a beacon of what evangelicals once were and of what they still aspired to be. The young (and still evangelical) John Henry Newman, for example, began reading Sargent's life of Martyn in May 1823 and found it both "improving" and humbling. In conversations with his friend E. B. Pusey over the next few months, Newman discussed whether he possessed the requisite qualities for the missionary office, "the highest privilege from God I can possess," and shared with Pusey his intention to "pray to God to make me a missionary." In Pusey himself Newman saw an "active, devoted spirit," but prayed, "God grant he may not, like Martyn, 'burn as phosphorus.'"[26]

Martyn's spiritual disciplines of self-denial and scrupulous self-examination burned with a consuming intensity that gave even Newman some concern, but they exhibited characteristics which were to become central motifs in the ascetic spirituality of the Oxford Movement. Perhaps the most prominent note struck by Sargent's *Memoir* is Martyn's devotion to prayer: "I felt the need of setting apart a day for the restoration of my soul by solemn prayer," runs a journal entry for 1804: "I was engaged in prayer in the manner I like, *deep seriousness*."[27] Before his departure for India, Martyn's prayers were the arena in which the imaginative contest between devotedness to God and the manifold attractions — both carnal and spiritual — of remaining in England was played out, and the contest is frequently described in graphic detail:

> Riding home from Lolworth, I was enabled to be in prayer much of the time. I was labouring to feel an entire indifference to all created comforts, even to be contented without the ordinances. I wanted to feel myself as having nothing on earth to do but to work for God, and as having to expect no comfort but communion with God. I endeavoured to realize my future life as a missionary, to ask whether I could be satisfied at resigning for ever all pleasing society, to roam about a desert looking for people to preach to, and to wait upon them, patiently enduring their scorn and ill treatment. My heart did not at all shrink from it, but on the contrary, improved and embraced it. It has been in general a blessed day.[28]

26. *John Henry Newman: Autobiographical Writings,* ed. Henry Tristram (New York, 1957), pp. 191-97.

27. Sargent, *Memoir,* pp. 60-61.

28. *Journals and Letters,* 1:232.

Carlyon wrote in his recollections of Martyn that "it may almost be said that Martyn stuck literally to the text, 'pray without ceasing.'"[29] Carlyon thought Martyn prayed too much, particularly on the long voyage to India, when godless and scoffing shipmates would have benefited far more from good ordinary conversation that followed the scriptural injunction to be all things to all men so as thereby to gain some.

Quite frequently Martyn's journal conjoins prayer and fasting.[30] How widespread the practice of fasting was among evangelical Anglicans of that era is an intriguing question, but there is no doubt that Martyn's regular practice of fasting was one of the features that made his life so attractive to a later generation of Anglicans of more Catholic inclinations. Samuel Wilberforce, editing Martyn's journals in 1835, found his observance of fasting convicting. Wilberforce's diary for Good Friday that year records that he read Pusey's tract *The Benefits of the System of Fasting,* number 18 in the *Tracts for the Times,* and was persuaded by it of the value of fasting for the realization of unseen things, prayer, and the subduing of the body to the spirit, and continues: "I have also been brought to this conclusion both by seeing in my dearest father's journals his difficulties on this very point, when he set himself to serve GOD in earnest, and comparing it with the mortified and unselfindulgent life he led afterwards; and also by Mr Martyn's experience recorded in his journals on the same point. I have, therefore, determined with God's help to make a conscience of observing the fasts of the Church."[31] For the Tractarians and their sympathizers, however, perhaps the most moving aspect of self-denial recorded in Martyn's journals was his wrestling with the apparent call of God to a life of celibacy. Sargent's *Memoir,* however, says rather little on the subject, apparently seeing Martyn's romantic entanglement as potentially injurious to his reputation for sanctity. Readers of Catholic sympathies would have picked up some hints of the theme from Sargent's biography, but for its full significance in Martyn's spiritual pilgrimage they had to wait for Wilberforce's edition of the journals, which cites the relevant passages at length. Wilberforce's extracts show how Martyn regarded his passionate love for Lydia Grenfell from its first flowering in 1804 as standing in stark opposition "to my devotedness to God in the missionary way."[32] Wilberforce records that Martyn at-

29. Carlyon, *Early Years,* 1:14.

30. E.g., Sargent, *Memoir,* pp. 114, 131, 150.

31. A. R. Ashwell, *Life of the Right Reverend Samuel Wilberforce, D.D.,* 2nd ed., 2 vols. (London, 1883), 1:83, cited in David Newsome, *The Parting of Friends: The Wilberforces and Henry Manning,* new ed. (Grand Rapids and Leominster, 1993), p. 173. Pusey's tract on fasting, number 18 in the *Tracts for the Times,* was in circulation from January 1834.

32. *Journals and Letters,* 1:145.

tended a meeting of the Eclectic Society on June 3, 1805, at which Richard Cecil warned him that he "should be acting like a madman, if he went out unmarried." Martyn spent the rest of the evening in much perplexity on the subject. The examples of his missionary heroes, David Brainerd and C. F. Schwartz, and of the apostle Paul himself, all pointed to the merits of celibacy, but the thought of being without female company "in a scene and climate of such temptation" as India was sobering. "But yet," writes Martyn, "voluntary celibacy seems so much more noble and glorious, and so much more beneficial in the way of example."[33] Confessing himself "utterly at a loss to know what is best for the interests of the Gospel," he wrote to Charles Simeon seeking the spiritual direction of his father in God, and waited on tenterhooks for the reply, "hoping of course that the will of God would coincide with my will, yet thinking that the determination of the question would be indifferent to me."[34] On this matter, Martyn had chosen the wrong spiritual director. Simeon, apparently influenced by the example of the early Cambridge evangelical John Berridge of Everton, had formed a determination to remain single for the sake of the gospel,[35] and his reply to Martyn made clear that in Simeon's view he should do the same. Martyn's journal entry on reading his letter is one of the most poignant and revealing of all those that survive in Wilberforce's edition:

> When the letter arrived, I was immediately convinced beyond all doubt, of the expediency of celibacy. But my wish did not follow my judgment quite so readily. Mr Pratt coming in, argued strongly on the other side, but there was nothing of any weight. The subject so occupied my thoughts, that I could attend to nothing else. . . . My heart was ready to break with agony, at being torn from its dearest idol, and at other times I was visited by a few moments of sublime and enraptured joy. Such is the conflict: why have my friends mentioned this subject? It has torn open old wounds, and I am again bleeding.[36]

The oscillation between transparent self-deception ("immediately convinced beyond all doubt" and "nothing of any weight") and painfully honest self-

33. *Journals and Letters,* 1:259-60.

34. *Journals and Letters,* 1:261, 263.

35. William Carus, *Memoirs of the Life of the Rev. Charles Simeon, M.A.* (London, 1847), pp. 230-31; Charles Smyth, *Simeon and Church Order* (Cambridge, 1940), pp. 269-70. For Berridge's views on marriage see *Dictionary of Evangelical Biography,* 1:87-88. For Simeon's recommendation of celibacy to missionaries, see also John Noble, *A Memoir of the Rev. Robert Turlington Noble* (London, 1867), pp. 45-46.

36. *Journals and Letters,* 1:263-64. Martyn refers to Josiah Pratt (1768-1844), secretary of the CMS from 1802.

diagnosis is entirely characteristic. It points toward the key to Martyn's fascination: for those keenly aware of the weakness of the flesh, the evidence of self-deception was (and is) reassuring, for it revealed the unmistakable human fallibility of a person whose piety at times teetered on the brink of priggishness; yet the accurate diagnosis of the pain within his soul appeared to confirm the rare depth of his spirituality.

The inner conflicts over Lydia continued after Martyn's departure for India. David Brown had from the outset urged Martyn to come out as a married man, and continued after his arrival in Bengal in May 1806 to recommend that he send for Lydia. By July 14 Martyn is well-nigh persuaded: "Mr B's arguments appear so strong, that my mind is almost made up to send for Lydia. I could scarcely have any reasonable doubts remaining, that her presence would most abundantly promote the ends of the mission."[37] But still Martyn vacillates, this time under the influence of his reading in Catholic missionary history: his journal for July 22 reads: "I passed the latter part of the day in the house, reading the life of Francis Xavier. I was exceedingly roused at the astonishing example of that great saint, and began to consider, whether it was not my duty to live, as he did, in voluntary poverty and celibacy. I was not easy till I had determined to follow the same course, when I should perceive that the kingdom of God would be more advanced by it."[38] Yet the journal for the very next day records: "Wrote out a letter for Lydia, but am not yet determined to send it." The letter, which was finally sent on July 30, requested her to come and join him as his wife.[39] Lydia, of course, never came. There is evidence, published only in the 1880s, that by 1809 Martyn had accepted that Lydia would never be his, even though he did not entirely rule out marrying some other person: he wrote to his cousin (who was also Lydia's brother-in-law) in October 1809 confessing that "after one disappointment I am not likely to try again, and if I do I will give her [Lydia] the earliest intelligence of it, with the same frankness with which I have always dealt (with her)."[40] Even if Martyn never arrived at a fixed resolution to remain celibate, his example of forgoing marriage for the sake of Christ undoubtedly inspired some of his more Catholic successors, including probably Newman himself, to view celibacy as an integral part of Christian devotion at its most complete.[41]

37. *Journals and Letters,* 1:468. See also 1:168, 467.

38. *Journals and Letters,* 1:470.

39. *Journals and Letters,* 1:471, 473-78.

40. Martyn to Rev. T. M. Hitchins, October 10, 1809, in Henry Martyn Jeffrey, *Two Sets of Unpublished Letters of the Rev. Henry Martin, B.D., of Truro* (Truro, 1883), p. 57.

41. I owe the point about the influence of Martyn's celibacy on Newman to Dr. Sheridan Gilley.

We should take note also of Martyn's question of whether he was called to a life of voluntary poverty as well as celibacy. As a chaplain of the East India Company, Martyn lived in moderate luxury on what James Stephen termed "an ugly allowance" of £1,200 a year. For Stephen, the generous salary was "a misfortune, and had been better avoided if possible."[42] For Martyn, the question of whether to accept appointment as a Company chaplain, with its ample remuneration, rather than be sent out as a poor missionary by the Church Missionary Society, was part of the dilemma of vocation with which he wrestled in Cambridge during 1804. Charles Grant warned Martyn in January 1804 that missionary life in India would not be cheap (though the terms of his warning are hardly self-consistent): "it would be absolutely necessary to keep three servants, for three can do no more than the work of one English; that no European constitution can endure being exposed to mid-day heat; that Mr Swartz [*sic*], who was settled at Tanjore, did do it for a time, walking among the natives."[43] At much the same time, Martyn received news that through some malpractice he had lost his inheritance from his father, apparently for good.[44] He had an unmarried sister to support, and his original intention of going to India as a CMS missionary no longer seemed feasible. Martyn's first reaction to the information that as a Company chaplain he would be earning £1,200 a year was fear that he "would be in danger of worldly-mindedness. At present I feel no desire after the riches of the world."[45] Nevertheless, he accepted the Company appointment, which was eventually confirmed on April 24, 1805, as the only means whereby his missionary vocation could be fulfilled. This evangelical saint reluctantly adopted, not the path of voluntary poverty, but that of voluntary riches, for the sake of the gospel, but it seems never had an entirely easy conscience about the lifestyle of palanquins and servants that came with his position.

We turn to our third and final question. How far is it possible to draw apart the hagiographic veil with which nineteenth-century Christians cloaked Martyn and discover something of his personality and the impact it made, both on Europeans and on the Muslims of north India and Persia who met him between 1806 and 1812? It is not difficult to find criticism of Martyn, even from some who deeply admired him. Newman, for example, was prompted by his reading in 1828 of the journal of another missionary pioneer

42. Stephen, *Essays in Ecclesiastical Biography,* 2:339.

43. *Journals and Letters,* 1:85-86.

44. Sargent, *Memoir,* pp. 54-55; *Journals and Letters,* 1:79; John R. C. Martyn, *Henry Martyn (1781-1812): Scholar and Missionary to India and Persia; A Biography* (Lewiston, N.Y.; Queenston, Ont.; and Lampeter, 1999), p. 24.

45. *Journals and Letters,* 1:179.

in India, Bishop Heber, to reflect in a letter to John Keble that Heber was superior to Martyn in what would now be called cultural adaptability: "most pious men who have gone out in ecclesiastical capacity to foreign countries . . . have hardly had that flexibility and elasticity of religious principle which can accommodate itself to this world, but from one cause or other have worked stiffly — H. Martyn, in spite of the romantic interest attending him, is (is he not?) an instance."[46] Newman, of course, did not know Martyn personally, but Clement Carlyon did, though only in the English context. Carlyon's chapter on Martyn in his autobiographical reflections repeatedly draws the same comparison as did Newman between Martyn's "stiffness" and Heber's congeniality as revealed in their respective journals. Heber was by far "of a happier temperament," and able to recognize how much good was to be done "by a judicious conformity with the usages of the world around him." In Martyn's life, on the other hand, "occasions constantly present themselves which excite regret that the earnest zeal of so good a man was not always tempered with that gentleness of manner which, without compromising the truth, found a way for Bishop Heber to every heart." Both men, judged Carlyon, were entitled to "the glorious appellation of saints," but Martyn, unlike Heber, was a saint who was "naturally prone to overlook our Saviour's injunction to 'combine the wisdom of the serpent with the innocency of the dove.'"[47]

Yet, how much weight should be placed on such verdicts is debatable. There is no doubt that Martyn had a propensity to make himself unpopular among some sectors of European society in India, not least because he made no secret of the fact that he found their sins almost as painful to behold as his own.[48] J. W. Kaye's history of Christianity in India records that his first public sermon in Bengal, delivered at the New Church in Calcutta, "not only gave offence to his congregation, but drew down upon himself the enmity of some of his brother-chaplains." His doctrines "did not consort with their notions, so they preached at and against him. They pronounced his discourse a rhapsody — a mystery; said that he would drive men to despair, destroy their hopes of salvation, and speedily empty the church."[49] Antipathy to Martyn's uncompromising evangelicalism was thus evident in the reactions he aroused, but this is not the whole explanation. According to Kaye, that other notable Cambridge ecclesiastical export to India, Daniel Corrie, who was no less of an

46. Newman to Keble, July 31, 1828, in *The Letters and Diaries of John Henry Newman*, ed. Ian Ker and Thomas Gornall, 2 vols. (Oxford, 1979), 2:86.

47. Carlyon, *Early Years*, 3:20-21, 36-37.

48. A. T. Embree, *Charles Grant and British Rule in India* (London, 1962), p. 240.

49. John William Kaye, *Christianity in India: An Historical Narrative* (London, 1869), pp. 190-91.

evangelical, "could find hearers" among the British soldiery, "where Martyn could find none. . . . he abounded in what Martyn most wanted, the tact to conciliate and the cordiality to attract."[50]

It is tempting to conclude from such writers as Kaye and Carlyon that Martyn was a religious bigot, a holy bigot to be sure, but a bigot nonetheless. But firsthand contemporary evidence from India paints a rather different picture. We have mentioned that Martyn's voyage from Calcutta to Bombay in 1811 was made in the company of the eminent East India Company official, Mountstuart Elphinstone, who was proceeding to take up the position of Company resident at Poona. Elphinstone, whose religious views were of a deistic or Unitarian variety,[51] found Martyn to be "a far better companion than I reckoned on, though my expectations were high. His zeal is unabated, but it is not troublesome, and he does not press disputes and investigate creeds." Elphinstone was impressed by Martyn's exceptional abilities as a linguist and mathematician, but even more by his "good sense," simplicity of manners and character, and cheerfulness of conversation. "We have in Mr Martyn," he wrote home to a friend, "one of the mildest, cheerfullest [*sic*], and pleasantest men I ever saw." Martyn was able to talk on "all subjects, sacred and profane, and laughs and makes others laugh as heartily as he could do if he were an infidel." He was in fact "disposed to join in every sort of innocent mirth."[52]

George Smith, author of the largest of Martyn's biographies, published in 1892, cites most of Elphinstone's commendation and then makes the shrewd observation: "He who, in the close intimacy of shipboard life in the tropics, could win that eulogy from a critic so lofty and so experienced, must have been at once more human and more perfect than his secret *Journal,* taken alone, has led its readers to believe possible."[53] Martyn's journal, whose intense and severe introspection was responsible for much of the adulation lavished on him by mid-nineteenth-century admirers, may in fact be a misleading indication of the man as he appeared to his contemporaries. It was, after all, written in conformity to a Puritan genre of private spiritual journals kept for the rigorous benefit of one's own soul; they were a Protestant variant of

50. Kaye, *Christianity in India,* p. 197.

51. M. McLaren, *British India and British Scotland, 1780-1830: Career Building, Empire Building, and a Scottish School of Thought on Indian Governance* (Akron, Ohio, 2001), pp. 146, 151-53.

52. T. E. Colebrooke, *Life of the Honourable Montstuart Elphinstone,* 2 vols. (London, 1884), 1:232-33; R. D. Choksey, *Mountstuart Elphinstone: The Indian Years, 1796-1827* (Bombay, 1971), p. 134.

53. Smith, *Henry Martyn,* p. 328.

the confessional, and were never intended for public consumption.[54] Martyn records that his object in keeping a journal was "to accustom myself to self-examination, to give my experience a visible form, so as to leave an impression on the memory, and so to improve my soul in holiness."[55] Constance Padwick, with this statement in mind, warned in her biography of Martyn that reliance on the journal as a source presented the danger that "we know our Martyn chiefly as the great penitent" and fail to discern the lighter dimensions of his personality.[56]

The same quality of cheerfulness that so impressed Elphinstone about Martyn also struck Sir John Malcolm, the British soldier and envoy to Persia to whom (with Sir James Mackintosh) Elphinstone introduced Martyn on their arrival in Bombay. Malcolm in his turn wrote a letter of recommendation for Martyn to Sir Gore Ouseley, the British ambassador at Tabriz. Martyn, he asserted, had a knowledge of Arabic "superior to that of any Englishman in India. He is altogether a very learned and cheerful man, but a great enthusiast in his holy calling." Malcolm, who was no supporter of missions,[57] assured Ouseley that Martyn had "no thought of preaching to the Persians, or of entering into any theological controversies," which would have undermined the current British objective of establishing a treaty with Iran. He had told Martyn that Ouseley would "not allow his zeal to run away with him." Nevertheless, he was confident that Ouseley would be pleased with him: "He will give you grace before and after dinner, and admonish such of your party as take the Lord's name in vain; but his good sense and great learning will delight you, whilst his constant cheerfulness will add to the hilarity of your party."[58] Ouseley was indeed pleased with him, for it was Ouseley who, after Martyn's death, secured the safe transmission of his Persian New Testament to St. Petersburg, where it was published under Ouseley's supervision in 1815.

European observers of like educational attainment but little sympathy for evangelical piety could thus find Martyn to be a much more attractive and indeed hilarious person than the introspective zealot who emerges from the pages of his journal and hence also from most biographies. The biographer of

54. See William Haller, *The Rise of Puritanism*, new ed. (Philadelphia, 1972), pp. 96-100; Owen C. Watkins, *The Puritan Experience* (London, 1972), pp. 18-25.

55. *Journals and Letters*, 1:52.

56. Constance E. Padwick, *Henry Martyn: Confessor of the Faith* (London, 1923), p. 10; see also pp. 77-78.

57. McLaren, *British India*, pp. 157-58.

58. J. W. Kaye, *The Life and Correspondence of Major-General Sir John Malcolm, G.C.B., Late Envoy to Persia, and Governor of Bombay; from His Unpublished Letters and Journals*, 2 vols. (London, 1856), 2:65-66.

John Malcolm, who recorded his subject's favorable impression of Martyn, was J. W. Kaye, the same author who deemed Martyn markedly inferior to Corrie in his ability to preach to the Company's troops. Perhaps aware of the implicit contradictions in his portrait of Martyn, Kaye summed up the man in the following paradoxical terms: "A strange, sensitive being — *all nerve* — was this young Cornish priest. Irritable and impulsive, of varying moods, sometimes sanguine and hilarious, at others despairing and dejected, he was wrenched and torn by gusts of passion which seemed almost to threaten his existence. His health was delicate, and he had overworked himself. He seemed to be always in an extreme state of tension vibrating to the slightest touch. His soul never rested."[59] But what evidence, if any, survives of how Martyn was regarded by the indigenous inhabitants of India and Persia? The standard European printed sources — and sadly, they are almost all we possess — give relatively little clue, for Martyn's sainthood was secured more by the charting of his inner spiritual life than by actual missionary achievement. In a rather unsavory way, J. W. Kaye again points us in the right direction. Writing of the mendicants who flocked to hear Martyn's preaching in front of his house at Cawnpore (Kanpur) in 1809-10, Kaye betrays the racial nastiness that after the Indian Rebellion of 1857 crept into British evaluations of Indians and to an extent also of those who took seriously their capacity to respond intelligently to the Christian message:

> They came to receive alms, and he distributed to them. Then they listened to what he said — those naked, squalid heathens — the halt, the maimed, and the blind — they flocked around him and listened. Or they pretended to listen — for what could they do less? And Martyn spoke to them, as one who could not help speaking, as one who felt it would be a sin to be silent. From the full heart gushed forth a torrent of words — not always perhaps with the strictest philological propriety — and, in sooth, only by rare snatches intelligible to his congregation. But the numbers increased, and so did the plaudits: and far be it from me to say that no seed fell upon good ground.[60]

If the mendicants were only *pretending* to listen, and unable to understand more than the odd snatch of what Martyn said, why did they keep coming, and in increasing numbers? This was no sycophantic audience: the evangelical writer of missionary tales, Mrs. Sherwood, describing the same series of ad-

59. Kaye, *Christianity in India,* p. 187.
60. Kaye, *Christianity in India,* p. 199.

dresses, records the utterance of "low murmurs and curses," "hissings and fierce cries."[61] Nevertheless, Martyn was evidently capable of exerting a hold of some kind on the beggars of Cawnpore, for George Smith notes that "When Mr Martyn collected these people he was most carefully watched by the British authorities."[62] Part of the key to Martyn's attraction to Indian audiences, whether poor or learned, is suggested by an even earlier historian of Indian Christianity, James Hough, another of Charles Simeon's protégés who followed Martyn into the Company's chaplaincy service. Hough's account (dating from 1845) describes Martyn's five weeks in Bombay in 1811, when he had repeated conversations with a Zoroastrian named Feeroz, "the most intelligent Parsee in the place," and a young and learned Muslim, Mahomed Jan, who was no less zealous in defending the tenets of the Qur'an. Hough records that, though such interlocutors did not yield to his arguments, "they all looked up to him with respect as a man of extraordinary learning and piety."[63]

As a dying man, Martyn appears to have made a similar but still deeper impression on the Sufi scholars of Shiraz, with whom he found himself in protracted religious debate, much against his better judgment, during the eleven months from June 1811 to May 1812. Martyn soon reached the conclusion that there was no hope of convincing Muslims of the truth of Christian doctrine by the power of rational argument alone. He relied increasingly upon prayer for the blessing of the Holy Spirit on all his scriptural logic. "I do use the means in a certain way," he wrote to Lydia Grenfell on September 8, 1811, "but frigid reasoning with men of perverse minds, seldom brings men to Christ. However, as they require it, I reason, and accordingly challenged them to prove the divine mission of their prophet. . . . With very little hope that any good will come of it, I am now employed in drawing out the evidences of the truth; but oh, that I could converse and reason, and plead, with power from on high. How powerless are the best-directed arguments, till the Holy Ghost renders them effectual."[64] Like many another nineteenth-century missionary after him, Martyn was discovering the hard way that rational appeal to the Christian evidences was a barren method of apologetic in an Islamic or Hindu context. Yet, for all the frustration his scriptural reasoning encountered, as the doctrinal controversies into which he was drawn ran their tortuous course, Martyn's learning, humility, patience, and resignation acquired for him a rare reputation among his opponents: he was increasingly de-

61. Smith, *Henry Martyn,* p. 283.

62. Smith, *Henry Martyn,* p. 284.

63. Hough, *Christianity in India,* 4:492; see Sargent, *Memoir,* pp. 299-301.

64. *Journals and Letters,* 2:373. See also Kenneth Cragg, *Troubled by Truth: Life-Studies in Inter-faith Concern* (Bishop Auckland, U.K., 1992), pp. 23-24.

scribed as *merdi khodai*, a "man of God," one who was filled with the divine drunkenness.[65] As the inscription on his tomb at Tokat read, "He will long be remembered in the East, where he was known as a man of God."[66] This external and non-Christian testimony to the sanctity of Henry Martyn, far more than the inferences that his Christian admirers later drew from his journal, deserves to be given most weight in our assessment of the spiritual legacy of this extraordinary and complex man.

65. Smith, *Henry Martyn*, pp. 373, 392, cited in Clinton Bennett, "Henry Martyn," in *Mission Legacies: Biographical Studies of Leaders of the Modern Missionary Movement*, ed. G. H. Anderson et al. (Maryknoll, N.Y., 1994), p. 267.

66. Smith, *Henry Martyn*, p. 530.

CHAPTER 6

Revival, Syncretism, and the Anticolonial Discourse of the Kherwar Movement, 1871-1910

PETER B. ANDERSEN

For a long time, "syncretism" has been a problematic term in the history of religion. This is because the term's present meaning — the mingling of religious traditions — carries strongly negative associations; and one may, therefore, be tempted to avoid the term in scholarly usage. It is, however, a practical term that opens for analysis the ways in which religious traditions mutually influence one another. To use the term constructively, it is necessary to recognize how and when "syncretism" acquired its present negative connotations, the essentialism in the background, and to discuss the degree to which it helps us move from an analysis of the mutual influence of religious traditions to an analysis of power and hegemony.

The Greek noun *synkrētismos,* which must have meant something like "mixing together," is first found in Plutarch (A.D. 45-125), who made a pun out of it when he stated that love among brothers involved helping each other

This essay is one result of a joint publishing project with Santosh Soren (Copenhagen) and Marine Carrin (EHESS-CNRS, Toulouse) that deals with portions of the late P. O. Bodding's folkloric collections. A fuller treatment of "The Story of the Babajis" is planned. For this essay, I have used the edition prepared by Santosh Soren; the translation is from a draft prepared by Mr. Soren and myself. My work in India benefited from collaboration with the late Prof. Ashok K. Ghosh, Calcutta University, who introduced me to fieldwork in 1982, and from the support of Dr. Ranjit Bhattacharya, former director of the Anthropological Survey of India, the joint director Dr. Jayankar Sarkar, and their colleague Dr. Das, of Ranjhi. At the Department of History of Religions, University of Copenhagen, Assoc. Prof. Tove Tybjerg and Assoc. Prof. Dr. Morten Warmind have offered helpful advice.

against mutual enemies, "imitating in this point, at least, the practice of the Cretans, who, though they often quarrelled with and warred against each other, made up their differences and united when outside enemies attacked; and this it was which they called 'syncretism.'"[1] The term had a decidedly positive meaning, which became commonplace, when the word reappeared in the writings of European Renaissance scholars like Erasmus of Rotterdam (1469-1536), who saw the classical heritage of the non-Christian philosophers as an achievement that strengthened Christianity. The negative connotations of "syncretism" originated during the seventeenth century when other Protestant theologians refuted the attempt of the Lutheran George Calixtus (1586-1656) to reestablish the consensus of the early Christian church — a position that in his time was hailed as well as condemned as "syncretism." And because Calixtus's position was formally condemned in 1645, the concept of syncretism has since carried a negative meaning in church history as well as in common language.[2]

Instead of asking whether syncretism is to be evaluated as a positive, integrative process or a dissolution of the doctrines of a particular Christian church or of another religious system, I shall direct attention to how new religious elements are continuously reworked into wholes when integrated into a different cultural or religious system. In this regard I follow some of the suggestions of specialists on syncretism in general[3] and of specialists on Christian missions to India. Among them, Robert E. Frykenberg has stressed that Christianity in India is the result of a long history of indigenization, perhaps dating as far back as the early centuries of the Christian era.[4] Such long-term changes in religions have been described by Richard M. Eaton in his analysis of the rise of Islam in Bengal over half a millennium from 1204 to 1760. Eaton argues for the existence of three distinct aspects of the process,

> each referring to a different relationship between Islamic and Indian superhuman agencies. One of these I am calling *inclusion;* a second, *iden-*

1. Plutarch, *Moralia* 490b (Helmbold translation). Quoted from the introduction, "Problematizing Syncretism," in *Syncretism/Anti-Syncretism: The Politics of Religious Synthesis,* ed. Rosalind Shaw and Charles Stewart (London and New York, 1994), p. 3.

2. In this paragraph, I am indebted to Shaw and Stewart, "Problematizing Syncretism."

3. Helmer Ringgren, "The Problem of Syncretism," in *Syncretism: Based on the Papers Read at the Symposium Cultural Contact, Meeting of Religions, Syncretism* (Stockholm, 1969), p. 13.

4. Robert E. Frykenberg, "Christians in India: An Historical Overview of Their Complex Origins," in *Christians and Missionaries in India: Cross-Cultural Communication since 1500 with Special Reference to Caste, Conversion, and Colonialism,* ed. Robert E. Frykenberg (Grand Rapids and Cambridge, 2003), pp. 33-61.

> *tification;* and a third, *displacement.* By *inclusion* is meant the process by which Islamic superhuman agencies became accepted in local Bengali cosmologies alongside local divinities already embedded therein. By *identification* is meant the process by which Islamic superhuman agencies ceased merely to coexist alongside Bengali agencies, but actually merged with them, and when the Arabic name Allah was used interchangeably with the Sanskrit Niranjan. And finally by *displacement* is meant the process by which the names of Islamic superhuman agencies replaced those of other divinities in local cosmologies. The three terms *inclusion, identification,* and *displacement* are of course only heuristic categories, proposed in an attempt to organize and grasp intellectually what was on the ground a very complex and fluid process.[5]

Eaton's three aspects of the process of religious change could easily be utilized for analyzing the process of indigenizing the Christian church in India, and his warning about the complexity and fluidity of the process alerts us to the fact that even his first two categories, which could be taken as different aspects of syncretism, may be divided into further subcategories if we took a closer look at the processes. Nevertheless, his systematization of one continuous process of religious change is illuminating and important for any study of syncretism in India.

In the following analysis of syncretism the evidence is taken from the Kherwar movement, an anticolonial movement among the Santals and low-caste Hindus in the last part of the nineteenth century and the beginning of the twentieth. For a number of reasons the Kherwars make a good fit for an analysis of the advantages and limitations of the term "syncretism." One is that it becomes possible to investigate the changes of the strictly political element in the movement over time. Another is that the Kherwars appeared in a time of other religious mass movements and may also be compared to contemporary mass conversions to Christianity and Hinduism in India. And the third feature that makes the Kherwars interesting for studies in syncretism is that they incorporated Hindu as well as Christian elements into their belief system. This entailed the introduction of a combination of "foreign" elements into Santal religion, a phenomenon that has often been underestimated because some of the early descriptions of the Kherwars were made by missionaries opposed to the Kherwars in one way or another. Missionaries either fought them, as the well-known specialist on the Kherwars, Rev. L. O. Skrefs-

5. Richard M. Eaton, *The Rise of Islam and the Bengal Frontier, 1204-1760* (Delhi, 1997), pp. 269-70.

rud, did during the 1870s and early 1880s,[6] or they assessed them as perverted forms of Christianity, as did his successor, Rev. P. O. Bodding, who downplayed the importance of Christian elements in their teaching by having them disappear.[7]

Background

The first mention of the Santals in Indian history comes from British reports of the 1790s. At that time, the Santals lived in the jungles covering the lower part of the Chota Nagpur Plateau. They were depicted as a people without caste, and it was generally stated that Hindus of higher caste did not allow them to stay in their villages but placed them between the village and the jungle. The reason that the Santals moved out of the jungle to stay among the Hindus was the agrarian policy of the East India Company. The Company acquired the function of collector of land rent — called "Divani" under the Moghul Dynasty in Delhi — in major parts of eastern India in 1765; and from the 1790s the Company initiated a change in the collection of land rent. This reform was called *The Permanent Settlement;* it made the position of land-rent collector inheritable and froze the land rent at an invariable rate. The reform was based on the rather naive idea that as soon as the *zamindars* (officials to whom the Company entrusted the collection of land rent) realized they could not be evicted from the soil, they would invest in it, which would in turn result in an increase of the Company's revenue from other sources. But to ensure that an adequate income would be immediately available, the Company settled the land rent at an amount many times greater than any land rent ever collected before the reform. Afterward, the land rent was increased at irregular intervals as well.

As a consequence, *zamindars* had to bring virgin soil under cultivation, and to do this in the interior of the country they employed Santals. Santals were employed as a group under the leadership of a headman *(manjhi)*, who negotiated the payment on behalf of the whole group. The most common result was that the headman and the *zamindar* (or more properly, his subcollectors) settled on a land rent that the headman had to collect from the rest of the group and settle on their behalf. After the Santals had cleared the

6. Olav Hodne, *L. O. Skrefsrud, Missionary and Social Reformer among the Santals of Santal Parganas: With Special Reference to the Periods between 1867 and 1881* (Oslo, 1966), pp. 265-87.

7. L. S. S. O'Malley, *Bengal District Gazetteer, Santal Parganas* (Calcutta, 1910), p. 150.

jungle, they laid out fields where they grew millet and in a minor degree paddy. Formally, the Santals were allowed to cultivate the fields and claim ownership of the soil at some later point. They were, however, given no support during the first year, which forced them to borrow on the soil or the crop to get through the long period after they planted the first beds of paddy until the first harvest some four to six months later. Moneylenders likewise moved into the land. This bound the Santals by mortgage in a situation very much like slavery as sons inherited the mortgages of fathers. When construction of a railway began in 1854, the condition of the Santals seemed to improve, as the wage work allowed them to pay back their debts. But the moneylenders would not allow them leave to earn extra money so that they could pay off all their debts, and this led to intensified conflicts between Santals and moneylenders as well as landlords. After the authorities had swept aside protests from the traditional headmen in an 1854 insurrection, the Santal *Hul* broke out in 1855. The *Hul* started with attacks on the moneylenders and landlords and with the burning of their private archives, but it soon swelled from a local protest to a regular insurrection, which in the end was severely crushed by the East India Company military. On their escape, many Santals moved farther east and settled in parts of the present West Bengal where previously there had been no Santal settlements.

At the local level, however, one could say that the insurrection led to improvements for the Santals. A so-called nonregulation district, the Santal Parganas, was created by Act XXXVII of 1855, which covered parts of an old nonregulation area, the Damin-i-Koh, that had been designated for tribals around Rajmahal, Pakur, Godda, and Dumka. The Santal Parganas was exempt from most of the laws governing Bengal, and the Santals were able to take their grievances directly to the British authorities without going through local courts. This was indeed an improvement because the local courts had often sided with the moneylenders and collectors. Moreover, headmen were given a formal position as they were nominated and paid by the Company, which enabled them to act as a kind of local arbitrator and police authority. Finally, it was prohibited to hand over farmland to nontribals. Ideally, this should have prevented a transition from the mortgaging of land to slavery. Yet in 1867, the Bengal legal system was applied once more, leading to widespread protest. Reforms were introduced again from 1871, but while they were intended to ameliorate the situation of the Santal cultivators by giving them full rights as *ryots* of the land, the imposition of the concept of private property probably accelerated the alienation of their lands to nontribals.

New Bengal laws introduced after India became a colony under the British Crown in 1858 were intended to protect the rights of the peasants and copyholders against the collectors and moneylenders. These laws, however, had only a minor impact, as the collectors successfully argued that the *Permanent Settlement* was based on the logic of land rent, which would become impossible to collect if the land could not be seized and the cultivators bound to it. That the agreements between the collectors and the Santals normally were informal and not based on written legal documents only added to the problems. The upshot was that Santals could be evicted from a well-defined farm they had cultivated for years, at the whim of the collector if he wished to increase the land rent.

Even if the development in Santal Parganas and the surrounding districts gradually came to follow the same lines, it is important to keep the differences between these administrative divisions in mind when considering the Santals in the last part of the nineteenth century.

Religion as a Denominator

As mentioned, high-caste Hindus kept the Santals out of their villages, but there are good reasons to doubt that "religion" in the sense of "religious community" was a denominator as such during most of the nineteenth century. This is strongly indicated by Rev. P. O. Bodding's Santali dictionary.[8] The entry on the word *dhorom*, which can now be used to designate a religious community, would probably not have been used in that sense at the time. Besides the possible meaning of "religion" as indicative of a specific religion (but not a "religious community"), the meanings aggregate around religious observances, proper conduct, and piety. When it comes to the meaning of "religion," the examples given often indicate that a more literal translation would be "to perform rituals on behalf of some deity." *Dibi sewa dhorom,* for instance, means "a religion that worships Durga"; *bonga sewa dhorom* means "a religion that worships spirits" (i.e., Bodding's Christian-flavored translation of the *bongas,* which are the central deities among the Santals); and Christianity may be designated *kiristan dhorom* or *Isor sewa dhorom,* that is, "a religion that worships God."[9]

In Bodding's time, as today, there was no common denominator for Hindus and Hinduism in Santali. High-caste Hindus were termed *deko* or *deko pusi,* which may be rendered "Hindu cats," because to the Santals they ap-

8. The collections underlying this dictionary were initiated by Rev. Skrefsrud in 1869 and continued by Rev. Bodding up to around 1930.

9. P. O. Bodding, *A Santal Dictionary* (Oslo, 1934), 2:183-84.

peared to be very fond of milk and fish. Also, high-caste Hindus were similarly seen as devious, as stated in the proverb "You may deceive a Santal, but never a Hindu cat."[10] *Deko* is, moreover, as much a term for a Bengali as for a Hindu, and low-caste Hindus are not included in the definition of the term. Bodding's examples of excluded Hindu castes are Doms, Bauris, and Hadis. Even now, however, the term has not been fixed in this regard.

When present-day Santals distinguish between Hindus (including low-castes) and Christians, who may be Santals or belong to any specified caste, they tend to turn to an Anglicized vocabulary that bears evidence to the fact that it is a product of the huge classificatory endeavor of the census, which began in 1871. Here the colonial government of India tried to account for its inhabitants in accordance with the scientific vocabulary of the time. For our present theme it is evident that H. H. Risley faced great difficulties in fitting the religions of the different castes and tribes into mutually exclusive categories when he published *The Tribes and Castes of Bengal* in 1891 in accordance with the systematic rules set up by a conference on the ethnography of northern India sixteen years earlier.[11] In his article on the Santals, Risley distanced himself from L. O. Skrefsrud, one of his correspondents for the Santal Parganas, who identified the supreme deity of the Santals as Thakur. Risley expressed his doubts as follows: "I am myself inclined to doubt whether a god bearing the Hindu name Thakur, and exercising supreme powers which mark a comparatively late stage of theological development, can really have formed part of the original system of the Santals."[12]

Regarding groups that later anthropology has come to consider low-caste Hindus, the classificatory situation in the late nineteenth century was not much better. Risley was in no doubt that the above-mentioned Bauri were of non-Aryan descent and professed "to be Hindus of the Sakta sect, but in Western Bengal, at any rate, their connexion with Hinduism [was] of the slenderest kind." They also sacrificed "fowls to Barpahari, which is merely another name for the 'great mountain' (Maran Buru) of the Santals."[13] It is evident from Risley's impressive article on the Brahmins of Bengal that he struggled with the fact that he regarded "Hinduism" proper — or the essence of Hinduism — as something represented by the higher castes, primarily the Brahmins.[14] In his work, the Brahmins are initially described in terms of nu-

10. Bodding, *A Santal Dictionary,* 2:10.

11. H. H. Risley, *The Tribes and Castes of Bengal: Ethnographic Glossary* (Calcutta 1981), vol. 2, appendix 2.

12. Risley, *Tribes and Castes,* 2:232.

13. Risley, *Tribes and Castes,* 1:80.

14. Risley, *Tribes and Castes,* 2:141-62.

merous historical references to the *Laws of Manu,* the *Mahabharata,* and the *Puranas;* the actual Brahmins of his own day were diligently classified in accordance with different groups of descent. The content of their religion and many of their religious practices, however, are simply left to our imagination of what the essence of the holy scriptures might be.

Historical Sources for the Kherwars

The Kherwars had existed as a distinct group with a large Santal element over a long period of time since the first census in 1871; well-organized forms of the movement could still be found collaborating with the independence movement in the 1930s. Even if it is mostly an assumption that the Jharkhand movement did in fact take over from the Kherwar movement after the 1930s, some facts still need to be acknowledged: even after independence, Kherwars were still being reported on as an existing group in 1966,[15] and the 1991 census noted the presence of 2,261 Kherwars among the Santals in Bihar. For the present argument, which mostly considers the history of the movement until the first decades of the twentieth century, it is important to recognize that scholarly study of the Kherwar movement and the teaching of the early Kherwar leaders was first systematized by Rev. P. O. Bodding in his correspondence to L. S. S. O'Malley, which the latter included in his *District Gazetteer of Santal Parganas* (1910). Bodding also dealt with the later development of the movement in a paper published in 1921. At a later point, Aditya Prasad Jha added important elements in his historical study based on the materials in the State Central Records Office in Bihar.[16] Olav Hodne has studied the relations between the Kherwars and one of the missionaries to Santal Parganas, Rev. L. O. Skrefsrud;[17] and Joseph Troisi has described them against the background of other social movements among the Santals.[18]

Besides these sources, which look upon the Kherwars from different outsiders' points of view, one of the sources underlying Bodding's description of the Kherwars exists as well. It is the narrative of a Santal written down in Santali and kept together with Bodding's collections of Santal folklore in the

15. Hodne, *L. O. Skrefsrud,* p. 275.

16. Aditya Prasad Jha, "Nature of the Santhal Unrest of 1871-1875 and Origin of the Sapha Hor Movement," *Indian Historical Records Commission (Proceedings)* 35, pt. 2 (1960): 103-13.

17. Hodne, *L. O. Skrefsrud,* pp. 265-87.

18. Joseph Troisi, "Social Movements among the Santals," in *Social Movements in India,* vol. 2, *Sectarian, Tribal, and Women's Movements,* ed. M. S. A. Rao (Delhi, 1979), pp. 123-48.

Oslo University Library. As this source enables us to get a Santal point of view on the Kherwars, it deserves some consideration.[19] The narrator of "The Story of the Babajis" was most probably Bodding's main collector, Sagram Murmu or Baharur Sagram Murmu. He settled in Mohulpahari in Santal Parganas where Bodding was a missionary in 1892 and continued to work for Bodding at least until 1927. But the present story can be dated more precisely, as Bodding quoted from it and rewrote parts of it using the anthropological vocabulary of the day in his correspondence with O'Malley for the *District Gazetteer* of 1910. A specific point is the way the *babajis* cured women possessed by spirits.

> Briefly, the woman confesses to having had sexual intercourse with a great number of *bongas* (in one case, it is said, the woman mentioned as many as 127 male *bongas,* each separately by name). During the confession the *babaji,* as a preliminary measure, draws figures on the ground, muttering *mantras,* spitting on the figures and wiping them out; after a night's preparation, he gives the woman a twig with which she draws figures on the ground according to his instructions, one to represent each of the *bongas* with whom she has lived; finally the *babaji* makes the woman break off her connexion with each *bonga,* and she repeats after him a long list of abusive epithets for each and every *bonga,* winding up with spitting and trampling on the figures.[20]

This is really the narration of a cure for *bongas* such as the Jogon Bonga, called "the big-bellied, the undersized with protuberant stomach, the stout and plump like a taro root, the dirty one, the broad-footed, the deformed one, the nose-less, the one with sunken cheeks, the big-toothed (etc.)."[21]

It is possible to date the manuscript more specifically: one of the last events described is a visit of the narrator to a named guru on January 28, 1906. And if the narrator really is Sagram Murmu, the story in itself throws some light on a case of personal syncretism. That Sagram Murmu had Christian leanings can be seen from a letter he wrote to Bodding sometime around 1907,[22] but in his presentation of the Kherwars he still gives evidence of his re-

19. *Babajuiko reak' katha* ("The Story of the Babajis"), perhaps authored by Sagram Murmu, Oslo University Library, MS. 8vo 1448-Y & MS 4to 1686-III-5, recorded as No. 0684 and 2203 in Sagram Santosh Kumar Soren, comp., *Santalia, Catalogue of Santalia: Manuscripts in Oslo,* Nordic Institute for Asian Studies, Report Series, no. 41 (Copenhagen 1999).

20. O'Malley, *Bengal District Gazetteer,* p. 149.

21. *Babajuiko reak' katha,* paragraph 66.

22. Johannes Gausdal, *The Santal Khuts* (Oslo, 1960), p. 9.

spect for and belief in the powers of the leaders, the Babajis. The narration begins, "I am going to tell you the story of the *babajis* whom I have seen with my own eyes and about whom I have heard with my own ears." Sagram Murmu then gives an extensive description of the first one, Bhagrit Babaji, who appeared as a *babaji* in 1871. The narrator seems to have continued to visit different *babajis* at his own initiative up to the time he wrote the story down. Whoever the narrator was, he saw clear parallels between the teaching of the Kherwars and that of the Christian church, which we know he attended as a regular churchgoer because he stated that Bhagrit Manjhi spoke about "the Ten Commandments about which we all hear daily in the church."[23]

In the following, I will try to relate the well-known descriptions of outsiders concerning the early history of the Kherwar movement and their implications for understanding syncretism, using "The Story of the Babajis." My argument will be that there are to be found a number of instances of syncretism between Santal religion and culture and Hinduism as well as Christianity, but that the meaning of the variations in religion was dependent on a time-specific political program for the empowerment of the Santals.

The Kherwar Movement

The term "Kherwar" is usually assumed to be derived from the self-designation of the Santals in their own language, Santali, as was reported to Rev. L. O. Skrefsrud by a Santal, Kolean guru, in 1869.[24] This may, however, be a result of the Kherwar movement, as the term is not recorded anywhere until this movement emerged, which can be dated to the Santal Bhagrit Manjhi's agitation at the time of the first census, which was conducted in 1871. He was by then already a known political leader as he had been imprisoned in 1868 for his participation in agrarian unrest. Evidently, however, it was not until 1871 that he appeared as a *baba,* or more properly, a *babaji,* which was the honorific title of the religious leaders of the Kherwar movement. Bhagrit forwarded demands to the British for Santal raj (self-rule) and demanded that the Santals should return to worshiping the (sun) god Chando (or Rama) and cleanse themselves from their sins instead of worshiping their traditional deities, the *bongas,* whom he considered evil. After a famine in 1874, he expanded his teachings as well as the sphere of his political actions. A shrine built according to Hindu principles was constructed under his supervision and a

23. *Babajuiko reak' katha,* paragraph 7.

24. P. O. Bodding, *Traditions and Institutions of the Santals* (Oslo, 1942), pp. 10, 12.

Santal was appointed as *panda* (priest).[25] Theologically, Bhagrit explained that the *Hul* had failed because Santals had had intercourse with non-Santal women; politically, he had himself anointed as raja and started to levy land rent. He was then arrested together with his brothers and the *panda*, and was sentenced to imprisonment for two years. In Sultanabad District, another leader, Gyan, ordered the Santals to cleanse themselves and stop paying rent to the government; for this, Gyan was sentenced to seven years of imprisonment. Nevertheless, the Kherwar agitation continued in 1875, and from 1874 to 1877 extra troops were stationed at Dumka, the main town of Santal Parganas. Bhagrit Manjhi died in 1879.

The Kherwar movement continued, however, and preparations for the census of 1881 led to new outbreaks of violence. There were by then Kherwars in many places in Santal Parganas, and a new leader, the Hindu Dubia Gossain, toured Santal Parganas before he settled in Hazaribagh District. Dubia Gossain smoked *ganja*, smeared his body with ashes, and let his hair grow long, all in accordance with the practices of Hindu *babajis*. In Santal Parganas, the house of the Jamtara magistrate was burned down, prisoners were freed from jail in Khatikund, and the magistrate was forced to cancel the census operations.[26]

In retrospect, it is difficult to know exactly which Kherwar groups stood for which activities, and what the relations between Santals and low-caste Hindus were, but there is no doubt that 40,960 people registered themselves as Kherwars during the 1881 census.[27] Even more telling for the breakdown of the census operations is the fact that 825,835 Santals were recorded in the 1871 census, and 1,450,351 in 1891, but only 202,752 in 1881. Some districts claimed what could be considered a natural increase of the Santal population, but in many others large numbers of Santals evidently recorded themselves as something else, or refused to be recorded at all. In Santal Parganas alone the change was from 455,513 in 1871 to 9,148 in 1881.[28] These figures are serious indicators of social unrest at a time when extra troops were stationed in Dumka (1881-82).

As stated, the Kherwar movement continued in different forms and there are great differences in the assessments of it as a political or religious movement. There is little doubt, however, that many administrators and missionaries regarded the early phase of the Kherwar movement in the 1870s and

25. Jha, "Santhal Unrest," p. 198.
26. Hodne, *L. O. Skrefsrud*, p. 272.
27. Hodne, *L. O. Skrefsrud*, p. 273.
28. Risley, *Tribes and Castes*, 2:234.

early 1880s as a dangerous political phenomenon. This view was stated in administrative reports, in letters from the missionaries to the authorities, and in newspapers. In 1874, for example, when the Kherwars were strongly opposing the Christian missions, the Church Missionary Society (CMS) missionary Rev. A. Stark stressed that the government should found Christian schools as a way of fighting the opposition,[29] and in the autumn of 1880 Rev. L. O. Skrefsrud observed that the Kherwars propagated "a rabid, socialistic, political agitation, the religion being only a means towards an end."[30] When one considers the situation of the census operations at the time, it is understandable that Skrefsrud considered the movement political. Other observers, however, had already pointed to the fact that parts of the movement had shifted their focus toward more peaceful aspects of religious life. The administration report of Bhagalpur Division for 1877-78 states that "He [Bhagirath] and his new sect, have been orderly and quiet; they have formed themselves into a separate community, they won't eat, drink or intermarry with the other Santals; they call themselves Kherwars, and in their religious and domestic practices are more and more approximating to the Hindoos and may almost be regarded as belonging to that religion."[31] As for Hindu influences, the Kherwars have often been seen as the original group from which three branches, Sapha Hor, Samra, and Babaji,[32] have split away. The Kherwars have already been introduced. The Sapha Hor, or Clean Santals, were those who were especially strict about avoiding commensality with non–Sapha Hor and excluding them from ceremonies and life-cycle events. It was also especially the Sapha Hor who refused to eat fowl and pork and drink rice beer. Instead of doing what common Santals do, they had to bathe in the morning before they could take any food.[33] The Samras' sacrifices consisted of sugar and sweetmeats, and they met regularly on one evening a week.[34] The latter innovation definitely can be seen as a step in the direction of a nascent organization of religious life into parish-like structures.

In retrospect, there is general agreement among scholars on the existence of these three groups and some of their characteristics. It is, however, difficult to know when they originated and whether they can be seen as the product of

29. Jha, "Santhal Unrest," pp. 108-9.

30. L. O. Skrefsrud, "The Kherwar Movement," *Statesman and Friend of India*, November 8, 1880.

31. Quoted from Jha, "Santhal Unrest," p. 111.

32. Troisi, "Social Movements," p. 135.

33. Troisi, "Social Movements," p. 135.

34. P. C. Roy Choudhury, *Bihar District Gazetteers: Santal Parganas* (Patna, 1965), p. 935.

schisms in one movement or as different developments in an open network of religious leaders, which Santals and non-Santals could participate in according to their choice. Troisi, who follows a chronological framework as to when the different branches appeared, stresses that the division in the three branches took place after the Kherwar movement went underground after their activities in 1897.[35] Hodne stresses that the three different branches had already been mentioned in 1880 by Rev. L. O. Skrefsrud,[36] who described them with some of the same characteristics as they were later known for. About 1906, Bodding's Santal informant used "Kherwar" as a designation for people who joined the *babajis*,[37] but he named the story after the leaders, the *babas*. For our purposes, the most relevant question is how far the Kherwars manifested indicators of non-Santal religious influence, and on that there is general agreement. The prohibition against killing fowls and pigs, and the consequent taboo against eating their meat, is one indicator of Hindu influence. Others are the ritual practices, the names of the gods worshiped, and the institution itself, which is usually considered borrowed from Hindu *babajis*.[38]

It is, apparently, only Rev. Bodding who argued that "several of the babajis had been pervert Christians, and the first, Bhagrit, either had been a Christian or at any rate had been in a Christian school."[39] This argument was strongly refuted by Hodne,[40] who stressed that the missionaries of the CMS, on whose field Bhagrit lived, never mentioned anything about his having a connection with Christianity in their reports to the government. Instead, basing his argument on the general census figures, which began including the Kherwars only in 1881, Hodne saw them as being part of a general movement of Santals toward Hinduism. In 1901, 11 percent of the 663,000 Santals in Santal Parganas were returned as Hindus, a figure that in 1931 grew to about 50 percent of the 754,004 Santals in Santal Parganas and the 796,656 Santals in Bengal. The Bihar census of 1931 recorded only that the Santals "are being

35. Troisi, "Social Movements," p. 135.

36. Hodne, *L. O. Skrefsrud*, p. 278.

37. *Babajuiko reak' katha*, paragraph 13.

38. There were, of course, varieties of low-caste religion that Risley would rather have considered as tribal than as Hindu. Later researchers, who have written after Hinduism had become a communal identity, have not seen any problems in designating religious practices as being Hindu or non-Hindu.

39. Quoted from O'Malley, *Bengal District Gazetteer*, p. 150. Bodding put forward a similar position in his own name in "The Kherwar Movement among the Santals," *Man in India* 1 (1921): 222-32.

40. Hodne, *L. O. Skrefsrud*, p. 281.

gradually 'Hinduized' and the further this process is carried, the more they are in danger of becoming identified with the depressed classes."[41]

Although the figures in later periods may indicate an ongoing Hinduization, I will return to Bodding's main source for his description of the early Kherwar movement in the hope that it will offer some hints for understanding his observation on Christian influences among the Kherwars. I will also consider what this might mean for our understanding of religious communities and syncretism in the latter part of the nineteenth century.

The Kherwars in the Santal Source

In "The Story of the Babajis" we meet Bhagrit Baba as a teacher of repentance in the time of the 1874 famine. The Burmese rice that the government provided for relief was, in the words of Bhagrit, a gift from the past:

> The rice the Europeans have brought now is the same that we sacrificed in the olden days; it is the same that they bring back to us. It is the rice we offered during our worship by giving a handful of it, which they now bring back to us; it is meant for maintaining our life. Take this rice when you have done proper rituals, fowls and pigs shall not tread on it. And, prepare your food everyday after taking a bath in order that you do not commit adultery; hold on to rituals and religious duties. Now that I have said everything to you, go and act accordingly.
>
> When the people of the country returned [to their villages], they began to slaughter fowls and pigs; they said, "If there are hungry fowls, they will probably eat the rice." Saying this, they each killed and ate one of the fowls, and they called themselves Kherwars.[42]

The reason for the demand for repentance was that God — the sun god Chando — had wanted to give the Santals the country in the time of the *Hul*. But the leaders Sido and Kanhu had failed to "carry out their office": "They could not control their greed and began to snatch away the daughters and daughters-in-law of others. They did unjust acts in the eyes of Chando, and therefore, he in turn did not give the country to them; and, as he did not approve of their misdeeds, they could not win their fight."[43] But now, in 1874,

41. Hodne, *L. O. Skrefsrud*, p. 279.
42. *Babajuiko reak' katha*, paragraphs 12 and 13.
43. *Babajuiko reak' katha*, paragraph 11.

when the Santals had repented, "The Europeans are trembling in fear, they bring the rice and deliver it to us, and they will shortly run away; it is because of this reason that they have made [roads and railways] for themselves like the tracks and passages of field rats. They know very well that one day the 'black' sons of this land will get the country — they know it definitely."[44] The known story of the arrest of Bhagrit Baba comes later, and even if it is cast more in the idiom of fraud than of political demands,[45] the modern reader is not in doubt that Bhagrit lost his case. The narrator, however, describes him and another eighteen specified and unspecified leaders all around the country as convincing men of God, and perhaps as victorious. The implicit reason is that all of them had the power to heal and had predicted that the effect of their actions would vanish after three[46] or five years[47] when they, too, would die, which the narrator states that they did. All of this appears to be convincing to the narrator, who at his own initiative had continued to visit the various *babajis* when they came forward, even if at some time he must have begun attending the Christian church as well. In this regard, his evidence on the Kherwars' preaching of repentance becomes important, because he seemingly saw it as just another formulation of the Christian message of repentance.

According to the narrator, the *babajis* claimed that it was God who had given them the power to heal. They could, however, only contact God in prayer and act as intermediaries between God and the ailing; healing was God's decision, and depended on the repentance of the ailing. Generally the *babaji* received visitors in the evening and promised them to contact God during the night. In the morning he could tell them: "Sirs, the Supreme Being descended in the middle of the night; did you hear or not hear what we were saying to each other? They answered: 'Where? When? We did not hear the conversation.' He said to them: Then, sirs, maybe you did doze a little, didn't you? They answered: 'Yes, maybe we slept right away.'"[48] The story of Pero guru, who healed the sick, says he could identify witches and that he celebrated Karam, one of the famous social rituals of Santal society. Importantly, the guru in the story stresses that such powers are not his, but God's: "Sirs, my folks, you say: 'If we go to Pero guru, he will heal us.' But, my folks, I say to you: I do not heal, it is Chando who heals; have faith in him and he will heal you. He has given me a blessing in order to tell you these words."[49] As stated, the Ten Commandments

44. *Babajuiko reak' katha,* paragraph 11.
45. *Babajuiko reak' katha,* paragraph 15.
46. *Babajuiko reak' katha,* paragraph 19.
47. *Babajuiko reak' katha,* paragraph 30.
48. *Babajuiko reak' katha,* paragraph 6.
49. *Babajuiko reak' katha,* paragraph 19.

were stressed by the *babajis,* and even if it is virtually impossible to recognize the commandments as they are listed in the Bible, the context often indicates a general moral precept that has a Christian character. The *babaji* known as Bariar guru taught that the things forbidden to eat were "these that we hear about in the Ten Commandments."[50] But when he continues to give rules about the dances that are permitted to be danced, he introduces new rules as to who are allowed to touch each other, and he stress that adultery is forbidden.[51] This is necessary because "Chando is . . . afflicting us with all kinds of sorrow because he is angry with us" — a moral God indeed, but historically the deities of the Santals had not been bothered by sexual transgressions. In traditional Santal lore, adultery was forbidden by God, but God did not become angry or punish Santals because of their misconduct.

Christian and Hindu Influence on Santal Religion

Bodding's narrator of "The Story of the Babajis" resided in Santal Parganas. Most of the place-names that can be recognized are in the vicinity of Dumka, and his information in many regards is limited to that area. Dubia Gossain, for instance, is not mentioned at all, and neither are the temples that he established or their pandits, not even the one known in connection with Bhagrit Baba. When the narrator stressed Christian elements, one may of course doubt that it was because he had made what could be termed an *interpretatio Christiana.* I think, however, that Bodding is right in supposing that the narrative on repentance and the Ten Commandments reflects historical fact. Still, it is Bodding's own theology that leads him to use the expression "perverted Christians." In this regard, Bodding was a missionary of his own time with his own specific Lutheran approach to Christianity. In retrospect, it is more fruitful to see the Kherwars as one of many modernizing movements in the colonial period, and in this regard they were drawing from many of the same sources as the missionaries. The preaching of morality would be one such source, and the glorification of God as the one who heals when people repent would be another.

In the Santal perspective, Christian missions and the Kherwar movement simply represented different pathways into modernity; both pathways would have had the effect of reforming the Santal community, and both would have had to come to grips with traditional elements in the Santal culture and reli-

50. *Babajuiko reak' katha,* paragraph 30.
51. *Babajuiko reak' katha,* paragraph 30.

gion as well as with each other. Simultaneously, the incorporation of new traits into contemporary Hindu culture gradually made it an alternative carrier of community identity for Christians, Kherwars, and even the Santals themselves.

Conclusion

One might ask if what we have seen was syncretism. It was, but not syncretism of a kind that destroyed Santal society. Rather, it was a syncretism that entailed the inclusion of new gods and ideas accompanied by new forms of belief suitable for the social changes Santal society was then undergoing. At the end of the nineteenth century these social changes included new forms of rent and agrarian exploitation of farmers, copyholders, and workers; the response to all this was visible in mass movements that combined demands for social reconstruction with a stress on individual repentance. In this way, the Kherwars and the Christian missions were in full agreement on the solution, except on one point: the name of God. For the missionaries, this was a serious point of divergence; for the Santals, the importance of repentance might have had greater weight. For the narrator of "The Story of the Babajis" the documented fact that he visited the *babajis* even after he had started to frequent the Christian church seems to indicate that to him repentance was the primary issue, and that repentance therefore functioned as a kind of common denominator shared both by Santal religion and Christianity.

One could go on to ask whether the Kherwars exemplify the categories that Richard Eaton formulated — inclusion, identification, and displacement — and discuss their usefulness for an analysis of the ways in which elements of Santal religion were integrated with non-Santal religious elements, Hindu or Christian. The important lesson from the story, however, is that the names of the deities and the names of the religions are of minor importance to the central religious message. A religious message fitting to the time and the actual social situation of individuals needs to appeal to them if they are to listen to it and accept unfamiliar religious elements in accordance with the importance of the message.

That the Kherwars have been on the decline at least since the 1930s is evidence that new forms of religious and political organizations have taken over. The Jharkhand movement is only one of them, and the political and religious excitement in contemporary Santal society is evidence that a new social situation has emerged and that the Santals are still searching for fitting answers within the context of modern Indian society.

CHAPTER 7

Caste, Catholicism, and History "from Below," 1863-1917

CHANDRA MALLAMPALLI

One of the hallmarks of Robert Frykenberg's career has been his inclination to examine India's modern political history "from below." It is not the decrees of imperial rulers or the grand story of the nation that has predominantly interested Frykenberg, but little stories, centered upon localities, where Indians have been the primary agents of change and influence. Frykenberg contests the usage of terms such as "colonial" or "Indian" throughout his work. He prefers to focus on the smaller, "hard pieces" of social identity — linguistic, regional, or local *jati* affiliations — upon which larger constructions of India rested. Nowhere does this history from below find finer expression than in *Guntur District* (1965), a brilliant local study, which describes how various groups of Telugu and Maratha Brahmins undermined the very structures of British rule through their superior mastery of traditional sources of power and influence.[1] *Guntur District* redirected the historiography of India away from national histories, largely centered upon Delhi or Calcutta, toward other local studies of South India.

Later in his career, Frykenberg extended his perspective from below to scholarly research on the history of Christian movements within Telugu and Tamil districts of South India, from 1500 on. Debates that have preoccupied historians of the Raj — local versus central power, indigenous agency and resistance versus colonial power, cultural imperialism, etc. — find many parallels within the history of Indian Christianity. As with his treatment of the British Raj, Frykenberg approaches Indian Christian history from below.

1. Robert Frykenberg, *Guntur District, 1788-1848: A History of Local Influence and Central Authority in South India* (Oxford, 1965).

Those holding center stage in this endeavor are not foreign missionaries or the higher echelons of ecclesiastical bodies based in Europe or North America, but Indian catechists, translators, evangelists, bishops, and converts from various caste backgrounds. By focusing on indigenous agency, Frykenberg's scholarship counters a tendency, prevalent within both Hindu nationalist and Marxist historiography, to regard Christianity purely as a "foreign" or "colonial" religion.

This essay explores the relevance of Frykenberg's approach to history to court cases addressing the legitimacy of caste practices of South Indian Roman Catholics. Tried during the late nineteenth and early twentieth centuries, these cases illustrate how the judiciary's increasingly rigid notions of Christian identity collided with Catholic observances of caste customs and distinctions. What implications do such cases pose for bottom-up approaches to history? On the one hand, they reveal the high degree to which Catholics had accommodated themselves to South Indian culture and their use of the courts to secure their "immemorial rights." On the other hand, they show the unwillingness of the courts to recognize caste distinctions among those who "profess the Christian religion." The emerging indigenous Catholicism, as seen from below, stood in constant tension, I argue, with taxonomies the Raj imposed from above. The story that emerged, ironically, is that of the Raj de-Indianizing an Indianized Catholicism.

Debating Difference

The topic of Catholics and the Raj can be situated within wider debates concerning the origins and nature of religious difference within South Asian society. How have modern institutions (e.g., law, print media, and electoral politics) engendered new self-consciousness among religious groups and a heightened sense of religious boundaries? An overview of recent scholarship illustrates the tension between those perspectives that stress Indian agency and knowledge and those that stress policies of the Raj and their impact.

This discussion has been particularly lively among scholars of Islam and Hinduism. Leftist historians such as Bipan Chandra or Gyanendra Pandey argue that Hindu-Muslim communalism was largely generated by the Raj through its policies of divide and rule.[2] Hindu and Muslim elites would later adopt the language of communalism to pursue their own political interests.

2. Bipan Chandra, *Communalism in Modern India* (New Delhi, 1984), and Gyanendra Pandey, *The Construction of Communalism in Colonial North India* (New Delhi, 1990).

Others such as Arjun Appadurai and Bernard Cohn have explored the divisive impact of census categories, personal laws, separate electorates, and other means of counting and classifying the Indian population. Through such means, the Raj nurtured new forms of group consciousness and conflict.[3] Other "postmodernist" perspectives have described how fluid and syncretistic social relationships between Muslims and Hindus during the premodern period became more segregated and fixed under British rule.

Scholars such as Chris Bayly, Francis Robinson, and Peter van der Veer, however, have challenged these explanations of difference. Their work has pointed to a prehistory of group consciousness.[4] From their perspective, religious identities of the nineteenth and twentieth centuries grew out of premodern ideas, practices, and symbols anchored in the real experiences of Indians. Robinson, for instance, has outlined the role of Islamic reform movements and print media in nurturing, from the eighteenth century on, a sense of Muslim distinctiveness throughout north India and other parts of the Islamic world.[5] A separate Muslim identity was neither invented by the colonial state nor contrived by urban elites to serve their sectarian interests. Well before the Muslim League's campaign for a separate "Land of the Pure," a distinctive Muslim identity had very much become a part of the religious idiom of popular classes.[6]

Frykenberg has contributed to this lively debate through his rich account of the emergence of "Hinduism" as a concept and as an institution. Originally the term "Hindu" (or "Hindoo") was used synonymously with "India" and referred inclusively to anyone or anything that was native to the Subcontinent. Just as there were Hindu vessels and Hindu flora and fauna, there were also Hindu Christians, Hindu Muslims, etc. Over the course of nearly two centuries of British rule, four complex historical processes — orientalist scholarship, reform movements, Hindu religious and charitable endowments, and revivalism — gave rise to an officially recognized "Hindu reli-

3. Arjun Appadurai, "Number in Colonial Imagination," in *Orientalism and the Postcolonial Predicament,* ed. Carol Breckenridge and Peter van der Veer (Philadelphia, 1993), and Bernard Cohn, *Colonialism and Its Forms of Knowledge: The British in India* (Princeton, 1996).

4. C. A. Bayly, *Origins of Nationality in South Asia: Patriotism and Ethical Government in the Making of Modern India* (Oxford, 1998), and "The Prehistory of Communalism?" *Modern Asian Studies* 19, no. 2 (1985): 177-203; Peter van der Veer, *Religious Nationalism: Hindus and Muslims in India* (Berkeley, 1994).

5. See Francis Robinson, "Technology and Religious Change: Islam and the Impact of Print," *Modern Asian Studies* 27, no. 1 (February 1993): 229-51.

6. Francis Robinson, *Islam and Muslim History in South Asia* (Oxford, 2000), pp. 161-65.

gion" or "Hinduism."[7] These processes, he observes, involved both European and Indian agents and forms of knowledge. A trenchant critic of Edward Saïd and his South Asianist protégés, Frykenberg stresses in his more recent work that understandings of Indian society and history have emerged through an Indo-European symbiosis, and not through a colonially imposed orientalism.

While the study of Indian Christianity has factored far less prominently in debates concerning the origins of communal difference, key studies have made important contributions. Susan Bayly's captivating study of religious practices in South India describes how Muslims, Syrian Christians, and Hindus participated in a common "sacred landscape," consisting of shared cult figures, relics, sacred shrines, and symbols of ritual power derived from multiple traditions.[8] Other scholars such as David Mosse and Ines Zupanov have similarly described how Jesuits and other Catholic orders embraced local knowledge systems and established South Indian domains that resembled patterns of Hindu temple establishments.[9] Early British rule, according to Bayly, contributed to the disintegration of this syncretistic culture and to the emergence of sharper boundaries and more rigidly observed orthodoxies.

Recently, Frykenberg, in collaboration with Brian Stanley, significantly expanded the historiography of South Asian Christianity through the publication of two edited volumes of exceptional quality. Without grounding their claims in the syncretism described by Bayly, contributors make a compelling case for the Indianness of Christianity. They do so by placing Indian converts, catechists, and translators — not foreign missionaries — at center stage of an "indigenous discovery" of Christianity. Inspired by Lamin Sanneh's work on West Africa, Frykenberg has promoted research that stresses the place of translation and appropriation in producing authentically South Indian Christian movements. Such translation has not only occurred within high traditions of persons such as the Tamil Vellalar, Vedanayakam Sastri, but also within low traditions represented by Dalits and tribals.[10]

7. Frykenberg, "The Emergence of Modern 'Hinduism' as a Concept and as an Institution," in *Hinduism Reconsidered,* ed. Sontheimer and Kulke (New Delhi, 1989).

8. Susan Bayly, *Saints, Goddesses, and Kings: Muslims and Christians in South Indian Society, 1700-1900* (Cambridge, 1989).

9. David Mosse, "The Politics of Religious Synthesis: Roman Catholicism and Hindu Village Society in Tamil Nadu, India," in *Syncretism/Anti-Syncretism: The Politics of Religious Synthesis,* ed. Charles Stewart and Rosalind Shaw (London, 1994); Ines Zupanov, *Disputed Mission: Jesuit Experiments and Brahminical Knowledge in Seventeenth Century India* (New York, 1999).

10. Among the volumes in the series edited by Stanley/Frykenberg are Frykenberg, ed., *Christians and Missionaries in India: Cross-Cultural Communication since 1500* (Grand

As much as such perspectives from below offer a corrective to Eurocentric interpretations of Indian Christianity, they run the risk of minimizing the very real impact of the foreign hand on the minds of converts and the direction of Christian movements. (Critics of bottom-up imperial history similarly argue that they downplay the extent of British impact upon the Indian social structure.) Many modern translators of Indian Christianity — Vedanayakam Sastri, V. S. Azariah, and Pandita Ramabai, to name only a few that have been featured in recent scholarship — endured heated and painful confrontations with missionaries and other Western church authorities over the cultural forms, theologies, and practices of their faith. In pursuit of a fictional autonomous history, a perspective from below must not ignore instances of cultural imperialism on the part of missionaries. Neither, however, should these confrontations form the basis of an entirely different construction of events, centered exclusively upon missionary power. Rather, they serve to show how India's discovery of Christianity, from the earliest times to the present, has been one of complex negotiations of power and difference involving multiple elements, both native and alien to the Subcontinent.

The Judiciary as a Site of Christian Difference

The relationship between Roman Catholicism and things Indian has not always been a smooth one. Under the *padroado* (the royal patronage extended to the Portuguese Crown to oversee missionary activity in the Far East), Hindus, Muslims, and Syrian Christians of Goa and Malabar confronted an imperial Catholicism that was often hostile to their beliefs and customs. It was primarily under the auspices of the Propaganda Fide (the society established by the Vatican, which sought to liberate Catholic missions from imperial control) and through the labors of Carmelite, Franciscan, and Jesuit orders that a more accommodating, Indianized Catholicism emerged.[11]

This more accommodative brand of Catholicism was expressed in ornate processions and public festivals celebrated by Tamil Catholics, which mirrored observances within South Indian "Hindu" domains. It was also seen in the Jesuit recognition of *varna-jati* distinctions observed by Tamil and Malayali converts during the seventeenth and eighteenth centuries. Fol-

Rapids and Cambridge, 2003), and Frykenberg and Judith Brown, eds., *Christians, Cultural Interactions, and India's Religious Traditions* (Grand Rapids, Cambridge, and London, 2002).

11. Samuel Hugh Moffett, *A History of Christianity in Asia*, vol. 2, *1500-1900* (Maryknoll, N.Y., 2005), pp. 16-17.

lowing the example of Robert de Nobili, who had made several converts among Brahmins and had honored their customs, later Jesuit missionaries in Tamilnad observed caste distinctions during Mass and other ceremonial contexts. Rather predictably, such accommodation was welcomed by higher-ranking Vellala converts but opposed by lower-ranking Parava fishermen, Shanars (toddy tappers, who were later called Nadars), and Pariah groups. Occasionally, tensions between these groups erupted into heated legal disputes.

This section draws attention to two ways in which the Indian judiciary derecognized caste observances of South Indian converts, thus undermining some of the accommodative tendencies of Catholic movements. The first deals with the quest for and enforcement of a Christian law of inheritance. Up until 1865, when the Indian Succession Act was passed, the Indian legislature had formulated no Christian law of inheritance. The courts had adopted an open-ended approach to inheritance disputes within Indian Christian families. In the absence of a universal law or *lex loci,* the law governing such disputes was either to be based upon the nationality of the family in question (French, Portuguese, Armenian, English law, etc.), upon the codified Hindu inheritance law, or upon local custom. If the family's identity or customs were ambiguous, the courts would admit evidence that would demonstrate that one law applied over another.

This open-ended approach to Christian inheritance occasionally subjected the judiciary to the enormous burden of determining which customs a family followed. Perhaps to relieve the courts of such a burden, this approach gave way in 1865 to the Indian Succession Act. The Succession Act subjected all "native Christian" families of British India, both Catholic and Protestant, to what was essentially an English law of inheritance. According to English law, the property (both ancestral and acquired) of a deceased father would go to his surviving spouse and children.

The problem with applying English law to native Christian families was that many of them continued to abide by the inheritance practices of their original castes. Roman Catholic converts from low-caste Telugu- and Tamil-speaking backgrounds fell into this category, often having converted to Catholicism in groups. Under the *Mitakshara* school of Hindu inheritance law, male members of an undivided household shared ancestral property (and sometimes acquired property as well) equally. Upon the death of a male head of the household, brothers and sons would divide shares of family property in equal portions. The wife, however, would be entitled only to maintenance within the family home. Whether *Mitakshara* law could apply to South Indian familial patterns was a hotly debated issue within South Indian legal scholarship.[12] With the relevance of textual Hindu law to South India's Hindus being called into question, the case for its relevance to Christian or mixed-race families was even more problematic.

An important case that illustrates the complexities of Christian inheritance law is *Abraham v. Abraham* (1863), decided only two years before the Succession Act was passed.[13] The case involves a mixed-race family from Bellary, a cantonment town near the border between present-day Karnataka and Andhra Pradesh. In 1854, Charlotte Abraham, an Anglo-Indian, along with her two sons, sued the younger brother (Francis) of her deceased husband (Matthew) for possession of her late husband's estate and distillery business. Charlotte argued that because her husband was Christian and because he, by marrying her, had embraced the customs of the Anglo-Indians, she was entitled to his property under English law. Francis responded that he and Matthew, in spite of having adopted Western clothes and many English customs, continued to function like undivided Hindu brothers with respect to the business. As such, Francis believed that he should become the head of the household and divide Matthew's property equally with Charlotte's two sons according to Hindu law. London's Privy Council ultimately ruled in favor of Charlotte and her two sons, but only after an exhaustive examination of the family's cultural habits and ways of relating to each other.

Court records describe Matthew and his relatives as "very dark-skinned" Tamil Pariahs from Madras, who were fourth-generation Roman Catholics.[14] Matthew and Francis, however, converted to Anglicanism before each of them married Anglo-Indian women. Of particular importance for our purposes are not the interesting facts of the case or the verdict, but the sources of evidence that each side marshaled to prove their cases. Charlotte's witnesses consisted primarily of Europeans and Anglo-Indians.[15] These witnesses tended to shun all aspects of "native" society. Many such witnesses argued that Matthew and Francis were imbued with the same sensibilities, having thoroughly assimilated into Anglo-Indian society.

Francis, by contrast, called witnesses who were primarily low-caste Roman Catholic converts. Many were members of the land-cultivating, Telugu

12. See, for instance, J. H. Nelson, *A View of the Hindu Law as Administered by the High Court of Judicature at Madras* (Madras, 1877).

13. *Abraham v. Abraham,* Privy Council Cases with Judgments, 1863.

14. Testimony of plaintiff's seventy-fifth witness, Mrs. Elizabeth McBride, forty-seven years old, Protestant East Indian residing at Madras. *Abraham v. Abraham.*

15. Of the 101 witnesses deposed by Charlotte's counsel, only 72 were found in the court records. Of these, 44 were taken from Protestants of whom only 8 were Indians. None of the Indians listed their caste backgrounds.

Mootatee Capu caste, who had converted en masse in Kurnool around the turn of the nineteenth century.[16] In his own deposition, Francis did not conceal elements of his assimilation into English culture, for example, his marriage to the Anglo-Indian, Caroline Platcher; his adoption of the Western dress; and his decision to baptize his seven children in the Church of England. Still, he maintained that he and his brother had retained key aspects of their Tamil heritage, particularly with regard to inheritance. As English as he had become in dress, speech, etc., he drew upon his family's former networks of indigenous Catholicism to construct a case for his enduring Indianness.

Indeed, one of Francis's key witnesses was the Reverend P. Doyle, the parish priest who had overseen the conversion to Catholicism of hundreds of low-caste Telugus near Kurnool. Doyle spoke at length about the continual observance of caste customs among converts and claimed to have known several Catholic families who divided their property like Hindu undivided families. In addition to Doyle, many converts themselves vividly described their observance of caste customs, including local approaches to family inheritance.

By deciding the case in Charlotte's favor, judges of London's Privy Council did not deny the existence of Christian families that followed the Hindu law of inheritance. On the contrary, Lord Kingsdown openly acknowledged the highly pluralistic character of the Christian population of British India.

What the judges did conclude, on the basis of the ethnographic evidence, was that the Abraham brothers had, in spite of their race, become members of the East Indian community and were to be judged by English law. Employees and clients referred to Matthew and Francis as "Pedda and Chinna Doray." The term "Doray" could designate someone holding official or high-ranking status or a white person. Both brothers had married East Indian women, adopted Western clothes, abandoned caste observances, embraced the Protestant faith and its work ethic, and associated primarily with East Indians and Europeans. Given the nature and extent of their assimilation in every notable way, it would be unreasonable to suppose that they divided their property according to Hindu law.

On the face of it, the decision does not appear to have militated against indigenous Catholic caste customs. It amounts to saying, "Yes, there are Indian Christians who continue to divide property like Hindu families, and this is legally valid; but the Abraham brothers do not belong to that class." When examined in hindsight after the passing of the Indian Succession Act only two years later, the Abraham verdict takes on a different meaning. By placing

16. Of the 150 depositions taken by the attorney for Francis, 104 were found in the court records. Of these, 53 were Roman Catholics, of which all but two were Indian.

Christians — including those witnesses called by Francis — under English law, the act effectively de-recognized Francis's evidence. The verdict in Charlotte's favor becomes a verdict on the cultural complexion of Indian Christianity, which, in her case, was decidedly English.

After the Succession Act came into effect in 1866, inheritance disputes within Catholic families were decided on a summary basis according to the English standards set forth in the act.[17] This was met with considerable resistance both in and out of court. T. R. A. Thumbu Chetty, a Roman Catholic Madrassi who had served as a judge on the Mysore High Court, consistently objected to the way the courts were treating "Hindoo Christians" (as he called them) as an entirely separate community with separate laws, simply because they had changed their "opinions" regarding religion.[18] By and large, the act affected propertied caste Catholic families far more than it did Protestant mass converts. The latter also retained many caste customs after conversion; but coming as they often did from Dalit and lower Sudra *jatis*, they possessed little or no ancestral property and remained unaffected by the Succession Act.

The other sense in which the Indian judiciary de-recognized Catholic caste practices was in relation to the celebration of Mass and the observance of sacred festivals. Church authorities had assigned separate roles and spaces to higher- and lower-ranking groups. Early Jesuits of the Madurai Mission had instituted such practices when they selected altar servers and catechists from among their more literate and pious Vellala converts. They preserved the higher-ranking status of Vellalas by assigning to them the nave of the church, while consigning Nadars and Pariahs to the peripheries with dividing walls. Within some churches, officials assigned separate entrances for high and low castes and served communion separately.[19] By the early twentieth century, non-Brahminism and anti-untouchable campaigns inspired low-caste Catholics to contest these practices both within the church and in courts of law. Occasionally, however, litigation worked in the opposite direction.

In *Michael Pillai v. Barthe* (1917), a group of Roman Catholic Vellalas

17. See *Ponnusami Nadan v. Dorasami Ayyan* (1880), *Indian Law Reports,* vol. 2, Madras, 209-212, and *Tellis v. Saldanha* (1887), *Indian Law Reports,* vol. 10, Madras, 69-73.

18. Chandra Mallampalli, *Christians and Public Life in Colonial South India* (London, 2004), p. 14.

19. This segregation was in fact the Jesuit answer to Benedict XIV, who in 1744 had insisted that everyone should attend Mass and receive communion at the same place and the same time. Kenneth Ballhatchet, *Caste, Class, and Catholicism in India, 1789-1914* (Richmond Surrey, 1998), pp. 111-12.

(which included both Pillais and Mudalis) sued the bishop at Trichinopoly, the parish priest, and several Nadar Catholics for the right to enforce caste segregation within the Holy Family Church at Vedakkankulam. The Vellala plaintiffs wanted the court to reerect walls that had separated caste Catholics from the so-called polluting castes. They alleged that such segregation was written into a series of agreements between the high- and low-caste parties with the approval of the bishop. The first agreement was in 1854, when the building plans were being drafted; the other in 1877, when the construction was completed. The 1854 agreement supposedly envisioned two adjacent churches with a common chancel so that both churches could observe Mass simultaneously. The southern nave would be reserved for Vellalas, the northern for Nadars. After the Nadars protested this arrangement, the second, compromised agreement was reached. In 1910, the dividing walls were demolished. The plaintiffs sought a declaration from the court identifying the first agreement as binding and designating the Vellalas as the sole owners of the church. They also sought court orders that would restrict the use of the altar, handling of sacred images, and performance of certain rituals and processions to the Vellalas.[20]

Two dimensions of the Vellala plaintiffs' arguments are noteworthy. First, in a manner similar to Francis Abraham (above), they appealed to the history and culture of indigenous Catholicism to uphold their observance of caste distinctions. They cited a bull issued by Pope Gregory XV in 1623, which allegedly recognized caste distinctions. They also invoked Robert de Nobili's missionary approach, which embraced the customs of Tamil Brahmins and sanctioned their caste prejudices.[21] Last, they cited directions issued by the Holy See (no dates) charging missionaries to preserve the usages, customs, and manners of their converts, "provided that they be not most evidently contrary to Religion."[22]

The second dimension of their case was their appeal to customary right, namely, the right to be free from contact with so-called "polluted" castes. Through their eyes, contact with Shanars was defiling and required ceremonial cleansing. Such observances of custom, as Justice J. Napier observed, far preceded their conversion to Catholicism and remained unaffected by it. In fact, judges of the Madras High Court were astonished to observe that the Vellalas saw no contradiction between notions of pollution and Christianity.

The Madras High Court rejected the Vellalas' claim for various reasons,

20. *K. Michael Pillai v. J. M. Barthe and others,* All India Reporter (1917), Madras, 432.

21. *K. Michael Pillai v. J. M. Barthe and others,* 436.

22. *K. Michael Pillai v. J. M. Barthe and others,* 436.

the most important being that notions of pollution were inconsistent with the Catholic religion. In expressing this view, judges dismissed the indigenous Catholicism cited by the plaintiffs as irrelevant to the nature and extent of the discrimination being practiced at Holy Family Church. Such overt discrimination, in their view, had never been sanctioned by papal decree. On the basis of various shreds of evidence, Judge Napier concluded that Vellalas had pressured the bishop in 1877 into making a temporary concession, which permitted separate spaces for higher and lower castes: "There can be no doubt that in his desire to see the new church built, the Bishop shut his eyes to the real foundation of a claim so inconsistent with his faith, in the delusion that time would remove the discard — a hope that has been falsified by the quarrels of the parties from that day to this."[23] In essence, Napier's comments defended church hierarchy against the efforts of the Vellalas to subvert it. By suing for the right to discriminate, they were essentially demanding the right to tell a bishop whom he could and could not employ at the altar, during festivals or in the serving of communion. This violated the very basis of authority in Catholicism. Hence, if Vellalas wanted to observe laws of pollution, they would have to secede from Catholicism and form a separate religion!

Courts may recognize castes as corporations, holding rights to property or easements, and all customary rights that go along with such ownership. Properties purchased and owned by and for a caste may be used by that caste according to its own laws and customs. The Vellalas sought such rights in connection to their church. The Madras High Court, however, could not extend the recognition accorded to Hindu castes to the Vellalas on account of their conversion to Catholicism. This, in the High Court's view, bound the Vellalas to the dictates of canon law and the authority of the bishops.

Conclusion

Robert Frykenberg's "bottom-up" approach to the study of modern India's political history also carries significant implications for the study of Indian Christianity. Instead of focusing on the activities of foreign missionaries, ecclesiastical bodies, or colonial authorities, his approach directs our gaze toward the initiatives, adaptations, and creativity of Indian converts. The story being told is not about the imposition of an alien religion (or state apparatus) upon passive Indians, but about complex processes whereby Christian movements have assumed local characteristics and grounding. The primary risk in

23. *K. Michael Pillai v. J. M. Barthe and others*, 436.

taking this approach, however, is to minimize the impact of British or foreign missionary policies upon the choices available to Indians.

Court cases addressing the validity of Roman Catholic caste practices can find a place within histories written from above and from below. Historians, for instance, may use these cases to stress the power of the colonial judiciary. The judiciary, after all, used resources at its disposal (including Indian *vakils*, translators and pandits) to interpret Indian laws and social practices, and to validate some practices over others. The cases discussed in this essay may illustrate what Thomas Metcalf calls the "creation and ordering of difference."[24] Just as the Raj institutionalized differences between Hindu and Muslim "communities," it reified a "Christian community" by defining its ethos in opposition to local caste observances.[25]

This top-down perspective remains intact even when we stress the judiciary's efforts to preserve or protect aspects of the Indian social structure.[26] "Immemorial rights" based upon custom or tradition belonged to the vocabulary of the new imperialism instituted under the East India Company's Raj. The courts had to discover what these rights were and who held them before they could "protect" them.[27] This process resulted in serious disagreements over how the courts were interpreting the nature and scope of Hindu law and the composition of South Indian society. The Madras High Court's decision not to recognize the claims of Catholic Vellalars may be located within the logic of this new imperialism. By rejecting Vellalar Catholic claims to immemorial rights, the High Court did not deny that such rights exist and should be honored; they merely denied that Catholics were entitled to them.

For the historian committed to Frykenberg's perspective from below, the same cases tell alternative stories. They describe how Indians such as Francis Abraham or the plaintiffs in *Michael Pillai v. Barthe* attempted to use the courts to secure their own interests. These plaintiffs invoked the history of indigenized Catholicism in hopes of benefiting from the judiciary's professed commitment to religious toleration. Their lack of success does nothing to diminish the fact of their efforts and the larger story such efforts tell about colonial subjects; that of Indians domesticating institutions of British rule to

24. See Thomas Metcalf, *Ideologies of the Raj* (Cambridge, 1995), chaps. 3 and 4.

25. This is an argument put forth in Chandra Mallampalli, *Christians and Public Life in Colonial South India, 1863-1937: Contending with Marginality* (London, 2004).

26. By the same token, "indigenization" as an aspect of missionary ideology or strategy must not be confused with "indigenous agency" in missions, which is centered upon the activity of converts.

27. David Washbrook, "South India 1770-1840: The Colonial Transition," *Modern Asian Studies* 38, no. 3 (2004): 487-88.

suit their communal interests, or of Indians rearticulating traditional loyalties within modern institutions.[28]

Historians from below can uphold the Indianness of Catholicism, even in the face of judicial attempts to invalidate Catholic caste observances. The significance of these decisions can be mitigated by highlighting several developments within the Madras judiciary. First, judges relied upon Indian informants and pandits, hired by the courts to interpret Hindu law. While this reliance was very strong during the years of *Abraham v. Abraham* (1854-63), it became less the case in subsequent decades as major works of Hindu law were translated and published in English. Still, the picture that emerges all along is that of dialogical relationship between Indian and European knowledge, rather than clear dichotomy between the two.[29] Second, from the 1860s, increasing numbers of Indians were serving as *vakils,* barristers, attorneys, and even judges.[30] The Indianization of the judiciary counters any tendency to view Catholics as victims of purely European assumptions and decisions. Finally, historians from below can downplay the significance of Madras High Court decisions by stressing the lack of training of many legal practitioners and the limited influence of legal decisions upon the society at large. In other words, Indian Catholicism remained highly Indian in spite of judicial attitudes and policies toward their customs.

In the face of perspectives stressing either state power (in this case, that of the judiciary) or Indian agency, historians are faced with an interpretive dilemma. The decision to embrace a perspective from above or below, or elements of each, depends upon the larger story one wishes to tell. If the historian's primary objective is to stress the "Indianness" of Catholicism, there is no better approach than Frykenberg's history from below. Still, a distinction needs to be made between the actual history of South Indian Catholicism and how that history was represented, used, and evaluated within imperial courts. The fact that litigants invoked this history to legitimate upper-caste domination also raises ethical questions about which dimensions of local culture Catholics themselves have attempted to preserve.

If, on the other hand, the historian wants to trace the origins of Catholic

28. Pamela Price describes how succession disputes within the South Indian kingdom of Ramnad were fought out within colonial courts in ways that resembled traditional competition for privilege and status. See *Kingship and Political Practice in Colonial India* (Cambridge, 1996).

29. This is in keeping with Eugene Irschick's perspectives in *Dialogue and History: Constructing South India, 1795-1895* (Berkeley, 1994).

30. John J. Paul documents these developments in *The Legal Profession in Colonial South India* (Oxford, 1991).

marginality from South Indian society, or how Christians in general came to be perceived as non-Indian, a history from above is vital. Perceptions of Christians as outsiders were popularized during the Indian nationalist movement and have found new life and vigor amid the current rise of Hindutva chauvinism. A history from above helps us to appreciate the imperial origins of such perceptions. Judicial knowledge about Hindus, Muslims, and Catholics often militated against their day-to-day practices, experiences, and aspirations. Court cases present historians with interesting records of the disjunction between the judiciary's official knowledge and the claims of religious litigants.

CHAPTER 8

Hindu Pundits and Missionary "Knowledge" of Hinduism

GEOFFREY A. ODDIE

The relationship between knowledge and power has been debated in South Asian studies for a very long time — well before the publication of Saïd's celebrated *Orientalism,* first published in 1978. Robert Eric Frykenberg, whose work we celebrate on this occasion, addressed the question in his *Guntur District, 1788-1848* (1965). His work is, among other things, a study of how Indian subordinates exploited the British officials' ignorance of local society to achieve their own personal objectives. "Probably the most significant feature of the early years of British rule in Guntur," we are told, "was the difficulty which they had in obtaining vital information."[1]

Like Frykenberg's contribution and other work, this paper raises questions about the nature and extent of European knowledge of India. Our focus is on British Protestant missionary knowledge of Hinduism in particular and the part Hindu pundits (or *munshis,* as they were commonly called) played in the missionaries' perception and understanding of Indian religion. What were the most important factors affecting missionary views of Hinduism? How important were the pundits in the formation of missionary views and models? And if pundits were influential, to what extent do missionary views and representations of Indian religion merely reflect a recycling of Brahminic or other high-caste ideas of Hinduism?

The paper begins by pointing out that the pundits' influence was only one element in a complex of factors affecting missionary knowledge and understanding of Hinduism. Nevertheless, for some missionaries, contact or study

1. Robert E. Frykenberg, *Guntur District, 1788-1848: A History of Local Influence and Central Authority in South India* (Oxford, 1965), p. 37.

with a pundit was an unforgettable and important part of their exposure to the Hindus' world of thought and practice. The pundits, it is argued, did not represent or teach the one overarching or coherent view of what Indian religion was supposed to be. In fact, their role was to reinforce the idea of diversity — a view of Indian religious phenomena that at least some missionaries came to accept in the second half of the nineteenth century. Indeed, pundits employed in the various missions as teachers and translators were not confined to any one Hindu religious tradition, sect, or school of thought. Their teaching and outlook varied greatly depending on their socioreligious background. Furthermore, what the pundit decided to communicate and the way this was done was not always a simple or straightforward process. Much depended on trust and rapport and on the nature of the relationship between pundit and pupil. Again, even if the relationship between the two was such that the pundit was prepared to divulge all he knew, there may have been gaps between what he thought he said and how the message was received or understood.

Sources of Missionary "Knowledge" of Hinduism

Knowledge and insights provided by pundits was one among a growing number of different sources of information on Hinduism in the late eighteenth century and during the nineteenth century.

In the earlier part of the period most missionary candidates appear to have known little about Indian religion, and judging from their application papers, tended to think more about the needs of the "heathen" generally than about Hindus in particular. The term "Hinduism," for example, rarely occurs in London Missionary Society (LMS) candidates' papers. As is apparent from Alexander Duff's account of his youth, there was a certain degree of general knowledge, especially among Christians. References to Brahmins and Hindu ascetics, the Jagannath procession, *sati*, hook-swinging, and other customs were available through travelers' accounts and in earlier missionary literature. But most missionaries, during the first half of the nineteenth century, were "trained" in ordinary theological colleges and, except in a few cases, were unable to acquire further knowledge of Hinduism in the college classroom. Furthermore, because of rapidly changing needs for staffing in the mission field, candidates eventually assigned to India seldom knew where they were going until shortly before their departure. In these circumstances preparation for their specific destination was difficult.[2]

2. For information contained in the above paragraph, see Geoffrey A. Oddie, *Imagined*

The missionaries' immediate task upon arrival in India was usually to study the local language. While taking lessons and perhaps also engaged with their *munshi* or pundit in religious discussion, newly arrived missionaries were therefore largely ignorant of the details and complexities of Indian religion. This situation was, however, partially rectified during the second half of the century. An increasing amount of missionary and other periodical literature and many other new Western publications referring to Hinduism became available during this period. As candidates' papers suggest, for young men considering the mission field, missionary biographies and missionary accounts were among the most popular sources of information.[3] But quite apart from missionary material there were other secular publications providing an increasing amount of information on the same subject. This was available, not only in newspapers and in a range of periodicals, but in parliamentary debates and official government of India publications. Furthermore, an ever-increasing number of Hindu religious texts or portions of scripture were available in translation. These included varied collections such as Max Müller's *Ancient Sanskrit Literature,* M. Monier-Williams's collection of texts in *Indian Wisdom* (1875), and John Muir's *Original Sanskrit Texts.*[4]

Another newly developing but less formal method of obtaining information for recruits to the mission field, was through friends or family already in India. Evidence suggests that as the century progressed a small but increasing number of applicants for mission work were born in India or had friends or relatives already there. For these candidates, all other sources of information on Hinduism could be supplemented informally and through personal contact.[5]

While therefore the knowledge young men and women had of Indian religions when they commenced mission work during the second half of the century varied considerably, there was some overall improvement — a greater

Hinduism: British Protestant Missionary Constructions of Hinduism, 1793-1900 (New Delhi and London, 2006).

3. See especially Stuart Piggin, *Making Evangelical Missionaries, 1789-1858: The Social Background, Motives, and Training of British Protestant Missionaries to India* (Oxford, 1984).

4. Though there is evidence that the reading of these texts was encouraged by missionary societies, it is not clear how much missionaries or mission candidates took advantage of them. However, even if many workers remained unacquainted with, for example, Max Müller's work, or unwilling to read it, his approach was undoubtedly one factor in encouraging more sympathetic views of Hinduism and possibly also an atmosphere in which the pundits' missionary pupils were more open and eager to listen. See Max Müller Papers, Ms. Eng. C2807 No. 24, Indian Institute, Oxford; also Oddie, *Imagined Hinduism.*

5. Oddie, *Imagined Hinduism.*

proportion of mission workers being better informed than their forebears had been in an earlier generation.

After the missionaries' arrival in India, a greater knowledge of Indian religions could be gained, not only through the pundit, but in other ways as well. The pundit's presence and commentary was usually the first challenging new source of information; but in the long run and over a longer period of time, other sources of information within India also played a part in the formation of missionary views and interpretation. To discuss in detail all these additional and varied sources of knowledge is beyond the scope of this paper. Much depended on where the missionaries were sent. If they became vernacular preachers in the countryside, they were often exposed to the views of lower- as well as upper-caste peoples.[6] If their work was in education, then they were more likely to gain insights into Brahminic and upper-caste belief and practice, and together with this, gain a more sophisticated understanding of Hindu reform and revival movements. The missionaries' own direct observation of Hindu practice, of forms of worship, temple festivals, and other activities, was also extremely important as a factor in their increasing knowledge of Indian religion. Though scattered in different parts of the Subcontinent, they also learned a great deal from each other — through their own conferences and India-based publications. Among other factors affecting their knowledge and understanding was the growth of the Christian community. Converts, catechists, and other helpers such as "Bible women," as well as Indian Christian scholars (such as K. M. Bannerjea, Nilakanth [Nehemiah] Goreh, and others), contributed to the missionaries' local or more general knowledge of India's religion and society.

The pundit was therefore but one source of information and comment. However, this does not necessarily mean that he had comparatively little effect on missionary thinking. The young missionary's initial encounter with him usually came at a formative and impressionable time in the missionary's career in the mission field. Much of the pundit's effect also depended upon what weight individual missionaries were prepared to give to his commentary — and clearly in some cases, his remarks were taken seriously, even treasured, as the best evidence on particular aspects of Hindu thought and practice.

6. In her recent study, *Contentious Traditions: The Debate on Sati in Colonial India* (Los Angeles and London, 1998), Lati Mani has refocused attention on the kind of comments and "feedback" missionaries received while preaching in the marketplace and on tour in and around Calcutta.

Munshis, Pundits, and Religious Tradition

The term *munshi* was Arabic in origin. In its strictest sense it applied to teachers of Arabic, Persian, or Urdu. However, it was also used more loosely in mission circles to refer to a "native" teacher of one or more of the languages spoken in different parts of the Subcontinent. While *munshis* in the stricter sense were usually Muslims, many of the so-called *munshis* who taught British missionaries throughout the nineteenth century were Hindus, or even, in a few cases, Christians.[7] The term therefore was used for both the *munshi* in the strictest sense and the Sanskrit "pundit" or "pandit" (from *pandita,* or "learned man").[8] Indeed, *munshi* and "pundit" were sometimes used interchangeably in the same passage simply to signify a "native" teacher of an Indian language or languages.[9] The focus of this paper is on the *Hindu* teacher or translations consultant — on the Hindu pundit sometimes known as *munshi.*[10]

Pundits as Translation Consultants

Protestant missionaries employed Hindu pundits for two main reasons during the period 1793-1900. One was for assistance in the work of translation, usually of portions of Scripture or the whole of the Bible into vernacular languages, or for translating vernacular works into English. The second major reason was to teach missionaries the local language. Some missionaries re-

7. See, for example, Ralph Wardlaw, *Memoir of the Late Rev. John Reid, M.Ar.* (Glasgow, 1845), p. 161; J. Abbs, *Twenty-Two Years' Missionary Experience in Travancore* (London, 1870), p. 51; and Frank Ashcroft, *Story of Our Rajputana Mission* (Edinburgh, 1909), pp. 30-31.

8. Henry Yule and A. C. Burnell, *Hobson-Jobson: The Anglo-Indian Dictionary,* 2nd ed. (1902), pp. 740-41. CWM (Council for World Mission, formerly LMS), Incoming Correspondence, South India, Tamil, Box 3, Folder 3. Report of the first general meeting of the Madras District Committee, 2/9/1827 and 4/10/1827.

9. See, for example, the LMS Madras District Committee's regulations in relation to missionary pay and conditions in 1827. CWM Incoming Correspondence, South India, Tamil, Box 2, Folder 3, Jacket B, J. Crisp, 15/10/1827.

10. It is important to note that these pundits, employed as assistants in mission, do not include another class of "learned men" whom the missionaries met while itinerating, or on some other occasion. A well-known example of one of these "learned persons" was Dayananda Saraswati, who had long conversations with the Scottish Presbyterian missionaries at Ajmere in 1866. *United Presbyterian Missionary Record,* n.s., 1 (September 1, 1866): 168-69; John Robson, *Hinduism and Its Relations to Christianity* (Edinburgh and London, 1893), pp. 218-19.

tained the services of their pundits for more diverse work or for longer periods than others. Indeed, it was not only the Serampore Baptists, committed to a major translations program, who employed *munshis* over long periods of time. Elijah Hoole, for example, who developed a lifelong passion for Tamil language and literature, remarked that during the whole of his time in Madras (1820-28) he "always considered it necessary to have a learned native assistant, on whom, though not fully employed by me, I could rely for help in any difficulties which might occur in Tamul reading or composition."[11] Apart from these duties, pundits were also known to help missionaries in their preaching.[12]

Fifty pundits were appointed to positions in the College of Fort William established by the East India Company in 1800.[13] William Carey, who shortly afterward was appointed professor of Bengali, employed ten of this number for work in the Bengali and Sanskrit departments. A few of the best of them were later appointed for work at Serampore where, along with other Hindu pundits, they were used in translating the Bible into the vernacular. Among these Fort William pundits also employed at Serampore were Mrtyunjay Vidyalankar, a much-esteemed and religiously conservative Sanskrit scholar who subsequently became pundit of the Supreme Court, and Ramram Basu, one of Carey's original teachers who was clearly influenced by the teachings of Christianity.

Less well known is the story of a similar though less ambitious missionary project developed by Church Missionary Society (CMS) missionaries some years later at Kottayam in Travancore. Here, once again, the missionaries were determined to translate the whole of the Bible into the local vernacular — in this case into Malayalam. In 1813, the British resident, Colonel John Munro,[14] conceived of the idea of founding a college for the education of Syrian clergy and laity. After negotiations with leaders of the Syrian community, a college was eventually established under the auspices of the CMS at Kottayam. Joseph Fenn was appointed principal and Benjamin Bailey, who had been in Travancore for a slightly longer period (and who was therefore supposed to

11. Elijah Hoole, *Madras, Mysore, and the South of India; or, A Personal Narrative of a Mission to Those Countries from MDCCCXX to MDCCCXXVIII* (London, 1844), p. 189.

12. Ashcroft, *Our Rajputana Mission*, p. 31.

13. S. Pearce Carey, *William Carey, D.D., Fellow of the Linnaean Society* (London, 1926), p. 242.

14. An evangelical and resident of Travancore state from 1811 to 1814, Munro believed that "the diffusion of genuine Christianity in India [is] a measure equally important to the interests of humanity and to the stability of our power." Robin Jeffrey, *The Decline of Nayar Dominance* (London, 1976), pp. 6-7.

be better acquainted with the local language), was appointed superintendent of the translations project.[15] The original work of translation undertaken by the *catanars* (or Syrian clergy) was eventually revised with the assistance of at least one influential Hindu pundit. The pundit who was initially described as "a respectable Brahmin" was Waidya Natha Iyer, a Tamil Brahmin who, according to Bailey, attended him regularly every morning to assist him in revising the translation.[16] After nine months, the missionary, with the pundit's much-needed assistance, had completed a revision of all four Gospels. Another notable Hindu pundit at Kottayam was the Sanskrit *munshi* whose services could always be called upon in times of need. A Nair, and native of British Malabar named Chatu Menon, he had been a *Kariyaka* or Tahilsadar in the Travancore service before accepting the position of *munshi* under Bailey. According to Cheriyan, other Brahmins and Nairs were also employed as pundits in the translations project.[17]

Pundits as Teachers

For the great majority of missionaries, the serious and sustained study of language was begun only after their arrival in the country and as a result of their securing or being given the services of a *munshi* or pundit.

The ability to function in the vernacular language had long been valued and recognized as a sine qua non for the professional missionary, and as the nineteenth century progressed, the need for formal qualifications and the use of pundits was increasingly recognized as an essential component of any missionary system. The usual practice of making arrangements with a *munshi* or pundit was increasingly formalized by the missionary societies and the local committees in different parts of India. Hence, some societies, like the LMS and the Society for the Propagation of the Gospel (SPG), provided the missionary with "a *munshi* allowance" and also began to insist on the need to pass language examinations. For example, the Calcutta Diocesan Committee (the local organization representing the SPG) declared in its regulations of about 1880 that "Every Missionary, ordained or lay, and every Catechist and School master of the Society is required to pass, within one year of the date of

15. E. Stock, *History of the Church Missionary Society: Its Environment, Its Men, and Its Work*, vol. 1 (London, 1899), pp. 232-34; P. Cheriyan, *The Malabar Syrians and the Church Missionary Society, 1816-1840* (Kottayam, 1935), pp. 178-79.

16. CMS archives, University of Birmingham, CMS Proceedings, Bailey to Parent Committee, April 23, June 27, November 10, 1818.

17. Cheriyan, *The Malabar Syrians*, pp. 178-79.

his arrival in the country, or of his entering the service of the Society, an examination as to his competency to read, write and converse in the vernacular of the Mission."[18]

There was also a move on the part of missionary societies to detail the specific outcomes required in language examinations. Thus, according to the CMS committee in Madras, missionaries belonging to the Church of England Zenana Missionary Society (CEZMS) and the CMS in the 1890s were expected to demonstrate that they had developed the following skills:

> To translate, within a given time, in English a page (8vo) from an approved Text Book. To translate, within a given time, with accuracy of grammar and fair accuracy of idiom, a page (8vo) of narrative English and ten English sentences. Etymology and syntax. To write, within a given time, a short exposition of one of the Parables. To read aloud with facility, and to translate from a book not previously studied and a selected portion of the Bible. To translate with readiness a paper of short conversational sentences to be read out by the Examiner. To read and translate an ordinary Vernacular letter. To converse with Natives, not employed in the Mission, on ordinary and religious subjects with such fluency and accuracy as to be easily intelligible.[19]

It was generally recognized that language studies would occupy a substantial part of the missionaries' time and attention — for one or two years, or even longer.[20] Language requirements were increasingly formalized and underscored in statements of mission society bylaws and policy, and, in a few cases, would-be missionaries, unable to pass their examinations, were "disconnected" or sent home.[21] Indeed, a successful career in the mission field came to depend more and more on the results of language examinations and, by implication, on the help or assistance of pundits or teachers, most of whom were Hindu.

18. SPG, *Annual Report*, 1880, p. xxii.

19. *India's Women and China's Daughters*, April 1899, p. 71.

20. S. F. Latham, *Memoirs of Zenana Mission Life* (London, n.d.), p. 23.

21. The CEZMS, established in 1882, was one missionary organization that adopted a hard-line approach toward its missionaries who failed to acquire the local language. In at least two cases prior to 1900, its missionaries were either sent home or forced to resign. Birmingham University Library; CEZMS, CEZ/C/AM1, vol. 1, Register of missionaries with particulars of service. See also the case of Elizabeth Coleman, who failed her language examinations and whose services the Madras Committee recommended should be dispensed with "at an early date" (UTC Bangalore, CEZMS, Madras Committee Proceedings, vol. 1, 20/12/1883).

Reading the Person:
The Pundit as an Example of "the Learned Hindu"

As the above comments suggest, the hiring of a *munshi* or pundit was a significant event that marked the beginning of what could become a long-term personal and developing relationship. Furthermore, it was an experience that in some cases could greatly color the missionary's understanding and ideas of Hinduism.

Even if the relationship between missionary and pundit failed to develop, even if the missionary's regular meetings with him never went beyond a business-like arrangement,[22] contact with the pundit was often important in conveying first impressions and in providing some insight into the Hindu religion and way of life. Newly arrived missionaries soon became familiar with "native" servants; but the pundit was different. In many instances he was the first learned or educated Indian the missionary met, the first representative of "real Hinduism" and a person with whom the missionary could have a considered and in-depth discussion about Hindu beliefs and customs. And more than a source of knowledge conveyed verbally, he was in his person, conduct, and appearance an example and symbol of the Hindu religion and way of life. While part of the missionary's world of educated persons and mentors, he was, at the same time, a significant representative of the missionary's "other."

It is hardly surprising, therefore, that some missionaries, eager to learn as

22. In spite of the *munshi*'s pleasure at having gained employment in the mission, available evidence suggests that missionary *munshis,* compared with some of their colleagues, were paid a very moderate salary. It is true that once having been appointed professor of Bengali in Fort William College, Carey was able to obtain and pay very learned *munshis.* The chief pundit or *munshi,* Mrtyunjay, received a salary of Rs 200 per month, the second pundit Rs 100, and the remaining six Rs 40 per month (S. Pearce Carey, *William Carey,* p. 206). But even the lowest-paid of these appear to have been much better off than ordinary pundits working in the missionary system during that period and later in the nineteenth century. The highest rate of pay for *munshis* employed by the LMS in Calcutta in 1893, for example, was only Rs 15 per month, in spite of the rise in prices, and the fact that some pundits could earn up to Rs 20 in aided vernacular schools in the early 1860s when the rupee was worth even more. (SOAS, CWM, Incoming Letters, N. India [Bengal], M. B. Phillips, August 8, 1893, and *General Report on Public Instruction in the Lower Province of the Bengal Presidency for 1861-62, with Appendixes* [Calcutta, 1863], appendix C.) In 1880 the SPG in Madras was paying its *munshis* Rs 15 per mensem, *Annual Report of the SPG,* 1880, p. 32, while CEZMS allowances for *munshis* in the same region appear to have varied depending on location. In the estimates for 1882 the two Miss Oxleys at Madras were allowed 120 rupees for sharing a pundit for the year (Rs 10 per mensem), and the two women at Masulipatam 150 rupees (Rs 12.5 per mensem). UTC archives, Bangalore, CEZMS, Madras Committee proceedings, 1882-1886, vol. 1, p. 203.

quickly and as much as possible, focused not only on the language they were studying but also on the *munshi* in the hope that he as a person, and in his behavior, would somehow betray the essence of what it was to be a Hindu. Recalling his experience of studying Hindi in Benares in 1839, James Kennedy (LMS) remarked that "I felt myself studying the native character as well." In working with his pundit Kennedy believed he had been given an illustration of "the patience, the courtesy, and also flattering, cozening character of the people."[23] Thomas Hodson of the Wesleyan Methodist Missionary Society (WMMS) and William Drew (LMS) also drew general conclusions from the experience of meeting their teacher. They interpreted their pundits' reluctance to be drawn out on the respective merits of Christianity and Hinduism as indifference to "the truth" — an indifference they came to believe was typical of Hindus generally.

Referring to the attitude of his pundit, Drew concluded that Hindus had reduced religion "to a most unmeaning thing." According to the missionary, they saw their "system" either as a path to the gratification of their worst passions, as a superstition in the most trifling forms, or as an unintelligible "mystery." It was in every way something to be laughed at. "'Tell me, Chiniah,' I said solemnly one day to my Moonshee, 'what are your hopes of salvation? — how do you expect to be saved?' An unmeaning laugh, with — 'I don't know,' was his indifferent but affecting reply. And as they do not know, so they do not care. They will turn aside the weightiest arguments with a smile or a stupid attempt at wit."[24]

Pundits' Social Background and Religious Tradition: Implications for Missionary Views of Hinduism

1. Hindu pundits in missionary employment were drawn from different Hindu communities and represented a wide variety of different Hindu religious traditions. As Claudius Buchanan (provost of Fort William College) discovered, even among the Brahmin pundits of northern India there were sharp differences of opinion, and different views of what constituted "the real Hinduism." In his *Memoir of the Expediency of an Ecclesiastical Establishment for British India,* published in 1805, he declared that the Hindus were "a divided people" and that "there is no such thing as a hierarchy of Brahminical

23. James Kennedy, *Life and Work in Benares and Kumaon, 1839-1877* (London, 1884), pp. 31-32.

24. J. S. Wardlaw, *Memoir of the Late Rev. W. H. Drew,* p. 56. SOAS, MMS Special Series (biographical) India, Box 21, Box. No. 625 (2), Journal of T. Hodson, August 1, 1831.

faith in Hindoostan, fixed by certain tenets, and guided by an infallible head. They have no ecclesiastical polity, church government, synods, or assemblies." Referring to Hindu schools of learning, he argued that the chief of these were Benares, Nadia, and Ujjain.

> Benares has acquired a higher celebrity for general learning than the other schools. But a Brahmin of Nuddeea or of Calcutta, acknowledges no jurisdiction of a Brahmin at Benares, or of any other Brahmin in Hindoostan. The Brahminical system, from Cape Comorin to Tibet, is purely republican, or rather anarchical. The Brahmins of one province often differ in their creed and customs from those in another. Of the chief Brahmins in the college of Fort William, there are few (not being of the same district) who will give the same account of their faith, or refer to the same sacred books. So much do the opinions of some of those now in the college differ, that they will not so much as worship or *eat* with each other.[25]

Much the same point about the different traditions among pundits was made some years later by James Kennedy, an LMS missionary of more than twenty years' experience of work in the Benares region. "Pundits as a class," he wrote, "keep themselves to one book, or books of the same order, and their knowledge of books outside their favourite circle is very limited."[26] Thus while we know that some Brahmin pundits employed by missionaries, for example Mrtyunjay Vidyalankar, were exponents of Advaita Hinduism,[27] others such as Waidya Natha Iyer, Benjamin Bailey's Tamil pundit, were almost certainly theists and followers of either Siva or Vishnu.[28] Nor was there a guarantee that those who were said to expound the same system of philosophy, or way of salvation, adhered to the same interpretation.

2. Some missionary pundits were drawn from the higher ranks of the non-Brahmin class. Richard Young has already explored the philosophy of Arumuka Pillai (commonly known as "Navalar"), Peter Percival's Tamil-speaking pundit.[29] It was he who became one of the best known and most ag-

25. Claudius Buchanan, *Memoir of the Expediency of an Ecclesiastical Establishment for British India* (London, 1805), pp. 25-26.

26. Kennedy, *Life and Work,* p. 163.

27. Dermot Killingley, *Rammohan Roy in Hindu and Christian Tradition* (Newcastle upon Tyne, 1993), p. 100.

28. Edgar Thurston, *Castes and Tribes of Southern India,* vol. 1 (Madras, 1909), p. 269.

29. R. F. Young and S. Jebanesan, *The Bible Trembled: The Hindu-Christian Controversies of Nineteenth-Century Ceylon* (Vienna, 1995).

gressive exponents of Saiva Siddhanta during the second half of the nineteenth century. While, in his view, salvation was through love of Siva as the supreme being, Elijah Hoole's long-term friend and pundit Govinda Moodley belonged to "the Vaishnava sect." He argued for the supremacy of Vishnu, and according to Hoole, "would sometimes assure me that all the worship offered to any being, was, in effect, received by Vishnu, as supreme, and that the worship of Christians was accepted by him."[30]

Apart from Arumuka Pillai and Govinda Moodley (both Tamil non-Brahmins), Kennedy's teacher and also Carey's first and perhaps most influential pundit were Kayasthas, or pundits belonging to the writer's caste. Throughout the late eighteenth and nineteenth centuries British missionaries were not therefore entirely dependent on Brahmin teachers as linguistic consultants. Clearly another important source of indigenous information was the non-Brahmin pundit; and, at least in the case of Ramram Basu (1757-1813), Carey's first teacher, he was strongly anti-Brahmin.[31] His views, fiercely critical of Brahmins, were reflected especially in the publication of a pamphlet that, according to Kopf's account, attacked the Brahmins, "who were portrayed as conspiring, like the medieval Roman Catholic clergy, to enshroud the world in ignorance and darkness."[32] While there can be little doubt that most Hindu "missionary pundits" were Brahmins, the appointment and use of non-Brahmin pundits raise questions about their influence on missionary thinking. How far, for example, was missionary criticism of the "Brahminical system" encouraged by non-Brahmin Hindus as well as by Christian pundits whom the missionaries employed from time to time?

3. The fact that Hindu pundits employed by missionaries, like Hindu pundits in general, were drawn almost exclusively, if not wholly, from the higher castes, has special significance for missionary views of Hinduism. It meant that, if anything, the pundits were likely to reinforce the convictions of those missionaries who viewed Hindu religion and society from the top down. While missionary preaching and the missionaries' contact with low and outcaste Hindus led them in a direction away from higher-caste culture, an initial and important countervailing influence was that of the Hindu pundit who

30. Hoole, *Madras*, p. 383.

31. For some biographical detail, see S. K. Das, *Sahibs and Munshis: An Account of the College of Fort William* (Calcutta, 1978), pp. 21, 74-75.

32. David Kopf, *British Orientalism and the Bengal Renaissance: The Dynamics of Indian Modernization, 1773-1835* (Berkeley and Los Angeles, 1969), p. 125. See also Richard F. Young's exposition of what is known of his views in "Was Rammohun Roy the 'True Successor' of Ramram Basu? A Critique of Certain Statements by David Kopf," in *Festschrift for Professor Ludo Rocher*, ed. R. Lariviere and R. Solomon (Madras, 1987), pp. 276-93.

for many inexperienced missionaries seemed to symbolize "the real Hinduism" or "the" Hindu tradition. James Vaughan (CMS), a missionary of twenty-one years' experience of work in India among lower- and higher-caste Hindus, was well aware of general differences in their theology and outlook. In his influential book *The Trident, the Crescent, and the Cross,* he drew a distinction between polytheistic and pantheistic beliefs and stated that "without doubt, the Pundits, and learned class, gravitate more towards pantheism than do the common people."[33] If this is in fact the case, then it would help explain why missionaries, influenced by pundits (and in common with many other European commentators), favored pantheism as the essence or kernel of Hinduism. Imbued with elitist assumptions about religion[34] and exposed to high-caste pundits from the very beginning, young missionaries were likely to adopt a high-caste approach and view of the world.

The learning of the vernacular in this context also had important implications for the missionaries' effectiveness in communicating with low-caste and outcaste Hindus, and in understanding their point of view. Describing his life and experience as a missionary in Mysore, William Arthur (WMMS) explained how he had become increasingly concerned with his pundit's Kannada, which he believed was not entirely appropriate for work among the lower classes:

> Feeling that an intimacy with a dialect of the ryots [cultivating classes] was essential to that familiar intercourse which is the surest way to confidence, I determined on acquiring it; and, among other means, requested my munshi to converse in it for an hour each day. To this he stoutly demurred, saying that it was an indignity to a learned Brahman, to be asked to speak the vulgar and broken Kanarese of the ryot; but, on being threatened with having a ryot munshi placed by his side, he first laughed heartedly at the idea of a ryot munshi, and then said he always thought the purpose of education was to gain polish, not vulgarity; but that if I were not content with a Brahman's education, without that of a ryot in addition, why then he could become a ryot, or anything else I pleased.[35]

33. James Vaughan, *The Trident, the Crescent, and the Cross* (London, 1876), p. 65.

34. Coming from Europe where the essence of Christianity was supposed to be preserved in written texts and also, for some missionaries, in the dictates of bishops or ecclesiastical councils, it must have appeared especially important to note what the supposed guardians of Hindu society were saying about the realities of the Hindu faith. Surely the *munshi,* more than most, was entitled to explain its teachings.

35. W. Arthur, *A Mission to the Mysore with Scenes and Facts Illustrative of India, Its People, and Its Religion* (London, 1902), pp. 207-8.

What therefore is striking in all this evidence is the extent to which indigenous knowledge and understanding, and even the way in which missionaries were taught the language, were tied to the pundit's social context and limited horizons. Indigenous knowledge, like European knowledge of "Hinduism," had its limitations. As Kennedy emphasized, the Brahmin pundits sometimes had little knowledge of other high-caste Hindu traditions. Nor could the Brahmin pundit be expected to know (and often did not want to know) about the nature of belief and practice prevalent among the common people. Indeed, the newly arrived missionary asking *munshi* questions about "Hinduism" and Hindu belief was likely to be given an answer reflecting all these limitations.

Further Indicators of the Pundits' Influence

Even if missionaries, writing reports for the consumption of supporters at home, were inclined to minimize the role of assistants, there is direct as well as circumstantial evidence in missionary records of the pundits' influence upon them. This influence was reflected in the pundits' translation of Hindu texts as well as in the role they played in explaining Hindu customs and teaching. As Marshman's son pointed out, William Ward was "but imperfectly acquainted with Sanskrit,"[36] and, in his journal, the latter readily admits that for the more abstract and philosophical parts of his work on the *Hindoos* he relied heavily on the pundits' translations and interpretation.

Secondly, there were discussions with pundits about a whole range of Hindu customs, rituals, and practice. For example, William Carey, who worked for some years in the Mofussil in comparative isolation from the company of other Europeans, was heavily dependent on the advice and comments of his first pundit, Ramram Basu. The relationship between the two men appears to have become increasingly close. Writing to the Baptist Missionary Society (BMS) in October 1793, Carey declared that "Ram Boshoo still keeps close to us; I have had much conversation with him, and find him a very sensible well informed man."[37] Three months later, when building his house at Debhatta in the Sundarbans, the missionary wrote that "though deprived of a personal intercourse with my European friends, I have at least one

36. John Clark Marshman, *The Life and Times of Carey, Marshman, and Ward* (London, 1859), 2:443.

37. Carey to BMS, November, 25, 1793, *Periodical Accounts of the Baptist Missionary Society* 1: 65.

religious friend, and that is Ram Ram Boshoo; he has indeed much timidity, but is a man of very good understanding, and well informed."[38] Ramram was, however, not the only pundit who described and explained different aspects of Hindu thought and practice, and for much of the period of his earlier life in Bengal, Carey learned a great deal from them. It was one of Carey's pundits who explained some of the details of the Charak Puja.[39] It was his pundits who argued that neither hook-swinging nor *sati* was sanctioned in the *shastras,*[40] and it was pundits who agreed to collect all the texts referring to *sati* and who were also involved in his survey of the circumstances and number of women who were burned annually.[41] Carey's understanding of different forms of Hindu worship was also enhanced by pundits who explained, for example, that, once used, the idol was not always thrown into the water.[42]

William Ward's diaries and other writings also provide evidence showing the importance of his pundits as a source of information. He drew heavily on the historical writings of Mrtyunjay, and also refers to the latter's exposition of Hindu ideas of God.[43] Ramnath Vidyavachaspati (another of his pundits at Fort William) discussed with him the extent of Krishna worship throughout Bengal and also provided him with what he claimed was evidence of human sacrifice.[44] Pundits also supplied Ward with further material that, like Carey, he used in his campaigns against a range of Hindu rituals and practices. These included details relating to *sati, thagi,* self-mutilation, infanticide, and the immoral nature of songs and dances performed at religious festivals.[45]

Thirdly, the pundits' influence on *some* missionaries was not confined to comments on the externals of popular practice. As noted in comments on pantheism, also important were their views of God or ultimate reality and their exposition of the different branches of Hindu philosophy. One example of a pundit who was influential in this respect was Govinda Moodley, whose friendship, views, and attitudes had a profound effect on the Methodist Elijah Hoole. In his narrative Hoole not only describes in detail their first meeting at

38. Carey to BMS, February 15, 1794, *Periodical Accounts of the Baptist Missionary Society* 1: 74-75.

39. "Answers to Various Questions Put to Mr. Carey," *Periodical Accounts of the Baptist Missionary Society* 1: 410-11.

40. *Periodical Accounts of the Baptist Missionary Society* 1: 423.

41. William Ward, *Literature and Mythology of the Hindoos,* vol. 4, 3rd ed. (London, 1817-20), pp. 114-15.

42. *Periodical Accounts of the Baptist Missionary Society* 1: 138, 410-11, 416.

43. Ward, *Literature and Mythology,* vol. 1 (1820), p. 30; vol. 3, p. lxxxvii.

44. Ward, *Literature and Mythology,* vol. 1 (1820), p. 288; vol. 4, p. 50.

45. Ward, *Literature and Mythology,* vol. 3 (1820), pp. xxvii, xlix, lv; vol. 4, pp. 50, 101-2.

the temple in Bangalore, but also expresses his feelings at their parting, when in 1838 Moodley traveled all the way from Bangalore to Madras to see his friend embark for the journey home.[46] It appears to have been largely as a result of Moodley's influence and the influence of other pundits he chose to employ that Hoole became one of the greatest early-nineteenth-century missionary enthusiasts for Tamil language and culture and one of the first British Protestant missionaries to draw attention to Tamil bhakti literature.[47]

Carey was also involved in discussion with pundits and others about more abstract Hindu teachings and philosophical ideas. These included Hindu ideas of life and death; the role of imagery in the inner reflection and life of the worshiper; and Hindu ideas of creation, the world, and the natural order. Judging from long entries in his diary, his early notion of Hindu cosmology was formed in discussion with pundits from Nadia.[48]

Ward's understanding of Hindu philosophy and of what he called "Hinduism" was, at the very least, reinforced by the pundits. Reiterating his views in the preface to the 1820 edition of his work, he declared that he had given "a rapid view of the Hindoo sacred code, as a grand system, regular in all its parts, and proposing a defined and magnificent object, nothing less than the yogee absorption into the divine nature, and, to the common people, a gradual advance towards the same state."[49] Ward was one of the earliest British Protestant missionaries, if not the first, to identify and describe what he believed was the core of the Hindu system. Based to a large extent on Shankara's interpretation of Vedanta in the *Vedanta Sara* (a text Ward quoted and had translated as an example of Hindu literature), it was an interpretation of "Hinduism" that he argued was validated in both ancient texts and in contemporary Hinduism. The doctrine, he claimed, was taught in many parts of Hindu writing, "especially in the Durshunus [*sic*]"[50] (often known as the six systems of Hindu philosophy), and was referred to "even in the conversations of the natives at the present time."[51]

Ward's adoption of this model of Hinduism was almost certainly influenced by his pundits. "Respecting the Divine Being," he wrote, "the doctrine of the vedantu [*sic*] seems chiefly to prevail among the best informed of the Hindoo pundits."[52] Two of his own "best informed" pundits were Mrtyunjay

46. Hoole, *Madras,* pp. 161-64.
47. Hoole, *Madras,* pp. 161-64.
48. William Ward, Journal, January 27, 1794. Baptist Historical Society (Oxford).
49. Ward, *Literature and Mythology,* vol. 1 (1820), preface, p. xxxiv. See also vol. 3, p. lxx.
50. Ward, *Literature and Mythology,* vol. 3 (1820), Introductory Remarks, p. ii.
51. Ward, *Literature and Mythology,* vol. 1 (1820), p. xxiv.
52. Ward, *Literature and Mythology,* vol. 2 (1820), p. 119.

Vidyalankar, who, as we have seen, was the head Sanskrit pundit at the College at Fort William, and Ramnath Vidyavachaspati, the second Sanskrit pundit in the same institution.[53] Both were Brahmins,[54] and while the latter's philosophical views are unknown, Mrtyunjay was an Advaita Vedantin.[55]

Lastly, John Robson, the Scottish author of *Hinduism and Its Relations to Christianity,* a book that went through three editions between 1874 and 1905, was also much in debt to pundits for his knowledge and understanding of "the Hindu system." A United Presbyterian Church missionary stationed at Ajmer, Rajasthan, from 1861 to 1872, Robson was a missionary of scholarly inclinations who mixed a great deal among pundits and other high-caste Hindus, as well as among the humbler sections of the population. His consistent and long-term view of Hinduism was not unlike that of William Ward, who believed that the summum bonum of the Hindu religion was Advaita Vedanta, a philosophy that, according to Robson, was "not very far removed from many European pantheistic systems."[56] Referring to his account of Hindu philosophy and its influence, he declared, "I have stated it as I have heard it explained by the more learned pundits and read it in their books of the subject, and the reader may imagine all the different stages of acquaintance with and belief in it down to the utmost ignorance."[57]

Some Complicating Factors

No doubt further research will continue to underline the missionaries' dependence on Hindu comment and pundits' views. However, one important qualification that needs to be kept in mind is the obvious point that the British missionaries had their own presuppositions and agenda and that the questions they asked helped predetermine the kind of answers they received. The parameters of the debate were dictated largely by missionary needs, and by what they were interested in learning. Their notions of "religion" and what aspects of thought and practice they thought important to understand were not necessarily the subjects Hindus themselves would have chosen to discuss

53. Ward, *Literature and Mythology,* vol. 1 (1820), p. 30; vol. 3 (1820), Introductory Remarks, p. lxxxvii; vol. 1 (1820), p. 288; vol. 4 (1820), p. 50. N. S. Bose, *The Indian Awakening and Bengal* (Calcutta, 1960), pp. 195-96.

54. Das, *Sahibs and Munshis,* p. 20.

55. Killingley, *Rammohun Roy,* p. 100.

56. John Robson, *Hinduism and Its Relations to Christianity* (Edinburgh and London, 1893), p. 85.

57. Robson, *Hinduism,* pp. 85-86.

or viewed as important for an understanding of Hindu religious and social life.

Secondly, while there were cases where the missionary's knowledge and understanding of "Hinduism" were greatly enriched as a result of a close and trusting relationship, this should not blind us to situations that were radically different, where the missionary was treated less readily with an honest and straightforward opinion. The relationship between some missionaries and pundits was clearly complex, and in some cases pundits may have felt pressure to deliberately misrepresent the facts, withhold information, or tell their "pupils" whatever they seemed to want to hear.

One of these undoubtedly more complex situations arose over the issue of Christian conversion. Missionary records are full of accounts of the way in which missionaries attempted to confront and convert their teachers.[58] They also contain evidence of the way in which pundits attempted to hose down the issue, often in the politest and least confrontational manner. But even if they avoided a response on the first occasion, the issue was still there as an undertone, and as a continuing part of the context in which the dialogue between missionary and pundit was taking place. One pundit strategy was noted by Rev. Warth (CMS), who declared that whenever he conversed upon religious topics or, in other words, attempted to convince his pundit of "the excellence" of the gospel scheme, his teacher became sleepy, in a way in "which I have observed in others."[59] Another strategy was to say nothing, or to pretend to agree. Thus, according to Rev. Richard Allnutt (CMS), Hindu *munshis* employed by the CMS, feeling threatened as a result of conversions to Christianity in the Tinnevelly district, bound themselves "with an oath before their gods" not to be persuaded by missionary arguments to become Christians. "Their determination," wrote Allnutt, "is to assent to everything and believe nothing."[60] Another strategy was to laugh (and then be accused of not taking religion seriously), to point to obstacles, or even to say that while Christianity is not for me, later generations of my family might be more interested in conversion.[61] Another perhaps more obvious reaction designed to resist pressure was not only to oppose Christianity, but to try to focus the missionary's attention on what he or she might think were the more commendable aspects of Hindu faith and practice; or even concoct an interpreta-

58. *Missionary Register* 24 (1837): 464; Kennedy, *Life and Work,* p. 32; *Harvest Field* 6 (1885): 105-6; Wardlaw, *Memoir of the Late Rev. W. H. Drew,* p. 56; M. R. Allnutt, *A Record of Sixty-Nine Years' Ministry: Memoirs of Richard Lea Allnutt* (London, 1911), p. 52.

59. *Missionary Register* 24 (1837): 464.

60. Allnutt, *A Record,* p. 52.

61. *Harvest Field* 6 (1885): 105-6.

tion of Hindu custom that would make it appear more like some acceptable aspect of Christianity.[62] In some circumstances, therefore, there was probably pressure to misrepresent. Indeed, a frank and open confession of what one really believed or how one felt, in front of a missionary sahib (especially an employer), could be difficult. Thus, according to Murray Mitchell, Krishna Sastri, an able pundit "much employed" by the mission, gave a series of lectures on "the relative claims of Hinduism and Christianity"; but later when the missionaries arrived, he abstained from attacking Christianity.[63]

But not all reactions were devious or completely negative. Over time some pundits became increasingly attracted to Christianity, thought about conversion, and in some comparatively rare cases were baptized.[64] This process of gradual rapprochement with Christianity inevitably raised in-depth questions not only about Christianity, but also about the nature of Hindu beliefs and practice.[65] Thus, in conversing with pundits who were questioning their own faith, or contemplating conversion, the missionaries themselves were almost invariably increasing their knowledge and understanding of the pundits' religious background.

The effect of what the missionaries learned from pundits on their overall

62. This may be one of the considerations that helps to explain why Robert Noble's pundit attempted to "Christianize" his depiction of Hindu practice. He claimed that during the great "annual ablutions" taking place by the sea, the people washed their sins away, not by bathing, but by entering the temple and offering prayers for "pardon of their sins," and secondly, that they used certain prescribed forms of prayer *understood by them and many of the people.* However, Noble, who had already studied Telugu, made his own independent inquiries, and as a result, was given a very different explanation. The Brahmins and "other respectable natives" he consulted declared, "without a single exception," that the people performed their ablutions not to cleanse themselves before going to the temple, but to wash away their sins. Furthermore, not even the Brahmins could enlighten the missionary on the meaning of the prayers involved. While Noble suggests that this episode demonstrated the unreliability of English-speaking pundits, this conclusion is not inconsistent with the idea that the pundit was attempting to deflect criticism of Hindu practice by making it appear more like Protestant Christianity. John Noble, *A Memoir of the Rev. Robert Thurlington Noble, B.A.* (London, 1867), p. 138.

63. J. Murray Mitchell, *In Western India: Recollections of My Early Missionary Life* (Edinburgh, 1899), p. 113.

64. A well-known example is Carey's first pundit, Ramram Basu, who, while attracted to Christianity, was never baptized. For the baptism of pundits see Ashcroft, *Our Rajputana Mission,* p. 31; Cheriyan, *The Malabar Syrians,* p. 179; *India's Women,* May 1899, p. 108; Irene H. Barnes, *Behind the Pardah* (London, 1897), p. 74; *Missionary Notices* 11 (1845-47): 80.

65. For a detailed account of the discussions that arose between Rev. W. Smith and his *munshi* ("an eminent pundit") in Benares in the 1860s, see *Church Missionary Record,* n.s., 13 (1868): 369-70.

evaluation or estimation of Hinduism is another issue that cannot be fully discussed in a short paper such as this. We know that the more Carey knew of Indian "paganism" (as he called it), the more he disliked it.[66] But sometimes the experience of working with pundits had a very different effect; and, ironically, while some pundits were attracted by Christian teachings, some missionaries were attracted by what they discovered in Hindu tradition. The evangelist was evangelized, and dedicated a part of his time and effort in trying to convince the British public, and especially people in missionary circles, that Hindu thought and practice were not always as evil or as bad as had been represented.

Two outstanding examples of this more sympathetic approach, encouraged through the encounter with Hindu pundits, are reflected in the spiritual journey and outlook of Elijah Hoole and J. Mackenzie Cobban, both Methodists, and both excited by their discoveries in Tamil literature. Having been inducted into the mysteries of Saivism and Saiva Siddhantha through the agency of his pundits, Hoole, writing in his book published in 1844, avowed that "there are however, some devotional compositions of his [Siva's] worshippers, in which, addressing Siven as the Supreme, they have attained to the truly sublime; and, in the most appropriate language, have displayed a correctness of sentiment and ardency of devotion, which we cannot but admire."[67]

More than forty years later, when conservative views were still widely prevalent in missionary society circles, Mackenzie Cobban greatly shocked the chairman of his panel at a conference in London by his "concessions" to Hinduism. Undaunted by the fact that his address had been cut short, and referring to Tamil literature in a subsequent session, Cobban declared that "I tell you I have met with expressions of truth yonder in those heathen books that have surprised me, but they have also delighted me, because they have given me the conviction that God has been in the country before I came. The Spirit of God has been speaking somehow, whether by fragments of prophecy or revelation I cannot tell, and I do not care."[68] Rejected by at least some of his own, Cobban was celebrated in India. "The title of Virama was conferred upon him by pundits of the Tamil country," wrote the editor of the *Madras Christian College Magazine,* "and though no particulars of how and when it was conferred have come down to us, there appears to be no reason for disputing the accuracy of the statement."[69]

66. Oddie, *Imagined Hinduism.*

67. Hoole, *Madras,* p. 380.

68. James Johnston, ed., *Report of the Centenary Conference on the Protestant Missions of the World* (London, 1888), pp. 89, 97-98.

69. *Madras Christian College Magazine* 9 (1891): 278.

Conclusion

While missionaries were drawn from a variety of different backgrounds and had different degrees of knowledge of Hinduism, the pundits also varied considerably in what they knew and felt was central in their religious or philosophical system. If some of them encouraged their missionary pupils to think of Advaita Vedanta as the essence of Hindu faith, others, such as Hoole's pundit, stressed the overriding importance of bhakti or loving devotion to a deity. As we have seen, the pundits were, possibly without exception, drawn from among the Brahmin or dominant non-Brahmin castes, and their way of viewing reality tended to emerge not from the struggles of the common people, but from the more privileged environment of upper-caste society. Their relationship with missionaries produced an interpersonal dynamic that also varied greatly and that, as in the case of William Carey, could affect the way some individual missionaries perceived or understood the details of Hindu thought or practice.

Research on the nature and extent of the pundits' influence on missionary knowledge and interpretations of Hinduism is difficult because of the scattered nature and scarcity of research material. Only in some cases do we know the names of the pundits involved, and even more rarely the detailed nature of the conversations that took place. While Carey, Ward, Hoole, Robson, and a few others indicate in some detail something of the nature and impact of their discussions with pundits, this kind of comment is rare and seldom appears even in missionary archival records. Furthermore, missionaries, like authors and commentators generally, were probably not immune from the temptation to claim credit for other people's ideas; and this suggests that, in some cases, they may have been unwilling to acknowledge the pundit as the real source of their ideas or information. However, as we have argued, there is clear evidence of widespread and sometimes long-term missionary contact with pundits. This suggests that the pundits' influence on the missionaries' knowledge of details of Hindu belief and practice extended further than the cases cited in this paper.

But did the pundits' influence go beyond providing missionaries with the details of Hindu belief and practice? What of the pundits' influence on the missionaries' overall model of Hinduism? Here there are at least three major considerations. Firstly, there is the role of the missionaries' preknowledge or presuppositions. For various reasons discussed elsewhere, it is likely that when he became involved with pundits, William Ward was, for example, already predisposed to interpret Hinduism as Brahminism, or a Brahmin system. This was not an interpretation likely to be disputed by his Brahmin pundits who espoused similar ideas. Hence the role of pundits in this instance, and possibly in Robson's and Vaughan's case, was to reaffirm the missionary's preexisting views. Robson, however, insists that the pundits' verdict was the deciding factor in the formation of his interpretation, and the reader is left with the impression that had the pundits' model of Hinduism been different, then the missionary may also have had a different view.

Secondly, it appears that on some occasions the missionaries' general interpretation was *modified* through contact with pundits. Indeed, both Hoole and Cobban, missionaries working in South India, were surprised and excited by what they found. Having in all likelihood inherited the view of Hinduism as a Brahminical intellectual system involving beliefs and outward practice, Hoole was delighted to discover, through his pundit, a religion of the heart, of the love of God through Vishnu or Siva. Cobban, for his part, having found much that was, for him, new in bhakti literature, began to draw distinctions between different traditions and to revise his notion of Hinduism as a unified and coherent whole.[70]

However, these cases of changing interpretation, partly or wholly through the pundit's influence, are almost certainly exceptional. Some missionaries were probably like Peter Percival, who, in spite of a long-term and close association with his pundit, appears to have remained largely untouched by his pundit's very different views of the nature and coherence of Indian religion.[71] Indeed, a missionary's changing paradigm or overview of Hinduism may have had little to do with his or her pundit. There were other influences and factors, including observation and experience, which sometimes proved more important in affecting the missionary's basic views and understanding. While, for example, the scholarly John Murray Mitchell appears to have had a long record of contact and discussion with pundits, one of the most trans-

70. *Madras Christian College Magazine* 7 (1889): 196-210.

71. Percival, author of *The Land of the Veda,* published in 1854, and highly regarded as a Tamil scholar, had previously spent six years with his pundit, Arumuka Navalar, revising the Tamil Bible. The pundit, while continuing his work of translation and maintaining a close and friendly relationship with Percival, became increasingly active and well known as the leading advocate of Saiva Siddhanta. See Young and Jebanesan, *The Bible Trembled,* pp. 108-26. However, in spite of Percival's close and lengthy period of collaboration with Ceylon's most celebrated exponent of the system, and notwithstanding the findings of more recent scholars (who emphasize the movement's doctrine of the continued separation of God and the soul in the state of liberation), he managed to squeeze his reference to Saiva Siddhanta into his preexisting monistic or Vedantic model. *The Land of the Veda* (London, 1854), pp. 204-5. For comments on Saiva Siddhanta, see especially Fred Clothey, "Tamil Religions," in *The Encyclopedia of Religion,* ed. M. Eliade (New York and London, 1987), and T. M. P. Mahadevan, ed., *Saiva Siddhanta* (Madras, 1960), pp. 287-88.

forming moments of his life was when he mixed with Hindu pilgrims in western India and, at least partly as a result, became convinced that bhakti was the essence of Hinduism.[72] In some cases, contact with the Hindu pundit was a significant event in the missionary's journey of discovery and understanding, but additional factors, presuppositions, context, observation and experience, and other influences all played a part in missionary constructions of Hindu religion.

72. For an account of Mitchell's visits to Pandharpur and of the devotional poetry of Tukaram, see Mitchell, *In Western India,* pp. 230-36, and *The Indian Antiquary* 12 (1884). For his references to bhakti, see also National Library of Scotland (Edinburgh), MS 7826, Folio 114, Mitchell to Smith, July 22-24, 1882.

CHAPTER 9

Proselytism in the History of Christianity in India

MICHAEL BERGUNDER

Preliminary Note

Up to recent times in the history of Christianity in India, there have been numerous cases in which significant numbers of Christians have jointly changed their church affiliation. However, this phenomenon — today usually covered by the term "proselytism"[1] — has long been neglected,[2] probably because of the strong denominationalism that pervades Indian church historiography. For a realistic and adequate discussion of proselytism within Indian Christianity, it is indispensable to overcome popular "sheep-stealing" polemics based on stereotypes; one needs to look at the complex historical dimension of this phenomenon, which the following essay attempts to do. A historical overview of the problem is first given, using specific case studies, followed by further reflections on how a fruitful analysis could be made.

1. "Proselytism" is a broad term that is often also used in the sense of "forced" conversion to Christianity; see, e.g., R. E. Frykenberg, "Introduction: Dealing with Contested Definitions and Controversial Perspectives," in *Christians and Missionaries in India: Cross-Cultural Communication since 1500,* ed. R. E. Frykenberg (Grand Rapids, 2003), pp. 17ff. In the present essay, the term refers to its narrower theological meaning.

2. But see K. Baago, "'Sheepstealing' in the 19th Century," *Bulletin of the Church History Association of India,* November 1966, pp. 17ff.; H. Grafe, *The History of Christianity in Tamilnadu from 1800 to 1975* (Erlangen, 1990), pp. 113ff.

Historical Overview

Proselytism between Orthodox and Catholic Christians

The history of Christian proselytism began in sixteenth-century India during the royal patronage *(Padroado)* of the Portuguese colonial power when Catholic missionaries entered the country. The missionaries soon paid attention to the old established Orthodox churches on India's West Coast, which traced their roots back to the apostle Thomas and were affiliated to the East Syrian (Nestorian) patriarchate of Babylon. Certainly, there were some individual East Syrian Indian Christians who joined the Catholic Church during the sixteenth century, but this was apparently a marginal phenomenon.[3] Of more serious consequences were the controversial but successful efforts of the Catholic side to enforce a merger and gradual Latinization of the East Syrian Indian church. In that regard, it was of some importance that the East Syrian mother church itself had experienced a split in 1553; as a result, a rival patriarch was established who brought his faction into union with the Catholic Church (becoming the Chaldean church of the East Syrian rite). It was this patriarch who succeeded in sending new bishops to the Indian branch church.[4] With a united bishop as its head, the East Syrian Indian church became Rome-friendly and even more susceptible to efforts of Latinization by the Goanese archbishops, whose aim was not a union in the traditional sense but a complete Latinization of the Indian East-Syrians. When in 1597 the Chaldean bishop Mar Abraham died after a long term in office, the Portuguese archbishop of Goa, Alexis de Menezes, saw his chance. In 1599, he staged the so-called Synod of Diamper, at which the East Syrian Indian church was put under direct control of the Portuguese *Padroado* and a radical Latinization of its rites and teachings was demanded.[5]

In the following decades, however, a virulent opposition arose against this development, and in 1648/49 a representative of the anti-Catholic resistance group wrote letters to several Oriental patriarchs, asking them to send an Or-

3. However, up till now this view is rejected by the Catholics of Kerala who belong to the Latin rite. See A. M. Mundadan, *History of Christianity in India,* vol. 1, *From the Beginning up to the Middle of the Sixteenth Century (up to 1542)* (Bangalore, 1984), pp. 348ff.; G. Menachery, ed., *The St. Thomas Christian Encyclopedia of India,* 2 vols. (Trichur, 1973), 2:58ff.

4. J. Thekkedath, *History of Christianity in India,* vol. 2, *From the Middle of the Sixteenth to the End of the Seventeenth Century (1542-1700)* (Bangalore, 1982), pp. 34ff.

5. S. Neill, *A History of Christianity in India: The Beginnings to 1707* (Cambridge, 1984), pp. 208ff.; Thekkedath, *History,* pp. 64ff.

thodox bishop for the church. Indeed, the request was granted, and after diverse complications the West Syrian bishop Mar Gregorius made it to India in 1665 and was recognized by a large number of congregations. Thereby, after a time of merger with the Catholic Church, many East Syrians became Orthodox West Syrians and also gradually took up most of the corresponding new rites. In the end, however, even though the majority of the East Syrians stayed within the Catholic Church, additional Latinization of a radical kind was prevented. In time, even a reintroduction or revival of the old East Syrian rite was promoted; this development led to the reestablishment of a (united) East Syrian (now called Syro-Malabar) Indian hierarchy in 1923.[6] Then, at the beginning of the twentieth century, among the Orthodox Indian West-Syrians, a split occurred that led to lengthy and paralyzing conflicts within the church. In reaction, a strong pro-Catholic union movement emerged; as a result, the West Syrian Orthodox bishop Mar Ivanios converted to Catholicism in 1930, hoping to become the metropolitan of a newly founded Syro-Malankar Church (in union with the Catholic Church), the rite of which was based on West Syrian Indian traditions.[7]

On the other hand, there were also significant transfer movements from Catholic to Orthodox churches, though in most cases these were only temporary.[8] In 1887, A. F. X. Alvarez (1837-95), probably an excommunicated Brahmin Catholic and ex-seminarian from Goa, started to attract a following among Catholics in Sri Lanka and present-day Tamil Nadu. He was able to establish good relations with the West Syrian Indian church, and in 1888 the main bishop of this church even consecrated him as a metropolitan of his own "Independent Catholic Church of Ceylon, Goa and India." From then on, he called himself Mar Julius. Afterward, the Indian West Syrian church repeatedly referred to its communion with this church as proof of its own strong missionary activism. The new sister church, which at times had several thousand members, did not survive the death of Alvarez in 1895.

6. See A. M. Mundadan, *Indian Christians: A Search for Identity and Struggle for Autonomy* (Bangalore, 1984), pp. 50ff.

7. Mundadan, *Indian Christians*, pp. 109ff.; Menachery, *Encyclopedia*, 2:71ff.

8. C. M. Agur, *Church History of Travancore* (Madras, 1903), pp. 367, 404ff.; J. A. Otto, "Mission und Kaste in Südindien," *Zeitschrift für Missionswissenschaft und Religionswissenschaft* 4 (1941): 116f.; P. F. Anson, *Bishops at Large* (London, 1964), pp. 105ff., 121, 132ff.; S. B. Kaufmann [Bayly], "Popular Christianity, Caste and Hindu Society in South India, 1800-1915" (Ph.D. diss., University of Cambridge, 1979), pp. 257f., 366ff.; Mar Aprem, *The Chaldean Syrian Church of the East* (Delhi, 1983), p. 39; S. Bayly, *Saints, Goddesses, and Kings: Muslims and Christians in South Indian Society, 1700-1900* (Cambridge, 1989), pp. 316ff., 449ff.

From Tiruchchirappalli (Trichy), we find another unusual case. In the 1930s Catholic Vellalar Christians separated themselves temporarily from their church because of caste quarrels and employed Orthodox West Syrian Indian priests from Kerala to conduct their worship services. In this connection, L. M. Soares should also be mentioned. Soares, originally from Goa, was nearly illiterate. For a time, he had worked as Alvarez's coworker, and like him he had been excommunicated from the Catholic Church. In 1889, he succeeded in being consecrated as bishop of the Chaldean Syrian Church of the East, which has its center around Trichur in Kerala. This church resulted from a schism in the Catholic United Indian East-Syrian Church and claims to continue the pre-Portuguese East Syrian Nestorian tradition as an independent Orthodox church. Soares, with the bishop's name Mar Basilius, had numerous adherents among Tamil Catholics; in 1900, he even became the head of the entire East Syrian splinter church. After his death in 1903, however, Tamil followers faded away and returned to the Catholic Church.

Proselytism between Orthodox and Protestant Christians

In 1813, the Church Missionary Society (CMS), which was supported by Anglican evangelicals, started to work with the West Syrian Indian church.[9] Their assistance consisted of teaching the prospective clergy at a theological seminary, translating the Bible into Malayalam, and pushing for liturgical reform. Cooperation with the CMS was decidedly welcomed by the head of the Indian West Syrians, because he expected advantages from the patronage of a Western mission society. For their part, the missionaries believed that certain teachings and rites they had found were indeed offensive, but could be attributed to long-standing Catholic influence and could be eradicated without detriment to the identity of this Orthodox church. Apart from the abolition of celibacy, which was achieved without major opposition, most of the suggested changes concerned the core Orthodox heritage. Over time, the Indian side became increasingly aware that the missionary reform program would result in Protestantization. After more than twenty years, cooperation between the Orthodox church and the CMS ended in open conflict and eventual separation. The CMS stayed in Kerala and decided to start a new mission to non-Christians. The first members of this new work, however, were former West Syrian Indian Christians who had left their mother church to join the CMS,

9. P. Verghese, ed., *Die syrischen Kirchen in Indien* (Stuttgart, 1974), pp. 85ff.; C. B. Firth, *An Introduction to Indian Church History,* rev. ed. (Madras, 1976), pp. 165ff.

sometimes even as entire congregations. Many of them later occupied leading positions in the new CMS mission. In 1889, as a delayed effect of this conflict, a large reform group within the West Syrian Indian church, heavily influenced by the teachings of Anglican missionaries, caused a major split that formed the independent Mar Thoma church. Later on, many other Protestant missions also started working in Kerala with the assistance of former West Syrian Indian Christians: the Plymouth Brethren, the Salvation Army, and the Pentecostal movement, among others. It is noteworthy, however, that none of the available sources report major transfers from Protestantism to Indian Orthodoxy.

Proselytism between Catholic and Protestant Christians

In many cases, Protestant missions started their work in India with Catholic proselytes. Often, the first Indian Protestant catechists had already worked in the same capacity within the Catholic Church. When the first regular Protestant missionary endeavor, the Lutheran Tranquebar Mission, began its work in the Tamil region, many of the newly won members, especially from the Thanjavur area, which had been a center of the old Jesuit Madurai Mission, came from the Catholic Church (e.g., 40 percent in 1727/28).[10] The first Indian catechist of the Tranquebar Mission was a former Catholic, and out of the first three Indian pastors of the mission, two came from originally Catholic families. The first half of the nineteenth century, when Catholic missions were in a massive crisis and many new Protestant mission societies were starting to work in India, was a peak period of proselytism.[11] When the CMS missionary James Hough stayed at Palayankottai from 1816 till 1821 to revive the old mission of the Society for Promoting Christian Knowledge, every sixth new member was a former Catholic.[12] Charles Mead, who worked for the LMS in south

10. H. Grafe, "The Relation between the Tranquebar Lutherans and the Tanjore Catholics in the First Half of the 18th Century," *Indian Church History Review* 1 (1967): 41ff.; A. Meersmann, "The Catholic Church in Tranquebar and Tanjore during the Formative Years of the Lutheran Mission," *Indian Church History Review* 1 (1967): 93ff.

11. For an assessment of this period by Catholic mission historians, see, e.g., A. Huonder, *Der einheimische Klerus in den Heidenländern* (Freiburg, 1909), pp. 71ff.; J. A. Otto, *Gründung der neuen Jesuitenmission durch General Pater Philipp Roothaan* (Freiburg, 1961), pp. 253ff.

12. J. Hough, *A Reply to the Letters of the Abbe Dubois on the State of Christianity in India* (London, 1824), pp. 197f. The figures given are probably too low, because Hough reports elsewhere that, in 1826, 59 non-Christians were baptized and 73 persons were admitted from other churches (mainly Catholics; see Baago, "Sheepstealing," p. 21 n. 17). Cf. also the mission work of Rhenius among Catholics in Madras, 1815-20 (Baago, p. 21).

Tranvancore from 1818 to 1852, systematically targeted Catholic Christians, and the many complaints by local Catholic priests to their bishop in Cochin prove that he was quite successful.[13] The Society for the Propagation of the Gospel (SPG) also had no objection to a concerted missionary effort among Catholics. C. S. Kohlhoff, for example, worked a long time in Irangalur (near Trichy), where the largest part of his congregation was recruited from Catholic Christians in the nearby villages.[14] In the American Madurai Mission, founded in 1836, the majority of all families that were accepted as new members came from the Catholic Church;[15] as a rule, they received new baptism.[16] Out of its first 100 Indian workers, 36 came from Catholic families (eleven of the fathers of these families had already been Catholic catechists), besides 24 with a Protestant and 40 with a Hindu background.[17] The Lutheran Leipzig Mission, which assumed control of the Tranquebar Mission in the 1840s, also had quite a few new members who came from the Catholic Church (see table). Apart from numerous new members in the area around Putukottai,[18] Catholic Maravars went over to the Leipzig Mission in especially great numbers.[19] This trend continued up to the twentieth century.[20]

When Catholic missionary work regained momentum in the second half of the nineteenth century, efforts were made to reverse the loss of members to

13. Agur, *Church History of Travancore,* pp. 820ff. Cf. also the activities of Samuel Flavel, an Indian LMS evangelist who aggressively proselytized among Catholics in Bangalore. See S. Laidler and J. W. Massie, *Religion in India: A Voice Directed to Christian Churches for Millions in the East* (London, 1827), pp. 24ff.; quoted by Baago, "Sheep-stealing," pp. 20-21.

14. J. A. Sharrock, *South Indian Missions: Glimpses into the Lives and Customs of the Tamil People* (Westminster, 1910), pp. 283ff.; H. P. Thompson, *Into All Lands: The History of the Society for the Propagation of the Gospel in Foreign Parts, 1701-1900* (London, 1951), p. 187.

15. J. S. Chandler, *Seventy-Five Years in the Madura Mission* (Madurai, n.d.), pp. 107, 221.

16. Chandler, *Seventy-Five Years,* p. 205. Rebaptism by LMS missionaries is also explicitly mentioned. See Laidler and Massie, *Religion in India,* p. 267, quoted by Baago, "Sheepstealing," p. 21. In most Protestant mission societies, except those that only accepted adult baptism, Catholics were not rebaptized. But, *sub conditione,* Catholics often baptized Protestant proselytes (Grafe, *History,* p. 116).

17. Chandler, *Seventy-Five Years,* pp. 97f.

18. R. Handmann, *Die Evangelisch-Lutherische Tamulen-Mission in der Zeit ihrer Neubegründung* (Leipzig, 1903), pp. 211ff.

19. Handmann, *Tamulen-Mission,* pp. 242f., 453.

20. P. Fleisch, *Hundert Jahre lutherische Mission* (Leipzig, 1936), pp. 227, 386f. See also Grafe, *History,* p. 118 n. 147, which reports that a large number of Catholic Dalits joined the Leipzig Mission in 1934.

the Protestants. Though statistics are generally unreliable, most reports give the impression that many proselytes indeed returned to the Catholic fold.[21] Catholic missionaries, moreover, did not hesitate to work systematically among Protestants with a non-Catholic background. From the middle of the nineteenth century we have reports from the area around Palayankottai, where the SPG and CMS were active, which tell us that entire Protestant villages became Catholic.[22] Many Protestants from the Krishnanagar CMS mission in Bengal and from the Punjab mission of the United Presbyterian Church went over to the Catholic Church.[23] Rather spectacular were the events in Chota Nagpur where Jesuits began to work in 1869. From the Lutheran Gossner Mission, which had worked in the area for decades, numerous catechists with their congregations joined the Jesuits and laid the foundation for further missionary work.[24] In 1950 in Nagaland, the Catholic Church started its work with three former Baptist families.[25]

Proselytism of Protestants by Protestants

Many of the major Protestant mission societies tried to coordinate their activities in India by acting on the principle of "comity," by which each mission was allotted certain territories. However, against this strong intra-Protestant ecumenical impetus, which even influenced the foundation of the Church of South India (CSI) in 1948,[26] one finds many cases of clear-cut proselytism. Most spectacular are the complex conflicts between Anglicans and Lutherans in the Tamil region. Here, in the first half of the nineteenth century, several Lutheran missionaries, most of them from the Tranquebar Mission, had started to work on behalf of Anglican mission societies (SPG and CMS), which lacked sufficient personnel of their own. As soon, however, as the Anglicans had enough personnel, they established their own administrative

21. See, e.g., Chandler, *Seventy-Five Years,* pp. 107, 217; Fleisch, *Hundert Jahre,* pp. 226f.

22. Otto, *Gründung,* pp. 335ff.

23. Baago, "Sheepstealing," p. 33; D. B. Forrester, *Caste and Christianity: Attitudes and Policies on Caste of Anglo-Saxon Protestant Missions in India* (London and Dublin, 1980), pp. 88ff.; F. Stock and E. Stock, *People Movements in the Punjab: With Special Reference to the United Presbyterian Church* (Pasadena, 1975), pp. 102, 314ff.

24. J. Richter, *Indische Missionsgeschichte,* 2nd ed. (Gütersloh, 1924), pp. 320ff.; F. J. Bowen, *Father Constant Lievens, S.J.* (St. Louis, 1936); Baago, "Sheepstealing," pp. 34f.

25. F. S. Downs, *History of Christianity in India,* vol. 5, pt. 5, *North East India in the Nineteenth and Twentieth Centuries* (Bangalore, 1992), pp. 123f., 130f.

26. Firth, *Introduction,* pp. 233ff.

structure; simultaneously, the "Lutheran" mission stations that had to that time enjoyed a great amount of freedom were gradually Anglicanized and put under episcopal jurisdiction. This development did not occur without strong opposition, especially from C. T. E. Rhenius, who had worked for the CMS in Palayankottai for many years. In 1835, Rhenius stopped collaborating with the Anglicans and gathered a considerable number of his congregation — though the majority remained faithful to the CMS — into an independent church for which he received support from German Lutherans. Only the early death of Rhenius in 1838 prevented a permanent split.[27] Rhenius's conflict became prototypical for further quarrels provoked by the Leipzig Mission, which, seeing itself as the legitimate heir of the Tranquebar Mission, demanded that all Anglican mission stations founded by Lutheran missionaries be handed back to its control. Equipped with this self-understanding, the Leipzig Mission systematically proselytized among Christians of the Anglican mission stations that formerly belonged to Lutheran missionaries, especially in Madras,[28] Thanjavur,[29] Coimbatore,[30] and Manikramam.[31]

Nevertheless, it was not only the Leipzig Mission that promoted intra-Protestant proselytism. Another Lutheran mission, the Missouri Evangelical Lutheran India Mission (MELIM), started its substantial mission work at the southern tip of India with former members and workers of the LMS in 1907.[32] And, from the High Church SPG it is known that it did not always comply with comity agreements:[33] it, too, targeted Lutheran Christians.[34] Moreover, in Chota Nagpur the SPG started its work by taking into its ranks three veteran missionaries from the Gossner Mission. The three had left their home organization in protest, taking with them several thousand Lutheran Christians.[35] When new evangelical missions came to India at the end of the nine-

27. Handmann, *Tamulen-Mission,* pp. 429ff.; J. Aargaard, *Mission-Konfession-Kirche* (Lund, 1967), pp. 354ff.; S. Neill, *A History of Christianity in India: 1707-1858* (Cambridge, 1985), pp. 222ff., 454f.

28. Handmann, *Tamulen-Mission,* pp. 196ff.

29. Handmann, *Tamulen-Mission,* pp. 245ff.; G. A. Oddie, *Hindu and Christian in South-East India* (London, 1991), pp. 175f.

30. Handmann, *Tamulen-Mission,* pp. 278ff.; Baago, "Sheepstealing," pp. 28ff., concerning conflict with the congregationalist LMS.

31. Handmann, *Tamulen-Mission,* p. 260.

32. J. W. Pickett, *Christian Mass Movements in India* (New York, 1933), pp. 323ff.; H. M. Zorn, "Relations between the Missouri Lutheran and the London Missionary Society," *Indian Church History Review* 1 (1967): 1ff.

33. Chandler, *Seventy-Five Years,* p. 222; Richter, *Indische Missionsgeschichte,* p. 247.

34. Handmann, *Tamulen-Mission,* p. 290; Baago, "Sheepstealing," p. 23 n. 19.

35. Thompson, *Into All Lands,* 349ff.; Baago, "Sheepstealing," pp. 23f.

teenth century, they normally ignored all territorial agreements between the established Protestant mission societies and practiced an overt proselytism (e.g., the Salvation Army and Plymouth Brethren).[36] In the twentieth century, it was the Pentecostal movement that enjoyed the largest share of intra-Protestant proselytism.[37] Even the CSI was not immune to the recurrence of proselytism in Kerala when the newly independent Anglican Church of India (ACI) split from it in 1966 under the instigation of American Carl MacIntire of the evangelical International Council of Christian Churches.[38]

Reasons for Proselytism

Before analyzing reasons for proselytism in the Indian context, it should be stated that, at least with regard to many Protestant mission societies, a strong ecumenical tendency could be observed already in the nineteenth century, which eventually resulted in the formation of two major church unions (the CSI and Church of North India). These unions were also made possible because, in contrast to Catholics, the confessional or denominational allegiance among Indian Protestants was never very strong.[39] This may explain, however, why Indian Protestants were relatively uninhibited about changing their church affiliations. Still, it does not adequately explain conscious and deliberate proselytism among certain Christian groups. In the following section, the complex ensemble of differing motivations behind this variety of proselytism will be examined. For pragmatic reasons, external and internal aspects will be differentiated, i.e., between missionaries and local communities, in order to clarify the agency of Indian Christians within the processes of proselytism.

36. Richter, *Indische Missionsgeschichte*, p. 241; Pickett, *Mass Movements*, pp. 323ff.; J. W. Gladstone, *Protestant Christianity and People's Movements in Kerala: A Study of Christian Mass Movements in Relation to Neo-Hindu Socio-Religious Movements in Kerala, 1850-1936* (Trivandrum, 1984), pp. 135f.

37. M. Bergunder, *Die südindische Pfingstbewegung im 20. Jahrhundert* (Frankfurt, 1999), pp. 280ff., 310.

38. Verghese, *Die syrischen Kirchen*, pp. 144f.; S. Vattappara, *The Great Anglican Tradition* (Kottayam, 1994); J. W. Gladstone, ed., *United to Unite: A History of the Church of South India, 1947-1997* (Chennai, 1997), pp. 280f. The founder of the ACI, V. J. Stephen, was consecrated as bishop by J. P. Dees from the Anglican Orthodox Church (Statesville, South Carolina).

39. L. Caplan, "Class and Christianity in South India," *Modern Asian Studies* 14 (1980): 650ff.

External Aspects

Western Confessionalism and Denominationalism

In most cases, Western mission societies were formed along confessional or denominational lines; accordingly, the European and North American ecclesiastical front lines were transferred to India. The strong anti-Catholic feeling of resentment in the Lutheran Tranquebar Mission did not originate in India but in German Lutheranism. The renewal of the Catholic Church in Europe in the nineteenth century, which led to a steady increase of mission work in India, was accompanied by an explicit anti-Protestant thrust that also showed its effects in India. That the Anglican High Church SPG did not stick to the agreed mission territories surely had something to do with its ties to the Oxford Movement and its strong reservations about the evangelical revivalism that had shaped many Western mission societies.[40] Similarly, the Leipzig Mission and the MELIM were founded as decidedly Lutheran-confessionalist mission societies, and their missionaries often had such a narrow understanding of Christian teachings that they questioned the orthodoxy of all other Christian churches. Ordinarily, they did not see any problem at all with their proselytizing activities.

Pressure on Mission Societies to Succeed

The mission societies in India were under enormous pressure to report successful conversions back home; only then could they hope to receive sufficient donations to continue their work abroad. Moreover, in many cases the missionaries themselves had come to India with very high expectations and noble ideals, only to become disillusioned after realizing that the conversion of "the heathen" had proven largely unsuccessful, at least in the beginning. This disillusionment often led to a kind of conversion pragmatism that did not hesitate to practice deliberate proselytism. As a rule, in such a situation membership applications from individual Christians or entire congregations of other mission societies were hardly ever refused. Even the Orthodox churches were affected by that pressure, which is seen in their consecration of Catholic priests to increase their numbers.

40. Neill, *History of Christianity: 1707-1858*, pp. 395f.

"Sheep-Stealing" Polemics

For centuries, cases of proselytism in the history of Indian Christianity have been defended by one and the same stereotypical polemic. The aggrieved party normally accuses the other side of luring away the members of their congregations by the offer of material incentives. For example, a Jesuit of the Madurai Mission in the South wrote in 1727: "Would to God that we could equally avert the ruin which threatens us from the Danish heretics, settled at Trancambadi [*sic*]. They have sent their catechists with their pockets well supplied, in order to sow trouble and disorder among the Tanjore Christians."[41] Two hundred years later the Protestant mission historian Julius Richter made the following judgment about the Chota Nagpur Jesuit mission in the North: "Money plays a major role in their subversive activities; temporarily they paid for all persons attending church, and every one who changed to them received not only new clothes on baptism but also a comparatively high amount of cash."[42] Such a stereotypical polemic reduces Indian Christians to a passive mass of people who can easily be bought; at the same time, it says a great deal about the implicit prejudices of Western missionaries. Unfortunately, it also confuses our understanding of the active strategies applied by Indian Christians when changing their church affiliations.

Internal Aspects

Socioeconomical Conflicts

Since for many Indians conversion to Christianity was connected with the hope of social and economic emancipation, proselytism was often used as an active strategy to satisfy this expectation. For example, the major shifts from Protestantism to Catholicism in Palayankottai in the South and Chota Nagpur in the North can both be largely accounted for by the superior legal representation of Christian affairs by the Jesuits. Moreover, any improvement of social status within Indian society is often connected with a breaking of caste *(jati)* barriers. Therefore, proselytism related to socioeconomic emancipation has often had something to do with conflicts between different caste groups. Among new converts to Christianity caste had not yet lost its plausibilities; it was apparently unavoidable that members of different castes

41. Annual Letter, 1727, quoted from L. Besse, *Father Beschi of the Society of Jesus: His Times and His Writings* (Trichinopoly, 1918), pp. 84f.

42. Richter, *Indische Missionsgeschichte,* p. 321.

in one and the same congregation came into conflict with one another. When one caste group felt marginalized or saw its privileges at risk, it often agitated for a change of affiliation. In that way, proselytism contributed to an ecclesiastical landscape in India that is still shaped along caste lines, though this can also mean that one and the same denomination is comprised of several dominant castes that vary from region to region or even from congregation to congregation. Examples have already been given of entire caste groups that changed their church affiliation, from the SPG to the Leipzig Mission in the Thanjavur area (Vellalars) and from the CSI to ACI in Kerala (Dalits). In this context, proselytism can be partly understood as a process that involved conflict in which certain caste groups failed to achieve access to the material resources of a certain mission society (e.g., schools and hospitals) to promote the social and economic emancipation of their own community.

Socioreligious Conflicts

Social discrimination in India is rarely based on unequal distribution of economic benefits alone; such discrimination may also have a specifically religious dimension. Though socioeconomic and socioreligious motives are generally closely interwoven, there is some heuristic value in differentiating between the two. In village communities especially, social status and religious privileges are closely linked together. In certain regions, as Bayly has shown, the church achieved recognition by Hindus and Muslims as an equal trustee of religious honors.[43] This often led to fierce disputes within the churches over who would exercise these privileges, which were considered expressive of social status. Religious privileges within a Christian congregation may involve, among others, the seating order in worship services, altar services, and other auxiliary services (collecting donations, ringing the church bell, keeping the church keys, etc.), and marriage procession routes and offices at

43. A particularly striking example is the South Indian village of Kalugumalai, where Hindus of a certain caste group (Nadars) converted to Catholic Christianity in 1895. Immediately afterward they built a chapel on the town's main procession street. When they were Hindus, their use of the street, which was also for ceremonial marriage processions, was prohibited at the instigation of another caste group (Maravars), which did not want to share its privileges. When the procession at the annual Hindu temple festival was about to parade through that street, the newly converted Christians erected a temporary bamboo marquee *(pantal)* in front of their chapel and conducted prayer meetings. The purpose of this marquee, which reached far into the street, was evidently to block the way of the temple car in order to claim the same right of way for the street as the other group. See Bayly, *Saints, Goddesses, and Kings,* pp. 446ff.

church festivals. In that way, many newly converted Christians obtained access to religious honors that were out of reach when they were Hindus. When no consensus could be reached within the church about the distribution of religious privileges, the losing party often arranged for a change of church affiliation.

Excursus: The Village of Vadakkankulam

The peculiarity of proselytism based on socioreligious conflict can be usefully illustrated through the example of the village of Vadakkankulam at the southern tip of India. Vadakkankulam is a village that now has a Christian majority.[44] Since the seventeenth century, Catholic Christians have lived there and church life is shaped by two caste groups, Vellalars and Nadars. Vellalars traditionally had exclusive right to religious privileges. In 1807, a Vellalar who had borrowed from Nadars and was unable to clear his debts had been disentitled from all religious honors. Because he felt that this treatment was unfair, he and his supporters approached the LMS and offered it a plot on the procession street where a small prayer house was then built. When the major Catholic festival with its car procession took place, the turncoats erected a temporary bamboo marquee *(pantal)* in front of their chapel and conducted prayer meetings in it with an LMS catechist they had invited from outside. Their real aim was to use the marquee, which reached far out into the road, to assert their religious rights to the procession street. This action followed a common pattern for conflicts about religious privileges.[45] The defectors, however, eventually gave in and returned to the Catholic fold after doing public penance.

In the course of the nineteenth century, when the Nadars began to question the traditional religious privileges of the Vellalars more insistently, some Vellalar representatives approached the SPG in 1865, registered as inquirers, and donated several plots in town to this society. This was meant as a warning to the Catholic leadership that the loss of their privileges would result in a mass exodus to the SPG. Analogously, in 1878, Nadars allowed the SPG to build two new schools in Vadakkankulam, this time as a warning that they would turn to the SPG if they continued to be deprived of religious privileges.

44. See Kaufmann, "Popular Christianity," pp. 178ff.; A. Sivasubramanian, "The Crusade against Caste Domination in the Holy Family Church at Vadakkankulam (1912-1913)," in *Jesuit Presence in Indian History*, ed. A. Amaladass (Anand, India, 1988), pp. 334ff.; Bayly, *Saints, Goddesses, and Kings*, pp. 420ff.

45. See above, n. 43.

For similar reasons, a group of Nadars from Vadakkankulam associated themselves with the controversial Bishop Soares, already mentioned above, to protest against the persisting socioreligious dominance of the Vellalars. At the beginning of the twentieth century, when the Vellalars feared the final loss of their privileges, they decided to give MELIM the chance to build a chapel at Vadakkankulam. For a while, a majority of Vadakkankulam's Vellalars moved over to MELIM but were won back by Catholic missionaries who assured them that they would be allowed to retain certain rights and prerogatives, which is still the case today.[46]

Religious Renewal

Any thorough examination of the social background of proselytism must not neglect its spiritual aspects, which are also quite important. In this regard, it is of interest that within the sociology of religion a model has become widespread that sees competition between different denominations as a positive factor for religious mobilization.[47] Applying economic concepts, this model explains that competition revives spirituality because the church and its officeholders have to satisfy the religious needs of their clients. Transferred to the Indian situation, this would mean that the often vigorous competition between the mission societies, along with the ever-present threat of proselytism, made it possible for Indian Christians to uphold their own religious interests. It can hardly be denied, however, that intermissionary competition also resulted in a number of problematic developments, especially when one keeps in mind the persistence of caste within the Indian church. Nevertheless, the fear of proselytism prompted many changes in the churches and missions that might otherwise not have taken place. A good example comes from the eighteenth century when the Jesuit C. J. Beschi introduced a new church festival to intensify Indian Christian spiritual life; Beschi did this because he suspected that many Catholics in the Thanjavur area might go over to the Tranquebar Mission. Furthermore, Beschi improved the formation of the catechists and even introduced them to Ignatian spiritual exercises. Another example comes from the smaller evangelical missions, the Salvation Army, the Plymouth Brethren, and others. These groups, though they encouraged proselytism, were actually responsible for quite a few revival movements within the established mission so-

46. When a group of Nadars tried to abolish all Vellalar privileges in 1940, they failed. Finally, in protest, this group apostatized, became Hindus, and erected a Shiva temple at Vadakkankulam.

47. See R. Finke and R. Stark, *The Churching of America, 1776-1990: Winners and Losers in Our Religious Economy* (New Brunswick, N.J., 1992).

cieties; consequently, such groups exercised considerable influence over the shaping of Indian Christian spirituality. In the twentieth century, this role devolved upon the Pentecostal and charismatic movements.

Conclusion

Proselytism has had a prominent place in Indian Christianity for the last five hundred years. Indian Christians frequently and consciously used the practice of proselytism to their advantage, as a means of resolving social conflict or as a way of voicing their religious aspirations. On the whole, one can seldom speak of a passive "flock of sheep" that was simply lured away to another church, tempted by nothing more than mere material incentives. When one understands that change of church affiliation is an active strategy that presupposes personal agency, one is then able to make a more analytically useful assessment of proselytism and its role in the history of the Indian church.

Baptisms of Non-Christians and Admissions from Other Christian Confessions in the Leipzig Mission in India, 1848-1860[48]

Year	*Baptisms*	*Admissions*
1848	288	400
1849	320	28
1850	154	81
1851	189	100
1852	68	371
1853	107	132
1854	723	94
1855	115	258
1856	127	421
1857	120	160
1858	128	139
1859	115	236
1860	185	181

48. Handmann, *Tamulen-Mission,* p. 465. Statistics for 1857 are estimated.

CHAPTER 10

Anticipating Independent India: The Idea of the Lutheran Christian Nation and Indian Nationalism

GUNNEL CEDERLÖF

In August 1946, just before M. K. Gandhi moved from his ashram at Wardha to Delhi, Johannes Sandegren, bishop of the Tamil Evangelical Lutheran Church, took the opportunity of visiting him to discuss again the situation of the Christians in India. In an atmosphere where "[Gandhi] spoke, and I mostly listened," the Mahatma and the bishop held an hour-long conversation. As most Christian missionaries, Sandegren was concerned about Gandhi's negative position on conversion. He reported having told Gandhi that he made the work hard for the missionaries and Gandhi replying, as on many other occasions, that he was not against Christianity as such but advised everyone to remain in his or her religion to improve it.[1] Gandhi said he had recently visited the Gossner Lutheran mission in Ranchi where the work and expression of faith had impressed him. He pointed to a young man in the room and remarked that the boy was a Christian and had come together with his brother to the ashram to serve India. But Sandegren noted that he knew the boys' family and that the brother had traveled on to Calcutta to find out if he needed to renounce Christianity and to have Indian nationalism as his religion.[2] In a

1. T. E. Yates, *Christian Mission in the Twentieth Century* (Cambridge and New York, 1994), pp. 75-77.

2. Johannes Sandegren was the third bishop of Tranquebar and the head of the Tamil

I am grateful for assistance and comments from Geoffrey Oddie, Sven Thidevall, Tore Furberg, Beppe Karlsson, Lars Berge, and Kajsa Ahlstrand. I have also benefited from comments by the participants in a seminar at the Swedish Institute of Missionary Research, autumn 2005, at which an earlier version of the text was presented.

later report, Sandegren recalled a meeting with Gandhi in 1941 at which Gandhi had been less diplomatic and stated, "Bishop, had I the power, I would institute laws that would stop the Christian mission's work." Sandegren was now searching for ways to make the Christian church and its work accepted in an anticipated independent India.[3]

Many foreign Christian missions felt squeezed from two sides. From the turn of the twentieth century, alongside growing Hindu and secular nationalist movements, concerns for the consequences for minority religions increased. And in the hostile relationships between the European powers in the First World War, non-British missions as well as all missionary activities sympathetic to the nationalist movement were targeted and increasingly controlled by the British government in India.[4] Positions on the question of nationalism varied greatly between missions and the individual missionaries in them, from a clear support for the British as the ruling authority in India to active support for the nationalist movement.[5] In 1925, Johannes's younger brother Paul, also a missionary in India, wrote of nationalism as an epoch-making force that would endanger the situation of Indian Christians as long as there were foreign links to the churches. He argued that autonomous Indian churches needed to detach themselves from the West.

> Will nationalism, which without doubt keeps India's future in its hands, take a decidedly hostile position against Christianity? Naturally, it stands opposed to all that is Western. It is therefore near at hand to in-

---

Evangelical Lutheran Church from 1934 to 1956. Church of Sweden Archive (hereafter CSA), Church of Sweden Mission (hereafter CSM), Johannes Sandegren Collection, Box J, "Manuskript 1920-1960: Utkast till Manuskript till föredrag, artiklar, etc. rörande Indien 1927-1961," Envelope 2, "Dr. Ambedkars utmaning," p. 2, author's translation. See also Gerald Studdert-Kennedy, *British Christians, Indian Nationalists, and the Raj* (Oxford and New York, 1991), p. 63.

3. CSA, CSM, Johannes Sandegren Collection, Box J, "Manuskript 1920-1960: Utkast till Manuskript till föredrag, artiklar, etc. rörande Indien 1927-1961," Envelope 1, "Biskop J. Sandegrens föredrag i Amiralitetskyrkan den 12 mars 1946. Det politiska läget och kristen mission i dagens Indien," p. 1, author's translation.

4. Arthur Jeyakumar, "Bishop Johannes Sandegren and the British Government of India," *Indian Church History Review* 30 (1996): 5-14; D. Arthur Jeyakumar, "The Attitude of the Government of India towards Indian National Movement — a Case Study: Dr. Everest Forrester-Paton," *Indian Church History Review* 30 (1986): 43-53; John Webster, "Presbyterian Missionaries and Gandhian Politics, 1919-1922," *Indian Church History Review* 19 (1985): 27-28.

5. William W. Emilsen, *Violence and Atonement: The Missionary Experiences of Mohandas Gandhi, Samuel Stokes, and Verrier Elwin in India before 1935* (Frankfurt and New York, 1994), chap. 6.

> clude Christianity, since it has evidently come to India and appeared in Western attire both with regard to cult and thinking. . . . Politics have for one hundred years favoured Christianity. It is about time and basically only an advantage, that it is made independent and free from all such outer assistance. The great danger lies in a situation where Christianity is branded not only as alien but also as anti-national.[6]

Like his brother, Johannes Sandegren perceived nationalism to be the crucial point for the destiny, even the survival, of Christianity in India, and that it threatened to force Indians into Hinduism or atheism. He argued that nationalism had made Indians into a people, while the Christians in India were divided among themselves by the many, often competing, denominations. Further increasing the split, these denominations had different positions in relation to Indian society and in particular to the question of caste.

As I will argue, in contrast to the main body of Protestant missions, the European-based Evangelical Lutheran mission had a dual stand on the question of nationalism partly because they had developed as church missions, built on national churches with a strong resonance of the north European nationalist movements. The idea of the folk church expressing the specific ethnic character of the people and place, also with roots in late-nineteenth- and early-twentieth-century romantic and nationalist notions of the *Volk,* gave the idea of an indigenous Christian nation a central place in their work. The goal, therefore, became to form an autonomous Tamil Folk Church of the Evangelical Lutheran confession.[7]

Johannes Sandegren had strong political views and expressed these in his many discussions with politicians, not least in South India where he lived and worked. However, he also lectured and published articles, and left behind many unpublished manuscripts on the issue of Indian nationalism and the situation of the Lutheran Christians in India. Working fifty years in the

6. Paul Sandegren, "Kristendomens Genombrott i Indien," in *Missionen en Livsmakt. Från Svenska Kyrkans Missions Femtioårshögtid,* ed. Svenska Kyrkans Missionsstyrelse (Stockholm, 1925), p. 76, author's translation.

7. Differences of opinion between the more orthodox confessional German mission and the ecumenical position of the leadership of the CSM is reflected in the controversy over the usage of "Lutheran" in the name of the church where archbishop Nathan Söderblom wanted to avoid the term. Tore Furberg, *Ett Ekumeniskt Tecken. Svenska Kyrkans Biskopsämbete i Mission och Ekumenik under Förra Hälften av 1900-Talet,* Studia Missionalia Svecana XCVII (Uppsala, 2004), p. 76; William Richey Hogg, *Ecumenical Foundations: A History of the International Missionary Council and Its Nineteenth Century Background,* 1st ed. (New York, 1952), p. 60; Herman Sandegren, *Svensk Mission och Indisk Kyrka* (Stockholm, 1924), p. 162.

Church of Sweden Mission (CSM) in South India, of which twenty-two were spent as bishop of the Tamil Evangelical Lutheran Church (TELC), he had a significant influence on decisions within the church and mission. But, interestingly, most of the manuscripts are written in Swedish and were most likely intended for a Swedish audience. Swedish was not Sandegren's first language, so the manuscripts he wrote in Swedish were hardly first drafts to be translated later. In spite of the quite detailed discussions of the situation in India, including many names and places that were well known in India but mostly if not completely unfamiliar in Sweden, Sandegren obviously intended to let the Indian situation have an impact on discussions also in Sweden. At times it is difficult to firmly establish whether or not Sandegren actually published a certain manuscript, but the careful editing that is characteristic of most texts indicates an intention to do so.[8]

The 1930s and 1940s, during the intensifying struggles for Indian independence, was the time when Johannes Sandegren most intensively wrote on the issue of nationalism. He questioned the Dravidian movement for its "atheism," feared the alliance between orthodox and "modern secular" Hindus, perceived the radicalism of Dr. Ambedkar as a challenge for the church on the integration of untouchable castes into the social order, and admiringly criticized Gandhi in correspondence and in personal meetings for his position on the shrinking maneuverability of Christians in India. However, Johannes's understanding of the roots of Indian nationalism differed in significant ways from that of his brother Paul. As "a sign of subordination" and "an ailment in the societal body," Johannes Sandegren saw the national movements as inevitable and an outcome of Britain's ruthless exercise of power and excessive violence, as in the massacre at Amritsar in 1919.[9]

As many other missionaries in India, Sandegren suggested Christianity as the unifying solution and moral leadership for the violently torn Indian nation. However, he did not speak of Christian faith at large but argued that Lutheranism in "its ecumenical form in certain Nordic countries" carried a message for both Indian nationalists and the national Indian church that would counter both syncretism (i.e., deviation from the Lutheran confession)

8. These manuscripts are kept in the Johannes Sandegren Collection in the Church of Sweden Archives in Uppsala, Sweden.

9. CSA, CSM, Johannes Sandegren Collection, Box J, "Manuskript 1920-1960: Utkast till Manuskript till föredrag, artiklar, etc. rörande Indien 1927-1961," Envelope 2, "Nationalismen och lutherdomen i Indien," p. 2. CSA, CSM, Johannes Sandegren Collection, Box J, "Manuskript 1920-1960: Utkast till Manuskript till föredrag, artiklar, etc. rörande Indien 1927-1961," Envelope 1, "Den politiska utvecklingen i Indien efter världskriget," p. 2, author's translation.

and atheism. The statement suggests the limited range of such ecumenism, and over the years the TELC came to carefully guard its limited boundaries against merging with other Protestant churches. Significant of his position, ideology had a national focus, while practice was mostly grounded in regional concerns. Even though he had not grown up in the same strict Lutheran confessionalism as his parents, Johannes Sandegren saw his mission to secure the "pure" Lutheran faith in India. The Federation of the Evangelical Lutheran Churches in India (formed in 1926) was a tool to promote unity among Lutherans. Significantly, "ecumenism" meant first of all to unite the Lutheran churches and to keep the boundaries strong against other denominations, even though a less hostile attitude to the Reformed churches could be seen in the early twentieth century.[10]

The methods Sandegren practiced to discipline the Lutheran Christians were detailed and almost hostile toward other churches. For example, marriages between Lutheran Christians and persons of other denominations were discouraged, even though kinsmen among whom brides and grooms were sought often belonged to different denominations, and a Lutheran who married a Roman Catholic had to pay a penalty. Irrespective of the social realities in which Christians made their decisions, such marriages were evidently seen as a threat to church unity.[11]

Johannes and Paul Sandegren were third-generation missionaries in the Leipzig mission. Their grandfather C. F. Kremmer was sent by the Leipzig Society to India in 1846, and his oldest daughter Theodora married a missionary from Sweden, Carl Jacob Sandegren, three years after his arrival in India in 1869. When the CSM was formed in 1874, Carl Jacob and Theodora came to form a strong link between the two missions in India, which relationship otherwise was marked by several conflicts, and six of their children worked for shorter or longer periods as missionaries in India. Johannes Sandegren's influence on church matters in the TELC, due to his ancestry, should therefore not be underestimated.[12]

Like many other younger missionaries who arrived in India and South Africa from the 1890s onward, Johannes and Paul Sandegren were influenced by

10. Gunnel Cederlöf, "The Politics of Caste and Conversion: Conflicts among Protestant Missions in Mid-Nineteenth Century India," *Swedish Missiological Themes* 88 (2000): 141-43; Sigfrid Estborn, *Johannes Sandegren och Hans Insats i Indiens Kristenhet* (Uppsala, 1968), pp. 188-89; Herman Sandegren, *Svensk Mission,* p. 230.

11. Herman Sandegren, *Svensk Mission,* p. 162.

12. Carl Jacob Sandegren worked sixty years in India, Theodora fifty-three, Johannes fifty. J. D. Asirvadam, *Johannes Sandegren: The Third Bishop of Tranquebar* (Madras, 1962), p. 3. Estborn, *Johannes Sandegren,* pp. 14-15.

the nationalist sentiments arising in Sweden and had begun to emphasize a specifically Swedish character of the Lutheran mission in India. The idea of creating a folk church remained strong in their writings. During his student years in Uppsala, Johannes Sandegren was impressed by and found strong support in Nathan Söderblom,[13] at the time professor of theology and later archbishop, who had proclaimed the young student as the forthcoming bishop in an Evangelical Lutheran church in India.[14] During these years the nationalistic and church-oriented Young Church Movement *(Ungkyrkorörelsen)* was under formation. Söderblom was a leading figure in this milieu, but was less inclined to adhere to strong nationalist sentiments than were two other leading theologians, J. A. Eklund and Manfred Björkquist. The movement grew out of the Uppsala Christian Student Association (Uppsala Kristliga Studentförbund, formed 1901) and came as a response to the deep societal changes in the late nineteenth century of agrarian transformation and a growing and increasingly church-critical working class. Many perceived the situation to be threatening and confusing. The aim was to regain Christian influence through the Church of Sweden and to promote an integrated and uniform Christian culture based on the Swedish nation. However, this was not a movement nostalgically intending to revive a past, homogenous, Swedish culture. They rather perceived a cultural synthesis of the present, industrialized Sweden. The vision was to ensure the church to be the "soul" of the nation.[15]

The national character of the European Lutheran churches had deep roots also in Germany. Karl Graul, the first director of the Leipzig Society, argued that the Lutheran mission should remain international, gathering all Lutheran churches into one mission headed by the Leipzig Society, while the Lu-

13. Nathan Söderblom (1866-1931), professor of theology at Uppsala University, 1901-14, professor of theology at Leipzig University, 1912-14, archbishop of the Church of Sweden, 1914-1931.

14. Asirvadam, *Johannes Sandegren,* p. 8. This part of Asirvadam's text is almost entirely identical with a manuscript in the Johannes Sandegren Collection, written by Sandegren. CSA, CSM, Johannes Sandegren Collection, Box J, "Manuskript 1920-1960: Utkast till Manuskript till föredrag, artiklar, etc. rörande Indien 1927-1961," Envelope 2, "My Grace Is Sufficient for Thee: For My Strength Is Made Perfect in Weakness," biographical notes of Johannes Sandegren's life.

15. Lars Berge, *The Bambata Watershed: Swedish Missionaries, African Christians, and an Evolving Zulu Church in Rural Natal and Zululand, 1902-1920* (Uppsala, 2000), pp. 162-63; Tore Furberg, *Kyrka och Mission i Sverige, 1868-1901. Svenska Kyrkans Mission Tillkomst och Första Verksamhetstid* (Church and mission in Sweden, 1868-1901: The origins and early years of the Church of Sweden mission) (Uppsala, 1962), pp. 401-2; Sven Thidevall, *Folkkyrkan, Vision och Verklighet. Ett Folkkyrkligt Reformprograms Öden 1928-1932* (Uppsala, 2000), pp. 21-23.

theran churches themselves should be founded in national custom. Just like similar terms, "folk" and "nation" are both exclusive and inclusive since they seek to unite people under a common identity of ancestry, territory, and language and, in doing so, reject those who do not belong to this group of people. The nation, or the *Volk*, should express the Lutheran confession through the uniqueness and individuality of the church in regard to its ethnicity and race. Thereby, the ideas of nation and race were intertwined in the identity of the folk church.[16] The Christian community — the church — was seen as the missionizing body, and the goal was to form new communities of Christians into indigenous churches that were independent both in decisions and finances. It has even been argued that in the implementation of Swedish contemporary missiology, the national folk-church rather became identified by territory than by confession.[17]

Graul's missiological visions shone through in contemporary Swedish missiology. The debates on the formation of a folk church in India drew much inspiration from the leading Swedish missiologist of the late nineteenth century, H. W. Tottie, who argued for the intimate relationship between the universal character of the Christian church and the particularistic identity of the actual national churches.[18] Thus, from the Swedish missionaries' perspective it would be an anomaly to assume a church, so identified with an Indian ethnic and national identity, to be antinational. Paul Sandegren's critical remark in 1925 was in fact a statement in support of liberating the church from the West so that it could become an Indian, or rather a Tamil, folk church. One may assume this nationhood of the church to be due to the fact that CSM and Leipzig Evangelical Lutheran Mission (LELM) worked in Tamil-speaking South India. However, the idea of the "nation" uniting a national church would hardly be able to encompass all India since India was divided by language, history, and culture.

On discussing the failure of Christianity in India, Paul Sandegren pointed specifically to the fact that the missions had failed to form national churches and remained without ordained Indian priests. During the last two hundred years, Indian converts had become attached to individual European missionaries rather than forming indigenous churches. "A deeper cause, making the

16. Yates, *Christian Mission*, pp. 35-36.

17. Berge, *The Bambata Watershed*, pp. 156-57, 166-69; Furberg, *Kyrka och Mission*, pp. 165-66; Herman Sandegren, *Svensk Mission*, p. 4.

18. H. W. Tottie was much inspired by German Lutheran confessionalism and Lund high-church theology; ecumenically, however, he was more open compared to the dominant German position. Furberg, *Kyrka och Mission*, pp. 196-97. See also H. W. Tottie, *Evangelistik* (Uppsala, 1892).

preservation of the congregations as a national church impossible . . . was the mission's complete dependence on Europeans, who at that point acted very aggressively. The missionizing Christianity in India . . . was culturally so tied to the European Christianity that the measure of independent Christian culture, necessary for a breakthrough, had not yet appeared."[19] Swedish Lutheran missionaries often pointed to the Nordic national churches as a model for Christians in India. However, Nathan Söderblom's ecumenical work in Sweden, including initiatives for intercommunion with the Church of England, did obviously not transmit into the Lutheran mission's work in India. Here, church boundaries rather became borders to defend than gateways to intercommunication with other denominations.

The Swedish mission held a slightly anomalous position with regard to the establishment of an independent church. In contrast to the German mission, they had wanted to involve Indian clergy and laymen at an earlier stage, when the Germans still perceived Indians as "immature" for leadership. But the controversial constitutional question of episcopacy, which created a cleavage in Swedish-German relations, had a double edge. The German mission was forcefully against establishing a church with a bishop, but had difficulties asserting their position since they were weakened by the anti-German regulations in India due to the First World War. An episcopal church was against a German-Lutheran tradition, and the Leipzig mission feared the influence of non-Lutheran faith and praxis. In contrast, in Sweden, it was particularly supported for its ecumenical dimensions by the Swedish archbishop, Nathan Söderblom. At the same time, when the Swedish mission succeeded in making the TELC an Episcopal church, they faced opposition also from influential, nationalist, Indian members of the church who anticipated a Swedish rule in disguise in a church with Swedish missionaries as successive bishops.[20]

In the late nineteenth century, as a consequence of the formation of a church mission and increasing demands for a Swedish-Lutheran character in the mission work, the Swedish mission claimed a more independent role in India in relation to the LELM. Claims for Swedish mission stations and a Swedish diocese in the mission field were made.[21] At the time Peter Hörberg was sent as an earmarked "Swedish" missionary to India in 1885, the question of a national church also received new significance. In contrast to the society missions, the CSM was formed as a church mission to be considered as a con-

19. Svenska Kyrkans Missionsstyrelse, *Missionen en Livsmakt* (Stockholm, 1925), p. 74, author's translation.

20. Furberg, *Ett Ekumeniskt Tecken,* pp. 73-101.

21. Furberg, *Kyrka och Mission,* chap. 4.

cern for the whole of the Church of Sweden, and as a mission aiming at forming new national churches where new communities of Lutheran Christians would grow. In its organization, the CSM was basically a copy of the society missions, relying on voluntary work and finance. Its structure ran parallel to the Church of Sweden, and only the Mission Board had a legal place in the church. But it was still important for the missionaries to claim legal sanction for the mission from the state and the state church, which may be why the older brother Herman Sandegren in his historiography emphasized that the mission was a part of the church's legal framework. Likewise, it made the Swedish position stronger in negotiations with the Leipzig mission when they could argue that Leipzig was in fact negotiating with the entire church. The formation of the CSM had grown out of disputes and consultations between representatives of missionary societies, many of them in the revivalist movement, and proponents of the national church. Similarly, the debates between Lund high-church and Uppsala low-church positions formed the theological field.[22]

However, the attempts to push forward the Swedish positions in India were not taken lightly by the Leipzig collegium. In the 1880s, nationalist sentiments grew significantly in both Germany and Sweden, and "German mission in German colonies" became a catchword as the German mission in East Africa grew. When the Leipzig collegium heard of the Swedish requests for their own mission stations, they responded that if the Swedes wanted their own mission, they should seek their own mission field. Along similar lines, Karl Graul's argument for an international, and not national, Lutheran mission became a tool for keeping "the field" under LELM control.[23] But as Swedish missionaries in South India began to outnumber their German colleagues, not least by the women missionaries, and the CSM emphasized that they were part of the Church of Sweden and not an isolated society mission, they could secure a Swedish diocese within the LELM in India in 1901. Yet, the goal remained to maintain unity and develop a "Tamil folk church of Lutheran confession."[24]

In the developments of the 1880s, other considerations for a future Lutheran church in India can also be seen. When Paul Sandegren argued that Christianity should be "made independent and free" of European assistance to gain legitimacy in an increasingly nationalist Indian nation in 1925, his ar-

22. Furberg, *Kyrka och Mission,* chap. 1, sec. 1; Cederlöf, "The Politics," pp. 140-41; Herman Sandegren, *Svensk Mission,* pp. 145-50.

23. Furberg, *Kyrka och Mission,* pp. 291-94.

24. Herman Sandegren, *Svensk Mission,* pp. 143-45, 150-51.

gument resonates of concerns to protect a Lutheran church from conflicts between European powers. In the Swedish mission conference in 1888, Director Hardeland stated that: "We must endeavour to form Tamil pastorates that are managed by Indian priests. . . . they should be strong enough to stand also in difficult times as, for example, during a major war in Europe."[25]

British "Enemy Nations" and Anti-Western Targets

When Paul Sandegren wrote of the danger of Christianity being perceived as alien and antinational, it was in view of both being associated by Indians with British colonial overlordship — which could result in expulsion — and the experience of British policy regarding "enemy nations" in the First World War. Already in 1914, the British government placed the first German missionaries in internment camps. All other German missionaries were interned the following year and sent back to Germany in early 1916. From 1915, all LELM properties, mission stations, and schools were administered by the CSM under the supervision of the Mission Trust in Madras.[26]

Johannes, Paul, and their older brother Carl Sandegren also faced restrictions due to the war. They were forbidden to work in the former German mission stations from 1916 onward[27] — presumably because they had a German mother and close connections in Germany. During the war years the British press in India became increasingly anti-German and demanded that all ties to Germany be cut. The restrictions facing the Sandegrens continued until 1922. In 1919, the government of Madras denied permission for Johannes Sandegren to become a member of the Executive Council of the Mission Trust, and in 1921 requests by the CSM to make Sandegren a member of the CSM mission board and the TELC church council were similarly turned down.[28] Declared "a very undesirable person on account of his pro-German sympathies," Johannes Sandegren found difficulties in obtaining a return permit after a furlough in Sweden in 1922. And in spite of having British nation-

25. Herman Sandegren, *Svensk Mission,* p. 125, author's translation.

26. CSA, CSM, Missionsstyrelsens protokollsbilagor (Mission Board Appendices) 1916:2, App. 198, "Svenska Kyrkans Tamulmission, årsberättelse [annual report] 1915," p. 2. Jeyakumar, "Bishop Johannes Sandegren," pp. 6-7.

27. Jeyakumar, "Bishop Johannes Sandegren," p. 10, referring to G.O. No. 1147, Public, 14.6.916.

28. Jeyakumar, "Bishop Johannes Sandegren," pp. 7-8, referring to G.O. No. 505, Public, 12.11.1919, and G.O. No. 496, Public, 5.8.21. Herman Sandegren, *Svensk Mission,* p. 234. *Svenska Kyrkans Missionstidning* 47 (1922): 318.

ality, being born in British India, to have had his name on the black list made it difficult for him and his wife to receive return permits to India again in 1940.[29]

The British government's attempts to suppress anti-British agitation among missionaries and persons connected with the mission institutions could be seen throughout British India; the regional differences, however, were significant. Restrictions remained the same throughout the British territories; missionaries were not permitted to engage in political affairs. Some missions and missionaries adhered strictly to this regulation by will or by need, while others openly displayed their disagreement with British rule and violent enforcement of law. But perhaps more important were the effects of the different regional situations on the missions' work and the political activities that had links to the institutions. In general, the United Provinces, Punjab, Bihar, and Bombay displayed more violence and anti-British political activity compared to Madras and the Central Provinces. As a result, missions were more affected by anti-British activities in the former regions.[30]

These regional differences also cut through missions. As John Webster shows, students in the Presbyterian mission schools in Punjab, a region where political tension was high, protested actively through demonstrations and strikes against the Rowlatt Bills in 1919 as part of the Rowlatt *satyagraha* initiated by Gandhi. The year 1919 was violent in Punjab; the massacre in Amritsar of unarmed people who had gathered for a public meeting only days after the *satyagraha* had been launched, left 379 dead according to the government's moderate estimates and marked a particularly brutal peak of events. This year came to mark a turn in national politics with Gandhi emerging as a political leader on a national level.[31] The Presbyterian missionaries, however, did not take part in the protest. In Lahore, for example, missionaries volunteered to aid the British army, arguing that honor bound them to be loyal to this Christian government, which had protected the mission from the start. In contrast, the Presbyterian mission in western India had nothing to report on anti-British protests, obviously working in a district unaffected by the political turmoil. After 1920, in addition to being politically "neutral," non-British missionaries had to pledge also to promote loyalty to the British government and make Indians good British subjects.[32]

29. Jeyakumar, "Bishop Johannes Sandegren," pp. 12-14.

30. Judith M. Brown, *Gandhi: Prisoner of Hope* (New Haven, 1989), p. 131.

31. Brown, *Gandhi*, pp. 128-31. Bipan Chandra, *India's Struggle for Independence, 1857-1947* (New Delhi, 1988), pp. 181-83.

32. The Rowlatt Bills, named after the chairman of the committee, restricted civil rights and the press for the sake of curbing terrorist activities. Webster, "Presbyterian Mis-

Also, the annual reports of the TELC spoke of unbounded loyalty to the British government in India and neutrality during the war. In 1917, the CSM India chairman Ernst Heuman discharged a lengthy attack on Annie Bessant and her work, and concluded that he was happy that not even the younger Christians in the town congregations had been attracted by the "Home rulers," and that the great masses realized that "'self-government' under Brahmin-rule would be anything but a gain." Two years later, Heuman wrote that the "super-national" character of the mission was easily misunderstood; he added, in a patronizing voice, that no one needed to doubt the mission's loyalty since it had "succeeded in fostering and keeping our Christians in allegiance, . . . during times of home-rule agitation . . . our Christians completely dissociated themselves from these movements." Much in line with a general attitude of indifference among Indian Christians, many of whom were poor and illiterate, and himself being more involved in rural than in urban congregational work, Heuman believed that economic inflation and drought together with imports of machine-loom textiles and kerosene had been a greater concern of people than the nationalist agitation.[33]

However, protests were not lacking in South India. An interesting report from Madras city in 1932, discussed by Arthur Jeyakumar, reveals the extent to which British authorities would go to suppress any display of support for the independence movement. The case is one of everyday significance rather than one of exceptional violence, which gives a view of the atmosphere in which missions in South India also worked. In January 1932, the government of India introduced four ordinances intended to curb manifestations of civil disobedience. The Emergency Powers Ordinance was implemented only in Bengal and Bombay presidencies. The three others, the Unlawful Instigation Ordinance, the Unlawful Association Ordinance, and the Molestation and Boycotting Ordinance, were put in place throughout India and gave the police and courts extensive power in their implementation. The last ordinance was particularly intended to curb not only picketing but also any support for picketers, including loitering near places of ongoing strike.

Ernest Forrester-Paton was a Scottish medical missionary of the "unrec-

---

sionaries," p. 28; John Webster, "American Presbyterian Missionaries and Nationalist Politics in the Punjab (1919-1935)," *Indian Church History Review* 34 (2000): 54-56; Emilsen, *Violence and Atonement,* p. 149.

33. CSA, CSM, Missionsstyrelsens protokollsbilagor (Mission Board Appendices) 1916:2, App. 198, "Svenska Kyrkans Missions arbete i Sydindien 1917," p. 1-5, and 1919:2, App. 206, "Översikt av arbetet på svenska indiska missionsfältet, 1918-19," p. 2, author's translation. Geoffrey A. Oddie, "Indian Christians and National Identity, 1870-1947," *Journal of Religious History* 25 (2001): 349, 363.

ognized"[34] National Missionary Society of India. Six years after his arrival in India, in 1921, he founded Christukula Ashram west of Madras. During the civil disobedience movement, the members and founders of the ashram were involved in picketing of toddy shops as part of a temperance campaign. However, the district collector deemed the activity political, and it was stopped after pressures from the collector. In January 1932, immediately after the new ordinances had been passed, Forrester-Paton, who displayed his support for the Gandhian movement by wearing *khaddar* (homespun cotton dress), went to Madras to find out if the many reports on excessive police violence against picketers were correct. Walking along the streets south of Parry's Corner and finding police armed with *lathis* (long bamboo batons) running toward an opening and there dragging a man out, he walked casually along the street to get a view of what was happening. One policeman came to question him about what he was doing there, if he was a European and from what country, why he was wearing *khaddar* and if he was a missionary. He reported having replied to all questions when another policeman arrived and both policemen began to beat him with their *lathis* and gave orders for a water cart to drench him in colored water. Finally, doused with green-colored water and limping, he managed to escape.

The next day Forrester-Paton found that a case had been filed against him in court where the police falsely testified that he and six Congress volunteers had blocked a shop selling foreign goods and lectured to people not to purchase these. On being told by a police sergeant to leave, Forrester-Paton was reported to have disobeyed the orders and persisted in his behavior. Thereby he had committed a crime against Ordinance Four of 1932 (prohibiting boycotts). The case went all the way to the House of Commons in London, where it was found that a mistake had been made. Subsequently, the case was withdrawn in Madras. Arthur Jeyakumar assumes the withdrawal may have been a way to avoid Forrester-Paton exercising his right as a European subject to appeal to higher court if convicted in Madras.[35]

Compared to Ernest Forrester-Paton, who was a Scot, Paul and Johannes Sandegren had German family relations and worked in a mission that the British saw as pro-German. This adds another dimension to their relationship to the Indian government and the question of nationalism. When Paul and Johannes Sandegren spoke about nationalism, they addressed two issues.

34. From 1919, restrictions were laid on the entry of Christian missions into British colonies, and the government subsequently issued a list of "recognized" organizations for missionary or philanthropic activities. Jeyakumar, "Attitude of the Government," p. 43.

35. Jeyakumar, "Attitude of the Government," pp. 47-53.

They believed their primary task was to form and strengthen a Lutheran church in India based on nationhood that could remain unaffected by anti-Western politics and inter-European conflicts. They further wanted to combat the pro-British conception of the European Evangelical Lutheran Missions as being pro-German. Nationalism implied thereby both a movement for the sake of the Indian people to gain independence from British rule and a movement intended to unite Indian Lutheran Christians into a church. Paul and Johannes Sandegren's perception was that the Lutheran Christians needed to become a people, or a folk, to meet the threat of the Indians becoming a people and a nation hostile to a Christianity they would label as alien and antinational.

However, the two brothers had somewhat different perceptions of the meaning of "nation" and its implications for the Christians in India. Their common political interest is evident in the many reports they wrote during their active years. But while Paul was deeply engaged in social issues, not least caste, and the regional situation of South India, Johannes focused mainly on national issues. Expressing far more radical views than his brother, Paul was highly critical of the Western character of the mission and church. He argued for accommodating and indigenizing the church, and for the Christian message to be conveyed in genuine Indian forms, but without deviating from the Evangelical Lutheran confession.[36] He asked, rhetorically: "Can there not be an Indian Christianity, free from the Western form? And is there not room for Christianity within Indian nationalism? Is not Sundar Singh a model for an Indian Christianity liberated from Western church characteristics and dogmatism?" His answer was that the destiny for Indian Christians would be decided by their stand for or against the coming, new Indian nation: "We would not in the least build our hope on any political, cultural or economic factors that perchance would make us wish that previous relations of power would be preserved."[37]

In contrast, Johannes Sandegren explained Indian nationalism as an inevitable consequence of a meeting between cultures, where Indians "guard their own values against a superior and insistent Western culture." With a metaphorical comparison of the Indian nationalist to a literary character, he

36. Cf. Oddie, "Indian Christians," p. 355.

37. Sadhu Sundar Singh (b. 1889; disappeared in 1929). Swedish missionaries and theologians such as Nathan Söderblom expressed admiration for Sundar Singh and saw him as a Christian mystic, practicing and preaching Christian faith as an Indian *sadhu*. Sundar Singh visited Sweden in 1922, invited by the CSM. See, for example, Karl Fries, "Sadhu Sundar Singh," *Svenska Kyrkans Missionstidning* 47 (1922): 118-21. Paul Sandegren, "Kristendomens Genombrott i Indien," p. 77, author's translation.

wanted to show that nationalist sympathies were merely the result of a lack of self-confidence and a form of self-preservation in the Indian when faced with the West. He compared the Indian reaction with that of the young Chinese character in Pearl Buck's *A House Divided* who, in the story, is confronted with the American society. Thereby, Sandegren chose only to emphasize the young man's negative reactions to America (a country with merits that were "hard to deny") and his glorification of China. He concluded: "His inferiority forced him to deny all the good things he saw in the West." Thereby, Sandegren could determine that the spread of nationalism in India was a testimony to England's success as a colonial power; its just, although foreign, government had awoken and, in consequence, turned India's "slave mentality" into protest.[38] Evidently, the Swedish missionary leadership in India looked toward an independent Indian nation with a high degree of apprehension.

For builders of a folk church, one may ask: "Who represents the folk?" Compared with the Reformed churches (later, the Church of South India), the TELC was late to ordain pastors from the "untouchable" or scheduled castes. And in their internal conflicts over the TELC constitution around 1920, one of Leipzig's arguments to confront the Swedish claim for an Episcopal church targeted the risk that once the bishop was an Indian, German confessional control would be lost.[39] In 1956, thirty-seven years after the inauguration of a Tamil folk church, Johannes Sandegren was succeeded by Raja B. Manickam as the fourth bishop of the TELC and the first Indian to be elected bishop of the church.

An Untouchable Nation *or* a Christian Nation

Closely connected with the question of how to relate the Lutheran Christian "nation" to the Indian "nation" was the issue of untouchability. Conversion, in particular of members of untouchable castes, had come under heavy criticism from both the secular and the Hindu nationalist movements. As several studies have shown, many of these conversions took place in community-based movements; large numbers came from extremely poor sections of society searching for social and spiritual liberation from oppressive economic, social, and ritual relationships by way of conversion to Christianity and Islam.

38. CSA, CSM, Johannes Sandegren Collection, Box J, "Manuskript 1920-1960," "Utkast till Manuskript till föredrag, artiklar, etc. rörande Indien 1927-1961," Envelope 2, "Nationalismen och lutherdomen i Indien," pp. 1-2. The document can be dated 1939. Author's translation.

39. Furberg, *Ett Ekumeniskt Tecken,* pp. 73-101.

This situation has also been given as an explanation for why the "untouchable castes" of South India were not keen on joining the Hindu nationalist movement and did not pressure the Western missions to leave as part of the agenda of the independence movement. A significant number of studies now emphasize the agency of these converts and their community-based conversions as conscious ways to achieve specific aims. Through conversion they found self-esteem, protection from caste oppression, and ways to improve their social and economic situation.[40]

During the struggle for Indian independence, Gandhi's criticism of Christian mission was made both on religious and on political grounds. He criticized in particular the exclusive claim for Christianity as being the only true religion. However, he was also most concerned with the missionary activities among "untouchable" castes, which he argued undermined unity and mobilization among these depressed classes in the nationalist movement. The constitutional provision of 1950 restricting conversion and making conversion by "coercion or undue influence" illegal caused concerns among the Christians since it questioned the right to propagate. As is discussed by Judith Brown in this volume, in postindependence India, the Indian National Congress opposed religious "proselytizing," while a major controversy remained on the implementation of equal civil rights for followers of minority religions within the secular state.[41] Obviously, the Lutheran missionaries in South India also faced criticism for their activities. Not only Gandhi made critical remarks to Johannes Sandegren about the proselytizing missions; the governor of the Madras Presidency also accused the missions of breaking up the unity of the untouchable castes into many denominations. However, for Johannes

40. See Sathianathan Clarke's overview and analysis in "Conversion to Christianity in Tamil Nadu: Conscious and Constitutive Community Mobilization towards a Different Symbolic World Vision," in *Religious Conversion in India: Modes, Motivations, and Meanings*, ed. Rowena Robinson and Sathianathan Clarke (New Delhi, 2003), pp. 323-50. See further Henriette Bugge, ed., *Mission and Tamil Society: Social and Religious Change in South India (1840-1900)* (Richmond, Surrey, 1994); Gunnel Cederlöf, *Bonds Lost: Subordination, Conflict, and Mobilisation in Rural South India, c. 1900-1970* (New Delhi, 1997); Duncan Forrester, "The Depressed Classes and Conversion to Christianity," in *Religion in South Asia: Religious Conversion and Revival Movements in South Asia in Medieval and Modern Times*, ed. Geoffrey A. Oddie (New Delhi, 1991), pp. 65-93; Dick Kooiman, *Conversion and Social Equality in India: The London Missionary Society in South Travancore in the Nineteenth Century* (New Delhi, 1989).

41. F. J. Balasundaram, "Gandhi's Attitude towards Christianity," *Indian Church History Review* 28 (1994); Judith M. Brown, "Indian Christians and Nehru's Nation-State," in this volume; George Oommen, "Minority Consciousness of Christians in Post-Independent India: A Historical Perspective," *Indian Church History Review* 19 (1985): 65.

Sandegren, it was not so much a question of unity among the downtrodden as a question of unity among Christians.[42]

In a substantial draft article written in 1946, "The Challenge of Dr. Ambedkar," Johannes Sandegren analyzes the doctor's challenge as well as his appeal to the untouchable castes.[43] Typically, his main concern was Ambedkar's criticism of Hinduism and his stand on religion. Having rejected Hinduism as a "contagious disease" and not a religion (in Sandegren's own quotation of Ambedkar), the bishop was optimistic that Ambedkar would choose Christianity, "at least in its Protestant form." The reason declared — which was far more optimistic — was that if a quarter million untouchables decided to become Christians, Ambedkar would follow suit. And if sixty million untouchables converted, the movement would turn into a full-scale migration from one religious "home" to another. However, checking his enthusiasm, Sandegren relates Ambedkar's apprehensions about the caste conflicts in the Christian churches. The only acceptable alternative for Ambedkar would be a religion free from the caste system.

The final observation has significance for the Lutheran mission and church of which Sandegren was bishop. Since the mid–nineteenth century, the question of caste had caused divisions within the Leipzig Mission and, even more, between the Leipzig and the majority of the Protestant missions. Still, in the 1940s, the general position of the Lutheran mission was to accept the caste system as a social order but to combat the "caste spirit."

As soon as the Swedish and German missionaries of the Leipzig Society began to work in South India in the 1840s, they came into conflict with the majority of the Protestant missions on the question of caste. The general Protestant position was strictly against all expressions of caste and the idea of a spiritual hierarchy inherent in Hinduism. The question came to a peak in 1833 when the Anglican bishop Daniel Wilson declared that no adult convert was to be baptized without first renouncing caste.[44] Most of the Leipzig missionaries (with a few remarkable exceptions), however, argued that the caste system was an organic part of Indian society comparable to the estates in

42. CSA, CSM, Johannes Sandegren Collection, Box J, "Manuskript 1920-1960: Utkast till Manuskript till föredrag, artiklar, etc. rörande Indien 1927-1961," Envelope 2, "Nationalismen och lutherdomen i Indien," additional notes.

43. CSA, CSM, Johannes Sandegren Collection, Box J, "Manuskript 1920-1960: Utkast till Manuskript till föredrag, artiklar, etc. rörande Indien 1927-1961," Envelope 2, "Dr. Ambedkars utmaning," author's translation.

44. Daniel Wilson was bishop of Calcutta from 1832 to 1858. Geoffrey A. Oddie, *Social Protest in India: British Protestant Missionaries and Social Reforms, 1850-1900* (New Delhi, 1979), pp. 45-46.

early modern European societies. Social hierarchies were a part of the civic or worldly sphere of life and not a matter for the church or mission to interfere with — a logic corresponding with Luther's doctrine of the two kingdoms distinguishing the spiritual from the worldly sphere. Immoral or cruel expressions of this order were criticized, but not the order itself.[45]

While the conflict within the Protestant missionary body — the LELM being part of it — died down over time and the general position became more pragmatic, the "Leipzig view" of the caste system is remarkably persistent in Johannes Sandegren's writing. In a text from the early 1940s, when community-based conversion movements had also reached the work of the CSM and radicalized both methods and analyses of the missionaries working in Coimbatore and the neighboring districts, Sandegren adhered to a conservative view of caste. Discussing the contribution of the caste system to civic order in light of the tension between the freedom of the individual and the right of solidarity of a community, he wrote: "From a Christian point of view a caste system is neither more Christian nor unchristian than an individualistic or communistic[46] form of society." He quoted Gandhi to explain that the caste system worked as a bulwark against the free competition of individuals in Western culture, which inevitably would exploit the weak, and added that it ought to work in a similar way to protect a society from Western communism. As an example of a way to counter "selfish individualism" in Europe, Sandegren refers to Nazi Germany. "In very conscious opposition to the selfishness often found in an individualistic order stands point 24 of the Nazi party programme in Germany: 'Gemeinnutz vor Eigennutz,' which may perhaps be translated: the common welfare comes before the individual welfare."[47] Being a remarkable statement to make in Europe around 1940, it is still difficult to assess the implications. This isolated statement in favor of Nazi ideology asks for further research with a broader documentation. Yet, it may be noted that the common logic of Sandegren's two examples of desirable systems that guard the community from individualism — the Indian caste system and the German Nazi party program — is the stress on ideas and ideology before social implementation and physical realities.

45. Cederlöf, "The Politics," pp. 136-37, 147-51.

46. "Communistic" is here to be understood in opposition to "individualistic" and not as a political ideology or polity.

47. CSA, CSM, Johannes Sandegren Collection, Box J, "Manuskript 1920-1960: Utkast till Manuskript till föredrag, artiklar, etc. rörande Indien 1927-1961," Envelope 2, "Has India, with Its Caste and Group Consciousness, Any Contribution to Make to the Solution of the Problem of How Best the Individual Is Fulfilled in the Community?" pp. 1-2, 8. The manuscript is difficult to date exactly, but was most likely written in the 1940s. This is one of the few unpublished documents from this period that is written in English.

Sandegren's main criticism of the caste system was directed against its expressions. When he spoke of "the tyranny of caste," he meant the oppressive attitudes and behavior of higher castes toward lower castes. Particularly the notion of untouchability and the doctrine of transmigration and karma could not be reconciled with the Christian religion. With reference to Gandhi, he wanted to see a reformed caste system. He argued that hierarchies — formulated in psychological terms as "superiority and inferiority complexes" — are found in all societies. But because of the loyalties to the caste community, in which "[p]oor and rich members of a caste, in high position and low, come together at all domestic festivals and solemnities," cleavages of such hierarchies would be bridged. The caste system cleansed of all religious implication was not evil as such. It was simply a civic order, a social and economic system that corresponded to Middle Age guilds in Europe. As a "village system" it would balance conflicts and become a valuable contribution to the problem of civic orders elsewhere in the world.[48]

In the discussions within the CSM and LELM, the situation in South India was often compared with the CSM acceptance of the custom in South Africa of polygyny. The custom itself had been condemned by all missions working in Natal and Zululand, except one, but locally the Lutheran missionaries did not make a condition for baptism that a man first had to divorce all but his first wife. It was argued that the consequences for the other wives and their children would be too severe; further, the CSM tolerance of the caste system in South India was argued to be an equivalent case. In line with the principle of a territorial folk church that reflected local social custom, the caste system, just like the institution polygyny, was to be accepted.[49] Herman Sandegren's remark in 1925 is significant of this position. He stated that the Leipzig Mission had chosen to attack the "caste spirit" rather than the caste institution, and added: "The Leipzig [missionary] field lies in the midst of Hinduism's most powerful strongholds and their congregations amount to more than half of Sudras, for whom giving up caste is a far greater sacrifice than for Pariahs."[50] In plain words, Herman Sandegren stated that since it is harder to give up caste for persons of high caste than for those of low caste, we have to accommodate the caste system within the Lutheran mission and church.

48. CSA, CSM, Johannes Sandegren Collection, Box J, "Manuskript 1920-1960: Utkast till Manuskript till föredrag, artiklar, etc. rörande Indien 1927-1961," Envelope 2, "Has India, with Its Caste and Group Consciousness, Any Contribution to Make to the Solution of the Problem of How Best the Individual Is Fulfilled in the Community?" pp. 5-6.

49. Berge, *The Bambata Watershed,* pp. 202-5.

50. Herman Sandegren, *Kast och Kristendom i Sydindien* (Stockholm, 1921), pp. 202-3.

The 1920s to 1940s were formative years for the Tamil Evangelical Lutheran Church, from the inauguration of the national church in 1919 to the early years of independence in India. In complex and often contradictory ways, the ideological and missiological heritage of Lutheran confessionalism, Romanticism, and European nationalisms was read into the South Indian social and political contexts, as they were understood by the European missionaries.

Conclusion

In this exploratory essay, I have taken the notions of folk, nation, and nationalism in the work of the Evangelical Lutheran mission in South India along three different paths: first, the ideological debates in Sweden and India regarding the fundamental character of mission and church in India; second, the Swedish-German mission in its complicated relationship to nationalism and British colonial power in the war periods; and third, the relationship between the Christian "nation" and the social order in India. All three paths are broad fields in themselves and ask for more research to be made.

As is evident from Sandegren's many manuscripts, the perception of the "nation" is prescriptively born out of the missionaries' ideas about the Tamil "folk." "Nation" and "folk" are almost identical and are used interchangeably — the folk is the nation and the nation is the folk. Yet, they draw their meanings from different and intercommunicating contexts of north European nationalism and ideas of a folk church.

It is particularly interesting to note how these Swedish missionaries experienced being foreigners in British India. To be born a British subject, like almost all members of the Sandegren family, was more a question of citizenship than of nation-ness. They were moving within the British Empire without being part of it and were not, like the missionaries from Great Britain, living and working within an extended Britain, but in a foreign land seen as extremely peripheral to Sweden. Their "pro-German sympathies" were more than family ties to a British enemy-nation. As was common among Swedish intellectuals in the early twentieth century, they adhered to and defended German philosophy, literature, theology, and culture against what they saw as the oncoming tide of brutal and demoralizing industrial development that was often associated with the developments occurring in Britain. It is from within this context that the notion of the folk and the nation — also the Tamil folk-church in India — may be understood, where the church was to be the soul that brought nations together into a higher union. To that extent, the "Tamil Christian nation" was often seen as being in conflict with the "Indian secular nation."

Tentatively, one may suggest that once the notion of the folk became an integral part of forming an independent church in India, it appears to have supported particularistic tendencies. When the Tamil "folk" was interpreted to encompass the caste system as a character of their people, the folk or the Lutheran Christian "nation" remained divided. Hence, the independent Indian nation was seen both as a threatening competitor and as Lutheran Christianity's salvation, for it could then become a legitimate and genuine national community. The Swedish missionaries never really decided on which leg to stand.

CHAPTER 11

Indian Christians and Nehru's Nation-State

JUDITH M. BROWN

The relationship of the nation-state to India's religious minorities has been of profound importance since Indian independence in 1947. It is a touchstone of national identity and national belonging. This is particularly so, given the circumstances of independence, when the nature of the nation was in part argued out in religious terms and a large area of the northwest of the Subcontinent was engulfed in intercommunal violence. Moreover, the Congress party's rhetoric insisted that India, unlike Pakistan, was a secular nation-state, where religious minorities had not only rights to religious freedom, but were equal citizens under the constitution.[1] Not surprisingly, historical study of issues relating to national identity and the position of religious minorities has normally focused on Indian Muslims, as they remained the largest of those minorities, while their presence in India was inevitably complicated by the presence of the new Pakistani neighbor as an overtly Muslim nation-state, and its perceived threat to India's national integrity. However, the position of Indian Christians after the departure of the British also reflects the nature of the Indian state, and the meaning in daily life of being Indian. Robert Frykenberg has been one of the main historians of India who has taken the history of India's Christians with utmost seriousness, rightly seeing them as an integral part of their country's history and as having a major cultural and religious role in the Subcontinent al-

1. The constitution, which came into effect in 1950, declared in the preamble that the people of India solemnly resolved to constitute a democratic republic that would secure for all its citizens among other things liberty of thought, expression, belief, faith, and worship. One of the fundamental rights guaranteed in the document, and made justiciable, was the right to freedom of religion. On the making of the constitution, see Granville Austin, *The Indian Constitution: Cornerstone of a Nation* (Oxford, 1966).

most from the start of the Christian era. Latterly he has been deeply concerned at the status of Christians in the later twentieth century when a renascent political Hinduism is reconfiguring the meaning of being Indian and — despite the constitution — exposing some Christians to harassment and violence.

It therefore seems appropriate in an essay in his honor to revisit Jawaharlal Nehru, one of the founding fathers of the new nation-state, to ask how he envisaged the role of Christians in the new India, and to see how he dealt with some major issues relating to them during his period as prime minister. We shall see the profound and complex problems Nehru had to face in relation to the Christian minority, given his genuine ideological commitment to a broad and encompassing vision of the national community and to a secular polity. We shall also be taken back to one of Frykenberg's earliest historical concerns and one of his most influential pieces of historical scholarship, the history of Guntur district in Madras Presidency in the late eighteenth and early nineteenth centuries.[2] He uncovered what he called the "white ant syndrome," whereby those Indian employees of the East India Company who were in actual control of the structures of administration in the district undermined the integrity and financial viability of that administration as well as nullifying the policies of the provincial center. Rather similarly in the 1950s Nehru's government at the national center in Delhi found itself confronted and undermined by those controlling the organs of party and state in the regional states of India in matters relating to Indian Christians. Nehru's position was made the more complex by the international aspect of Indian Christianity: India was in a sense an international stage, where Christian groups outside India watched keenly the experiences of Indian Christians, and could have an influence on India's domestic decision making.

Indian Christians and the Prospect of Independence

Christians had been one of the fastest-growing minorities on the Subcontinent from the later nineteenth century. After partition, numbering just over 8 million, they formed the second-largest minority in the new India, just over 2.3 percent of the population in 1951. This was considerably smaller than the remaining Muslim population but larger than the Sikh minority.[3] As with In-

2. R. E. Frykenberg, *Guntur District, 1788-1848: A History of Local Influence and Central Authority in South India* (Oxford, 1965).

3. See S. C. Dube, ed., *India since Independence: Social Report on India, 1947-1972* (New Delhi, 1977), pp. 29, 143.

dian Muslims, India's Christian minority was not a single monolithic "community." They varied in numerical strength from region to region, and also had different socioeconomic positions and influence within regional society, dependent on their local histories. These varied from the Christians of parts of southern India whose presence often dated from early in the Christian era and who had for centuries been accepted and often influential members of local society, to the recent converts of the Protestant and Catholic mass movements in the late nineteenth and early twentieth centuries. Not surprisingly, the most vulnerable were those who prior to conversion to Christianity had been outcastes in Hindu society, and had depended heavily on foreign missionaries for access to resources such as education and health care, which had helped them raise their expectations of life as well as their socioeconomic status.[4]

Like other Indians, Christians were nationalists in a broad sense of the word, and welcomed the end of imperial rule, as did most expatriate missionaries. Indeed, ecclesiastical "decolonization" had occurred almost twenty years earlier, in 1930, in the case of the Anglican Church of India, Burma, and Ceylon. Indian Christians and their missionary colleagues were working in the environment of a newly autonomous church within the Anglican communion well before political independence, and there were attempts to build up an Indian church leadership, despite the failure to achieve an Indian rather than an expatriate episcopate until well after 1947. Nonetheless, the prospect of independence and the end of the British Raj was fraught with problems for Indian Christians. Some of these lay in the mind, in the sense of apprehension about what the future might hold for indigenous Christians in an environment where nationalism was shot through with the imagery of Hinduism and the identification of the motherland with the mother goddess, and where many of the local politicians within the dominant Congress party clearly saw India in terms of the Hindu majority. As Bishop Azariah, the first Indian Anglican bishop and himself of low-caste background, said in a sermon in Madras Cathedral in 1938, "Nationalism is apt to be identified with loyalty to the ancient religion of the land" and could produce suspicion and hostility toward "any religion which is not supposed to belong to the soil, and which . . . is pledged to propagate itself among all outside it."[5] He was particularly anx-

4. On the making of new Christian communities in Andhra out of the converts of the mass movements, see the study of the first Indian Anglican bishop, who himself came from a lowly family in the Hindu hierarchy; Susan Billington Harper, *In the Shadow of the Mahatma: Bishop V. S. Azariah and the Travails of Christianity in British India* (Grand Rapids and Cambridge, 2000).

5. October, 18, 1938, cited in Harper, *Shadow of the Mahatma,* p. 344. See also my essay "Who Is an Indian? Dilemmas of National Identity at the End of the British Raj in India,"

ious about the future for his own flock of former untouchables in Andhra, fearing that once again they might suffer persecution and oppression, as they once had, at the hands of high-caste Hindu landlords. Even the European bishop of Bombay looked to the future with apprehension, writing home in 1946 to the Society for the Propagation of the Gospel (SPG), of his fears that after independence local Congress leaders might make evangelistic work difficult, with encouragement from the higher echelons of the all-India party, and that grants for Christian schools might be withdrawn and religious teaching might be forbidden in school hours.[6]

Other concerns at the prospect of independence were more evidently material. Under the new constitution all Indian adults were enfranchised, thus giving many Christians the vote for the first time. However, reserved seats for religious and ethnic minorities were done away with, in the belief that these special political provisions for minorities, which had been in place since the constitutional reforms of 1919, had been at the root of many of the political divisions among Indians in anticipation of the devolution of political power from imperial hands, and in the case of Muslims had enabled Muslim politicians to build up a powerful sense of separate identity. Consequently Christians would now have no specific institutional mechanism for registering their views in the legislatures in Delhi and the state capitals. Given their numbers and socioeconomic status, they were likely, therefore, to be at the mercy of the Hindu majority in the processes of democratic politics. It is noteworthy that a Christian member of the Constituent Assembly was one of the sponsors of the move to abolish reserved seats, a reflection of educated Christian understanding of the dangers of claiming any separate political status in the new environment.

More immediately difficult for the Indian Anglican church was the ending of the Indian Ecclesiastical Establishment (IEE), that is, that department of the imperial government of India that, under the Raj, had provided chaplains to minister to the civilian and military European communities, and had maintained some of the key church buildings. In anticipation of independence and the ending of the IEE, the Diocese of Lucknow, for example, was warned by its bishop as early as August 1946 of the likely financial impact on church work; for under the terms of the Indian Church Act of 1927, the diocese enjoyed government help for some buildings, the salary of twenty priests,

---

in *Missions, Nationalism, and the End of Empire,* ed. Brian Stanley (Grand Rapids and Cambridge, 2003), pp. 111-31.

6. Bishop of Bombay to SPG Overseas Secretary, August 17, 1946, USPG Archives, Rhodes House Library, Oxford, Box No. D 517, Letters — Bombay Diocese.

and a bloc grant (of Rs 92,250 in 1943/44) for diocesan work. The latter paid partly for the bishop, the diocesan chaplains, and offices. The bishop of Bombay similarly warned the Church Missionary Society (CMS) back in its London headquarters of the "tremendous burden" that would fall on the church as government assistance ended.[7] The Ecclesiastical Establishment was formally ended on March 31, 1948, and the new government was generous in the matter of handing over church buildings to the Indian Anglican church, giving with them a year's grant for maintenance. Nonetheless, the church was hard hit financially by the new burdens of salaries and building upkeep now laid upon it. As anticipated, the Lucknow diocese found itself in financial trouble, and this was exacerbated by general inflation in India.[8] But it was a similar story throughout the Anglican Church on the Subcontinent. After much discussion the SPG agreed to establish a reserve fund of £25,000 to help alleviate the consequences. This money, available for ten years, was intended largely for salaries and would be administered by the metropolitan of Calcutta (the equivalent of the archbishop).[9] Evidence from the archives of the Anglican missionary societies also indicates that the Anglican Indian church faced fundamental and long-term problems of finance and manpower during the Second World War and after independence. It now paid the price of earlier dependence on British missionary societies. As the British bishop of Assam from 1924 to 1945, George Hubback, lamented in 1940, "The habit of depending on the Mother church is so deeply engrained that it is not easy to eradicate it."[10] Not only were British sources of money gradually drying up. It

7. Circular from Bishop of Lucknow to clergy and church committees of Lucknow diocese, August 1946, CMS Archives, Birmingham University, Asia 1935-59, File G2 I7d1 (Lucknow). See also Bishop of Bombay to CMS Area Secretary, September 2, 1947, File G2 I 3/1 (Bombay Mission 1935-59). Little has been written about the Indian Ecclesiastical Establishment, but see G. Studdert-Kennedy, *British Christians, Indian Nationalists, and the Raj* (Delhi, 1991), pp. 95ff.

8. West Asia Secretary of CMS to Rev. S. H. Dixon, London, January 7, 1948, CMS Archives, Asia 1935-59, File G2 I7d1 (Lucknow).

9. File of letters on the financial problems of the Church of India, Burma, and Ceylon, subsequent to the ending of the Ecclesiastical Establishment, USPG Archives, Box No. D 512, Letters General — India 1939-1966. The SPG grant was enabled by the generosity of the Missionary Society of the Church of Canada, which released the SPG from the obligation of a grant to one of its own clergy funds.

10. Letter of September 15, 1940, to SPG headquarters from Bishop Hubback, USPG Archives, Box No. D 513, Letters received from Diocese of Assam. This box is full of evidence of the financial problems of the Assam diocese. It was not a major area for SPG work, but it provided money for stipends of Indian clergy and lay workers, Christian boys' hostels, pensions, property upkeep, and specifically from its Medical Department for medical work. Similar evidence comes from the CMS Archives: see the correspondence be-

became harder to find missionary recruits, although the Indian church was still demanding them. When the Indian metropolitan asked SPG for an expatriate priest, youth worker, and woman worker, the overseas secretary told him bluntly in 1954, "we could find you neither the workers nor the money for the posts you would wish to establish."[11]

For Nehru, too, the prospect of independence was fraught with apprehension. As he said in his famous speech at midnight as India gained freedom, his country's "tryst with destiny" was only partially accomplished as religious identity had divided the Subcontinent. Within days he was overwhelmed by horror at the violence that broke out in the Punjab as Muslims, Sikhs, and Hindus turned on each other with unexpected savagery. To him this was totally unexpected and sickening, and he admitted to a close Congress colleague, "I must confess that I have no stomach for this leadership. Unless we keep to some standards, freedom has little meaning, and certainly India will not become the great nation we have dreamt of for so long."[12] Two months after independence he still felt that "Life here continues to be nightmarish. Everything seems to have gone awry . . . our foundations have been shaken and all our standards seem to have disappeared."[13] His life's work seemed to be collapsing, as he had for years struggled alongside his mentor, Gandhi, to create a sense of Indian national identity that was not predicated on religion but that welcomed India's religious pluralism as a source of cultural strength. A composite nation would, in his long-term view, find its proper political shape in a secular state that safeguarded all religious minorities. He had spelled this out a year before independence in a London-based Catholic newspaper, reassuring Indian Christians about their future in an independent India, and acknowledging that they "form one of the many enriching elements in the country's cultural and spiritual life. In a country where there are so many creeds we must learn to be tolerant."[14]

---

tween the Nasik Mission and the CMS headquarters on the decline in the grant from CMS compared with the mission's increasing financial needs; Asia 1935-59, File G2 I 3/3 (Nasik Mission). The projected support by CMS for the Nasik Mission was 25 percent less than in 1951, for example: see letter of December 8, 1951, from the Bishop of Nasik and the CMS Secretary of the Mission to Canon Max Warren, General Secretary of CMS, ibid.

11. SPG Overseas Secretary to Metropolitan Aurobindo, July 6, 1954, USPG Archives, Box No. D 518, Letters — Calcutta Diocese.

12. Nehru to Rajendra Prasad, September 17, 1947, Nehru Memorial Museum and Library, New Delhi, J. Nehru Papers post-1947, 2nd Instalment, File No. 231, Correspondence with R. Prasad.

13. Nehru to K. P. S. Menon, October 12, 1947, *Selected Works of Jawaharlal Nehru* (hereafter *SWJN*) (2) (New Delhi, 1984-), 4:585.

14. Interview with Nehru in the *Catholic Herald,* before May 1946, *Selected Works of Jawaharlal Nehru (1)* (New Delhi, 1972-82), 15:171.

Throughout his years as India's first prime minister, Nehru strove to articulate this vision of India as a composite nation, drawing on all its cultural and religious diversities as a source of strength. He argued that to predicate national identity on religion was not only impossible in such a complex society as India's, but was also in principle retrograde, harking back to a "medieval" age rather than embracing modern ideals and forms of polity.[15] Much of his time was taken up with chiding his compatriots for their old and divisive loyalties, including religion, which in his eyes harmed the new inclusive nation that was coming into being. He also expended much precious energy in exhorting the Congress ministers in the state governments to recognize the understandable fears of religious minorities after the British departure, and their very real problems — in such matters as language, or recruitment to the governmental services.[16] One of his most forceful letters to his chief ministers was on this subject in September 1953, when he spoke of his fear that the position of India's minorities was deteriorating, and his apprehensions about "a more insidious form of nationalism [which] is the narrowness of mind that it develops within a country, when a majority thinks itself as the entire nation and in its attempt to absorb the minority actually separates them even more."[17] In this letter he specifically mentioned his "apprehension" that large numbers of their Christian compatriots were uncertain about their place in the new India, and reminded his chief ministers of their need to remember the composite nature of India, and the threat to the inner unity of the nation if majority groups tried impose their values on others. Nehru was also profoundly aware of the international dimensions of issues relating to India's religious minorities. In the case of Christians, their ties with foreign missionary societies, particularly those within Britain and the developing British Commonwealth (in which India was a key player), meant that any Indian Christian grievances would be publicized on a broad international stage and in the domestic political arenas of countries whose support India needed. Very specifically the support of the Catholic hierarchy in India and of the Vatican was a significant element in his long-term hope to achieve the peaceful integration of Portuguese Goa into the Indian Union.[18]

15. Speech by Nehru at Aligarh Muslim University, January 24, 1948, *SWJN* (2), 5:26.

16. On Nehru's work for national integration and his vision of the Indian nation, see Judith M. Brown, *Nehru: A Political Life* (New Haven and London, 2003), particularly part 4, chaps. 10 and 12.

17. Nehru to Chief Ministers, September 20, 1953, in G. Parthasarathi, ed., *Letters to Chief Ministers, 1947-1964* (hereafter *LCM*), vol. 3 (New Delhi, 1985-89), pp. 373-81.

18. See Secret Note by Nehru, March 14, 1955, about his meeting that day with the car-

However, Nehru's position in Indian politics was often ambiguous after independence, as it had been before. Despite his manifest standing in India and his great popularity, as prime minister, his actual power to control events and to ensure the implementation of policies was greatly limited by the constitutional division of powers between the center and the states, and by the nature of the Congress party itself. Over key issues ranging from the treatment of minorities to important economic and social policies he had little practical control, despite the thrust of all-India policy and his own exhortations to his countrymen. Moreover, Congress had within its ranks local groups with their own agendas and understandings of India, who often worked to nullify his policies, even when the all-India party had endorsed them. These tensions were evident on such issues as the legal reform of the status of women or the abolition of untouchability, over land reform in principle and in practice, or over education. Perhaps nowhere was it more evident than in the treatment of religious minorities, given the great spectrum of Hindu opinion within the Congress and particularly its state parties, which sheltered many whose vision of India was one rooted in Hindu tradition and observance, where minorities were barely accepted as proper Indians. Even in its highest ranks there were those whose idea of India seemed to Nehru to be inimical to the minorities — hence his bitter battle with P. D. Tandon for supremacy in Congress in 1950-51, or his difference of opinion with the president, Rajendra Prasad, over the latter's attendance at the opening of a new temple at Somnath in 1951, which Nehru deemed supportive of Hindu revivalism and inappropriate for one whose office should be above sectional and particular interests.[19]

Some Significant Issues

Nehru evolved a very personal style of prime ministerial exercise of power, interesting himself and often intervening in issues that, some later observers think, could have been more appropriately delegated to Cabinet colleagues. But for him these issues were often symbolic of a much wider matter of great significance for the new nation-state. (Cleanliness in government offices, ministers' consumption of electricity, and the nature of advertising by the na-

dinal archbishop of Bombay and other Roman Catholic bishops: J. Nehru Papers post-1947, 1st Instalment, File No. 326, Part 1.

19. On the conflict with Tandon, see Brown, *Nehru,* pp. 194-95; for Nehru's views on the Somnath Temple issue, see *SWJN* (2), vol. 16 i, pp. 603-12.

tional airline were cases in point, where he was interventionist on minute details.) Moreover, he insisted that he should be open and accessible to his compatriots, as befitted the leader of the new democratic nation-state, and in contrast to the style of the former imperial regime. Ordinary people were allowed into his home to present petitions, and an enormous amount of correspondence flowed across his own desk and was dealt with personally by him. Consequently he was very aware of the problems experienced by Indian minorities. In the case of Christians a further channel of communication was an old friend and colleague from the days of the nationalist movement, who had been a close associate of Gandhi, the Punjabi Christian, Raj Kumari Amrit Kaur. For a decade, 1947-57, she was minister for health in the union government and thus in a position of daily access to the prime minister. Not only did Indian Christians make their problems known to the prime minister through her; she also had connections with international missionary organizations. Nehru did not like the fact that she had become "a kind of representative of Christians in India," but could not object because of her wide contacts.[20] Her presence in government made him unusually sensitive to the problems perceived or experienced by Christians.

However, Nehru soon became aware that despite his own sensitivity to minority problems, and despite the national rhetoric of unity, there were occasions relating to Christians (as indeed to other minorities) where he had little leverage over specific local situations, often because state governments and local Congress parties and officials would not cooperate with him. Early in 1955 Amrit Kaur made him aware that Christians in Meerut district of his own home state of Uttar Pradesh (UP) were being harassed by members of the Arya Samaj, a Hindu revivalist movement, with the connivance or encouragement of the district authorities. In particular they complained of antimissionary activity and forcible reconversion of Christians to Hinduism. (Many UP Christians were recent converts from among low or untouchable castes and therefore particularly vulnerable to local pressures.) Nehru forwarded two letters from Amrit Kaur to his home minister, G. B. Pant, who had recently left the post of chief minister of UP, indicating that he felt there was a good deal of truth in the complaints. Pant assured him that he had spoken to the district magistrate and also spoken in the area himself and hoped that everything would now be all right.[21] Within days Nehru felt he had to

20. Nehru to K. N. Katju, February 17, 1954, *SWJN* (2), 25:226.

21. Nehru's letter to Pant of March 10, 1955, is cited on p. 497 of *SWJN* (2), 28:497; Pant's reply of April 3, 1955, is in *Selected Works of Govind Ballabh Pant,* ed. B. R. Nanda (New Delhi, 1993-), 16:308.

write again on the matter, this time to the UP chief minister, indicating robustly that he thought "that something fairly effective should be done to prevent this kind of harassment and victimisation."[22] He received an assurance nearly two months later that the state government had indeed done so.

Far more problematic was the experience of Christians in central India, where local Hindu activists and the state government all seemed to be implicated. Complaints poured in to his office in the mid-1950s about harassment of Christians, particularly at the hands of members of the RSS, the militant Hindu nationalist organization that had been temporarily banned after Gandhi's assassination, and had strong roots in the area. The Roman Catholic cardinal archbishop of Bombay, Cardinal Gracias, who had spoken to Nehru personally about his anxieties about the treatment of Christians in various parts of India, in 1952, 1953, and 1954, now in 1955 requested a further meeting, and gave him in writing and in person a long catalogue of problems specifically in Madhya Pradesh, including actual violence against Christians, a spate of court cases, nonrecognition of and lack of grants for Catholic schools, and refusal to give scholarships to Christian tribal converts. He also emphasized the way a state government inquiry, appointed in 1954, into Christian missions was experienced as harassment of the local Christian minority. Nehru was deeply troubled that Christians as a large group in Indian society should be suffering such a sense of apprehension and insecurity, and largely blamed the RSS and Arya Samaj for generating local tension. But he was also concerned about the impact of such problems on the question of Goa, for Catholic bishops had been helpful in this matter, and Nehru also recognized the importance of Vatican support for the molding of Indian Catholic and international opinion.[23] However, repeated letters to Ravi Shankar Shukla, the chief minister of Madhya Pradesh (MP), led nowhere, and by late May 1955 Nehru was reluctantly convinced that the state government "approves of all these anti-Christian activities," as he told the Congress president, U. N. Dhebar. He hoped that the state Congress party could be used to counter the anti-Christian movement. "If the Government fails to do its duty, the Congress at least should not equally fail."[24] (Here again he mentioned the prob-

22. Nehru to Sampurnanand, April 12, 1955, *SWJN* (2), 28:497.

23. Cardinal Gracias to Nehru, February 21, 1955, J. Nehru Papers post-1947, 1st Instalment, File No. 320; Note by Cardinal for Nehru prior to their meeting, March 10, 1955, File No. 325, Part 1; Secret Note by Nehru on his meeting with cardinal and other Roman Catholic bishops on March, 14, 1955, dated same day, File No. 325, Part 1.

24. Nehru to U. N. Dhebar, May 27, 1955, Nehru Memorial Museum and Library, New Delhi, AICC Papers post-1947, 2nd Instalment, Correspondence of Congress Presidents, File 1955, No. 4307. On the same day Nehru also wrote a very strong letter to the MP chief

lem of Goa and the danger that Goan Catholics might become hostile to any merger with India.) Dhebar in turn talked to Pant, the home minister, who was also worried about what was going on in MP, but he reported bleakly to Nehru that the president of the Nagpur Provincial Congress Committee was a hard worker but had neither the standing nor the ability to tackle the issue, and in the circumstances he did not know what he could do.[25] So on an issue Nehru felt to be crucial, for both the country's national identity and also in the longer term her territorial integrity, he found himself hamstrung by local opinion, manifested in overtly Hindu activism and more insidiously in the local government and the Congress party. Indeed, when the inquiry into missionary work in Madhya Pradesh was eventually published, Nehru was adamant that the government of India had nothing to do with it and was not committed to its remarks or recommendations.[26]

Another aspect of the problems faced by minorities in the new India was underrepresentation in the structures of the state and its public services. If minorities were found to be underrepresented in the actual structures of decision making and governance, discriminatory treatment was the more likely, as was minority alienation from rather than incorporation in the new nation. Nehru recognized this clearly and was concerned at the small numbers of Christians who were elected to the legislatures. As he wrote in 1954 to a prominent Madras Christian legislator, who later became governor of Maharashtra, "I do not like the idea of any kind of communal or reserved representation. But certainly I shall exert such influence as I have to see that they [minorities] are properly represented."[27] This was a considerable admission from one who had fought the idea of communal electorates for decades and had helped to ensure that they were removed after independence. However, the problem was not resolved at the next general elections of 1957, and a Christian association from Bangalore complained to Nehru of the small number of Christians elected. The hapless Congress president, Dhebar, again

---

minister, detailing his extreme disquiet and telling him that such anti-Christian activity in MP did his government little credit; *SWJN* (2), 28:501-2.

25. U. N. Dhebar to Nehru, June 4, 1955, AICC Papers post-1947, 2nd Instalment, Correspondence of Congress Presidents, File 1955, No. 4307. G. B. Pant's concern was evident after he had also seen Cardinal Gracias when Gracias had come to see the prime minister; he had written a letter telling Shukla of the cardinal's complaints, including his emphasis on the problems created by the state government's inquiry into Christian missions: Pant to R. S. Shukla, March 20, 1955, *Selected Works of Govind Ballabh Pant,* 16:307.

26. Note by Nehru, October 23, 1956, J. Nehru Papers post-1947, 1st Instalment, File No. 481.

27. Nehru to P. V. Cherian, March 24, 1954, *SWJN* (2), 25:228.

had to tell his prime minister of the political reality and noted that the main failures were in Bombay and Andhra, where the local Congress parties could not be persuaded to support Christian candidates.[28] Nehru was also deeply worried at the small numbers of minorities in the military and civil services and in the police, as well as the effective barriers to members of minorities winning seats in the state and central legislatures and to holding office in Congress. He acknowledged it was worst in the case of Muslims, but worried about Christians also (except in Travancore-Cochin, which later became the state of Kerala). In his view this was serious for Congress, for India as a whole, and also for India's international reputation. But what really troubled him was that most of his countrymen appeared not to recognize the importance of the problem.[29]

Islam and Christianity were both Indian religions with international dimensions and connections, a fact to which Nehru, as his own foreign minister, was very sensitive. For Indian Christians their main connections with a wider Christian world came through the continuing work of foreign missionaries, who were in turn supported by Christian congregations abroad who were anxious to know about missionary work in India and the experience of their fellow believers in the new nation-state. Many missionaries were profoundly sympathetic toward the new India, and had spent years of their lives working for and with the Indian churches: their hope was to continue to do so after independence.[30] However, for many Indians who were not Christians, and particularly for those who envisaged the new India in specifically Hindu terms, missionaries were a dangerous relic of imperialism and a cultural threat to national identity. This had been abundantly clear in Madhya Pradesh, in the appointment and inquiry of the Nyogi committee into the working of foreign missions. As the astute leader of the CMS, Canon Max Warren, realized, the hostility to Christians in that particular area was sharpened by the presence of a significant tribal population, whose conversion was an abhorrent and dangerous prospect to a local government manned by or-

28. U. N. Dhebar to Nehru, August 25/26, 1957, AICC Papers post-1947, 2nd Instalment, Correspondence of Congress Presidents, File 1957 No. 4309.

29. Nehru to Chief Ministers, April 26, 1954, *LCM*, 3:535-36.

30. One example among many was the Cambridge Brotherhood in Delhi. Originally a missionary brotherhood of Anglican priests, supported by the SPG, it became a religious community within and serving the Anglican Church of India (and later still the united Church of North India), recruited Indian members, and also demonstrated its beliefs by service of the poor and destitute in Delhi. Its British members without exception remained after 1947 to serve their adopted land until their deaths. At the time of writing (2004), one such still remains in the community.

thodox Hindus. He noted that CMS could not work among the Gond tribespeople of Nagpur partly because it was in the state that had "the most anti-foreign Government of any in India, and they are particularly suspicious of foreigners in the tribal areas."[31] Hostility to missionaries was, however, a far wider issue than the actions of one state government. Nehru consequently became caught up in the whole question of the government's postindependence policy toward missionaries, much to his discomfort.

The policy issue became an urgent one early in 1953 largely because of the specific situations in the northeastern hill regions of the country, and in Madhya Pradesh, where there were significant tribal populations. In the Northeast, tribal communities had been profoundly influenced by Christian missionary work from the late nineteenth century, and many had actually become Christian. But they remained isolated from the settled Hindu society of the plains, and deeply suspicious of its creeping influence. From the time of Indian independence some of these groups, principally the Nagas, had called for their own autonomy, and no compromise between the tribal leadership and Nehru's government had proved possible. This was perhaps not surprising, given Nehru's passion for India's physical integrity and its simultaneous vulnerability in the northwest; and given the pressure from the Assam state government for greater control of the tribal area. The presence of Christian missionaries in areas of such contestation came to be seen as a serious threat to the new nation-state. The home minister, K. N. Katju, when pressed in Parliament on April 21, 1953, was clearly unwilling to say much, but did insist that it had been made clear to the missionary societies that missionaries who contributed to social welfare, particularly medical and educational work, were welcome, but that "evangelical prosyletising activities" were undesirable.[32] Not surprisingly this sparked off criticism from Christians in India and abroad, and Nehru found himself having to field intense criticism and to explain his government's attitude. He insisted that there had been no change in government policy as a whole toward missionaries, but that the Northeast was a particularly sensitive area from a political and military perspective, and that no new foreigners would be allowed in that area; this was because they were foreign and not because of their religious affiliation. He believed that in other tribal areas where state governments were hostile to missionary activity and there was a danger of local conflict, they should proceed carefully and not encourage mission activity, while in other areas his government should inter-

31. Note by Canon Max Warren, July 28, 1958, CMS Archives, Asia, 1935-59, G2 I 8 d1 (Nagpur).

32. Lok Sabha Debates, 3rd Series, 1953, vol. II, Part 1, p. 2306.

fere very little with missionaries. Social and humanitarian work by missionaries was always welcome, but not hostility to Indian culture. He was particularly insistent that India would stick to its principle of full religious tolerance.[33] A further dimension of Nehru's own response to this crisis was the evidence that the numbers of missionaries had been increasing since 1947 and that many of them were Americans. Privately he was prepared to admit that he found American attitudes, and their sense of superiority, culturally unpalatable. "I am not concerned with their religion, but politically they are becoming more and more irritating. They carry their politics and their peculiar outlook of the world wherever they go. I am afraid that if this continues, we shall have to be much stricter with them. That, I repeat, has nothing to do with religion."[34]

Nehru's was an unenviable position, caught between members of his own central government and local governments who were far more hostile to missionary work than he was, and harassed by criticisms from Christians at home and overseas, just when he was arguing for an inclusive and tolerant nation-state. His discomfort was evident when he felt it essential to write to the president of India himself, Rajendra Prasad, whose overt support for Hindu revivalism he had already deplored (see above). Prasad had presided in August 1953 over a meeting at the president's official residence where members of a Hindu social work organization had discussed conversion to Christianity among tribal movements and suggested that missionaries offered them material inducements to become Christians. Nehru said he was "concerned with the effect that your association with this matter might have on a large number of Christians. The President, whatever his personal views and convictions might be, is above religion and is the Head of a secular State, which treats all religions alike. He is in fact the symbol of that secular State." If that symbol was compromised, it "would no doubt create apprehensions in the minds of many of our citizens."[35] Prasad agreed that he should be careful that his conduct did not undermine the presidential position, but somewhat ingenuously said that the members of the organization could not help talking about an issue on which they felt they had grounds for complaint.

33. For Nehru's attitude in mid-1953, see Nehru to T. T. Krishnamachari, August 1, 1953, *SWJN* (2), 23:245-46; and his attempts to assuage the anxieties of Christians in India and abroad. Note of an interview with the Cardinal Archbishop of Bombay, July 30, 1953, pp. 243-44, and Nehru to Archbishop Brillioth of Sweden, August 22, 1953, pp. 248-50, and in SPG Archives, Box No. D 518: Letters — Calcutta Diocese.

34. Nehru to Amrit Kaur, August 30, 1953, *SWJN* (2), 23:250. See also his letter to her of October 25, 1953, 24:326-27.

35. Nehru to Rajendra Prasad, August 10, 1953, *SWJN* (2), 23:246-47.

Toward the end of 1953 Nehru sent a major policy note to his Home Ministry.[36] The starting point for policy should be the fact that Christianity was a major religion in India, indeed the third largest. So missionaries had to be judged not on the grounds that they were evangelists (for the preaching of Christianity was legitimate in a plural society where freedom of religion was guaranteed), but on secular, social, and political grounds — whether there were too many foreigners in the country, as he believed, whether they were taking employment from Indians, or whether they came from countries that were politically undesirable in one way or another (such as the United States or Spain). Frontier and tribal regions were a special case where political sensitivities had to be taken into account. The regulations governing the entry of missionaries would have to be redrafted and made tighter — but without reference to evangelical work. He felt that his government was in a profoundly uncomfortable position: the state had been too lenient in the past in permitting the entry of foreign missionaries, yet it had created the impression among many Indian Christians of being intolerant. A formula was needed that provided for stricter controls but did not give the impression of a shift to a less tolerant position. As he explained some weeks later to a prominent Indian Christian leader, there was no question of considering Christianity an alien religion in India or of prohibiting evangelism. The real question was that of missionaries as foreigners, and too many foreigners was undesirable from a political and social point of view.[37]

The controversy rumbled on through 1954 and Nehru found he had to put himself in the front line on an issue that went to the heart of the nature of the Indian nation-state, publicly pleading for tolerance toward Christians, and an approach to missionaries based on India's political sensitivities. He argued this in Parliament in May;[38] and several weeks later wrote to chief ministers on the matter, noting that the controversy was troubling him.[39] Dealing with the issue as a religious one would go against the constitution and the fact that

36. Note, October 25, 1953, *SWJN* (2), 24:322-25.

37. J. Nehru to Bishop S. K. Mondol, president of the Christian Council of India and Pakistan, November 21, 1953, included in SPG Archives, Box No. D 518: Letters — Calcutta Diocese. Interestingly Nehru said that the number of foreign missionaries had nearly doubled since 1947. In this same box there is also an undated statement by K. N. Katju, which had been sent to SPG in London by the metropolitan in Calcutta sometime in the second half of 1953. It stated that Christians were an integral part of the Indian nation with a right to profess, teach, and propagate their faith, but not to offend other Indians' religious sensibilities. He wanted Christians to stand on their own feet and not to rely on foreigners, though missionaries would still be allowed into India who helped the country.

38. Statement by Nehru in the Lok Sabha, May 18, 1954, *SWJN* (2), 25:411-12.

39. Nehru to Chief Ministers, June 15, 1954, *LCM*, 3:568-69.

India was a secular state, and "might encourage all kinds of aggressive tendencies in our people." He was trying to deal with it on the political grounds of where foreigners should and should not be allowed to go. Although he personally did not like evangelism, he did not feel that they should worry about this as missionaries had never had much success, even under British rule, whereas now public opinion and most state governments were opposed to them. "Therefore, nothing much can happen, and all this fear and apprehension of what the Christian missionaries might do seems to be grossly exaggerated." A little later he addressed presidents of provincial Congress committees, who were the core Congress leaders in the states, on the need for unity in India and Congress's role in pursuing this. Again he underlined the principles of the state's policy to Christian missionaries and warned against aggression toward missionaries, which he saw in some areas: "this kind of thing should be sternly discouraged. It is no part of our nationalism and it gives reign to a narrow and bigoted approach to a problem which should be dealt with calmly on the national level."[40]

In late November 1954 the Cabinet had laid down new policy guidelines on the admission and treatment of foreign missionaries. New missions had to have permission from the government of India — intended to preserve frontier and tribal areas from any new foreign work. State governments could withdraw recognition of a mission. Missions had to be sponsored by Indian church organizations, but in general missionaries already working in India should be permitted to continue their work, while doctors and nurses should be freely admitted. Commonwealth missionaries would now need visas, as did foreigners from outside the Commonwealth. Not surprisingly, Nehru faced criticism inside and outside India. The cardinal archbishop of Bombay complained that restrictions on missionaries prejudiced the exercise of normal Catholic Christian life, and particularly noted the new restrictions on Commonwealth missionaries.[41] Meanwhile in Britain, the heart of the Commonwealth, there was real concern about this new imposition, and the archbishop of Canterbury took it up with Nehru while he was visiting London. A formula was achieved at Nehru's behest between the Foreign and Home Ministries, designed to assuage Commonwealth opinion. The visa requirement was dropped for Commonwealth missionaries, and instead they would need special endorsements in their passports. Those who had worked in India be-

40. Nehru to PCC Presidents, August 5, 1954, *SWJN* (2), 26:200-204.

41. Cardinal Archbishop of Bombay to Nehru's Private Secretary, March 10, 1955, J. Nehru Papers post-1947, 1st instalment, File No. 325, Part 1; Secret note by Nehru on a meeting with the Archbishop on March 14, dated same day, File No. 326, Part 1.

fore would need a "no objection to return" certificate from the state in which they had worked. This system was presented as a mechanism for collecting information about missionary numbers. Moreover, the Indian High Commission in London was to be liberal in issuing special endorsements for British missionaries, as Britain herself placed no restrictions on the entry of Indians. Nehru insisted that his government should inform the major missionary societies of this as a matter of courtesy but also to elicit their cooperation.[42]

For Nehru the question of foreign missionaries touched on the core value of tolerance in a plural society, and the very nature of the new Indian nation and the nation-state. It mattered immensely to him that Indian Christians felt a valued and integral part of that nation, and believed that they would be fairly treated by the nation-state. But he also recognized that the issue had repercussions abroad, and that India's standing and policies would be judged abroad within the international context of Christianity. On no subject was this more vital than the vexed question of Goa and its continuation as a Portuguese enclave, and he was deeply anxious lest Indian Catholic opinion about the domestic treatment of Christians and missionaries should adversely affect the Vatican's supportive stance on Goa and its capacity to influence world Catholic opinion.[43] Many Goans were of course Christians, including the cardinal archbishop of Bombay, and in his attempts to integrate Goa into the nation-state Nehru was evidently concerned to carry them with him, whether they were inside the territory or outside in western India. When he eventually and reluctantly authorized the use of force in 1961 to end Portuguese rule, amid outcry abroad, he was deeply grateful for the support of the archbishop.[44]

Conclusion

Focusing on a number of critical issues relating to Indian Christians during the period of Nehru's prime ministership sheds light on many aspects of the

42. On this reworking of policy toward Commonwealth missionaries, see J. Nehru Papers post-1947, 1st instalment, File No. 323, in which there is a Minute of an interdepartmental meeting on the issue with representatives from the Home and Foreign Ministries, February 21, 1955, and a note by Nehru, March 5, 1955, for the Commonwealth Secretary.

43. Secret Note by Nehru, March 14, 1955, on meeting that day with Cardinal Archbishop of Bombay and other Catholic Bishops, J. Nehru Papers post-1947, 1st instalment, File No. 326, Part 1.

44. Nehru to Cardinal Gracias, December 22, 1961, J. Nehru Papers post-1947, 1st instalment, File No. 728.

emerging nation-state as well as on his own ideas and vision of a new India, and the complex position in which he found himself. Although he was not personally a religious person, he recognized the sensitivities of India's minority religious groups, and feared deeply the sort of Hindu nationalism that would have shut minorities out of the rhetoric and reality of the nation-state. To him such nationalism was narrow and obscurantist, a denial of India's rich and plural cultural heritage, and a serious threat to national integration in a context where the new nation encompassed significant minority groups. Moreover, as India's two largest minority groups belonged to international faith communities, any ill-treatment of them or threat to their position was bound to have international repercussions on India's world standing. Yet as this brief essay has shown, he found it extraordinarily difficult to persuade many of his Hindu countrymen of the multifaceted necessity of tolerance in the context of a plural society, and to imbue them with his vision of a composite nation, despite his extraordinary standing in public life. Even more disquieting was the fact that the very structures of the state and of his own party were often controlled by colleagues who did not share his vision or priorities. During his own lifetime it was clear that he could only work through people who were positioned to undermine his policies and authority in their local situation, where their interests and vision of the future clashed with his. Madhya Pradesh showed this most starkly in relation to Christians, just as Guntur district had over a century earlier shown the government of Madras how reliant it was on Indian subordinates who in turn could use the structures of government for their own ends. The rhetoric of Nehru's nation-state was predicated on tolerance, the value of pluralism, and the goal of integration in a broad community above narrow loyalties of region, caste, religion, and language. The reality was very different. Consequently the position of Indian Christians, even then, foreshadowed many of the potential problems now starkly apparent in India, when those who control state power and public communications have fostered a vision of India less plural and less tolerant than Nehru's.

CHAPTER 12

Christian Interpretation of "Hinduism": Between Understanding and Theological Judgment

JOHN B. CARMAN

A Role for Non-Indian Scholars?

What can scholars outside of India contribute to Christian interpretations of Hindu traditions? Indian Christians' risky involvement with a minority religious community gives them a greater right to speak than less involved outsiders, but outside scholars can bring a useful perspective. Many of them share in a long scholarly tradition that has struggled with the tension between "objective" history and "faith-filled" history. When they turn their attention to the Hindu tradition, this tension becomes more complicated. In addition to their Christian faith, they are concerned both with "objective" Hindu history and with Hindus' understanding of their own religion. This helps them to appreciate Hindus' understanding of their own history at the same time they are looking at Hindu religion in the light of their Christian faith.

The attitudes of Indian Christians toward their Hindu neighbors are diverse. Behind those attitudes are the various Western theological positions regarding other religions, but they are now voiced much more by Indian Christians themselves than by Western missionaries. Western scholarly approaches to Hindu traditions have become increasingly less theological and in some cases entirely secular. Scholarship related to Christian theological reflection is largely in the hands of those who are members of Indian Christian churches. Some of the continuing contribution of Western scholars has come in more thorough exploration of Indian church history. In this, Robert Frykenberg has played an important role, not only by his own work, but also by the encouragement he has given to young Indian scholars, both Christians and Hindus, to study church developments in the larger context of cultural, political, and religious developments in modern Indian history.

As one whose personal biography and scholarly interests have intersected with Bob Frykenberg's, it may be appropriate for me to consider the question of the current role, if any, of "outside" students of the Indian scene, including those like us who began our lives in India and continue to regard it as a second home. For me this is obviously a personal as well as a scholarly question. It is the more pressing because I have long postponed my attempt at a Christian theological interpretation of Hindu traditions. Questions that fifty years ago seemed exotic in an American seminary setting are now of much greater relevance to an increasingly diverse American society, but it may be that the best persons to answer these questions are Christians in India. My question is, then: Should assessments of Hinduism be left to Indian Christians?

There is no doubt that many of the condemnations of Hindu beliefs and practices by my missionary predecessors were both insensitive and ill informed, and that even those opinions based on greater factual knowledge and closer acquaintance with Hindus in their vicinity often did not present a fair picture because of their preconceptions. There are also cases where the evidence of objectionable practices was exaggerated or distorted in order to stimulate greater support from the missionaries' home countries.[1] There were, however, some missionaries who made a careful scrutiny of the religious practices and customs they observed,[2] as well as others who made scholarly studies of Hindu sacred texts and moral treatises.[3] It should be noted, moreover, that Hindu reformers shared in the sharp critique of significant features of nineteenth-century Hindu life.[4] There were a few missionaries from abroad who went still further in their sympathetic portrayal of Hindu social courtesies and religious quests.[5]

1. For example, the British Baptist missionary William Ward (1769-1823), whose writings were instrumental in convincing the British Parliament to lift sanctions against missionary involvement in Bengal. This has been discussed by Norvin Hein in an unpublished paper entitled "Protestant Views of Hinduism, 1600-1825," presented at Yale Divinity School in 1956.

2. Cf. the work of the pioneer Protestant missionary Bartholomaeus Ziegenbalg (1683-1719) and the Roman Catholic missionary Abbé Dubois (1765-1848). More recent examples would include the descriptions of South Indian village religion by Bishop Henry Whitehead (1853-1947) and W. T. Elmore (1871-1935).

3. Cf. the work of J. N. Farquhar (1861-1929) and Nicol Macnicol (1870-1952). See Eric Sharpe's discussion of Farquhar's predecessors in *Not to Destroy but to Fulfill* (Lund, 1965).

4. See, for example, Bruce Robertson, *Raja Rammohan Ray: The Father of Modern India* (New York and Oxford, 1995).

5. See Richard DeSmet's unpublished dissertation on Sankara, and the many recent publications of Francis X. Clooney.

In almost no case, however, did Christians from elsewhere in the world have as much at stake personally as did Indian Christians, some of whom experienced ostracism from their families and persecution from more senior family members or higher-caste Hindus. Many who were never physically attacked faced the constant criticism of their Hindu neighbors. Even today, the decision to be an active member of a small Christian minority can prove costly. It is this potentially risky involvement with the Christian community that gives Indian Christians a greater right to speak than less involved outsiders, whether or not their opinions of their neighbors' religion are well founded.

Nevertheless, there are good reasons for keeping Christian theological interpretations international. It is the genius of Christianity to be local and to express its universal character in terms intelligible to every "family, tribe, and nation." Yet that localization can lead to a subordination of what is universal to some particular *local* interest. In the current situation in India, many Christians identify either with the country's Hindu majority (and sometimes with the Hindu nationalists claiming to represent that majority) or with the very large "outcaste" group at the bottom of the traditional social structure, a group some of whose leaders now refer to themselves by the new collective name of Dalit (the "crushed" or "oppressed"). Identification with Hindu India can weaken the church's concern with other religious minorities, especially the Muslims, as well as concern for the church's universal message. Identification with the Dalits, on the other hand, can lead to a wholesale rejection of the high-caste (Brahmin) contribution to the church's own existence, as well as to a theology that bemoans the oppression of the Dalits but does not articulate their distinctive cultural and religious resources. An outside perspective on Hindu life is less likely to be affected by the need for solidarity with some larger group outside the Christian community.

There is value in having a number of outside perspectives from different national and confessional backgrounds. Each will have its own cultural prejudice, to be sure, but may also have the benefit of experiencing some other kind of interreligious encounter. Present Western perspectives may still be influenced by colonialist or neocolonialist attitudes, but they do benefit from the resources of knowledge and understanding accumulated in the modern Western study of many religious traditions. This potential advantage is in many cases unrealized because until recently few Western theologians had enough specific knowledge of other religions to interpret them theologically. This judgment depends, of course, on my assumption that adequate theological interpretation requires a close acquaintance with that which is being interpreted. While this may seem obvious to most theologians of this generation, it was not so in the past. Even today, theologians whose approach is that of applying a priori judgments concerning other religions continue to act as though detailed knowledge was unnecessary for reaching confident conclusions. This seems to me as true of very positive Christian assessments of other religions as of very negative ones.

Those who do want their theological interpretation to be informed by empirical and historical studies also have a significant problem: the difficulty of utilizing non-Christian believers' self-understandings of their faith to inform an evaluation of their faith from a Christian perspective. If such understanding is considered a prerequisite for evaluation, the inability to reach adequate understanding can lead to indefinite postponement of theological judgment. For many years I believed that this was an important reason for my postponing a systematic Christian interpretation of Hindu life and thought. I still think inadequate understanding should put a brake on theological interpretation, but I have recently become convinced that more important than the presumed degree of understanding is its nature. This change of view came after my dismaying discovery of an important difference between the scholar who has influenced my own approach to the history and phenomenology of religion, W. B. Kristensen, and a number of his Dutch students who wanted to utilize his general understanding of religion for their diverse theological interpretations. Kristensen did not, like a host of modern students of religion, reject the possibility of a theological approach. He thought, however, that such theological interpretation was necessarily meant to defend one's own religious position. He did not wish to engage in such theological defense because he saw his task as one of understanding others' religious positions, and he believed that such understanding requires one to recognize that the adherents of the religion one is studying regard their own religious practices as encountering absolute truth, never a lesser truth coming to full expression in Christian faith.[6] Kristensen's approach discloses his serious vocational commitment to understanding other religions, but it leaves a theoretical disjunction between the universal implication of one's own faith and the "truth" of the other faith one is trying to understand. The Dutch scholars who utilize a general understanding of religion for specific theological purposes

6. John B. Carman, "Modern Understanding of Ancient Insight: Distinctive Contributions of W. B. Kristensen's Phenomenology of Religion," in *Man, Meaning, and Mystery: 100 Years of History of Religions in Norway; The Heritage of W. Brede Kristensen*, ed. Sigurd Hjelde (Leiden, 2000), pp. 157-72, referring to various articles included in W. Brede Kristensen, *Symbool en Werkelijkheid: Een bundel godsdiensthistorische studiën* (Symbol and reality: A collection of studies in the history of religion) (Arnhem, 1954).

have tried to avoid that disjunction.[7] Certainly we should recognize that a truth affirmed or a practice borrowed to be incorporated into a Christian context is changed from its original setting, and may well appear to those in that setting to be grievously misunderstood.

I believe that the Christian student of another religion must live with the awareness that theological incorporation of some aspects of Hindu beliefs and practices into Christian life involves an understanding of those elements different from that of the Hindu believer. The Christian scholar's task is to come to an appreciative understanding of viewpoints that at some points seem very similar and at other points very different. There are multiple Hindu views of reality and the religious person's place in it. Christian scholars also need to be acquainted with the variety of Indian Christian perspectives. I shall illustrate the complexity of this task by attempting to interpret within a Christian framework Ramanuja's Vaishnava stance toward the modes of divine self-disclosure and divine-human relationships.

What Can Christians Learn from Ramanuja?

When I discovered devotional Hinduism during an introductory college course, my first question was: What could I, as a Christian, learn from Hindu bhakti? My first Christian theological guide was Rudolf Otto's *India's Religion of Grace and Christianity Compared and Contrasted,* which begins with an emphatic presentation of the religious profundity of this Hindu tradition but goes on sharply to contrast "India's religion of grace" with Protestant Christian faith.[8] A few years later, when I came to the stage of choosing a topic for my doctoral dissertation, I proposed a study of Ramanuja's doctrine of incarnation *(avatara)* as a test case for a general Christian interpretation of other religions.[9] Once embarked on my project, however, I not only had to restrict myself to the thought of one Hindu theologian, but I also had to confine my study to trying to understand this Hindu theology, postponing to a later work its evaluation from a Christian perspective. That "later work" is now finally in progress, and, like the earlier distinction between understanding and evalua-

7. Here I have in mind G. van der Leeuw, C. J. Bleeker, H. Kraemer, and K. A. H. Hidding. See my article noted in note 6 above.

8. Rudolf Otto, *Die Gnadenreligion Indiens und das Christentum* (Munich, 1930). English version entitled *India's Religion of Grace and Christianity Compared and Contrasted,* trans. Frank Hugh Foster (London, 1930).

9. Published as *The Theology of Ramanuja: An Essay in Interreligious Understanding* (New Haven and London, 1974).

tion, my approach depends on the theological sketch of the Dutch Reformed theologian and phenomenologist of religion, Gerardus van der Leeuw.[10]

In my current work, I am exploring the potential in the ancient Christian doctrine of the "seed-bearing Word" *(logos spermatikos)* for positively assessing Hindu traditions, especially the devotional tradition of Ramanuja. I hope to develop further the Christian interpretation of Ramanuja's teaching that I first presented at a conference in India over thirty years ago (January 1977 in Bangalore).[11]

My understanding of Ramanuja's thought is written in English and deliberately uses English terms with Christian theological meanings when I consider them the most appropriate translation for Ramanuja's concepts. That Christian terms often are appropriate implies that there are significant similarities between Christian and Vaishnava theology. For the same reason Vaishnava terms have often been used to express Christian doctrines in Indian languages. Those similarities do not mean that individual concepts or the larger doctrines are identical. Considering how different are their respective religious and cultural contexts, however, the similarities have to be taken seriously by the Christian theologian: they raise the question of the presence of the *Logos* in Ramanuja's theology and the subsequent tradition based upon it. We can certainly see Vaishnava terminology contributing historically to Indian articulations of Christian faith. Whether that is also a contribution in a spiritual sense — a genuine enrichment of the Christian community in India — is something about which Christians have differed and which they will continue to reconsider in every generation. My assessment is in some respects at a greater distance than those of Christians who have lived their lives alongside the community of Ramanuja's followers. I have tried to note the details of specific doctrines and their role in his total system.

Ramanuja's interpretation of the Vedanta affirms both the reality and the value of the world, which is both subordinated to, and connected with, the infinite reality of Vishnu-Narayana. I concur with those Christians who hold that his teaching provides the most adequate integration of the twin emphases of the Vedanta on pluralism and monism and thereby gives a promising basis for expressing the metaphysical dimension of Christian faith. How Christians are to appropriate and incorporate this metaphysical vision is far from clear, however, for it is not based on a rational interpretation of reality

10. See John B. Carman, "The Theology of a Phenomenologist," *Harvard Divinity Bulletin* 29, no. 3 (1965): 13-42.

11. Published as "Ramanuja's Theology and Christian Theism," *Journal of Vaisnava Studies* 2 (1993): 5-16.

comparable to Platonic and Aristotelian philosophy, but on the Vedic scriptures, which are not open to all rational persons, but only to that privileged minority qualified to hear, understand, and experience the eternal Vedic words. Should Christians reinterpret Ramanuja's metaphysics, against his explicit statements, as nevertheless based on a rational interpretation of reality? Or, alternatively, should Christians accept the Vedic vision as the eternal truth about both infinite and finite reality? A third possibility would be to demonstrate that the same metaphysics is implied in the biblical revelation of God. In any case, Ramanuja elaborates a view of souls as presently in bondage to their accumulated negative karma and thus forced to return to the world in birth after birth, but he maintains that the entire world of material bodies and embodied souls is intended to glorify God: that is, to express in the finite realm God's power and goodness. For those who believe in the truth of Vedanta, the finite world is *now*, along with God's infinite world, a realm of glory. Despite his horror of linking the Supreme Lord with anything defiling, Ramanuja insists that the entire finite universe is the body of God, who is its indwelling Self, as its supporting ground, its ultimate controller, and its owner.[12]

This soul-body relation between God and the world is the doctrine for which Ramanuja is best known by Indian philosophers outside his own community. It is less well recognized how Ramanuja interprets the same concepts in his understanding of devotion (bhakti). He considers devotion to be the realization at the level of intense feeling of what is always true metaphysically. Each of the three aspects of the soul-body relationship needs to be personally realized. First, all finite beings rest on the divine Support, but the serious devotee yearns for the divine Presence, feeling that his very life depends on that experience. Second, while all creatures are under the divine control, the devotee consciously acknowledges that all his actions are not his own doing and do not belong to him, for it is the Lord himself, as the Inner Controller, who is the active agent in the devotee's life. Third, the devotee is not satisfied with the metaphysical truth that the whole universe is the Lord's property and every creature is at the Lord's disposal. The devotee yearns to serve, believing that the highest privilege of any creature is eternal service to the Lord and the Lord's servants.

Both the metaphysical and the devotional dimensions of Ramanuja's teaching concerning the divine-human relation are somewhat different from the comparable doctrines in most Western Christian theologies (in part because of a different doctrine of creation). In Ramanuja's doctrine of divine

12. Carman, *The Theology of Ramanuja*, pp. 124-33.

descent into the finite world, the similarities to Christian faith seem to me more striking but the differences more significant. I have explored in *Majesty and Meekness*[13] some of the similarities between Ramanuja's conception of God's supremacy and accessibility and the expressions of some Christian theologians, but I have also noted the differences in the conceptions of the ways God enters the finite and fallen world.[14] The orthodox Christian view of God's incarnation in Christ has always affirmed the full humanity of Jesus. In the Vaishnava view, the body of the *avatara* consists of real matter, but of a special kind, made only of the noblest of the three elements that in various proportions combine to form ordinary matter. For many Christians, Jesus' being "bone of our bone and flesh of our flesh" is essential to the efficacy of Jesus' sacrificial death for his followers.

This doctrine is related to another important difference. The "descent" of God in Jesus is to a life ended by humiliation and sacrificial death, followed by resurrection and glorification. The "descent" of the *avataras* of Vishnu is to a challenging contest, usually with demonic forces, against whom they are always victorious. In the case of Rama, the *avatara* suffers psychologically when his royal consort Sita is abducted and again, according to some accounts, when he has to send his wife into exile "to uphold *dharma*" (because of a few citizens' suspicions that she had been violated by the demon-king Ravana). Ramanuja states the double purposes of Vishnu's descents succinctly: "Although the immediate occasion of His descents is to relieve the earth's burden of evildoers, their deeper intention is to provide a refuge for those who resort to Him, even for such creatures as we, by becoming a visible object to all mankind and accomplishing such Divine feats as captivate the hearts and eyes of all creatures high and low."[15] Ramanuja here emphasizes two frequent Vaishnava themes. The strength of the *avatara* enables him to restore dharma, the "right order" of human society and the cosmos. Even more important for later Vaishnavas, however, is the beauty of the *avatara.* Strength and beauty combine in making the *avatara* supremely attractive to his devotees. Divine beauty in Vaishnava theology applies not only to the *avataras* but also to Lord Vishnu's proper form in his heavenly realm. At least as important is the purpose of this beauty: to attract creatures to wholehearted and single-minded devotion to the Lord. While a few Christian theologians have emphasized the divine beauty, both verbal descriptions and ar-

13. John B. Carman, *Majesty and Meekness: A Comparative Study of Contrast and Harmony in the Concept of God* (Grand Rapids, 1994).

14. Carman, *Majesty and Meekness,* passim.

15. Carman, *The Theology of Ramanuja,* p. 78.

tistic representations of Jesus focus on the marring of Jesus' handsome face in his suffering and death.

The apparently sharpest contrast with Christian views of the incarnation occurs in the Srivaishnava doctrine (elaborated explicitly in the centuries after Ramanuja) of "image incarnations," the faith that consecrated images of Lord Vishnu contain his "real presence," that is, his special material nature that only appears to be ordinary stone, metal, or wood.[16] Here there is a concept of "incarnation" that Protestant Christians find difficult to comprehend, let alone accept. Catholic and Orthodox Christian theologians also object because they consider that it exceeds the legitimate notion of divine presence, either in sacred icons or in the consecrated and transformed bread and wine of the Eucharist. Do we face so sharp a contrast here that Christians have nothing to learn from the Srivaishnava doctrine of divine descent into the consecrated image? As it happens, it is this very issue, embedded as it is in the larger issue of the ways in which God "descends" to finite and sinful humanity, that has led me, as a Protestant Christian, to a greater appreciation of Roman Catholic and Greek Orthodox Christians. I have, at the same time, tried to explore the theological foundations of my inherited Protestant "iconoclasm," an exploration that has revealed diverse biblical and postbiblical Jewish views of idolatry and its prohibition, as well as the more and less radical extensions of this prohibition in Islamic thought and practice.

To *learn from* Ramanuja and his religious community requires that we first *learn about* them; "learning from" does not require our agreement, but it does suggest a process in which we seek to understand what a particular belief or practice has meant to these Hindus and what positive significance this might have for Christians. Indeed, either a quick condemnation or too easy a decision that this is "a beautiful Hindu custom" can short-circuit the process of learning to which I am pointing.

There may also be a *learning from* of a different kind, when we learn that Srivaishnavas have differed and divided over their interpretation in a way that many Christian students have found reminiscent of the disputes between Augustine and Pelagius, between Protestant reformers and Catholics in the sixteenth century, or between Calvinists and Methodists in more recent times. When we pursue this subject, we soon find that the Srivaishnava dispute involves far more than the doctrine of grace, including cultural differences between diverse groups of Brahmins, extending from the sensitive issue of

16. Vasudha Narayanan, "Arcavatara: On Earth as He Is in Heaven," in *Gods of Flesh/Gods of Stone: The Embodiment of Divinity in India,* ed. Joanne Punzo Waghorne and Norman Cutler in association with Vasudha Narayanan (Chambersburg, Pa., 1985), pp. 61ff.

whether widows should shave their hair to the apparently trivial matter of whether the rice or the curried vegetables should be served first at a meal.[17] Even so, the key issues about the relation of divine grace to human action look remarkably similar to those in the Christian community.

There is a certain ambiguity in one of Ramanuja's central metaphors: the relation of the human servant or supplicant to his wealthy or royal master. Often Ramanuja follows the Hindu tradition emphasizing the law of karma, which makes devotion (bhakti) look like a higher path of karma: service done to please a divine lord, whose grace is the favor rewarding such service. Equally basic to Ramanuja's thought, however, is another concept of service: the devotee's conscious realization of the service the entire cosmos is obligated to offer to its divine Master, whose love for his creatures precedes and stretches far beyond his subjects' small acts of service.[18] Service is therefore here seen as the consequence of grace instead of its cause.

Ramanuja has powerfully presented both the previous traditions concerning divine grace and human effort, but they remain separate in his thought, not yet fused into one. This lack of a synthesis made it easy for his later followers to differ with each other on this subject. On the whole Ramanuja is a very systematic thinker, much concerned with logical consistency. In the oral tradition he is represented as correcting what he sees as inconsistencies in the interpretation of the community's hymns in their spoken language of Tamil.[19] What is more, the Srivaishnava tradition after him, like the Christian tradition, wants to maintain a harmony between its devotional practices and its elaborately argued doctrines. Both traditions base themselves on revelation in the form of oracle, story, and song, and both try to "make sense" of a vast array of scriptures and traditions. The community's need to "make sense" of its traditions rests in part on the assumption that the divine Lord wills order for the cosmos, for human society, for the community of devotees, as well as for himself. The need for a rationally consistent teaching has also been important in defending the community against its critics and commending its teachings to potential adherents.

Ramanuja was quite successful, both as a teacher of consistent doctrine and as the organizer of an expanding religious community. Within a tradition of great poets, both before and after him, he wrote only in prose. Some of that

17. Alkondavilli Govindacharya, "The Astadasa-Bhedas," *Journal of the Royal Asiatic Society,* October 1910, pp. 1103-12.

18. John B. Carman, "The Dignity and Indignity of Service: The Role of the Self in Hindu Bhakti," in *Selves, People, and Persons: What Does It Mean to Be a Self?* ed. Leroy S. Rouner (Notre Dame, Ind., 1992), pp. 107-22.

19. Carman, *The Theology of Ramanuja,* pp. 210-11.

prose is quite lyrical, but it is rational discourse intended to reconcile apparent contradictions in the revealed texts and traditions it interprets. Why then did he fail to achieve a unified doctrine of divine grace? To put it differently, he seems to have failed to see the ambiguity in his understanding of the master-servant relationship. This "failure" can, however, be interpreted more positively. Despite his penchant for consistency, Ramanuja seems to have accepted and internalized some of the inconsistencies in the diverse traditions of his religious community. While Ramanuja tried to resolve other paradoxes, he seems to have been content simply to live in the paradox of grace.

Both Ramanuja and his successors tried to relate the paradoxes of religious experience to the theologian's urge for rational consistency. Their effort can provide a mirror for Christians seeking to understand their own doctrinal controversies, not only in the past but also in the present. Looking in that mirror, Christians might discover unexpected facets of our own struggle with similar tensions in the life of faith. For both Christians and Srivaishnavas, concern for doctrinal clarity has come at a high price, contributing to the division of the community. It is true that there have been other nondoctrinal reasons for controversies and splits, but we may still ask whether both Srivaishnavas and Christians might have avoided community divisions if they had been less concerned with doctrinal agreement in areas where poetic metaphors lend themselves to diverse interpretations. This is clearly a modern Christian question, both in its concern for ecumenical unity and its critique of earlier insistence on doctrinal uniformity. It is worth noting that there is also an "ecumenical" disposition among some Srivaishnavas, who seek to emphasize all that the two branches of the community have in common, which includes the teaching of Ramanuja. Both groups accept his authority as their preeminent teacher-scholar, and, more than that, as their primary spiritual guide on the path to salvation.

This effort to go behind the interpretation of Ramanuja in their own branch of Srivaishnavism has some similarities to the dual aims of the outside students of Ramanuja, who must balance the scholar's picture of this outstanding Hindu teacher with the figure who can be appropriated by Christians, and most specifically by Christians in India. What may be new in our modern consciousness is the ability to distinguish between the historical figure and the theologically interpreted guru. In Christian language, this is referred to as the distinction between "the historical Jesus and the Christ of faith." There has been much discussion about the viability of this distinction. It may be misnamed, since both views are historical, but one is history seen from within the community that is the result of that history, while the other is history seen from outside, without the community's faith in the salvific character of the founding events. When we are concerned with Christian scholarly approaches to the history of a different religious community, such as Ramanuja's, the distinction may have to be further complicated. In addition to concern for supposedly "objective" history, there is the Christian scholar's effort at empathetic understanding of Srivaishnava belief and practice, and there is the effort of the Christian theologian to incorporate some aspects of the Srivaishnava religious experience into Christians' own ongoing history. The theological incorporation may be aided by both the modern objective and the Srivaishnava subjective approach to history, but Christian appropriation or rejection of some other religious witness is a different task. If there is ever a "Christianized Ramanuja" comparable to the Christianized Plato and Aristotle of many Christians, that figure may appear strange, both to "objective" historians and to Srivaishnavas. The difference from the intellectual situation of medieval Christian scholastics is that they thought they were studying the "real" Plato and Aristotle. With a modern sensibility we realize that our Christianized appropriation is only one more perspective on the utterance of the divine Word in what seems to be outside the Christian tradition, but not outside God's saving history of humanity.

Early Christian theologians who recognized Christian "borrowing" from Greek and Roman culture justified it with the example of the Israelites robbing from the Egyptians who had kept them in slavery, once they were given permission to leave. The "spoiling of the Egyptians" is a graphic metaphor, but it more accurately describes colonial practice in removing oriental treasures and transporting them to Western museums. We Christians do not have the Israelites' excuse. If our enrichment from the spiritual resources of other religions is to be justified, it had best be respectful borrowing, especially if we necessarily modify what we borrow. Perhaps Srivaishnavas might eventually see the divine Word in a Christianized version of Ramanuja just as Martin Luther King heard God's message in Gandhi's Christ. In the meantime, it behooves Christian scholars, especially those participating in the strong tradition of modern Western historiography now spreading around the world, to engage with Srivaishnavas in the continuing task of mutual understanding of one another's religious heritage. This is a task different from the theologian's appropriation, but it is essential to it, and it requires that we utilize to the utmost our religious imagination.

Concluding Reflections

My brief survey of Ramanuja's teaching touches on several issues relating to a Christian theology of religion. These may be grouped together under two headings: how to proceed, and what to accomplish.

A. How to Proceed
   1. Applying the modern historian's distinction of "subjective" and "objective" history to the outsider's interpretation of another religious community's history.
   2. Understanding similarities and differences between religions in an atmosphere of respectful dialogue and mutual learning; learning from both programmed and unintentional encounters.

B. What to Accomplish
   1. Christian appropriation
      a. using key terms (representing concepts and/or metaphors) that have been or could be used to express central affirmations of Christian faith;
      b. determining the appropriateness of a particular metaphysical view from a non-Christian source to express the implicit or explicit assumptions in Christian faith;
      c. respectful borrowing, recognizing that what is borrowed is changed from its original context and may not be recognized as authentic by the tradition from which it is borrowed.
   2. Revisioning and broadening one's Christian denominational identity through the "mirror" of another religious community
      a. being reminded by another religious position of other Christian traditions different from one's own;
      b. discovering in the controversies within another religious community a "mirror" for Christian doctrinal disputes, one that may illuminate the problem of trying to systematize faith in rational concepts.

This very list, which would not have occurred to theologians of previous generations, indicates both the complexity of this kind of theological interpretation and the distinctive perspective we have in this postcolonial era.

Many Christian theologians in the past have assumed that they could make sweeping theological judgments about other religious traditions and their adherents. Whether negative or positive, these judgments were made with little effort to understand how those being evaluated regarded their own faith. One Western scholarly reaction to this theological past has been to refrain from any kind of evaluative judgment. While there is much in favor of minimizing judgments about other people, especially when they are negative, the actual situation of encounter is one in which our traditions are not hermetically sealed boxes. In such encounters both positive and negative judgments are inevitably made. We must make a conscious decision to refrain from evaluating what we do not understand. Both Indian Christians and Christians from elsewhere need to explore *together* where evaluations can and should be made. Educated Indian Christians have hitherto been introduced to both classical and recent Western Christian perspectives. It is important that Western Christian scholars become acquainted with the way these issues appear in the history of Christianity in India and in contemporary Indian Christian discussion. Historians of Indian Christianity are necessarily concerned with the ongoing efforts of Indian Christians to define themselves both positively and negatively in relation to Hindu traditions. Christian theologians and historians of religion can share in the next chapter of this Christian engagement as they provide factual description, empathetic understanding, and patient theological interpretation.

CHAPTER 13

An Overview and Analysis of Missionary Collections in the United Kingdom Relating to South Asia

ROSEMARY SETON

India was the preeminent mission field for British Protestant missionary societies[1] for the greater part of the nineteenth century, and a very major field thereafter. Since the nature of missionary work required conscientious reporting, a rich archival legacy from the eighteenth century onward can be expected. Despite considerable opposition from the East India Company, both the Baptist Missionary Society and the London Missionary Society had sent missionaries to the Subcontinent before 1800. Prior to that date there had been support from within Britain for the German missionaries of the Danish

1. There are few archival resources in the U.K. relating to the history of Catholic missions in South Asia. Examples are manuscripts of Abbé Jean Antoine Dubois (1765-1848), whose *Letters on the state of Christianity in India in which the conversion of the Hindoos is considered as impractical,* published in 1823, found favor with the East India Company while provoking fury with English evangelicals: these are to be found in the India Office Collections at the British Library. Manuscripts collected by William Marsden at London's Kings College include letters and other material, 1627-68, relating to Portuguese Catholic missionaries in India, including a seventeenth-century martyrology. The archives of the British Province of the Society of Jesus, which has existed since 1623, contain materials relating to work in India (particularly Calcutta) from 1832, while those of the Mill Hill missionaries, or St. Joseph's Missionary Society, founded by Cardinal Herbert Vaughan in 1866, document activity in what is now Pakistan and Kashmir from 1878.

A very early draft of this paper was given at a conference entitled "Cultural Interactions: Christianity and South Asia's Religious Traditions" organized by Bob Frykenberg and Judith Brown at Balliol College, Oxford, in 1999. At this conference, as so often in all he said and wrote, Bob laid great stress on the importance of archival resources to the scholar. I am delighted that this present paper is appearing in a collection honoring him.

mission at Tranquebar. King George I had sent an earnest letter of support, the mission had received financial support from the Society for the Propagation of the Gospel, while the Society for Promoting Christian Knowledge became a patron. With the gradual easing of restrictions in the first quarter of the nineteenth century, removed altogether in 1833, the pioneering missionaries were followed by missionaries of the Church Missionary Society (1814), the Wesleyan Methodist Missionary Society (1814), the Society for the Propagation of the Gospel (1817), the Church of Scotland Foreign Mission (1829), the Irish Presbyterian Mission (1841), the Welsh Calvinistic Mission (1841), the Christian Vernacular Education Society (1858), and the Friends' Foreign Mission Association (1866).

By 1933, forty-two British societies were actively engaged in or supportive of mission work in South Asia:[2]

All Nations Missionary Union
Assemblies of God in GB and Ireland
Baptist Missionary Society
Bible Churchmen's Missionary Society
British and Foreign Bible Society
Calcutta Diocesan Mission
Cambridge Mission to Delhi
Ceylon and India General Mission
Christian Literature Society for India
Christian Missions in Many Lands (Brethren)
Churches of Christ in Great Britain and Ireland, Foreign Missions Committee
Church Missionary Society
Church of England Zenana Missionary Society
Church of Scotland Foreign Mission Committee
Conference of Missionary Societies in Great Britain and Ireland
Free Church of Scotland, Foreign Mission Committee
Friends' Service Council
India Christian Mission
Indian Church Aid Association
Kurku and Central India Indian Hill Mission
Lakher Pioneer Mission
London Missionary Society
Methodist Missionary Society
Missionary Settlement for University Women (Bombay Presidency)
Mission to Lepers
National Bible Society of Scotland
Oxford Mission to Calcutta
Presbyterian Church in Ireland, Foreign Missions Committee
Presbyterian Church of England, Foreign Missions Committee
Presbyterian Church of Wales, Foreign Missions
Regions beyond Missionary Union
Salvation Army
Scripture Gift Mission

2. [International Missionary Council], *Directory of Foreign Missions* (London, 1933).

Society for Promoting Christian Knowledge
Society for the Propagation of the Gospel in Foreign Parts
Strict Baptist Mission
Trust Society for the Furtherance of the Gospel (Moravians)
United Original Secession Church of Scotland, Foreign Mission Committee
Worldwide Evangelization Crusade
Young Men's Christian Organisation, Overseas Department
Young Women's Christian Organisation, British Overseas Committee
Zenana Bible and Medical Mission

A significant number of these organizations have left archives, though by no means all. Those that survive are not always complete or accessible. The trend over recent decades has been for missionary societies to deposit their archives in research libraries willing to house and maintain them and to make them available for public consultation. Complementing these official archives are the personal papers of individual missionaries. Viewed as a whole, personal papers form a valuable research resource since in unofficial correspondence or in personal diaries a missionary might confide views or describe events that would not appear in official reports or in correspondence with mission administrators. Many personal collections also include photographs, oral recordings, and other visual materials. Some collections are in private hands while others have been deposited in a very wide range of records offices and libraries scattered through the United Kingdom. Their existence, location, and content can be hard to establish.

Although the scholar-researcher may deplore the fact that the missionary documentary heritage in the United Kingdom is so scattered and dispersed and that survival itself has been somewhat haphazard, a number of recent developments tend to lighten the research task. First of all, there is the emergence of leading centers at Birmingham, Cambridge, Edinburgh, London, and Oxford, which have built up substantial collections of missionary materials all of which offer research facilities. Secondly, a variety of printed, electronic, and other tools have been created in recent years to centralize knowledge about the location and content of missionary holdings and to facilitate access to them.

A survey carried out during the Mundus project (for details of this project, see below) identified some 130 significant collections of materials in libraries, record offices, and other institutions in England, Scotland, and Wales relating to the history of Christian missions in South Asia, most of which are available for consultation. Papers of individual missionaries and others were included in the survey, as were archives of missionary societies and collections of printed and visual materials. Of the 123 named collections, more than half are held at the five major centers: the University of Birmingham, the University of Cambridge, Edinburgh's New College, the School of Oriental and African Studies in London, and the University of Oxford. Researchers starting out on an investigation of primary source materials might well be advised to base themselves at one or another of these centers, while remaining aware that significant collections are to be found elsewhere.

The resources of the University of Birmingham Library's Special Collections and those of the Orchard Learning Centre at Selly Oak combine to make Birmingham a key center for missionary research. The main University Library houses the archives of the Society for Promoting Female Education in the East, the Church of England Zenana Missionary Society, the Bible Churchmen's Missionary Society, as well as the extremely large archive (250 linear meters) of the Church Missionary Society. The library also holds the unofficial papers of the CMS. These include, inter alia, the forty-one journals and photograph albums of Edith Baring-Gould from her travels, many of them in the company of her father, a CMS secretary; an unbroken sequence of the personal diaries of Agnes Lees as a CMS missionary teacher in India from 1916 to 1947; the reminiscences of Arthur Le Feuvre as CMS missionary in Ceylon and Bengal from 1881 to 1908; and the diaries of Charles Shaw from 1912 to 1959. Missionary collections at Birmingham's Selly Oak have been accumulating for some years. Hitherto hardly accessible, they have recently been catalogued as part of the Mundus project and now await the attention of researchers. Exciting as any among these are the twenty-eight boxes of papers, photographs, and audio recordings left by the leading churchman and early bishop of the Church of South India, Lesslie Newbigin (1909-98), some of which were deposited by him in 1992 and the rest by his family after his death. It should be noted that restrictions apply to part of this collection, which comprises family and personal correspondence from 1936 to 1998 and official correspondence from 1919 to 1998, as well as research materials, and thus covers all phases of his life and career.

Cambridge and Oxford Universities also offer rich resources to the student of mission history. Cambridge University Library houses the archive of the British and Foreign Bible Society and the Society for Promoting Christian Knowledge (the latter archive awaits detailed cataloguing), while the Henry Martyn Centre at Westminster College holds a growing number of private collections. There has been a determined effort at the Centre to bring together a body of materials, including copies from other archives, relating to Henry Martyn (1781-1812), the Anglican chaplain, missionary, and scholar after whom the center is named. At Regent's Park College in Oxford is to be found the archive of the Baptist Missionary Society, while at the Bodleian Library of Commonwealth and African Studies at Rhodes House are the archives of the United Society for the Propagation of the Gospel and the Cambridge Mission to Delhi. Papers relating to the missionary and political campaigner Charles Freer Andrews can be found in the archive of the Cambridge Mission to Delhi as well as in the papers of William and Isabella Ross. The new Crowther Center for Mission Education in Oxford houses Church Mission Society library collections, formerly in Partnership House Library, Waterloo Road, London, as well as those previously held in Crowther Hall. There are around 29,000 volumes and 250 current journals as well as back copies of missionary journals. The Center also holds microfilm copy of the CMS archive and other supplementary archival materials.

Researchers wishing to examine the archives of the leading Scottish missionary societies should turn to the National Library in Edinburgh. Here are to be found records dating back to the 1820s when, after decades of campaigning, the Church of Scotland appointed a committee to inaugurate overseas mission work. Papers of its first missionary, Alexander Duff, who arrived in Calcutta in 1830 and who was to work zealously for his brand of Christian mission both in India and Scotland, are also held by the library. So are the records of the Free Church of Scotland's Board of Missions, which Duff and other Calcutta colleagues joined following the Disruption of 1843. For further information about Scottish missionary archives, see the *Catalogue of Manuscripts Acquired since 1925*, volume 6, *Manuscripts 7530-8022, Scottish Foreign Mission Records, 1827-1929* (Edinburgh, 1984). Researchers should be aware that there are considerable gaps in the archives, particularly of that most valuable of all series, *incoming correspondence,* for large portions of the nineteenth century. At New College, Edinburgh, missionary collections are to be found in the Centre for the Study of Christianity in the Non-Western World and also in New College Library itself.

Despite the wider dispersal of some, the London area remains a base for a number of missionary societies retaining their own archives. Among these are Quaker Peace and Service, the Salvation Army Overseas Work, the British Province of the Society of Jesus, and the Trust Society for the Furtherance of the Gospel (Moravian). Access conditions to these private archives vary as do the quality and quantity of extant material, and researchers are advised to contact the organization prior to visiting. At the British Library, in what are now termed the Asia, Pacific and African Collections, can be found records of the Lakher Pioneer Mission, the Missionary Settlement for University Women at Bombay, and the Women's Christian Colleges in Madras, as well as relevant official records of the East India Company and India Office, particularly the Public and Judicial Department. At Lambeth Palace Library can be found papers donated by the Indian Church Aid Association and early minutes and correspondence of the Society for the Propagation of the Gospel.

The School of Oriental and African Studies (SOAS) has been absorbing missionary society collections since the early 1970s. Those relevant to South Asian studies include such major archives as those of the Conference of British Missionary Societies and International Missionary Council, the London Missionary Society, now the Council for World Mission, the Methodist Missionary Society, and Interserve (incorporating the Indian Female Normal School and Instruction Society and the Zenana Bible and Medical Mission). Also of significance are the archives of the Presbyterian Church of England's Foreign Missions and the United Society for Christian Literature, which incorporates the archive of the Christian Vernacular Education Society for India. In addition there are a large number of personal collections, and a considerable quantity of photographic and printed materials. SOAS has also been the base for a number of initiatives culminating in the Mundus project to facilitate and improve access to missionary collections in the U.K., funded by the Research Libraries Support Programme during the academic years 1999-2002. During the project, previously unlisted collections in the five centers mentioned above were sorted and catalogued, some 40,000 photographs were listed and repackaged, and around 15,000 missionary-related printed works were catalogued. Detailed online catalogues were created for the archive of the Church Missionary Society at Birmingham and the British and Foreign Bible Society at Cambridge. In addition a Web-based guide to Missionary Collections in the U.K. was created, containing descriptions of more than 500 collections in over fifty institutions in England, Scotland, Wales, and Northern Ireland.[3] Many of the archives of British missionary societies are now available in microform. The archives of the London Missionary Society, the Methodist Missionary Society and a number of other missionary archives were copied several decades ago by Inter Documentation Company while, more recently, Adam Matthew Publications have performed the same service for such archives as those of the Church of Scotland, the Church Missionary Society and the Regions Beyond Missionary Union.

3. The Web site for the Mundus Gateway is http://www.mundus.ac.uk.

The Nature, Variety, and Usefulness of Missionary Collections: The London Missionary Society

It is well known, but perhaps bears repeating, that the London Missionary Society (LMS; originally known as the Missionary Society) was founded in 1795 "not to send Presbyterianism, Independency, Episcopacy, or any other form of church order and government . . . but the glorious gospel of the blessed God to the heathen."[4] With the rise of the denominational missionary societies, the LMS became almost by default the missionary arm of the Congregational Union of Churches, though about 10 percent of its missionary recruits throughout its existence were not Congregationalist. The LMS was not only "one of the oldest Protestant missionary societies; it was also one of the largest agencies in the Protestant missionary movement having sent out 2,400 missionaries . . . in the period down to 1923."[5] The LMS was governed by a board of directors and administered by salaried officials, preeminent among these a home and foreign secretary. In 1810 separate committees were appointed to oversee particular aspects of mission work, including the important overseas regional committees and the Examinations Committee, which appointed missionaries to the field. The constitution of the LMS was revised in May 1870, as a direct result of financial pressures and the expansion of overseas mission work; the work of the Investigation Committee (1866) in turn led to a new administrative policy and the emphasis on the development of self-governing and self-financing indigenous churches. In 1966 the LMS merged with the Commonwealth Missionary Society to form the Congregational Council for World Mission (CCWM), which, following unity with the Presbyterian Church of England in 1972, was changed to the Council for World Mission (Congregational and Reform). In 1977, all the member churches of the Council for World Mission were given "equal responsibility for the witness in their own areas and equal rights to the concern and resources of all."[6] A final change took place in 1980 when the official title became simply the Council for World Mission (CWM).

4. Every Annual Report of the Society included this statement of its *Fundamental Principle.*

5. Andrew Porter, *The Council for World Mission and Its Archival Legacy* (London, 1999).

6. B. Thorogood, "Whom God May Call," in *Gales of Change: Responding to a Shifting Missionary Context; The Story of the London Missionary Society, 1945-1977,* ed. B. Thorogood (Geneva, 1994), p. 249.

The Missionary Archive

The content and structure of the archives of Protestant missionary societies reveal some common characteristics, but other features set them apart. To understand why certain records are created or kept in a particular way, it is necessary to understand denominational differences and to appreciate the culture, hierarchy, and methodology of the body that created the records. One cannot expect to approach the records of the Methodist Missionary Society (MMS), for example, in the same way one would those of the London Missionary Society or the Church Missionary Society.[7] A common distinction in the archives of most missionary societies is that between the records of the home and overseas administrative departments. In home mission records one can expect to find board or committee minutes, financial records, papers relating to the recruitment and training of missionaries, internal U.K. correspondence, letter-books containing copies of outgoing letters and the records of editorial and publishing departments. Though home records do not wholly relate to overseas matters, the researcher cannot ignore them. They are particularly informative on the discussion and development of policies, correspondence with home supporters and the home government, financial operations and structures, and the selection, recruitment, and training of missionaries. The larger societies frequently set up committees that had a specific regional remit. The London Missionary Society, for example, had an India, China, and Ultra Ganges Committee from 1827 to 1840 and an India Committee from 1840 to 1954, whereas the Church Missionary Society's Committee of Correspondence directed all work until 1880, after which South Asian missions came under its West Asia Committee. Editorial and publishing records may contain drafts of publications as well as details of publications policy. It was frequently these departments that accumulated large collections of photographs used so often as illustrations in missionary magazines and other missionary publications. Home Office records also include copies of the letters sent out to overseas mission stations from missionary officials. These are often known as letter-books. In some organizations they may be the only correspondence series that survive. Copies of correspondence from LMS Home Office to missionaries in the field were organized as: Eastern Outgoing Letters: India from 1822-1830; Eastern Outgoing Letters: India, Russia: 1831-1843; and Eastern Outgoing Letters: India: 1843-1914. In 1941 the LMS offices in Livingstone House received a direct hit from a German bomb, and all that

7. CMS letter-books, for example, are to be found in the Overseas division.

survives of outgoing Indian correspondence from 1914 to 1939 is a letter-book containing "Oddments saved from the Blitz."

LMS work in India developed into two distinct mission fields: North India and South India. While the first missionary, Nathaniel Forsyth, went out to Calcutta in 1798, establishing himself in the Dutch-controlled area of Chinsurah, the major LMS impact was to be in southern India where, in the words of one of the society's historians, Richard Lovett, mission agents "received a much more cordial welcome among the devil-worshippers of Travancore than among the haughty Muhammedans of the North."[8] Only a handful of letters and a journal survive of the Society's pioneering agent in the princely state of Travancore, the German-born and Halle-educated Wilhelm Tobias Ringeltaube, who, with the help of the Indian convert Vedamanickam, established an LMS mission station there in 1806. After 1813 the LMS expanded its mission stations in both North and South India, and this is reflected in the arrangement of the archive. North India materials are arranged into the subgroups General, Bengal, Gujerat (Gujarat), and United Provinces (Uttar Pradesh). Support for missionary work in North India was, however, gradually withdrawn in the first half of the twentieth century. Resources were effectively withdrawn from the missions in the United Provinces for use in South India. Mission stations were gradually transferred to other societies; for example, work in Mirzapur was passed to the Bible Churchman's Missionary Society in 1925, and in 1926 the American Methodist Episcopal Mission took over work at Almora. By 1945, the Society's work in North India was confined to Bengal and Calcutta; the remaining LMS churches joined the United Church of Northern India in 1944. The move toward church union was completed in 1970 with the final establishment of the Church of North India.

The various fields of London Missionary Society work in South India were largely defined by linguistic region. Records are divided into the subsections of General, Canarese, Telugu, Tamil, and Travancore. Geographically, missions were concentrated in the Madras Presidency, the Bombay Presidency, and the Native States of Mysore and Travancore. Following Ringletaube's early work at Mayiladi, a mission was established at Nagercoil in 1819. This later became a training center for indigenous clergy, a significant factor in the success of the missions in South India. The administrative areas of LMS activity in South India were not rigorously defined; different linguistic groups could be of significance in a particular linguistic area: there were, for example, missions to Tamil- and Malayalam-speaking peoples in Travancore. Medical missionary work was particularly significant in Travancore with a central hospital at

8. R. Lovett, *History of the London Missionary Society, 1795-1895* (London, 1899), p. 52.

Neyyoor and outlying branches around. By the early 1900s Neyyoor hospital and its associated units were, in numbers of patients treated, "the largest medical mission in the world."[9] Other LMS medical centers in India included a large leper settlement in Almora, and hospitals at Jammalamadugu, Chikka Ballapura, and Erode. Travancore was also an important center for women's work with the development of "cottage" lace and embroidery industries with distinctive styles at Nagercoil, Trivandrum, Neyyoor, and Parassala.

The first major step toward church union in India was taken with the establishment in 1908 of the South India United Church, formed of church councils with congregational and Presbyterian traditions. This was to be followed by the "Tranquebar Manifesto" of 1919, calling for wider church union and the eventual establishment of the Church of South India in 1947. During the same period there was a transfer of responsibility from the mission to the church, with administrative control passing from missionaries with their district committees to church councils.

Incoming Letters

The strength of the LMS archive lies in the survival with relatively few gaps of correspondence from all missionaries in the field. This is known as "Incoming Correspondence" and is arranged chronologically and by region down to 1927. From approximately the last quarter of the nineteenth century, each letter has a cover sheet, which gives it a unique number, date sent, date received by the Home Office, the appropriate governing region (Eastern, Southern, etc.), and a précis of contents. From 1928 onward, incoming correspondence from the field is no longer stored in chronological order, but in alphabetical order by sender. This means that the letters from a particular missionary are filed together. This series contains copies of some outgoing letters so that to a certain extent it is both an incoming and outgoing correspondence series.

Journals and Reports

The series of journals provide a day-by-day account of the work of an individual missionary or mission station. Many were then sent back to the LMS headquarters for publication, and edited extracts from journals can often be

9. Norman Goodall, *A History of the London Missionary Society, 1895-1945* (London, 1954), p. 515.

found in missionary publications such as the *Missionary Magazine*, the *Chronicle*, and published *Annual Reports*. As a result of continuing financial pressures in the mid–nineteenth century and the growing need to audit missionary work, the board of directors decided that the missionaries should create an "annual report" of significant work occurring in their missions. This administrative change began in 1866, when the reports series was begun. The reports subsequently drawn up were sent to the LMS headquarters, and a significant number, around ten thousand, survive. There are approximately three thousand Indian reports, though some of these were damaged as a result of the May 1941 bombing.

Records, 1941-70

Since the first deposit of LMS records were received at SOAS in the early 1970s, three subsequent deposits have followed, taking the period covered by original documentation down to 1970. Moreover, all this later material is catalogued and available for consultation. Few other missionary societies have deposited materials of this late date; the cutoff date for CMS records available at Birmingham is 1949. From 1941 to 1950 the records remain divided between the fields of South and North India, with a single India field after 1950. A new series of subject files can be found in the later deposits, which take the researcher directly to such issues as the situation in India, 1941-44; the integration of church and mission; the issue of permits for missionaries (from 1950 onward "missionaries were required to obtain entry and re-entry visas and to register with the head of police in the locality of their work");[10] papers of the South India Missionary Council, 1927-1950; relations with the Church of South India and the United Church of North India; files on Christian Colleges, hospitals, and district missionary/church councils. Prior to 1940, similar subject files can be found in the Miscellaneous Series (formerly known as "Odds"). These papers are miscellaneous indeed, being a mixture of subject files, documents that have strayed from elsewhere, and bundles of illustrative material.

Like the CMS "Unofficial Papers" and the MMS "Biographical series," the LMS/CWM archive contains the private papers of individual missionaries. Among these can be found: letters written by Sadhu Sundar Singh to his "Dearest Mother," Rebecca J. Parker, an LMS missionary in South India, 1918-1929; papers and correspondence of T. Howard Somervell, from 1922 to 1954, a

10. Iorworth Thomas, "The Struggle for Freedom: Adventure in Unity," in *Gales of Change*, p. 92.

medical missionary in South India, and a noted mountaineer (he was a member of the 1924 Everest expedition); papers of Miss M. L. Butler, principal of London Mission Girls School, Bangalore, 1908-40; and papers relating to Elizabeth Jones, who taught women to make lace in Nagercoil and Travancore. Other personal papers of missionaries have been directly deposited in SOAS Library.

Visual Materials

Early-nineteenth-century missionary magazines and other publications often contained drawings and engravings as a graphic way of educating their readership and stimulating their support. During the last quarter of the nineteenth century photographs were increasingly used, first as the basis of engravings and subsequently directly as photographic reproductions. The LMS/CWM photographic archive at SOAS comprises some 15,000 images taken between the early 1860s and 1970. While this is a relatively low figure compared to the Basel Mission Archive, where there are "about 50,000 images created before 1950,"[11] it is high compared to the surviving photographic archive of the CMS and the MMS. The MMS photographic archive at SOAS contains around 3,000 images, although there are more awaiting sorting and cataloguing. The CMS photographic archive was not deposited with the written archive at Birmingham. Some images have been retained in the Waterloo Road offices, where they are used for current publishing and promotional purposes; others (mainly albums) have been deposited in the Royal Commonwealth Society Collections now in Cambridge University Library.

In the LMS/CWM collections there are about 2,000 images taken in India: views of mission compounds, church and school buildings, and hospitals; individual and group portraits of missionaries, church members, school pupils, hospital staff, and patients; as well as views of the countryside, Indian festivals, street scenes, modes of transport, and views of Indian towns before and in the early stages of modern development. Scholars are turning increasingly to these sources not as mere illustrations but as innovative and fertile ways of interpreting the past. As a way of assisting and stimulating this process, SOAS has joined with other partners[12] to create an Internet Missionary Photo-

11. Paul Jenkins, "Much More Than Illustrations of What We Already Know: Experiences in the Rediscovery of Mission Photography," *International Bulletin of Missionary Research* 26 (2002): 157.

12. The Catholic Foreign Missionary Society of America, Inc. (Maryknoll Fathers and

graphic Archive (IMPA) under the leadership of Professor Jon Miller of the University of Southern California. To date, around 10,000 images from these collections have been digitized. Of these, several hundred relate to South Asia and have been made available on a Web site hosted by the University of Southern California. The Web site, officially launched in 2005 and hosted by the University of Southern California, can be accessed at http://www.usc.edu/isd/libraries/archives/arc/digarchives/mission.

The Missionary Library

Most leading missionary societies built up libraries of works relating to the countries and cultures with which they engaged for the education and information of missionaries, mission administrators, and supporters. These libraries were also important repositories of the many works completed by missionaries. "Of the 1,120 [LMS] missionaries despatched by 1900 it is conservatively estimated that at least 13 per cent produced books" varying "from the elementary to the formidably learned."[13] By 1899, a catalogue of the LMS library had been compiled by Goodeve Mabbs. A heavily annotated copy of the printed catalogue still exists. The LMS Library has been deposited in SOAS Library almost in its entirety and is now accessible online as part of the library's online catalogue. Here can be found the Society's periodical publications including the *Annual Report of the LMS, Transactions of the Missionary Society, Chronicle of the London Missionary Society* and the *Juvenile Missionary Magazine.* Of particular significance to the South Asian scholar is a comprehensive range of printed reports on LMS hospitals, schools, and other aspects of mission work, known as India Local Reports, covering the period from the 1860s through the 1930s. Other strengths worth noting are an extensive collection of grammars and dictionaries; Bible and other translations; works written in vernacular languages, for example, hymnals and school primers; biographies and memoirs; and works on travel and exploration, some of which are rare early printed books.

Brothers), the Leipzig Mission, the Moravian Church at Herrnhut, the Norwegian Missionary Society, and Yale Divinity Library.

13. Porter, *Council for World Mission,* p. 15.

The Missionary Museum

The LMS was the earliest society to set up a missionary museum in Britain. Its pioneer missionaries had collected and sent back interesting curios, including "specimens in natural history, various idols of heathen nations, dresses, manufactures, domestic utensils, and instruments of war."[14] By 1826, these objects had been arranged in a "Missionary Museum," which could be viewed at the Society's premises (then in Austin Friars, but later in Blomfield Street) every Wednesday from 10 A.M. to 4 P.M. Admission appears to have been free, though tickets had to be signed by a director or officer of the Society. The existence of the museum is noted in an 1855 guidebook *London as it is Today,* in John Timbs's *Curiosities of London,* published in 1876, where it is considered "remarkable for its great number of idols (some 12 feet high) and objects of superstitious regard," and in Charles Dickens's *Dictionary of London, An Unconventional Handbook,* published in 1880. The museum served a dual purpose: to stimulate interest and curiosity but perhaps more importantly to display the "numerous, and (in some instances) *horrible* IDOLS . . . and those especially which were actually given up by their former worshippers." These "trophies of Christianity" would, it was hoped, raise "in pious minds, feelings of deep commiseration for the hundreds of millions of the human race, still the vassals of ignorance and superstition."[15] These included a large collection of idols from India, featuring among others: "Choitunyu the wise . . . multitudes flock to his temple in Bengal"; "Juguddhatree, the Mother of the World, dressed in red, sitting on a lion"; "Shivu Lingu, the Destroyer, has three eyes, rides on a bull, his Eyes inflamed with intoxicating herbs; he bears a strong resemblance to Bacchus"; "Guneshu, in the form of a fat short man, with an Elephant's head"; "Hunoomanu, the Monkey God . . . in some places his image is worshipped daily . . . Bears some relation to Pan." The collections also included a statue of the Virgin Mary and child "that belonged to two Native Roman Catholics [from Mysore] who embraced the Christian religion and sent the same to the Missionary Museum."

The London Missionary Society was not the only missionary society to assemble collections of ethnographic materials. The Wesleyan Methodist Missionary Society maintained a display of missionary memorabilia and curios at its Bishopsgate offices from 1838, while the CMS kept a repository of images and other objects at its Salisbury Square headquarters, which were lent to exhibitions or to illustrate lectures. In the early 1900s this repository

14. *Catalogue of the Missionary Museum* (London, 1826).

15. *Catalogue of the Missionary Museum,* pp. iii-iv.

was converted into "a rest and writing room for missionaries." The objects on display, though they included "instruments of self-torture connected with the dark and cruel religions of a heathen people" and "hideous" masks, were now being viewed rather differently from similar objects in the earlier LMS missionary museum.[16] While both the LMS and the CMS museum collections were eventually broken up, with objects being sold or transferred to the Horniman, the Pitt Rivers, and the British Museums, both societies were still able to furnish and organize spectacular missionary exhibitions into the twentieth century.[17]

In conclusion, one can only remark on the copious and detailed nature of missionary documentation that accumulated in the LMS mission house, as in other missionary headquarters. Not only did the distance between those serving in the mission field and those administering mission direction and policy at home necessitate full communication, there was also the need to keep thousands of home supporters as widely informed as possible of mission news. That there was some conflict between full reportage and what was deemed prudent to disclose to the wider public is evident in the heavy editing of some of the letters and journals before they appeared in the *Missionary Magazine* or the Society's *Annual Report.* During the course of the nineteenth century there was an increasing emphasis on the production of detailed statistical information in the society's own reports and in the statistical tables furnished for surveys of Protestant missionary work generally. One of the leaders in this regard was the Reverend Joseph Mullens, for many years an LMS missionary in India and foreign secretary of the Society from 1868 to 1879, who first prepared statistical tables on Protestant missionary work in India for the *Calcutta Christian Observer* of 1850. Such tables appeared at intervals of roughly ten years before being published separately as *Statistical Tables of Protestant Missions in India, Burma, and Ceylon* from 1900 onward.

The solemn and visionary purpose of missionary work has ensured the survival, in the case of the LMS and of most of the other major missionary societies, of vast quantities of letters, reports, papers, and other materials, long after their immediate purpose was at an end. That the sheer bulk of the documentation has caused problems for the Society's historians is borne out by the fact that few of them finished the task in time to meet commemorative

16. See Irene H. Barnes's account of the CMS, *In Salisbury Square* (London, 1906), p. 210.

17. For a description and analysis of the "Orient in London" (LMS) exhibition, 1908, and the "Africa and East" (CMS) exhibition of 1909, see chap. 8 in Annie Coombes, *Reinventing Africa: Museums, Material Culture, and Popular Imagination* (New Haven and London, 1994).

dates, or finished the task at all.[18] While some scholars may complain that while missionary archives "produce interesting information on the history of the Christian mission . . . it far from satisfies our need for information on developments in local society,"[19] others continue to uncover information to elucidate not only all aspects of the history of Christian mission including education, medical, and humanitarian work and relations with other faiths, but also such broad concerns and topics as gender, race, language, architecture, music, genetics, and climatology. The LMS collections have been at SOAS since 1973, and over the years I have not noted any diminution in their appeal as a research entity — quite the contrary.

18. Porter, *Council for World Mission*, pp. 1-4.

19. Dick Kooiman, "Who Is to Benefit from Mission Education? Travancore in the 1930s," in *Missionary Encounters: Sources and Issues*, ed. Robert A. Bickers and Rosemary Seton (London, 1996), p. 154. The same author goes on to explain that "patient and careful scrutiny of missionary correspondence" can reveal "a few glittering particles."

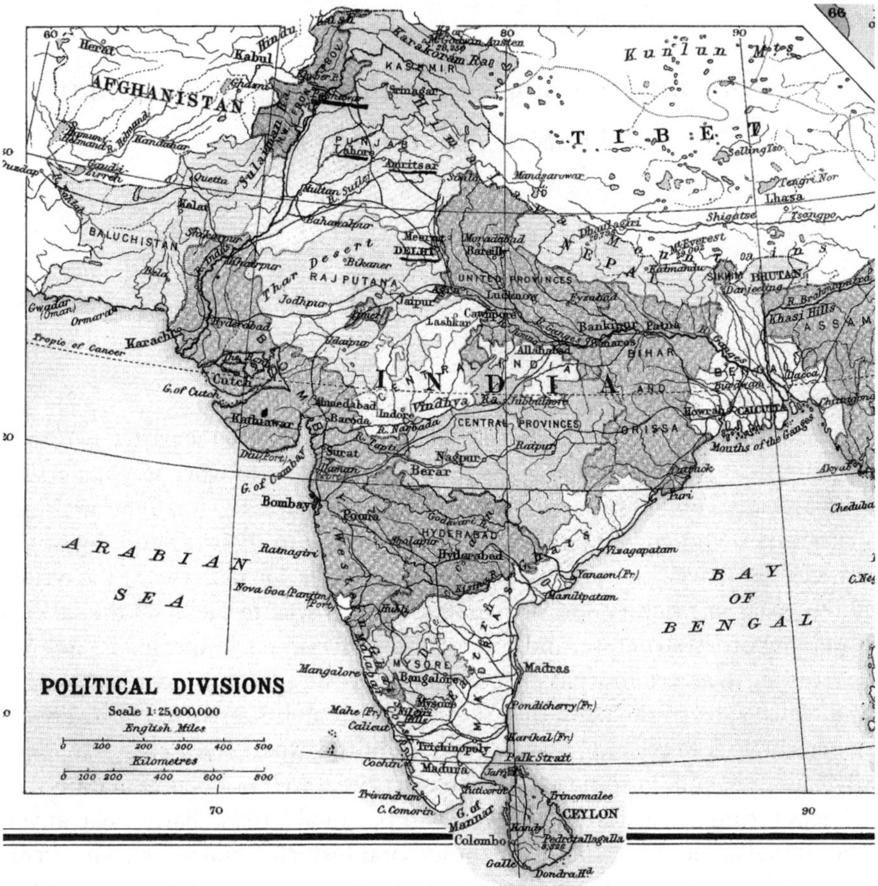

India, circa 1923. This map showing political divisions in India is an insert in a detailed map of Protestant mission stations in the western section of India.

Source: *World Missionary Atlas,* edited by Harlan P. Beach and Charles H. Fahs (New York: Institute of Social and Religious Research, 1925), plate 13.

North American Sources for the Study of Protestant Christian Missions in India

MARTHA LUND SMALLEY

The historian has been described as "a bringer of order to the past, a perceiver of patterns."[1] It is the fortunate historian who is able to work in partnership with archivists and librarians to pursue these tasks. It is the fortunate archivist or librarian who encounters the historian willing to discover and digest the sources that have been preserved.[2] Historians seek for patterns in the amorphous mass of primary sources while archivists seek to facilitate the task by providing order, structure, and preservation. Historians immersed in archival sources try to ascertain what part of the whole the available records represent and which sides of the truth they illuminate; archivists strive to clarify provenance and link to related records. The task of the expert researcher is to identify, navigate, and, in some cases, help to create a web of documentation that stretches from official archival records to personal letters, diaries, narratives, photographs, reports, pamphlets, theses, oral histories, and so on. The archivist and librarian assist the historian not only by preserving these elements but also by describing them and making them accessible.

The primary sources for study of North American mission activity in India are as amorphous a mass as a historian may ever wish to encounter. The political and cultural complexities of India, the diverse and evolving natures of the North American agencies, and the long period of their interaction all conspire to complicate the tasks of bringing order and perceiving patterns. Whereas researchers investigating mission activity in some areas of the world can get their initial bearings by consulting substantial reference works, such works seem to be less available for South Asia. And, alas, no North American

1. John A. Cannon, "The Historian at Work," in *The Historian at Work,* ed. John A. Cannon (London, 1980), p. 2.

2. Certainly Robert E. Frykenberg is a historian with whom archivists have felt fortunate to work, an exemplary model of willingness to pursue sources tirelessly and to work collaboratively with archivists and librarians.

corollary to the Mundus project described in Rosemary Seton's essay in this volume exists. Lacking the funding and time required for a comprehensive survey, this essay will seek to provide a simple baseline of information about archival records of North American Protestant missions in India, following a brief discussion regarding the types of documentation that are available for the study of missionary activity.

The North American contribution to missionary activity in South Asia was significant in its size and diversity. Protestant North American missionaries arrived in India in 1813, and by 1938 nearly fifty different North American groups were working in India, with a total of just over 2,000 staff. Some of these agencies respected comity agreements while others spread their work throughout the country. In comparison, British missions began about a decade earlier than the Americans and had 2,390 missionaries active in India in 1938. The "Continental Societies" are reported as having entered India two decades after the North American missionaries and employing 351 active missionaries in 1938. Of twenty-two union medical and educational institutions noted in the 1938 survey, fourteen had North American partners.[3]

How can we begin to assess the types, quantities, and accessibility of records that document this activity? Archival records and personal papers exist side by side with published reports and narratives spawned by a confusing array of sources, creating layers of diverse information. It is important to note that these various types of sources were generated for different purposes and different audiences. Ideally, the historian studying activity in a particular geographic area hopes to find (a) personal letters and diaries of individuals working that area, (b) letters, reports, and financial information related to the agencies for which they were working, (c) periodicals and reports distributed by those agencies, and (d) newspapers or other records that reveal outside reaction to the agencies' work. These different types of records reveal various angles of the story. Diaries and personal letters written to family members are likely to contain more introspective and unguarded reflection. Communications with a mission board may offer more thorough, but also more "politically correct," reporting. Periodicals, brochures, and reports prepared for distribution to the general public and financial supporters of the mission board are designed for a particular purpose. Newspapers and reports that go beyond the control of the mission board offer yet another perspective.

Let us take as an example the historian interested in Christian activity in

3. Statistics taken from the *Interpretive Statistical Survey of the World Mission of the Christian Church* prepared under the auspices of the International Missionary Council in 1938.

Tamil Nadu in the late nineteenth century. This historian will seek to determine which mission agencies were working in that area; which missionaries served those agencies; what personal papers, archival records, periodicals are extant for these players; and what additional materials are available to provide perspective on the mission records. For the novice researcher, evolving terminology for geographic areas and variant spellings can present an initial barrier. Under the British colonial rule, most of South India was integrated into the region called Madras Presidency. When India became independent in 1947, Madras Presidency became Madras State. In 1956 Madras State was reformed to present-day Tamil Nadu on linguistic lines. So for the late nineteenth century, the researcher looks for agencies working in Madras Presidency. How can the historian determine which mission agencies and missionaries were working in that area? B. H. Badley's *Indian Missionary Directory* (1886) provides valuable information, but it is arranged by the names of the agencies, and focusing in on a geographical area is somewhat laborious. Harlan P. Beach's *A Geography and Atlas of Protestant Missions* (1903) provides a map of India where the cities with "American Societies" are noted, along with an index of the cities providing the abbreviation of the specific agencies at work there. If our theoretical researcher is interested in the Chittur area, the index reveals that "RCA" worked there. Frustratingly enough for the novice researcher, there is no relevant mission agency listed under "R" in the alphabetical list of agencies provided in the beginning of the Beach volume. Thorough scanning of the list reveals the "Board of Foreign Missions of the Reformed Church in America (RCA)" listed under "B."

Now the researcher proceeds to determine where the Reformed Church in America archives related to India might be located. Researchers fortunate enough to have access to the *Proquest Archive Finder* database can quickly determine that New Brunswick Theological Seminary Library in New Brunswick, New Jersey, holds forty-eight linear feet of Reformed Church in America Board of Foreign Missions archives. The collection description in *Archive Finder* provides names of missionaries who worked in India, including Jacob Chamberlain, Joseph Mayou, Henry M. Scudder, John Scudder, Joseph Scudder, and William W. Scudder. Badley's directory and volumes of the *Protestant Missionary Directory* provide more detailed information about individual missionaries.

If our researcher wishes to find papers of a particular missionary, further searching in the *Archive Finder* and *OCLC's ArchiveGrid* databases — in fact, a simple Google search for "jacob chamberlain india mission" — reveals, for example, that personal papers of RCA missionary Jacob Chamberlain are located at the Billy Graham Center Archives in Illinois and the Yale University Divinity

School Library, as well as at the RCA archives. A search in the *WorldCat* database reveals more then ten published works by Chamberlain, many of which are also cited in online catalogues freely available to the public, such as the Yale University Library catalogue (http://orbis.library.yale.edu) and the Library of Congress catalogue (http://catalog.loc.gov/). A search in the same catalogues reveals that the Reformed Church in America missions periodical in the late nineteenth century was *De Heidenwereld,* chiefly in Dutch, and a general newspaper published in Madras, the *Hindu,* is available beginning in 1878. Annual reports of the Board of Foreign Missions of the Reformed Church in America are found to be held at various U.S. libraries. So our researcher begins to assemble a group of primary resources that may shed light on the topic at hand, and these materials will lead to others.

The past decade has seen a revolution in the archival field as the power of advancing technology has been applied to providing information about documentation. Methods of discovering archival materials have changed radically since the era of dependence on the multivolume National Union Catalog of Manuscript Collections and collection level records in scattered card catalogues. A half hour of Internet searching at a well-endowed academic library easily results in the identification of numerous caches of documentation of North American mission activity in India. Libraries now have electronic access to numerous university catalogues and can purchase access to national union catalogues such as *WorldCat* and extensive online information databases such as *ArchiveGrid* and *Archive Finder.* Increasingly, these databases contain not only brief records pointing to the existence of archival materials, but also detailed finding aids.

Yet what is most easily retrieved using the new technology is at best a hodgepodge of scattered information, very uneven in its quality and almost overwhelming in its quantity. A search for "india and missions" in the *ArchiveGrid* database, for example, results in more than 500 hits, yet we have no idea how these papers relate to the total universe of existing documentation, and the descriptive records retrieved are sometimes hopelessly vague. The researcher (or at least the archivist/librarian who is trying to assist the researcher) feels desperate for some structure to aid in evaluating the context and relevance of the information that has been retrieved.

A recent article on information sources for historians notes that "in 1750 Lord Chesterfield dismissed history as 'only a confused heap of facts,' unless there were maps and chronologies at hand to organize it."[4] Maps and chro-

4. Margaret Stieg Dalton and Laurie Charnigo, "Historians and Their Information Sources," *College and Research Libraries* 65 (2004): 400.

nologies are useful, but maybe even more to be desired are statistical atlases and comprehensive directories as tools to advance the historian's work of bringing order and finding patterns. Much as historians may consider the sorting out of the "confused heap" to be their task, the painstaking work of compiling statistics and directories to advance the task is not an attractive prospect. Unfortunately, not enough of this painstaking work has been done in documenting North American mission activity in India.

Researchers with an interest in China can become oriented to the broader picture of mission activity in their area and quickly learn about available documentation by using works such as the International Missionary Council's *The Christian Occupation of China* (1925), Archie Crouch's massive *Christianity in China: A Scholar's Guide to Resources in the Libraries and Archives of the United States* (1989, and now available in an updated version online from the Ricci Roundtable), Peter Mitchell's *Guide to Archival Resources on Canadian Missionaries in East Asia, 1890-1960,* and Kathleen Lodwick's detailed indexes to the broad-based China missionary periodical the *Chinese Recorder.* Works such as these make it easier for researchers to understand the lay of the land and begin to investigate how mission activity affected a wide range of social, political, religious, and economic issues.

Comprehensive reference works such as those mentioned above do not seem to be available for South Asia — or, if they exist, they are not widely known. B. H. Badley's nineteenth-century work *Indian Missionary Directory* provides useful basic information, and is available on microfilm, but few libraries in the United States hold it. Also of importance are the volumes of the *Protestant Missionary Directory and Directory of Christian Missions in India, Burma and Ceylon,* later known as the *Christian Handbook of India;* yet these works are very rare in the United States, and microfilm is apparently not available. Guides produced by denominations, such as *The Global Mission of ELCA and Its Predecessors,* provide valuable overviews of their own work, but the researcher who desires a broader overview is faced with the task of synthesizing widely scattered data. Missions atlases such as Harlan P. Beach's *Geography and Atlas of Protestant Missions* (1903); the *Statistical Atlas of Christian Missions* (1910), produced in conjunction with the Edinburgh World Missionary Conference; the *World Missionary Atlas* (1925) produced by the Institute of Social and Religious Research; and the *Directory of World Missions and Interpretative Statistical Survey of the World Mission of the Christian Church* (1938), produced by the International Missionary Council, provide broad-based but necessarily sketchy information.

When Archie Crouch prepared the massive *Christianity in China: A Scholar's Guide to Resources in the Libraries and Archives of the United States,* more than 1,200 libraries, archives, historical societies, religious orders, and denominational headquarters were surveyed to learn of the collections described in the repositories in the guide. The information was solicited through correspondence and phone calls, and personal visits were made to repositories as necessary. In comparison to the results of this level of effort, any information contained in this essay will be very meager, yet perhaps it can be considered to be a first step toward providing the type of consolidated, compiled information that might help any researcher in locating and evaluating relevant documentation, and would certainly assist archivists and librarians in pointing nonexpert researchers in the right direction.

The most basic task is to identify the players and the location and duration of their work in India, and the complexity only increases thereafter. What types of records exist for each agency? And, if records do exist, how well described are they, and how accessible to researchers? Documentation that shows up on the Internet and in printed directories is just the tip of the iceberg and can only lead one to wonder what is missing. Is any repository actively soliciting and collecting the personal papers of missionaries to India? What documentation is available in South Asia that complements North American holdings? How did the agencies interact in union enterprises; where and how are these activities documented? The compilation of data about agencies and their records is a mundane task, but such a base of knowledge can act as a springboard for comparative and intensive investigations.

We can begin with a listing of the North American agencies at work in India noted in the 1938 directory and survey published by the International Missionary Council. The table on pages 272-74 provides the name of the agency, the size of its foreign staff, and its areas of work within India.

Each of the agencies noted in the table, and each of the individuals who served these agencies, had a distinctive and often convoluted interaction with India. The cold facts of agency staff size and geographical locations can barely hint at the stories to be discovered. Certainly the usefulness of the list as an impetus for discovery would be aided by adding details and examples. The Advent Christian Denomination, Woman's Home and Foreign Mission Society's India Mission began in Guindy and Velacheri, both in Madras, in 1882 and included elementary schools, medical dispensaries, a printing plant, an industrial school, and boarding schools. The story of missionary John E. Clough is just one of hundreds that could be told about the American Baptist Foreign Mission Society's interactions with India. Clough's work among the Madigas, a Dalit group in Ongole, South India, triggered a mass movement toward Christianity. In one day, July 3, 1878, 2,222 individuals were baptized. Robert Wilson Hume of the American Board of Commissioners for Foreign

Name of Agency	Size of Staff[5]/Areas of Work
Advent Christian Denomination, Woman's Home and Foreign Mission Society	6 staff: Madras Presidency
American Baptist Foreign Mission Society	179 staff: Assam (61), Bengal (16), Hyderabad (21), Madras Presidency (66), Orissa (15)
American Board of Commissioners for Foreign Missions	81 staff: Bombay Presidency (36), Madras Presidency (43), Mysore (2)
American Lutheran Church, Board of Foreign Missions	26 staff: Madras Presidency
Assemblies of God, Foreign Missions Department of the General Council	79 staff: Bihar and Orissa (18), Bombay Presidency (15), Madras Presidency (8), Mysore (3), United Provinces (35)
Associate Reformed Presbyterian Church, Board of Foreign Missions	12 staff: Punjab
Brethren in Christ, Foreign Mission Board	13 staff: Bihar, Orissa
Canadian Baptist Foreign Mission Board	82 staff: Bihar and Orissa (6), Madras Presidency (76)
Christian and Missionary Alliance	58 staff: Berar, Bombay Presidency
Churches of God in North America, Board of Missions of the General Eldership	7 staff: Bengal
Church of England in Canada, Missionary Society	14 staff: Punjab
Church of God, Missionary Board	3 staff: Assam, Bengal, Bihar, Orissa, Madras Presidency
Church of the Brethren, General Mission Board	37 staff: Bombay Presidency

5. For the sake of comparison, the twelve largest British agencies in 1938 were: (1) Methodist Missionary Society (295 staff); (2) Church Missionary Society (281); (3) Church of Scotland (267); (4) Society for Propagation of the Gospel (238); (5) Church of England Zenana Missionary Society (216); (6) Baptist Missionary Society (190); (7) Brethren (176); (8) London Missionary Society (124); (9) Presbyterian Church in Ireland (61); (10) Zenana Bible and Medical Mission (59); (11) Presbyterian Church of Wales (51); (12) Bible Churchmen's Missionary Society (46).

Name of Agency	Size of Staff/Areas of Work
Church of the Nazarene, Department of Foreign Missions of the General Board	9 staff: Bengal, Bombay Presidency, Central Provinces
Evangelical and Reformed Church, Evangelical Synod of North America, Board of Foreign Missions	35 staff: Central Provinces
Evangelical Lutheran Synod of Missouri, Ohio, and Other States, Board of Foreign Missions	85 staff: Madras Presidency (85)
Free Methodist Church of North America, General Missionary Board	11 staff: Berar
Friends Foreign Missionary Society of the Ohio Yearly Meeting	5 staff: Central India
Heart of India Mission Band	1 staff: Madras Presidency
Hephzibah Faith Missionary Association	4 staff: Bihar
International Church of the Foursquare Gospel, Foreign Missions	2 staff: United Provinces
Mennonite Board of Missions and Charities	32 staff: Central Provinces
Mennonite Brethren Church of North America, Board of Foreign Missions	22 staff: Hyderabad
Mennonite Brethren in Christ, United Missionary Society	4 staff: Bihar
Methodist Episcopal Church, Board of Foreign Missions	277 staff: Bengal (18), Bihar and Orissa (11), Bombay Presidency (55), Central Provinces (31), Hyderabad (23), Madras Presidency (4), Mysore (14), Punjab and Kashmir (16), Rajputana (5), United Provinces (98)
Methodist Protestant Church	8 staff: Bombay Presidency
Metropolitan Church Association	18 staff: United Provinces
Missionary Bands of the World	17 staff: Central Provinces
North East India General Mission, Inc.	2 staff: Assam, Bengal
Pentecostal Assemblies of Canada	4 staff: United Provinces

Name of Agency	Size of Staff/Areas of Work
Pentecostal Assemblies of the World, Inc., Foreign Missionary Department	1 staff: United Provinces
Pilgrim Holiness Church, Department of Foreign Missions	3 staff: United Provinces
Presbyterian Church in Canada, General Board of Missions	25 staff: Central India, United Provinces
Presbyterian Church in the U.S.A., Board of Foreign Missions	235 staff: Bombay Presidency (52), Punjab (85), United Provinces (98)
Reformed Church in America, Board of Foreign Missions	39 staff: Madras Presidency
Reformed Episcopal Church, Board of Foreign Missions	3 staff: United Provinces
Reformed Presbyterian Church in North America, Board of Foreign Missions of the Synod	27 staff: United Provinces
Scandinavian Alliance Mission of North America	20 staff: Bombay Presidency
Seventh-Day Adventist Denomination	149 staff: Assam (2), Bengal (14), Bihar and Orissa (11), Bombay Presidency (31), Madras Presidency (27), Mysore (14), Punjab and Kashmir (13), United Provinces (35)
United Christian Missionary Society	50 staff: Central Provinces, United Provinces
United Church of Canada, Board of Foreign Missions	70 staff: Central India, Rajputana
United Free Gospel and Missionary Society	2 staff: United Provinces
United Lutheran Church in America, Board of Foreign Missions	82 staff: Madras Presidency (82)
United Presbyterian Church of North America, Board of Foreign Missions and Women's General Missionary Society	111 staff: Northwest Frontier Province (1), Punjab (110)
Wesleyan Methodist Connection of America, Missionary Society	8 staff: Bombay Presidency

Missions did literary work in Bombay, managed schools, and was secretary of the Bombay Temperance Union and Bombay Tract and Book Society. Time and space do not permit the comprehensive listing of the kind of detailed information that would provide a more accurate glimpse of the variety of issues and events that could be traced.

The varying staff sizes of the agencies listed above are a good indication that there were major players and minor players in the game. It seems prudent in this space to focus on the agencies that had the largest staffs as we provide basic information about the location of their archives and other pertinent sources. The top ten are listed below according to size of staff. The location of their archives is provided, along with an indication of whether finding aids or guides to the archives are available and whether at least portions of the archives are available in microfilm format. The names of the agencies' periodicals are followed by (M) if the periodical is available in microfilm format; libraries holding these periodicals in print or microfilm format can be identified through the *WorldCat* database.

Name of Agency	**Location/Accessibility of Archives**	**Periodicals**
Methodist Episcopal Church	United Methodist Church General Commission on Archives and History, Madison, N.J.; http://www.gcah.org; finding aids available online; microfilm available	*The Gospel in All Lands* (M), *Woman's Missionary Friend* (M)
Presbyterian Church U.S.A. / United Presbyterian Church of North America	Presbyterian Historical Society, Philadelphia; http://www.history.pcusa.org; finding aids available online; microfilm available	*Church at Home & Abroad* (M), *Woman's Work* (M), *Women and Missions* (M), *Women's Missionary Magazine*, *Missionary Horizons*
American Baptist	American Baptist Archives Center, Atlanta; http://www.abhsarchives.org/; finding aids not evident from site; microfilm available	*Missions* (M)
Seventh-Day Adventist	General Conference — Office of Archives & Statistics, Silver Spring, Md.; http://www.adventistarchives.org; finding aids and online documents	*Advent Review and Sabbath Herald* (M)
Missouri Synod Lutheran	Concordia Historical Institute, St. Louis; http://chi.lcms.org/collections/; finding aids available online	*Lutheran Witness* (M)

Name of Agency	Location/Accessibility of Archives	Periodicals
Canadian Baptist	McMaster Divinity College, Hamilton, Ont.; http://www.macdiv.ca/students/baptistarchives.php; finding aids not evident from site	*Canadian Baptist* (M)
United Lutheran Church in America	Evangelical Lutheran Church in America Archives, Chicago; http://www.elca.org/Who-We-Are/History/ELCA-archives.aspx; finding aids not evident from site	*The Foreign Missionary* (M), *Lutheran Woman's Work*
American Board of Commissioners for Foreign Missions	Houghton Library, Harvard University, Cambridge, Mass.; http://oasis.lib.harvard.edu/oasis/deliver/~hou01467	*Missionary Herald* (M)
Assemblies of God	General Council of the Assemblies of God, Springfield, Mo.; http://www.ag.org; archival holdings not evident from site	*Pentecostal Evangel* (M)
Christian and Missionary Alliance	C&MA National Archives, Colorado Springs; http://www.cmalliance.org/whoweare/archives/index.jsp; finding aids not evident from site	*The Alliance Weekly* (M)

Clearly, these archival resources are scattered geographically and have varying degrees of description and control. The situation for personal papers of missionaries is even more complicated. Only a small portion of missionary papers are preserved in places where researchers may access them, and there is no particular logic to where they may be housed. Databases such as *ArchivalResources, ArchivesUSA,* and *WorldCat* are great research tools, but they are not comprehensive in recording holdings, particularly for smaller and non-academic repositories. As always, the historian must be a detective in order to track down all relevant resources.

There is some evidence that historians are becoming less willing or able to devote the time and expense necessary for such detection work.[6] But the use of primary sources will always be important to the true historian. Much work remains to be done as archivists, librarians, and historians work in partnership to uncover the sources crucial for historical research, but we are fortunate in having models for success.

6. Dalton and Charnigo, "Historians," p. 407.

Index